Margaret Thatcher

Margaret Thatcher (*Source:* Lady Thatcher's Office.)

Margaret Thatcher

Prime Minister Indomitable

EDITED BY

Juliet S. Thompson
and Wayne C. Thompson

Westview Press
BOULDER • SAN FRANCISCO • OXFORD

Copyright © 1994 by Westview Press, Inc.

Published in 1994 in the United States of America by Westview Press, Inc., 5500 Central Avenue, Boulder, Colorado 80301-2877, and in the United Kingdom by Westview Press, 36 Lonsdale Road, Summertown, Oxford OX2 7EW

Library of Congress Cataloging-in-Publication Data
Margaret Thatcher : prime minister indomitable / edited by Juliet S.
   Thompson and Wayne C. Thompson.
     p.   cm.
   ISBN 0-8133-2347-9
   1. Thatcher, Margaret.   2. Prime ministers—Great Britain—
Biography.   3. Great Britain—Politics and government—1979–
I. Thompson, Juliet S., 1971–   .   II. Thompson, Wayne C.
DA591.T47M37   1994
940.085'8'092—dc20
[B]   94-5649
                                                                                              CIP

Printed and bound in the United States of America

The paper used in this publication meets the requirements
of the American National Standard for Permanence of Paper
for Printed Library Materials Z39.48-1984.

10   9   8   7   6   5   4   3   2   1

To Harry V. Jaffa and Catherine Leamy Lowe,
intellectual models whose politics were
always anchored in principle

Contents

List of Figures

Introduction and Acknowledgments

Referring to the forebears of today's Britons, Tacitus noted in *Agricola*: "Neque enim sexum in imperius discernunt" (They recognize no distinction between the sexes in choosing their leaders). Two millennia later, in 1969, an ambitious opposition Member of Parliament (MP), Margaret Thatcher, had still not convinced herself that this was true. She stated then that "no woman in my time will be prime minister." Six years later she became the first woman to win leadership over a British political party. Four years thereafter she was her country's first woman head of government and would become Britain's longest-serving prime minister in the twentieth century, the only one to win three consecutive general elections. Until she was forced to step down on November 22, 1990, after eleven and a half years in office, Margaret Thatcher had been the most innovative, successful, and unpopular prime minister since 1945. In the view of *The Economist*, she was "Britain's outstanding peacetime leader of the twentieth century."[1]

This book seeks to present and evaluate the policies and ideas of this extraordinary politician. It is divided into two parts. The first is composed of chapters by scholars who have studied British politics and Margaret Thatcher's career. In the second part, she speaks for herself. This work is not organized around a single, unified view of Thatcher. The authors analyze various aspects of her prime ministry and offer differing assessments, perspectives, and conclusions about her policies and leadership, as would befit such a multifaceted and controversial political figure.

In the opening chapter, the editors examine the uniqueness of Mrs. Thatcher as a leader and survey the principal stages of her political career. They provide a context within which the chapters and speeches which follow can be better understood. Jorgen S. Rasmussen describes her family and educational background, her entry into politics, and the personal qualities which made her successful. James E. Alt analyzes Thatcher's ideology and the economic changes which she attempted to bring about. Alan J. Ward describes and evaluates her high-profile foreign and defense policy. She

---

1. Tacitus quote in Ernle Money, *Margaret Thatcher—First Lady of the House* (London: Leslie Frewin, 1975), in front material. Thatcher's 1969 quote on promotional insert in *The Economist*, July 24–30, 1993. Final quote in "Margaret Thatcher's Ten Years," *The Economist*, April 29, 1989, 19.

herself asserted that "once again Britain stands tall in the councils of Europe and of the world."[2] She was clearly a political figure with far more than national significance. Her importance in the Cold War is examined by Trevor Salmon and William Macnair. Sir William Nicoll, who was director general in the Secretariat of the Council of the European Community (EC) in Brussels, describes the roots of her reservations about Europe. Lewis G. John provides a detailed description of why Thatcher lost the support of her Tory colleagues in November 1990 and was hoisted out of the prime minister's chair. Finally, James E. Cronin looks back to assess Thatcher's legacy, the reasons she was viewed as a success in her time, and the standards against which her government should be judged. He puts her into the context of British history.

Thatcher Speeches

Part Two of this book is composed of a selection of her most important speeches. Thatcher was not a natural orator. Her speeches were not known for extraordinary eloquence or humor, although the reader will see that they are not devoid of those qualities. She took voice lessons to lower the pitch of her voice, which enabled her to have a more effective and pleasing delivery. The strengths of her oratory were meticulous preparation, overwhelming mastery of facts, an underpinning of righteousness, morality, and principle, and a sharply combative approach. She seldom lost an exchange in Parliament and deserved her reputation in the House of Commons for prodigious forensic competence. Her words in Parliament were always her own, but she sometimes hired speechwriters to sprinkle her other speeches with quotations or sharp, catchy images. Her speeches are a record of the ideas that inspired British politics for a long time.

The political importance of her speeches was recognized by the publication of two previously edited volumes, which are useful to Thatcher scholars.[3] The selection in Part Two of this book gives greater emphasis to the seeds of her political and economic thinking before becoming prime minister, and it includes speeches delivered in the final years of her prime ministry and after. The selected speeches are presented in chronological order. These have been abridged to delete repetitions and most amenities, such as "I am delighted to

---

2. "It Is Time to Go," *Time,* December 3, 1990, 61.

3. Margaret Thatcher, *In Defence of Freedom: Speeches on Britain's Relations with the World 1976-1986,* introduced by Ronald Butt (London: Aurum, 1986). Margaret Thatcher, *The Revival of Britain: Speeches on Home and European Affairs 1975-1988,* compiled by Alistair B. Cooke (London: Aurum, 1989).

be here today." Her language has not been changed, but subheadings have been added to some lengthy speeches to aid the reader.

We open with her maiden speech to Parliament in 1960. Taking advantage of a rare privilege for an MP less than a year after entering the House of Commons, she introduced her own Private Member's Bill to give the press access to local government meetings. She displayed her legal mind and mastery of detail, and she received much praise for her freshman *tour de force*.[4] Her 1968 speech was one of the few instances before 1974 when she spoke out on the new direction her party, then in opposition, should take. The Conservative Political Centre lecture at the 1968 party conference was a prestigious occasion, and it was a sign of her importance that she was invited to deliver it. The speech revealed the way she linked morality and public policy, her aversion to excessive governmental and bureaucratic power, and her contempt for consensus politics, which, in her words, "could be an attempt to satisfy people holding no particular views about anything."[5]

She was the secretary of state for Education and Science in the Heath government from 1970 to 1974. Because of the tradition of collective responsibility, her public statements were invariably supportive of the prime minister's policies. That changed after the Labour Party regained power in 1974. Once she had emerged the surprising victor in the Tory leadership race in 1975, she began elaborating more explicitly the economic and foreign political views that later became known as "Thatcherism."

She brought to her new role as leader of the opposition no clearly deliberated and enunciated foreign policy priorities. The only consistent theme in her speeches since 1950 had been anticommunism. As a cabinet member in the early 1970s, she began reading the novels of Alexander Solzhenitsyn, who wrote about egregious human rights violations in the Soviet Union. She also had discussions with Professor Robert Conquest, a historian of Stalin's purges and terror.[6] Both strengthened her conviction that the Soviet Union was wicked and dangerous. Anticipating the 1975 Conference on Security and Cooperation in Europe (CSCE, or popularly "Helsinki Conference"), she expressed her thoughts on the Soviet threat in her speech to the Chelsea Constituency Association on July 26, 1975. It was the virulence of this address which won her the invaluable sobriquet from the Soviets themselves: Iron Lady. Their reaction to her speech established her international importance and undermined the domestic attacks directed

---

4. Hugo Young, *The Iron Lady: A Biography of Margaret Thatcher* (New York: Farrar, Strauss Giroux, 1989), 44–46. This book was first published in the U.K. under the title, *One of Us* (London: Macmillan, 1989).

5. Ibid., 62–65, and chapter by James E. Cronin in this book.

6. For influence of Solzhenitsyn, see her memoirs, *The Downing Street Years* (London: Harper Collins, 1993), 290, 452, 813; for Conquest, 451–52.

against her that, as a woman, she would be weak and indecisive. She therefore savored this epithet.

She responded to the Moscow leaders' protestations to her hard-line position in another important address to her Finchley constituency on January 31, 1976. In this she elaborated her foreign policy approach more stridently, accusing the Soviets of aiming for world domination. More than any other, this speech defined her international posture. On June 2, 1979, she made clear that this approach would continue through her first term as prime minister. "Communism never sleeps." Therefore, Europeans must be ready to sacrifice for their own defense. "Our first duty to freedom is to defend our own."[7]

Her highest priorities as Tory leader were to change the economic direction in which Britain was going and to lessen her compatriots' dependence on the state. We include three speeches she made in the United States in September 1975, as well as her first address to a Conservative Party conference as leader, on October 10, 1975, in which she defined the economic problems, as she saw them, and prescribed the solutions. They reveal her grasp of complicated economic theory and the moral implications of a "business as usual" approach to the nation's economy. She frequently returned to America, where she always found admiring and receptive audiences. Her two interviews on September 14, 1977, reveal the interest Americans had in her and gave her opportunities to speak to her own voters, via the New World, on a broad range of issues, from human rights to labor unions.[8]

Some of her speeches, such as her address to the October 10, 1980, Conservative Party conference and her 1985 speech in London to the American Bar Association, are remembered and quoted because they represent the heart of her beliefs. Her address to the 1980 party conference, her first as prime minister, came after several days of irreverent and scarcely concealed attacks on her ideologically oriented policies, which were causing severe damage to the party's standing in the polls. She was under intense pressure to moderate her policies, to make a "U-turn," to return to centrist, corporatist, consensus-oriented policies, as a frightened Edward Heath had done in 1972. With one phrase, she stopped her Conservative critics in their tracks: "Turn if you like. The lady is not for turning."[9]

She did not always take a combative approach in her speeches. In her

7. Young, *Iron Lady*, 169–71. See also *Downing Street Years*, 60–61.

8. After becoming prime minister in 1979, she was exasperated at having to devote as much attention to foreign policy as to domestic and economic issues. She confessed wistfully in December 1980: "I want to spend more time on the economy, but foreign affairs have taken over." Young, *Iron Lady*, 183. For her frequent trips to the U.S., see ibid., 120–21.

9. This turn of phrase, penned by speechwriter Ronnie Millar, was taken from a popular play in London at the time, *The Lady's Not for Burning*, by Christopher Fry. Thatcher, *Downing Street Years*, 122. See Jorgen Rasmussen's chapter in this book, and Young, *Iron Lady*, 208–9.

lecture to the St Lawrence Jewry in the City of London on March 4, 1981, she argued "as both a Christian and a politician" that "we must always beware of supposing that somehow we can get rid of our own moral duties by handing them over to the community." She pleaded for public life to be grounded in values, which young people must be taught: "I want this nation to continue to be heard in the world and for the leaders of other countries to know that our strength comes from shared convictions as to what is right and wrong, and that we value these convictions enough to defend them."

In her lecture on July 26, 1982, honoring Dame Margery Corbett Ashby, a Liberal feminist, she made one of her infrequent pronouncements on a woman's role in the modern world. From the beginning of her political career, she had stridently asserted that men were not more entitled than women to succeed in public life. She had remarked in 1965 that "if you want something said, ask a man. If you want something done, ask a woman." At her party's 1969 conference, she had even quoted Sophocles: "Once a woman is made equal to a man, she becomes his superior." Herself a wife and mother, she argued thirteen years later in her Dame Ashby lecture that "the home should be the centre but not the boundary of a woman's life." But she derided any notion of positive discrimination toward women, having clawed her way to the top without any such favoritism. "I hate those strident tones we hear from some Women's Libbers!" Elsewhere she asked: "What's women's lib ever done for me?"[10]

Some women argue that Thatcher never did anything for women. She only included one female in her government: Lady Janet Young, who was leader of the House of Lords from 1981 to 1983. But polls showed that she had softened reservations against women in politics. Asked the question in 1977, "I don't like women leaders," 28 percent of respondents answered in the affirmative; in 1985, only 16 percent did. By 1985, 40 percent believed that "it's time we had a woman in power, up from 37 percent in 1977. Some, such as President Jimmy Carter's national security adviser, Zbigniew Brzezinski, overlooked the fact that she was a woman: "In her presence you pretty quickly forget that she's a woman. She doesn't strike me as being a

---

10. First two Thatcher quotes in Young, *Iron Lady,* 311; see also 224–25. Third and fourth quotes in text of lecture in this book; final quote on women's lib in "Life at the top," *Maclean's,* December 3, 1990, 41. In *Downing Street Years,* 18, she noted that "more nonsense was written about the so-called feminine factor during my time in office than about almost anything else." When asked what it felt like to be a woman prime minister, her standard reply was, "I don't know: I've never experienced the alternative." She explained further, 129, that "a number of men I have dealt with in politics demonstrate precisely those characteristics which they attribute to women—vanity and an inability to make tough decisions. There are also certain kinds of men who simply cannot abide working for a woman. They are quite prepared to make every allowance for the 'weaker sex': but if a woman asks no special privileges and expects to be judged solely by what she is and does, this is found gravely and unforgivably disorienting."

FIGURE 0.1 Margaret Thatcher, 1988. (*Source:* British Information Services, New York.)

very female type." But she was certainly feminine. Although she was decisive and tough in a man's world, she felt free to cry in public (such as when the first casualty figures arrived from the Falklands, when her son was reported missing during an auto rally in Africa, or when she left 10 Downing Street for the last time in 1990), and she laid heavy stress on her appearance. Former Labour minister, Barbara Castle, admired her femininity. In a 1975 diary entry she wrote: "What interests me is how blooming she looks—she has never been prettier. I am interested because I understand this phenomenon. . . . She is in love: in love with power, success—and with herself. . . . If we have to have Tories, good luck to her."[11]

Her addresses to the joint meeting of the U.S. Congress in 1985, to the House of Commons at the time of the American bombing of Libya in 1986, and to the Aspen Institute in 1990, reveal both her convictions and the extent to which she saw a common destiny shared by her country and the United States. She was vigorously attacked at home for allowing U.S. planes to strike Libya from British bases only three months after having stated that "I do not believe in retaliatory strikes that are against international law." Her decision to support a grateful U.S. President Ronald Reagan in this matter showed not only her unfailing support for him, but her willingness to act without fully informing her own cabinet. Despite the battering her government took in popularity polls because of this episode, her loyalty strengthened the special British-American relationship.[12]

In her interview on Soviet television March 31, 1987, which was aired uncut, she displayed her mastery of defense issues, particularly nuclear deterrence. She underscored her support for Mikhail Gorbachev's political and economic reforms. Her interview highlighted a highly successful trip to the Soviet Union, and the aura of her sterling performance helped her win the 1987 parliamentary elections, which she called only six weeks after her return.[13]

Her famous September 20, 1988, speech at the College of Europe, Bruges, is an articulate elaboration of her objections to what she considers to be an excessive centralization of power in the hands of unelected leaders

---

11. Polling statistics in Gordon Heald and Robert Wybrow, *Gallup Survey of Britain* (London: Croom Helm, 1986), 30. Brzezinski quote in Young, *Iron Lady,* 304; see also 303-11. Castle quote from her February 5, 1975, entry in the *Castle Diaries* (London: 1980), quoted also in Bruce Arnold, *Margaret Thatcher: A Study in Power* (London: Hamish Hamilton, 1984), 144-45.

12. She worked especially hard on her address to Congress and borrowed Ronald Reagan's Autocue for the occasion. *Downing Street Years,* 468-69. See 441-49, 560, for the Libya raid and her speech. For Aspen speech and discussions with George Bush on the Iraqi invasion of Kuwait, see 800, 816, 819. See 157-58, 813, for her relationship with Reagan, as well as Young, *Iron Lady,* 251-58. Young, 475-78, 482, for Libya.

13. See Young, *Iron Lady,* 389-95 and 512-14, and Thatcher, *Downing Street Years,* 478-85, 772-74, 755.

in Brussels. She later wrote that the reaction to this speech "in polite European circles . . . was one of stunned outrage." But she claimed that it elicited "a great wave of popular support" from those who sought an alternative view of Europe's future.[14] Some of her parliamentary speeches have been included, not only for their substance, but because they provide the flavor of parliamentary discourse in Britain and show how she thrived in such an environment of debate and repartee. Finally, her 1992 address to the corps of cadets of the Virginia Military Institute (VMI) contains a summary of her aims and her underlying political philosophy.

Acknowledgments

We are grateful to the British Information Services in New York, especially Ray Raymond, Peter McInally, and Janet Bacon, for providing us with useful advice, the texts for some of the speeches included in Part Two, and most of the photographs used in this book. We thank Lady Thatcher's private office in London, especially Clare Lowther, who provided us with a photo, the texts of the speeches to the Conservative Party Conference in 1980, the Margery Corbett Ashby Memorial Lecture in 1982, and the American Bar Association in 1985, and permission to publish the transcribed text of her VMI address, which has heretofore been unavailable to the public. Other speeches were provided to us by Dr. Sarah Street, the Conservative Party Archivist at the Bodleian Library in Oxford. The Conservative Political Centre in London gave us Lady Thatcher's 1968 lecture, "What's Wrong with Politics." The House of Commons Library was most kind to provide us with the texts of her parliamentary speeches for use in this book. The Central Office of Information in London, especially Barry Cole, provided us with three useful photos. We are grateful to Lord Norman Tebbit of the Conservative Party and Nick Sigler of the Labour Party for their willingness to share their insights on the Thatcher legacy. The VMI Research Committee was generous in granting funds for a research trip to London, and Peter and Maureen Ward and Wolfgang and Gerda Goldbach provided the logistic backup which made that trip a success. Janet S. Holly and Elizabeth S. Hostetter of VMI's Preston Library were extremely helpful to us in compiling the bibliography. Catherine D. Thompson lent us a much needed hand in editing the page proofs and constructing the index. Larry I. Bland helped with copyediting and did the typesetting and pasteup. We owe special thanks to VMI's H. B. Johnson Lecture Committee for funding both her speech and the scholarly symposium on the Thatcher decade at VMI.

Juliet S. Thompson
Wayne C. Thompson

---

14. Thatcher, *Downing Street Years,* pp. 746, 742–46, 755.

About the Editors and Contributors

James E. Alt is professor of government at Harvard University and author of many books and articles on British politics and political economy, including *Cabinet Studies* (London: Macmillan, 1975), *The Politics of Economic Decline* (Cambridge: Cambridge University Press, 1978), *Political Economics* (Berkeley: University of California Press, 1983), and *Perspectives on Positive Political Economy* (Cambridge: Cambridge University Press, 1991).

James E. Cronin is professor of history at Boston College. His works include *Industrial Conflict in Modern Britain* (London: Croom Helm, 1979), *Labour and Society in Britain, 1918-1979* (New York: Schocken, 1983), and *The Politics of State Expansion: War, State and Society in Twentieth-Century Britain* (New York: Routledge, 1991).

Lewis G. John is professor of politics at Washington and Lee University, where he teaches courses on the British political system, as well as comparative public policy and American government. He has published a number of articles in journals both in the United States and abroad.

William Macnair is a retired British Army officer with experience in operations and intelligence. His graduate degree in international relations is from the University of St. Andrews.

Sir William Nicoll, C.M.G., M.A., LL.D., was appointed in 1972 to the U.K. delegation to the EC in Brussels. In 1977 he became deputy U.K. permanent representative and served a period as chairman of the Committee of Permanent Representatives (COREPER). In 1982 he was appointed director general in the Council Secretariat in Brussels. He retired from EC service in 1991. He is author, with Trevor C. Salmon, of *Understanding the New European Community* (Old Tappan, N.J.: Prentice Hall, 1993), and he has contributed a score of articles to European journals.

Jorgen S. Rasmussen is Distinguished Professor of Political Science at Iowa State University. One of the founders of the British Politics Group, he has been its executive secretary for more than a decade and a half. He comments on American political developments for the BBC Scotland news. Among the books he has written are a comparative politics text, now in its eighth edition, and an analysis of British government and politics, *The British Political Process: Concentrated Power Versus Accountability* (Belmont,

Calif.: Wadsworth, 1993). In addition, he has contributed to several other books and published in scholarly journals both in the U.S. and abroad.

Trevor Salmon is senior lecturer in international relations and Jean Monnet Professor of European Integration Studies at the University of St. Andrews. His recent books include *Unneutral Ireland* (Oxford: Oxford University Press, 1989); *International Security in the Modern Age,* co-edited with Roger Carey (New York: St. Martin's, 1992), and *Understanding the New European Community,* with Sir William Nicoll (1993).

Baroness Thatcher of Kesteven, Margaret, The Lady Thatcher, O.M., P.C., F.R.S., was Conservative Member of Parliament for Barnet, Finchley, and was Britain's first woman prime minister. She was appointed prime minister, first lord of the treasury and minister for the civil service on May 4, 1979, following the success of the Conservative Party in the general election of the previous day. When the Conservative Party subsequently won the general elections of June 9, 1983, and June 11, 1987, she became the first British prime minister this century to contest successfully three consecutive general elections. She resigned as prime minister on November 22, 1990. In December 1990, the Queen awarded her the Order of Merit. On June 30, 1992, she was elevated to the House of Lords to become Baroness Thatcher of Kesteven. In 1993 she was named chancellor of the College of William and Mary in Williamsburg, Virginia, an honorific office once held by George Washington. In October 1993, her memoirs, *The Downing Street Years* (London: Harper Collins), were published.

Margaret Hilda Thatcher was born on October 13, 1925, the daughter of a grocer who was active in local politics as borough councillor, alderman, and mayor of Grantham. She was educated at Kesteven and Grantham Girls' High School. She won a scholarship to Somerville College, Oxford, where she obtained a degree in natural science (chemistry). She is also a Master of Arts (MA) of Oxford University. In June 1983 she was elected a Fellow of the Royal Society (FRS). On leaving Oxford she worked for four years as a research chemist for an industrial firm, reading for the bar in her spare time. She was called to the bar by Lincoln's Inn in 1954 and practiced as a barrister, specializing in taxation law. While an undergraduate, she was president of the Oxford University Conservative Association. As Miss Margaret Roberts she contested two parliamentary elections of the Conservative Party, in 1950 and 1951, before being elected (after her marriage in 1951) to the House of Commons in 1959 as Member for Finchley. Lady Thatcher's husband, Sir Denis Thatcher, served in the Second World War as a major in the Royal Artillery. He is a former director of Burmah Castrol and is a director of other companies. He was made a baronet in December 1990. Sir Denis and Mrs. Thatcher have a twin son and daughter, Mark and Carol, who were born on August 15, 1953.

Mrs. Thatcher's first ministerial appointment came in 1961, when she became a parliamentary secretary to the then Ministry of Pensions and National Insurance, remaining in this position until the change of government in 1964. From 1964 to 1970, while the Conservatives were in opposition, she was a front-bench spokesman for her party and from 1967 a member of the shadow cabinet. When the Conservatives returned to office in June 1970, she was appointed secretary of state for education and science and was made a privy counsellor. After the general election of February 1974, she was appointed to the shadow cabinet and became opposition front-bench spokesman, first on the environment and later (in December 1974) on treasury matters. She was elected leader of the Conservative Party and thus became leader of the opposition in February 1975.

Juliet S. Thompson is a graduate of Davidson College and is a Ph.D. candidate in international studies at Old Dominion University. She is coauthor of *The Historical Dictionary of Germany* (Meteuchen, N.J.: Scarecrow Press, 1994) and collaborated in the editing of *Perspectives on Strategic Defense* and *Space: National Programs and International Cooperation* (Boulder, Colo: Westview Press, 1987 and 1989).

Wayne C. Thompson is professor of political science at the Virginia Military Institute. Among his books are *Kurt Riezler and the Crises of Modern Germany* (Iowa City: University of Iowa Press, 1980), *The Political Odyssey of Herbert Wehner* (Boulder, Colo: Westview Press, 1993), and the annually updated *Western Europe* and *Canada* volumes in the World Today Series (Harpers Ferry, W.Va.: Stryker-Post Publications).

Alan J. Ward is the Class of 1935 Professor of Government at the College of William and Mary. Born in England, he received his B.S. and Ph.D. degrees from the London School of Economics and Political Science. Among his writings are *Ireland and Anglo-American Relations* (Toronto: University of Toronto Press, 1969), *The Easter Rising: Revolution and Irish Nationalism* (Arlington Heights, Ill.: Harlan Davidson, 1980), *Northern Ireland: Living with the Crisis* (New York: Praeger, 1987), and *The Irish Constitutional Tradition: Responsible Government and Ireland, 1792 to 1992* (Washington, D.C.: Catholic University Press, 1993).

FIGURE 0.2 Margaret Thatcher. (*Source:* British Information Services, New York.)

PART ONE

Evaluations of Margaret Thatcher

1

Thatcher's Leadership

Juliet S. Thompson and Wayne C. Thompson

In the literature on Margaret Thatcher's rule, no word appears with greater frequency than "revolution." Her leadership dealt with change, not with mere stewardship. Many viewed that change as "radical." Her message of "radical conservatism" bore her name: "Thatcherism." No other British prime minister has had the suffix "ism" attached to his name. Oxford historian, John Roberts, described her as "above all a disturbing, much-needed questioner and mould-breaker."[1]

The first woman to lead a British political party or a major Western nation, Thatcher had the determination of a visionary and the ruthlessness of an outsider. She did not come from the establishment and never owed her success to it. She was ready to admit that modern Britain was a failure, and she could not understand why its leaders were so content with themselves while the country performed so poorly. To her, they seemed interested only in managing Britain's decline. Part of her appeal was that she represented a new kind of Conservative Party. The image of the party as the preserve of the landed gentry, bankers, or high-level civil servants, who could display charity toward the lower classes when needed, and who assembled in prayer in the Church of England, had changed.

Thatcher was an example of the "new" kind of Tory, who worked her way up in the world. The daughter of a dressmaker and grocer from Grantham, Lincolnshire, she had lived with her family in an apartment above the shop and worked all her childhood in her father's store. The only scientifically trained prime minister in British history, she studied chemistry

---

1. Roberts quote in "Mrs Thatcher's Place in History," *The Economist,* April 29, 1989, 59. For "Thatcherism," see Harris, Kenneth, *Thatcher* (London: Weidenfeld and Nicolson, 1988), 1, and the Rasmussen chapter in this book.

at Oxford, where, as leader of the Conservative Association, she advocated party reform following the 1945 election debacle and demanded "more working-class officers" in the Conservative Party. She later acquired a law degree after marrying a successful businessman, Denis Thatcher. Her marriage moved her from the struggling to the affluent middle class and eliminated any financial restrictions which might have stood in the way of a full-time political career. Because of her own background, she was better able to forge an alliance between skilled workers and the middle class in a society which is becoming more and more middle class.

She did not club with her party's elite. As a woman lacking fraternity with her male colleagues, she was an outsider, who harbored a bias against inherited wealth and Tory paternalism. She served three years as parliamentary secretary in the Ministry of Pensions from 1961 to 1964 and four years from 1970 to 1974 as Secretary of State for Education and Science before winning the party leadership in 1975. Only because she was an outsider was she able to enter the leadership race against Edward Heath, who demanded the party elite's support despite the fact that he had lost three elections. During her years in Number 10 Downing Street, the residence of the prime minister, she was opposed by many establishment institutions who felt the sting of her attacks: the civil service, the universities, the British Broadcasting Corporation (BBC), and the Church of England. She herself announced in 1981 to a startled private gathering in Number 10 that "I am the rebel head of an established government!" as she kicked off her shoes and stood on a chair to deliver an impromptu speech.[2]

She benefitted from the transformation within the party, which now extends from the grass-roots all the way up to Parliament. Its seats in the House of Commons are no longer occupied primarily by traditional local notables, but increasingly by insurance agents, housewives, teachers, salespersons, and self-made middle-management people. A good example of this new kind of Tory was Speaker of the House Bernard Weatherill, a former tailor who always carried in his pocket a thimble to remind himself of his humble background. It is said that when he entered Parliament, one aristo-

---

2. Quote in Hugo Young, *The Iron Lady: A Biography of Margaret Thatcher* (New York: Farrar Strauss Giroux, 1989), 242; for her activities at Oxford, see 14–27; for Thatcher as an outsider, see 100, 137–38, 412. In *The Downing Street Years* (London and New York: Harper Collins, 1993), 832, she wrote that "if the great and the good of the Tory party had had their way, I would never have become party leader, let along prime minister." She argued on 129–30 that in the eyes of the "wet" Tory establishment she was "of a different class, a person with an alarming conviction that the values and virtues of Middle England should be brought to bear on the problems which the establishment consensus had created. I offended on many counts." In the October 17, 1993, issue of *The Sunday Times,* which published weekly excerpts from her memoirs beginning October 10, political editor Michael Jones described her as a "renegade," a "guerrilla fighter operating deep behind enemy lines."

cratic Conservative was overheard saying to another: "I don't know what this place is coming to, Tom: they've got my tailor in here now!" The point is that the tailor to whom they were referring was a Tory. Unlike Heath, who worked hard to escape his humble origins, Thatcher gloried in hers although she did take elocution lessons to bury her Lincolnshire lilt. She never advocated a classless society and does not disdain classes. But she sought to replace the class-driven mould of British politics with a more fluid, open, upwardly mobile society in which merit and money are more important than tradition and class. She broke the grip of upper-class Tories and transformed the party into a more middle-class organization.

Like most British, she is a supporter of constitutional monarchy and got along well with Queen Elizabeth II, whose "formidable grasp of current issues and breadth of experience" she admired. "I always found the Queen's attitude toward the work of the government absolutely correct." It is possible that her attacks on self-perpetuating inherited privilege and vested interests weakened deference toward the monarchy, which found itself severely battered in the 1990s. Upon retirement, Lady Thatcher saw nothing inappropriate about accepting a mark of royal honor for the service she had rendered to her country. This is a standard reward for a former prime minister. She no doubt preferred a seat in the House of Lords to one in the House of Commons because the former allowed her the freedom to criticize her successor's Tory government. She did violate recent tradition, and perhaps her own meritocratic convictions, by conferring on her trusted first deputy prime minister, William Whitelaw, a hereditary peerage. The knighthood she conferred upon her husband, Denis, was likewise hereditary and will pass to her son Mark.[3]

Leadership Style

In the 1980s, Thatcher dominated her country and party like no leader since Winston Churchill. Her kind of leadership involved leading people where they initially did not want to go. Former Tory cabinet member Norman Tebbit said that "she has changed not only her own party but her country and has compelled the others to adjust themselves to that agenda." She did so by the sheer force of her personality and the rock-hard conviction of her ideas. She was a "conviction politician," a term which she herself coined. In a speech given shortly after her election in 1979, she asserted that

---

3. Thatcher's remarks about Queen Elizabeth II in *Downing Street Years,* 18. For Thatcher and the monarchy, see Young, *Iron Lady,* 489–93. The speaker elected in 1992, Betty Boothroyd, also came from a non-traditional mould, having been a West End chorus line dancer before becoming a Labour Party activist.

FIGURE 1.1 Margaret Thatcher, Queen Elizabeth II, and Bal Ram Jakhar at a reception in London following the opening of the Thirty-second Commonwealth Parliamentary Conference. (*Source:* British Information Services, New York.)

"in politics it is the half-hearted who lose. It is those with conviction who carry the day."[4]

She rejected the cozy politics of compromise and repudiated the very foundation of politics in Britain: the consensus under which it was governed since the 1950s. She startled the British ambassador to Iran in May 1978 by remarking that she regarded "people in my party who believe in consensus politics" as "Quislings, as traitors." Former Labour foreign minister, David Owen, noted that "conviction and courage are considerable virtues for any politician and Mrs Thatcher has them in abundance. A readiness to compromise is also a virtue, but this she disdains with as much vehemence as she despises consensus."[5]

---

4. Tebbit quote in "Thatcher's Place in History," 58. Thatcher's 1979 quote in June 2, 1979 speech in Part II of this book.

5. Quote in Iran in Young, *Iron Lady,* 223. Owen quote in "Thatcher's Place in History," 58.

She announced in the House of Commons on November 20, 1979: "I hope that one quality in which I am not lacking is courage." She coined the contemptuous term, "wets," for moderates in her party who wished to continue along the middle-of-the-road course charted by Harold Macmillan and Edward Heath. She stated flatly in 1984 that "I go for agreement, agreement for the things I want to do." She relished divisiveness if it furthered her causes. "The adrenalin flows when they really come out fighting at me and I fight back and I stand there and I know: 'Now come on, Maggie, you are wholly on your own. No one can help you.' And I love it." The British public became increasingly aware of this proclivity toward divisiveness. A poll showed that while 31 percent of respondents believed in October 1977 that "she divides the country," 71 percent thought that in January 1985.[6]

Conviction, Ideology, Philosophy

Her politics was always inspired by strong convictions. In 1945 the *Grantham Journal* reported on "the presence of a young woman of the age of 19 with such decided convictions" and "a gift for oratory" in the campaign against the local incumbent MP. In the 1950 and 1951 elections, she was, at ages twenty-four and twenty-five, the youngest woman to contest the elections, a fact that gained her nationwide publicity, despite her predicted defeats. Her campaign speeches were filled with anticommunist, antisocialist rhetoric, asserting that the choice to be made was between slavery and freedom. Although her beliefs changed little over the years, she expended far more effort than most politicians in seeking philosophical and even theological underpinnings for her ideas. She was determined to link principle with policy, to approach important political and economic questions from the standpoint of "rightness."[7]

As an Oxford student, she enthusiastically read Friedrich von Hayek's 1945 book, *The Road to Serfdom.* This Austrian refugee from National Socialism, who was teaching at the London School of Economics, argued that all forms of economic planning and socialism lead inevitably to tyranny. In the aftermath of Macmillan's and Sir Douglas-Home's loss of power in the early 1960s, serious debate again took place within the Tory party over the question of what alternative could be offered to the seductive socialism

---

6. First quote in Young, *Iron Lady,* 198; for "wets," see 198–200, 204, 209, 503. Agreement and adrenalin quotes in "Margaret Thatcher in Her Own Words," *The Economist,* November 24, 1990, 20. Polling statistics in Gordon Heald and Robert Wybrow, *Gallup Survey of Britain* (London: Croom Helm, 1986), 30–31.

7. Young, *Iron Lady,* 31; *Grantham Journal* quote in Young, 21.

preached by the Labour Party. In these debates Thatcher listened more than she spoke. A revealing exception was her 1968 Conservative Party Centre lecture, entitled "What's Wrong with Politics." This was her first comprehensive effort in public to spell out the political philosophy which would later guide her as prime minister. She bemoaned the absence of firm beliefs, emphasized the moral flaws of an incomes policy, and attacked the evils of consensus politics and government bureaucratic power.[8]

A member of Heath's government from 1970 to 1974, she respected the requirements of collective responsibility and did not criticize the prime minister's policy. But after his second defeat within a year's time in 1974, her interest in philosophy and ideology took on new fervor. Her most inspiring colleague in this enterprise was Keith Joseph, who immediately after Heath's fall as prime minister began speaking in public about the crisis in conservatism and the need for radical change. She called him her "closest political friend." His message was hers, although her break from Heath's views was more cautious than Joseph's. She joined the Conservative Philosophy Group, a semi-conspiratorial dining club which brought together philosophers and politicians to seek a new conservative direction for the party. She declared that "we must have an ideology. . . . The other side have got an ideology they can test their policies against. We must have one as well." Her interests in philosophy were less speculative than utilitarian. She examined philosophies for approaches and phrases she could use to undergird her own political ideas with more force and persuade the public of the rightness of her course. The result was a practical philosophy relevant to pressing public issues which most people could understand.[9]

She delighted in delivering bad news and stern lectures, and her driving ambition and moral certitude threw her opponents on the defensive. She was frequently criticized for simplicity and for infusing morality into complicated issues. But one of her greatest arts was the ability to crystallize and glamorize profound ideas and sell them to the voting public in terms of good and evil and as notions which are easily comprehensible, obvious, and

---

8. For influence of Hayek, see her *Downing Street Years,* 12, 618, 716, and Young, *Iron Lady,* 22, 405-7. For 1968 speech, see text in Part II of this book, as well as Young, 62-63, and the Cronin chapter in this book. The Conservative Political Centre is a policy study group within the party which has the liberty to be critical of party policy. For her role in it, see Young, 86, and *Downing Street Years,* 14.

9. Quote on need for ideology in Young, *Iron Lady,* 406. Because of her admiration for Joseph, she did not declare her candidacy for the party leadership until he had disqualified himself politically by stating publicly that the high birth rate among the poor was diminishing the quality of the British population. Thatcher eliminated Heath on the first ballot on February 4, 1975, and won easily on the second ballot a week later. See Rasmussen chapter in this book and Young, 91-98. In her cabinet, Joseph served in minor posts until 1986. For his influence on her, see Young, 75-80, 93, 102-3, 144; Thatcher, *Downing Street Years,* 14, 26, 562; and the Rasmussen and Cronin chapters in this book.

FIGURE 1.2 Thatcher meets in the garden of her London home with Tory leaders, April 22, 1979. They are (left to right): Angus Maude, James Prior, Humphrey Atkins, Lord Thorneycroft, Thatcher, Keith Joseph, Lord Carrington, Francis Pym, Ian Gilmour (back), and Geoffrey Howe. (*Source:* British Information Services, New York.)

utterly necessary. She once said that "I am in politics because of the conflict between good and evil, and I believe that in the end good will triumph." The fervor of her conviction paralyzed those who wavered. Her biographer, Hugo Young, called her greatest gift her "inspirational certainty."[10]

Popularity and Image

Thatcher was always a populist who had an uncanny knack for capturing the public mood, whether the issue was nuclear weapons, South Africa, hanging, union reform, law and order, or selling public (council) housing. Nevertheless, she was the ultimate example that a political leader need not be popular. She was charismatic and successful, but she was autocratic, unbending, and unloved. At election time in 1979, her popularity lagged 19

---

10. First quote in Young, *Iron Lady,* 352. Final Young quote in "Thatcher for President," *Time,* May 15, 1989, 90.

percentage points behind that of her opponent, James Callaghan, and by the end of 1981 she was the most unpopular prime minister since polling had begun. But she declared: "I will not change just to court popularity."[11]

Author Anthony Burgess wrote that "the trouble with her is that, despite allure and purposefulness, she's not likeable. Churchill, with all his faults, was even lovable. So was the Edwardian dandy Macmillan. But we have had ten years of a middle-class lady with an affected accent who chills the heart and stultifies the imagination." That Burgess was not writing fiction here is confirmed by opinion polls taken in 1985. Most British respondents found her tough, determined, "sticks to her principles," decisive, and shrewd; they agreed that she has a strong personality, speaks her mind, was trying hard, and knows what she's talking about. But they also identified her greatest deficiencies in terms of caring, listening to reason, being likeable as a person, and being sympathetic and in touch with working class, ordinary people. Only a third would want her as a friend.[12]

She never enjoyed "popularity," as her many nicknames reveal: "Attila the Hen," "the blessed Margaret," and "Nanny," to mention a few of the "kinder" ones. Many saw her as uncaring, insensitive, self-righteous, cold, obsessed, bossy, heavy-handed, and domineering. But she did not care. For her, fear and respect were far more important in politics than love and affection. She had won leadership over a divided party, most of whose senior leaders had voted against her. During her first government she led a divided cabinet, most of whose members opposed her economic policies and the methods she employed to put them into action. Many considered those policies to have been responsible for the depression and poverty of the 1930s, which had badly damaged the Tory party. Nevertheless, she often treated leading Tories in her cabinet like errant schoolboys, hectoring them and making decisions for them.

She had authority and respect because of her courage and what she accomplished and represented. She strode resolutely forward to remake her country in her own self-image: brisk, hard-working, frugal, and self-sufficient. She combined some of the best nineteenth-century values with twentieth-century energy. She rejected the spirit of failure. She was a strong leader who entered office with a sense of mission: to make Britain great again, or as she noted: to put the "Great" back into Britain. "I came to office with one deliberate intent: to change Britain from a dependent to a self-reliant

---

11. Thatcher quote in Young, *Iron Lady*, 240; see also 241–42 for popularity and 545 for populist.

12. Burgess quote in "Thatcher's Place in History," 59. Polling results in Heald and Wybrow, *Gallup*, 27–36, 45–46. For polling during 1979 elections, see Robert M. Worcester and Martin Harrop, eds., *Political Communications: the General Election Campaign of 1979* (Cambridge, Mass.: Basil Blackwell, 1991).

society—from a give-it-to-me to a do-it-yourself nation; to a get-up-and-go, instead of a sit-back-and-wait-for-it Britain."[13]

Luck

Thatcher won respect because of her combination of decisiveness and luck. Napoleon's standard question about his generals, "Has he luck?" could be applied also to her. She had luck! First she had only to face the Tories' B-team to win the party leadership in 1975 because a mortally wounded Heath prevented the top leaders from throwing their hats into the ring. As prime minister, she benefitted from an opposition which was in disarray and which, combined with the electoral system, gave her three consecutive election victories although at least 55 percent of the voters always voted against her party. She had the luxury of governing without an effective parliamentary opposition.

It has been said that the world stands aside for a man who knows where he is going. By the spring of 1979, British voters were prepared to do just that, with the ironic twist that the new leader was a woman. When she moved into the prime minister's office, she promised "three years of unparalleled austerity," and for three years the pain of Thatcherism was far more evident than the benefits. Unemployment rose and economic conditions worsened. She was unable to cut government spending significantly because of greater numbers on welfare and pay raises for government workers to bring them into equity with the private sector. Nevertheless, she held firm to her monetarist policies, vowing that "I will not stagger from expedient to expedient." She declared that the voters did not want "a government to be so flexible that it became invertebrate. You don't want a government of flexi-toys."[14]

By 1982 her party was well behind the Labour Party and the new Social Democratic Party (SDP)–Liberal Alliance in the polls, and she seemed to be heading for sure defeat in the next elections. Then the unexpected occurred.

---

13. "Thatcher in Her Own Words." Biographer Russell Lewis wrote of her capture of the leadership: "The widespread enthusiasm which her election aroused was partly due to her novelty and partly to her striking looks, but more than all else, it was due to her being the embodiment of many hopes." *Margaret Thatcher: A Personal and Political Biography* (London: Routledge and Kegan Paul, 1975), quoted also in Patrick Cosgrave, *Margaret Thatcher: A Tory and Her Party* (London: Hutchinson, 1978), 1. She wrote in *Downing Street Years,* 15: "We stood for a new beginning, not more of the same. . . . If we failed, we would never be given another chance."

14. "Thatcher in Her Own Words." Monetarism, which calls for enforcing financial discipline by restricting the money supply, is a term popularized by University of Chicago economist Milton Friedman, whom she knew and admired. Because many in her first cabinet neither understood nor embraced this theory, she formed an inner economic circle of believers within the cabinet which made all important economic decisions. See Young, *Iron Lady,* 149.

The Argentines gave her the chance to reassert herself and soar in the polls. Their troops invaded a small group of off-shore islands which had long been settled and ruled by the British. Until then Thatcher had neglected this festering problem and was unprepared to deal with it. Nevertheless, she responded quickly and galvanized the nation with her firmness and resolution in organizing the recapture of the Falkland Islands. The British basked again briefly in imperial glory, and she became an international figure who startled a world which had become almost supine in the face of naked aggression. An overwhelming majority of them applauded their leader for her ability to handle the crisis. Her wartime leadership, combined with the first signs of economic recovery and the public perception of Labour Leader Michael Foot as likeable but incompetent, greatly improved her electoral prospects. In December 1981 her approval rating had stood at 25 percent, making her the least popular prime minister since the war; six months later her popularity had doubled.[15]

Economic Policies and Trade Unions

The economic upsurge came, despite her own initial anxiety: "Supposing I put the ball at their feet, and they don't kick it?"[16] The electorate became convinced that her economic medicine had been a harsh necessity. Sensing the political winds blowing briskly at her back, she took advantage of the prime minister's privilege to set an election whenever it suits his or her party. Her electoral triumph in June 1983, which made her the first Conservative prime minister in the twentieth century to be reelected to a second term, revealed both the leadership image she had established in the Falklands War and the extent to which most social and economic groups in Britain accepted her diagnosis of the nation's problems. Most voters did not blame her for the country's most pressing problem: continuing unemployment, which had shot up from 4.3 percent to 13.3 percent during her four years in office. They patted her on the back for bringing inflation down to the lowest level in fifteen years. While the Labour Party focused on class-based rhetoric in a nation in which class significance is declining and in which the traditional working class is shrinking, the Conservatives aimed their appeal at the burgeoning middle class. Thatcher was in closer touch with the British people.

To her benefit, the Labour Party ripped itself apart when the extreme left

---

15. Heald and Wybrow, *Gallup,* 27–28; Robert M. Worcester, *British Public Opinion: A Guide to the History and Techniques of Public Opinion Polling* (Cambridge, Mass.: Basil Blackwell, 1991), 76, 83–84, 89–93. For Falklands War, see chapters by Ward and Salmon-Macnair in this book.

16. "A Legacy of Revolution," *Time,* December 3, 1990, 66.

tried to take it over, and the right split off to form the SDP. Labour was also dragged down by its links to the trade unions. Soaring inflation and rising unemployment, accompanied by increasingly strident union demands, had alienated people. Their revulsion at the excessive "unelected power" wielded by union bosses, who had toppled the governments of her two predecessors, had boiled to the surface in "the winter of discontent," 1978–1979, when coal and transportation strikes threatened to paralyze the entire nation. When the coal miners' unions tried this again in the winter of 1984–1985, she ultimately forced them to back down, granting no concessions after having encouraged the Coal Board and electricity industry to boost their stocks before the strike began. This humiliating defeat left the unions demoralized and on the defensive, as many of their members quit.

Backed by a nation which admired her strength, she attacked this unpopular enemy by expertly applying "salami tactics" to the laws that protected their collective rights and legal immunities: those that backed the closed shop, required employers to recognize unions, and permitted political strikes and secondary picketing. Her legislation made the unions more democratic. Secret ballots of all members have to be used whenever union bosses are elected, funds are given to political parties, or strikes are approved. National unions became financially responsible for the actions of their members, and labor contracts are enforceable in court. She rooted out one of the main causes of the "English disease" by taking on the bosses of the most powerful unions and crushing them: the steel workers in 1980, the coal miners in 1985 and the teachers in 1986. By 1987 strikes were at a fifty-year low; workdays lost to union disputes declined from 29.5 million in 1979 to 1.9 million in 1986.

The reduction in the number and length of strikes was, in part, due to workers' and employees' fear of losing their jobs and to their realization that real earnings for those with work had risen almost 35 percent between 1980 and 1987. There had also been a change of attitudes: many workers began to associate unions with strikes and therefore turned their backs on the unions, whose membership continued to decline. An important result for the overall economy was that the unions were no longer able to block the introduction of state-of-the-art technology in order to protect jobs. Thus, while from 1974 to 1980 output per worker in British manufacturing did not increase at all, from 1981 to 1987 it grew by 40 percent.

Reducing the State's Role in the Economy

The failures of the 1970s had prepared the way for a party leader who would advocate a policy based on the notions that the best help was self help, that initiative deserved rewards, that an economic pie must be baked before it is divided, that welfare could not produce prosperity, that free enterprise and competition are the engines of prosperity, that private business is better than nationalized industries, that the problem of inflation is greater than the problem of unemployment, and that the government cannot control the economy. She regarded traditional Keynesian economics as no cure for British problems, but as part of the disease.

Thatcher argued that the state was overspending, and the shortfalls were being covered by public borrowing and expanding the money supply, rather than by taxes. These expedients stimulated inflation and absorbed the capital which was desperately needed to finance industrial innovation. The cure, she argued, was to restrict the money supply and cut public expenditures, which would both reduce inflation and free investment capital. To create economic incentives, income taxes should be cut. Trade union power had to be curbed. Most important, an "enterprise culture" had to be created. Britain had to become a self-reliant, property-based democracy of popular capitalism in which good housekeeping would be best guaranteed by commercial self-interest, and success would have to be won in the market. She said in March 1980: "We should not expect the state to appear in the guise of an extravagant good fairy at every christening, a loquacious companion at every stage of life's journey, the unknown mourner at every funeral."[17]

At the heart of Thatcherism was the conviction that the country will be better off when individual citizens pursue wealth and are permitted to enjoy it. Thus, people would have to be given incentives to prosper, and commercial success should be admired, not scorned as vulgar. She announced that her vision was "a free, classless, open Britain." She claimed that her policies "are not based on some economic theory but on things I and millions like me were brought up with: an honest day's work for an honest day's pay; live within your means; put a nest egg by for a rainy day; pay your bills on time; support the police."[18]

Thatcher's Economic Success

Shortly after capturing the leadership of the Tory party in 1975, she announced that "I have changed everything."[19] By the time she stepped

---

17. Young, *Iron Lady*, 147.

18. Vision in "Legacy of Revolution." Second quote in "Thatcher's Ten Years," 19–20.

19. "Thatcher's Ten Years," 20. There had always been division within Tory ranks between proponents of more state intervention and those who favor less regulation and a much freer market economy. It was publicly perceived in 1975 when Thatcher defeated Heath for the party leadership that the new leader represented a different Toryism than Heath. But in some important ways he had helped pave the way for some of the changes she effected. He had favored a revamped conservatism, curbs on union power, changes in the welfare state, and an emphasis on business interests. For a comparison of the two leaders, see Young, *Iron Lady,* 51–65.

down in 1990, how much had she changed, and how lasting were those changes? Despite the legends which developed around this extraordinary leader, she did not come to power with a master plan. "Thatcherism" evolved through improvisation, happenstance, and pragmatism. For example, privatization went much farther than anyone had imagined in 1979. By 1990 fifty large companies had been sold or scheduled for sale, more than two-thirds of all industrial assets the state owned in 1979. Believing that making money should be rewarded, not penalized, she lowered the top tax rate on earned income from 83 percent to 40 percent and the basic rate from 33 percent to 25 percent. She reduced public spending from 44 percent of Gross Domestic Product (GDP) to 39.5 percent in 1990. Her government abolished wage, price, credit, and exchange controls, and in 1988 it reported a budget surplus of £3,000,000,000.

By election time in 1987, Thatcher evoked a nation with revived spirit and restored reputation. What many people had seen as an irreversible British economic decline had been stopped. Her pride and her optimism were borne out by the facts. She had inherited low economic growth and high inflation. Since the country began pulling out of recession in 1981, manufacturing output had shot up, and annual productivity had increased 3.5 percent, the highest in Europe in 1987–1988. Work stoppages had dropped to the lowest level since the late-1930s. The economy had grown at an annual rate of 3 percent and in 1988 was Western Europe's fastest growing economy, with 4 percent growth in real GDP. Inflation, which her Chancellor of the Exchequer Nigel Lawson called the government's "judge and jury," was down from a high of 24.2 percent to 3.5 percent in 1988, the lowest level in two decades. The average voter's real pretax income had increased by 25 percent since 1979.[20]

Unemployment was still higher than the 4.3 percent when she took office, standing at 11 percent at election time in 1987. However, in part because of incentives to small enterprises, a million new jobs had been created. Also, the jobs of the 89 percent who were employed in 1987 seemed far less threatened than in the early 1980s. Interest rates were falling, and the pound was much stronger. The British stock market was booming, and the U.K. had again become a leading creditor nation. Public borrowing had fallen to 1 percent of national income. Most important, she had restored morale and seemed to have ended decades of relative economic decline.

After her 1987 victory, London's *Sunday Times* proclaimed that Thatcher had brought about Britain's "biggest transformation since the Industrial Revolution." Indeed, her economic performance had profoundly changed her country. She had advanced what she called a "property-owning democracy," in which "every earner shall be an owner." Because her government

---

20. Harris, *Thatcher*, 214–16.

permitted many persons living in public (council) housing to buy their homes, more than two-thirds of Britons owned their homes, compared to 52 percent in 1979. Car ownership had also risen from 54 percent to 66 percent.

In 1979 four times as many Britons belonged to trade unions as owned shares in the stock market. By 1990 the number of stock-holders had tripled from 7 to 22 percent. During the Wilson-Callaghan years, trade union membership had grown from 24 to 30 percent of adults. As a result of a fall in union membership by one-fourth to fewer than nine million and 22 percent of adults during the Thatcher years, the number of union members and stock-holders became equal. Most people (88 percent) still believed that the unions were essential for protecting workers' interests. But while seven in ten respondents thought in 1979 that the unions had "too much power," only a third (31 percent) thought so in 1990. Thatcher's party made impressive inroads into the union vote. In the 1987 elections, the Tories commanded an 11 percent lead among working-class homeowners, compared with a 37 percent Labour lead among working-class council renters. Also, during the Wilson years, the majority of union members voted Labour; in 1987 only 42 percent did (up from 39 percent in 1983).[21]

Thatcher's rule had an impact on Britain's class structure. Robert Worcester argues that during her decade in power, the social categorization of the population underwent more change than at any time in British history. In 1979, a third of the public were in the middle social class, and two-thirds were in the working class. A decade later approximately 40 percent of households were middle class, while about 60 percent were working class. A "swing" of 7 percent had taken place. In terms of self-perception, the percentage of Britons who considered themselves to belong to the middle class had increased from 30 percent of the population in 1979 to roughly 50 percent in 1987.[22]

Many of her economic changes will survive. She herself had confidently predicted in 1986 that "I think, historically, the term Thatcherism will be seen as a compliment." Privatization, reform of the trade unions, and the central role of the market will not be fundamentally questioned. Nor will incomes policies and exchange controls be reimposed and tax rates brought back to 1970s levels. She was a chief spokesperson of an era which revealed that the invincibility of socialism was a myth, both in foreign and domestic policy. She had declared her goal to be nothing less than "the death of socialism," and she partly succeeded. She destroyed the old presumption that the U.K.'s mixed economy would continue to drift leftward. This had a profound effect on the Labour Party, which had to move toward the political center to survive and be electable. It was forced to transform itself

---

21. Worcester, *British Public Opinion,* 109, 116–17.
22. Ibid., 115–16.

by abandoning its antinuclear stance, unilateralism, hostility to the EC, and passion for nationalizing the "commanding heights" of the economy. It had to accept the notion that the state must work with and encourage the private market rather than seek to dominate it. As she broke off the handle of the "ratchet of socialism," Labour had to shed its identity as a socialist party.[23]

Incomplete Economic Revolution

Thatcher's "economic miracle" was restricted mainly to southern England, with Wales, northern England, and especially Scotland having benefitted far less from the revival. She herself admitted that there had been "no Tartan Thatcherite revolution." In her final year and a half in office, economic growth went flat again, and inflation climbed. She bequeathed upon her successor what became Britain's longest recession in decades. Her attempts to shake inflation out of the economy had created much pain. She had persuaded many British to worry less about unemployment. But double-digit joblessness combined with insufficient retraining of persons put out of work, especially those in the manufacturing sector, represents a significant underutilization of the nation's economic resources.[24]

The living standards of those with work rose, but economic inequality also increased. Although three-fourths of respondents said in a 1987 poll that they were satisfied with their standard of living, which had risen, almost nine out of ten agreed that "the gap between the rich and the poor in Britain is too wide." The poorest families in the U.K. saw their real income drop 14 percent, while the average household experienced a 36 percent increase. In 1991 the lower half of the population received a quarter of the total income, versus a third in 1979; thirteen million Britons lived on less than half the average income, versus five million in 1979. By the end of the 1980s more and more British began focusing their attention on the neglected infrastructure resulting from insufficient public investment. They became concerned about a decline of their roads, schools, and hospitals. Anthony Sampson, who had produced a series of books since 1962 entitled *Anatomy of Britain,* concluded a survey of the Thatcher years: "London is now the showplace for every inner-city malaise: declining transport and services, poverty, homelessness and non-planning blight."[25]

---

23. Thatcher prediction in "Legacy of Revolution." "End of socialism" in "Thatcher Revolution," 31.

24. Quote about Scotland in Thatcher, *Downing Street Years,* 618; see also 619–24. For economic turndown after 1988, see Alt chapter in this book.

25. See 1987 polling results in Worcester, *British Public Opinion,* 112. Other statistics in "When the Lustre Fades," *Maclean's,* April 20, 1992, 25, *The Guardian,* July 1, 1993, 1, and *The Economist,* July 10, 1993, 50. That these are relative figures is shown by another point in the last

She hated the term, "welfare state," and she swore that she would move the country away from it. She was not in principle opposed to welfare assistance, even for the "undeserving poor." But she argued that public assistance must not reinforce the dependency culture and should aim to restore the needy's self-discipline and self-esteem. "If the irresponsible behaviour does not involve penalty of some kind, irresponsibility will for a large number of people become the norm. More important still, the attitudes may be passed on to their children." She was sharply criticized for saying once that "there is no such thing as society." Largely unreported, however, was what she went on to say: "No government can do anything except through people, and people must look to themselves first." She was objecting to the view that the helper of first resort should be the state (a term often confused with "society") instead of individuals, families, and neighbors. The result, in her opinion, was that individuals and communities, which constitute a society, became discouraged and disoriented.[26]

In any case, she did not savage the budgets for welfare services, as her critics charge. In fact, total public spending actually rose by a fifth during her time in office although it had declined as a percentage of GDP. Social security and the National Health Service (NHS) consumed a third more, in real terms, in 1990 than in 1979, and spending on education also grew. Her efforts were directed toward getting more business-like management and more performance for the money spent. Efficiency and value-for-money audits became frequent, and competition forced the public sector into market discipline. Some public services were put out to tender in the private sector. She ordered that those persons really in need be targeted. Nevertheless, she left a Britain which was still less an enterprise society and more a welfare society. Such plans as education vouchers and workfare were not enacted, and the basic educational and health systems remained intact. The social security system was tightened up but not dismantled.[27]

Perhaps her greatest failure was that, despite three consecutive election victories won in part because voters saw economic improvement since 1979, she had failed to stamp her values permanently on the public's mind. She had declared that "economics are the method, but the object is to change the heart and soul." But most British were not converted to "Thatcherism." In a 1988 MORI survey, taken a year after 58 percent of the voters had voted against her party, seven in ten respondents saw Britain as "Thatcherist,"

---

two articles that ownership of consumer durables rose among the poorest tenth of the population between 1979 and 1991: ownership of washing machines rose from 69 to 85 percent of households, cars from 39 to 49 percent, and central heating from 29 to 69 percent.

26. Quotations in *Downing Street Years,* 626–27; see also 628–32 for the family, Young, *Iron Lady,* 534–36, and her March 4, 1981, speech in Part II of this book.

27. See *Downing Street Years,* 590–617 for her education, housing, and health policies.

while only four in ten wished it to be so. Asked about the "ideal society," 49 percent favored one that is a "mainly socialist society in which public interest and a more controlled economy are more important"; 45 percent favored a "mainly capitalist society in which private interests and free enterprise are more important." Almost eight in ten (79 percent) preferred a "society in which the caring for others is more highly regarded" to one in which the creation of wealth is emphasized; 55 percent chose collectivism over self-sufficiency. The survey concluded that 54 percent of the British public held essentially socialist values, while only 39 percent were essentially "Thatcherist." In her memoirs she confessed that she had failed to persuade even her cabinet of "Thatcherism": "I believed that they had generally become convinced of the rightness of the basic principles as I had. Orthodox finance, low levels of regulation and taxation, a minimal bureaucracy, strong defence, a willingness to stand up for British interests wherever and whenever threatened. . . . The arguments for them seemed to me to have been won. I now know that such arguments are never finally won."[28]

After she left office in 1990, public opinion polls revealed that more people favored increasing government services, even at the cost of higher taxes, than when she had taken office. In November 1992, the annual study of public opinion, *British Social Attitudes,* registered a marked shift of support toward intervention in the economy and away from free enterprise. Only one Briton in three agreed that private enterprise is the best way to solve economic problems. Partly because of renewed recession, her efforts to change the economic culture of Britain did not entirely succeed.[29]

Centralizing Political Power

Thatcher enlarged economic freedom for the individual, but this was not accompanied by a similar expansion of political freedom. She trimmed the central government by reducing the size of the civil service in Whitehall and gaining greater prime ministerial control over the top jobs. She promoted high achievers and transferred almost half of all civil servants to new agencies working at a greater distance from the traditional civil service. By privatizing many state industries, she reduced the role of government ministries in the nation's industries.

---

28. First Thatcher quote in "The Thatcher Revolution," *Maclean's,* May 8, 1989, 33. Final quote in *Downing Street Years,* 755. MORI poll in Worcester, *British Public Opinion,* 113–15; see also Young, *Iron Lady,* 529–30. Thatcher responded in 1986 to the charge of insufficient "caring" by saying that "caring isn't measured by what you say; it's expressed by what you do." Harris, *Thatcher,* 219.

29. "Stepping Out," *Maclean's,* 38. *British Social Attitudes* in "Thatcherism RIP," *The Economist,* November 21, 1992, 70.

Committed to tight central control over all government spending, she changed local government fundamentally, beginning with the abolition of the Greater London Council. She saw local government as one of the three institutions (the other two being the trade unions and Labour Party) in which the "hard left," which she was determined to crush because it sought to impose a Marxist system on Britain, was entrenched. The main idea behind the hated flat-rate community charge (poll tax) was to make the spending increases of local governments brutally clear and costly to all voters, thereby strengthening political pressures against local tax levies. But the sale of public housing, the "opting-out" for local schools (which enhanced the authority of the Ministry of Education), the tendering-out of services, and financial controls greatly weakened local governments and diminished their financial independence. This added up to a net strengthening of central political power in the U.K., including the power of the prime minister.[30]

She distrusted government and sought to reduce the dead hand of the state in order to encourage people "to stand on their own two feet." She accomplished this in the economic sphere, especially through her privatization program. But she actually broadened government power in the political sphere. This was abetted by the absence of an effective opposition in Parliament. Hers was a very activist law and order government, which legislated on a broad scale, including gun control, capital punishment, football hooliganism, homosexual rights, broadcasting guidelines, and secrecy laws. It did so without the usual British search for a consensus before charging off in a new direction.[31]

In the field of civil rights, her government prohibited alleged terrorists from broadcasting statements; this was directed primarily at the Irish Republican Army (IRA). Although she always enjoyed a sympathetic press in Britain, her government pressured television editors more than her predecessors had. It advocated censorship of publications deemed as security violations and tightened the Official Secrets Act to make it more difficult for journalists to publish such leaks. For example, her government pursued the author and publisher of the book *Spycatcher* even after it had been published and sold

---

30. A poll tax is paid by renters and homeowners alike regardless of income. It is a case where her moral sense, which had been the source of much of her dynamism, had blinded her to political realities, endangered her party's electoral prospects, and helped bring her down. It was phased out by her successor. See Thatcher, *Downing Street Years*, 339, for "hard left" and 642–67 for poll tax. See also Rasmussen and John chapters in this book.

31. *The Economist,* in "The Thatcher Legacy," October 2, 1993, 65–67, argued that her gathering of powers in central government hands was done to further the interests of the middle, lower-middle, and aspiring working classes. Her claim to have "rethought the state" was false, but "no implacable defender of the middle class can roll back the state."

FIGURE 1.3 Thatcher signing the Roll of Honorary Freemen at Kensington Town Hall in London, October 15, 1979. With her is Mayor Christopher Walford. (*Source:* British Information Services, New York.)

to the public.[32] Finally, she dominated her own cabinet far more than had any previous prime minister, giving new meaning to the concept of "prime ministerial government." She reduced anyone in her own cabinet who could rival her. Only one person (Geoffrey Howe) survived her eleven years in power.

Foreign Policy

In foreign affairs, she was the first British prime minister since Harold Macmillan to have real influence over both superpowers. She came to office with no clear set of foreign policy priorities, and her moral approach to

---

32. Young, *Iron Lady,* 459–63, 510, 537–39. Harris, *Thatcher,* 216–17. See K. D. Ewing and C. A. Gearty, *Freedom Under Thatcher: Civil Liberties in Modern Britain* (Oxford: Oxford University Press, 1990).

politics was less suited to this complicated arena than to domestic politics. Nevertheless, she set a bold example of resolution, as she strode the world stage commanding respect and exercising influence out of all proportion to the U.K.'s power and size. Her frank, personal diplomacy enhanced her and her country's influence.[33]

Anticommunism had strongly shaped her opinions since the war, and these sentiments were strengthened in the mid-1970s by Alexander Solzhenitsyn's attacks on Marxism-Leninism. During her first term, she continually criticized Moscow's leaders for their blustering, menacing behavior and human rights violations. But after her 1983 victory, she became convinced that Western nations should encourage change in the Soviet Union in a more constructive way. Her government began advocating an opening to the East and a search for practical forms of cooperation. She recognized Mikhail Gorbachev as a different kind of Soviet leader. She invited him to visit London in December 1984, four months before he became leader of the Soviet Communist Party. He impressed everyone with his candid and independent thinking. At the conclusion of his visit, she told the BBC that "I like Mr. Gorbachev; we can do business together." She called for a realistic assessment of the U.S.S.R. and warned against "starry-eyed thinking that one day Communism will collapse like a pack of cards, because it will not."[34] She assumed a role as interlocutor between the superpowers and convinced President Ronald Reagan that he too could get along with the new Soviet leader. She thus played a significant part in winning the Cold War. Because she was the West's most forceful spokesperson for individual rights, democracy, and the virtues of capitalism, she was greatly respected in the ex-communist world.

She was implacably hostile to the IRA, but she signed the 1985 Anglo-Irish declaration which, for the first time, accepted the Irish Republic's claim to have a say in Northern Irish affairs. She was respected in the British Commonwealth. However, Britain's relations with many of its partners deteriorated because of her opposition to economic sanctions against South Africa.[35]

She was admired abroad, especially in America, more than she was at home. Her political instincts had been shaped when Britain's allies were across the Atlantic and the enemy in Europe. At a time when most of

---

33. In *Downing Street Years,* 486–87, she wrote that "one should never lose sight of the importance of personal chemistry" between leaders, but that "personal relations must never become a substitute for hard-headed pursuit of national interests." See also 8–9 for her description of the U.K.'s foreign policy weaknesses she inherited.

34. Young, *Iron Lady,* 169–70, 185, 389–95, quotes on 393. See also her description of Gorbachev's first London visit in *Downing Street Years,* 459–63.

35. See Thatcher, *Downing Street Years,* 383–415 for Ireland; 512–24 for Commonwealth affairs and South Africa.

FIGURE 1.4 Mikhail Gorbachev visits Thatcher at Number 10 Downing Street, April 1989. (*Source:* Central Office of Information, London.)

Britain's foreign policy and business elite had long accepted that the U.K.'s relations with Europe were at least as important as its Atlantic ties, she gave absolute priority to the alliance with the U.S. "No one of my generation can forget that America has been the principal architect of a peace in Europe which has lasted forty years." The Americans appreciated her unflagging support, but the "special relationship" was not what it once was. Washington relied on Thatcher to block the threat of a closed "fortress Europe," which, it was feared, could be created by the EC's move toward a single market in 1992. But her obstreperousness toward her European counterparts risked driving Britain toward the periphery, not the heart of Europe, where it could have real influence. Also, the end of the Cold War somewhat diminished America's need for a trusty British ally in Europe. Increasingly important for the U.S. were relations with the EC itself and with such new powers as Germany, whose unification in 1990 Thatcher had opposed.[36]

Her image in the EC suffered because of her battles to change the Common Agricultural Program (CAP), to reduce the U.K.'s budget bill to Brussels, and to oppose the transfer of power to community institutions. She was in favor of European economic and political cooperation, and she never contemplated taking the U.K. out of the EC. As a member of Heath's cabinet, she had been bound by collective responsibility and had therefore supported British entry in the 1972 referendum. But she insisted that "we must look after British interests," and she was sensitive about grants of British sovereignty to bureaucrats in Brussels. "I do not believe in a federal Europe, and I think to ever compare it with the United States of America is absolutely ridiculous." Always the consummate populist, she was also well aware that her critical stance toward the EC was popular with British voters. This domestic political bonus helped inspire her to take an uncompromising stance toward her EC counterparts. Roy Jenkins said in 1985, while he was president of the European Commission, that "as a proponent of the British case, she does have the advantage of being almost totally impervious to how much she offends other people. . . . I have seen her when she was a new prime minister surrounded by others who were against her and being unmoved by this in a way that many other people would find difficult to withstand."[37]

---

36. Andrew Thomson, *Margaret Thatcher: The Woman Within* (London: W. H. Allen, 1989), 155. See chapter by Sir William Nicoll in this book. Her relations with George Bush were not as close as those with his predecessor, Ronald Reagan; see her *Downing Street Years,* 768, 782–84. For her reflections on the changes wrought by the collapse of communism, see 812–15, and the Salmon-Macnair chapter in this book. For her objections to German unification, see 768–70, 791–96, and 813–15 in her memoirs.

37. Quotations from Young, *Iron Lady,* 189–90. See also her 1988 Bruges speech in Part II of this book.

FIGURE 1.5 U.S. Ambassador Charles Price and Secretary of State James Baker (left) meet with Prime Minister Thatcher and (right) Foreign Secretary Geoffrey Howe and Denis Thatcher at the prime minister's weekend retreat, Chequers, February 1989. (*Source:* British Information Services, New York.)

Her objections to European unification did not endear her in European capitals. Piet Dankaert, president of the European Parliament from 1982 to 1984, described her as "the witch in the European fairy tale—always clearly recognisable and always the person liable to turn everything upside down." She had no sympathy for her continental colleagues, as she made clear in 1984: "There are nine of them being tiresome, and only one of me. I can cope with the nine of them, so they ought to be able to stand one of me." Even at home she was never able to persuade all her cabinet to embrace her views on Britain's role in the EC. Her deputy prime minister, Sir Geoffrey Howe, who launched her downfall because of unbridgeable differences on European policy, accused her of seeing a continent "positively teeming with ill-intentioned people scheming, in her words, to extinguish democracy."[38]

Resignation

On Thatcher's fall, former Foreign Secretary David Owen commented: "The Greeks understood it all. Great men and women are not brought down by lesser mortals. They are brought down by themselves."[39] Thatcher's cabinet was rocked by high-level resignations stemming from disagreements over Europe: In 1986 Michael Heseltine stormed out because he wanted a European consortium, not one from the U.S., to purchase a British helicopter company, Westland. In 1989 Nigel Lawson left because he insisted that the pound be included in the European Monetary System (EMS), to which Thatcher eventually agreed. The fatal resignation and the catalyst for her downfall was that of Sir Geoffrey Howe, the last surviving member of her original 1979 cabinet and an architect of "Thatcherism." He charged in Parliament that her obstruction in Europe carried "serious risks for our nation." His devastating speech led to a successful challenge to her leadership in November 1990. After the longest prime ministry since the Victorian era and the longest consecutive one since the Napoleonic age, Thatcher resigned.

The events leading to her fall related to Europe, but the underlying reasons why 45 percent of her parliamentary party colleagues voted against her were her domineering style and the likelihood that she was guiding her party toward defeat in the next elections. She admitted this at the time of her resignation: "The unity of the party and the prospects of victory in a general election would be better served if I stood down."[40] For eighteen months her party had trailed a Labour Party that had become more moderate, had overthrown its suicidal commitment to nuclear disarmament, and had embraced the EC. Her country was experiencing high inflation, a growing trade deficit, a slow-down in economic growth, and intense domestic opposition to her overwhelmingly unpopular poll tax for local governments.

Her compatriots had once greeted her brave radicalism and had supported her single-minded and often ruthless crusade to fashion a new social fabric in Britain based on property ownership, freedom of choice, and responsibility. She was forced to resign when her firmness turned into rigidity, and conviction became deafness. She had drifted increasingly out of touch with the mood in her country and her own party. She was toppled when she

---

38. Dankaert in "Thatcher's Place in History," 58. Thatcher in "Margaret Thatcher in Her Own Words." Howe in "It Is Time to Go," 63. See Young, *Iron Lady,* 382–88 for her basic objections to the EC. In her memoirs, she devoted two chapters to the EC with the derisory titles, "Jeux sans frontières" (Games without Borders) and "The Babel Express." She made no effort to conceal her distrust for "that un-British combination of high-flown rhetoric and pork-barrel politics which passed for European statesmanship." *Downing Street Years,* 727.

39. "Astride the World Stage," *Washington Post,* November 23, 1990, 1. See Lewis G. John's analysis of her fall in this book.

40. "Margaret Thatcher in Her Own Words," 34.

thought she knew what was best for Britain, even if everyone else disagreed. One of her MPs, William Powell, commented: "She's reached the point where everyone else is wrong and she's right. None of us want it, but there comes a point when simply we have to say, 'Enough.'" In his lengthy and highly readable memoirs, *The View from No 11, Memoirs of a Tory Radical,* Nigel Lawson calls her "one of the greatest prime ministers this country has known." But he provides a devastating chronicle of Thatcher's progressive deterioration as prime minister. She

> came increasingly to believe that she *was* the government and had no need of allies. . . . These traits led to the isolation and behaviour pattern that contributed to her eventual downfall. . . . Increasing numbers . . . of voters saw her as disagreeably strident, excessively authoritarian and unbearably bossy.

After winning three elections, she was sad and perplexed about having to quit. "It's a funny old world," she was reported to have mused at the time.[41]

Retirement

For a person with her conviction and drive, a quiet retirement was unthinkable. No one could believe in 1990 that he had heard the last of Mrs.

---

41. Powell quote in "It Is Time to Go," 60. Peter Jay's review of Lawson's memoirs, published in London by Bantam Press (1992), appears in "Ardent Author of a Revolution," *Financial Times,* November 6, 1992, 12. See also David Lennon, "The Thatcher Years," *Europe,* December 1990, 17. Thatcher quote in "Stepping Out," 34. The final chapter of her *Downing Street Years,* which appeared in October 1993, is devoted to her forced resignation. Unlike most politicians' memoirs, hers is characteristically bold, unforgiving, and aggressive. It sheds light on her hands-on style of leadership, her grasp of detail, her instinctive caution, and her voracious appetite for work. But she systematically alienated most of her supporters, and in the end only a handful of cabinet members wanted her to stay on. Her bitterness at the way she was dismissed shows in the contemptuous comments she makes about other leading Tories: Heseltine "was not a team player and certainly not a team captain" (423–24, 755); Howe's "clarity of purpose and analysis had dimmed" (756–57, 834); Lawson "had no interest in the job [of prime minister], and I had no interest in encouraging him" (755). John Major was "relatively untested and his tendency to accept the conventional wisdom had given me pause for thought." He was not "at ease with large ideas and strategies," and he was "unexcited by the sort of concepts which people like Nigel [Lawson] and I saw as central to politics." Nevertheless, she supported Major because he was the candidate most likely to "share my approach" (757–58, 831–32). See *The Sunday Times,* October 10, 17, 1993, Section III. No wonder most of her cabinet members publicly struck back at her after the book appeared. See "Lady Thatcher's Victims Bite Back," October 20, and "Howe Gives Damning Account of Thatcher's Last Term at No. 10," October 23, 1993, both in *Financial Times,* and the review of her book in *The Economist,* October 30, 1993, 102–3. When asked by David Frost on television about these counterattacks, she answered that "I'm sure I was wrong on a number of occasions, but I can't think of any immediately." "Out, Out, Out," *The Economist,* October 23, 1993.

Thatcher. She herself had said at the time of her "retirement": "There comes a time when you have to move on, but I shall still be fighting for everything I believe in." That was no idle warning. She reportedly went through a phase of grief, shock, and conspiratorial paranoia after her fall. But then she set out on lucrative speaking tours, wrote her memoirs, and reentered the national political debates as a kind of permanent sore to her successor. In March 1991, Conservative Party chairman Chris Patten emphasized his party's break with Thatcherism by pledging that it would direct its appeal to the electorate's "heart as well as the head," and Foreign Secretary Douglas Hurd affirmed that the U.K. would play a central role in building a more integrated Europe. Facing a general election, John Major's government promised to safeguard the achievements of the Thatcher years while ridding itself of what was unpopular, such as the poll tax. In April 1991, she stood up in the House of Commons and directed an electrifying attack. While mouthing words of support for her successor, she warned that the EC was seeking a "massive extension" of its power and that if Britain made the mistake of agreeing, it would be "the greatest abdication of parliamentary and national sovereignty in our history." In November 1991, she demanded a halt to the "conveyor belt to federalism" and continued: "What we are talking about is the rights of the British people to govern themselves under their own laws made by their own parliament."[42]

She chose not to contest her seat in the April 9, 1992, general elections, and she dutifully campaigned for John Major, visiting more than thirty constituencies. But no sooner had he been elected than she granted a devastating interview to *Newsweek,* entitled "Don't Undo My Work." To a prime minister who was attempting to distinguish himself from his successor, she said: "There isn't such a thing as Majorism." She effectively took credit for the Tory victory in the April election and criticized Major's consensus style of politics and his increased public spending.[43]

Thatcher expressed her views on Europe in an interview with *The European* on May 21/24, 1992: "We are just as idealistic about Europe as the federalists—we are just less federal." This position reflected many Britons' feelings: MORI opinion polls showed that when asked which part of the

---

42. First Thatcher quote in "After 32 Years, Thatcher to Quit Britain's House of Commons," in *Washington Post,* June 29, 1991, A14. Quotes from April speech in "Thatcher's Dark Shadow," *Maclean's,* July 8, 1991, 33. Quotes from November speech in *Financial Times,* November 21, 1991, 1. See text of this parliamentary speech in Part II of this book. Some compare her untimely criticism of John Major to Heath's driving resentment toward her after 1975. "Maggie, Mad or Magnificent?" *The Economist,* April 24, 1993, 63.

43. On reaction in Britain to the *Newsweek* interview, see "A Not So Funny Old World," *The Economist,* April 25, 1992, 66. After another year of criticism, Major retaliated, claiming that the Thatcher years were "a golden era that never was." See *The Economist,* April 24, 1993, 63, and July 31, 1993, 14.

outside world was most important to them, 34 percent said America and 21 percent Europe in 1969; in 1991 only 23 percent said America and 54 percent Europe. But surveys in the fall of 1992 revealed that two-thirds of Britons also remain leery of losing national sovereignty and identity to a European superstate, while nevertheless wanting to participate in a unified Europe. In September 1992, she rejoiced when a run on the pound forced Britain out of the EC's Exchange Rate Mechanism (ERM), which she called a "ruinous straitjacket." In her opinion, this gave Britain the chance to reclaim its "economic destiny." She reopened a split within the Tory party over Europe, leading the attack by about forty Tory MPs against the Maastricht Treaty. This EC agreement, which Major had helped negotiate, called for a common EC foreign and defense policy as well as single European currency. Threatening to resign if he lost, Major put the question of moving toward its ratification to the House of Commons in November 1992 and won by only three votes. Before it was finally ratified in the summer of 1993, she called for a referendum, charging again that "this treaty would undermine our age-old parliamentary and legal institutions" and "diminish democracy and increase bureaucracy." Her attacks against Major's policy toward Europe severely hurt his government.[44]

She was ennobled in the House of Lords as Baroness Thatcher of Kesteven, from which she could continue her attacks against "wets" from any party, including her own. But she worked hard for her Thatcher Foundation, which she created to keep her philosophy alive. She helps finance this foundation through highly lucrative speaking engagements, especially in America. Aiming particularly at the emerging democracies in eastern Europe, its objective is to "promote the widest possible acceptance of principles of economic and political freedom, democracy and the rule of law" through a program of research, conferences, and grants.

Lauded as "a pioneer others are likely to follow," she was installed as Chancellor of Buckingham University, Britain's only private university. She was also named honorary chancellor of the College of William and Mary in Williamsburg, Virginia. The most highly educated prime minister in British history, she had been denied an honorary degree by her alma mater, Oxford University. Many of Britain's intelligentsia, especially those who earn their living at institutions of higher learning, rejected her because of her education

---

44. MORI polls in "Time to Choose?" *The Economist,* September 26, 1992, 59. Other surveys in "Victor Beware," *Time,* November 9, 1992, 56. Thatcher quotes on Maastricht in the *Globe and Mail* (Toronto), June 8, 1993, A5. Quoting Edmund Burke that "it is necessary only for the good man to do nothing for evil to triumph," she reflected widespread frustration at the EC governments' inaction in the face of atrocities in Bosnia. She demanded strong action against the Serbs and a lifting of the arms embargo against Bosnian Muslims. See "Bosnia Burns, Just Fiddles," December 17-20, 1992, 9, and "Fury as Suffering Goes On," April 15-18, 1993, 1-2, both in *The European.*

FIGURE 1.6 President Franklin D. Roosevelt talks with Prime Minister Winston S. Churchill on board the HMS *Prince of Wales* during the Placentia Bay "Atlantic Charter Conference," August 10, 1941. The two generals behind them are George C. Marshall, U.S. Army Chief of Staff, and Sir John Dill, Chief of the Imperial General Staff. (*Source:* Franklin D. Roosevelt Library.)

reforms, the budget cuts she forced on them, and her insistence that they ask themselves the hard questions about why things, such as tenure, must continue in academia as they always have been. Many intellectuals underestimated her. Lord King, who chaired and privatized British Airways, recalled a letter to *The Times* in 1981 in which 364 economists warned that her deflationary budget would lead to recession and possibly even civil disorder. "History soon proved Margaret Thatcher right and 364 economists wrong. Our intellectuals have never forgiven her for that."[45]

---

45. "Thatcher's Place in History," 59. See also "Fashioned in Her Own Image." For the controversy concerning the Oxford honorary doctorate, see Young, *Iron Lady*, 401–4. The confidence with which she spoke on scientific matters was shown in her initial opposition to Reagan's Strategic Defense Initiative (SDI). She told him personally that "as a chemist" she knew it would not work. Young, *Iron Lady*, 398–99. Despite her different approach to SDI, she wrote in *Downing Street Years*, 462–68, that it was the single most important decision of Reagan's presidency and proved to be "central to the West's victory in the Cold War."

2

Margaret Thatcher and the Transformation of British Politics

Jorgen S. Rasmussen

In the spring of 1993, a politician who had been out of power for two and a half years denounced the European Community and the United States for cowardice in failing to protect the Muslims from the Serbs in Bosnia. Usually the views of has-been politicians are of little interest to anyone. In this case, however, the comments were widely reported in newspapers and magazines and earned interviews on morning television. Furthermore, those office-holders in Britain responsible for making policy felt compelled to defend themselves from the charge.

The event was vintage Margaret Thatcher. Both the fact of and the moral fervor of the outburst were typical of her. Unlike other former office-holders, she would not fade away into retirement, and, as always, anything she did was newsworthy. Her complaints concerning Bosnian policy were not an isolated attack. Within months of being driven from power, she had set up a foundation to propagate her views and had been among the leading critics of her handpicked successor's policy on the European Community. The political establishment still had to reckon with this elemental force.

Not until Franklin D. Roosevelt became president did Americans refer to their chief executive by initials. Subsequently, American politics saw JFK, LBJ, and, even, HST. But none of these sets of initials had the aura—for either supporters or enemies—that attached to the letters FDR. Similarly no British prime minister before Margaret Thatcher had become an "ism." Since her fall from power, the term "Majorism" appeared—primarily in journalistic speculations concerning the main components of her successor's policy objectives. It was only a pale replica, failing to conjure up the visceral feelings, both pro and con, that reference to Thatcherism could.

31

Just as Franklin D. Roosevelt played a unique role in twentieth-century American politics, so did Margaret Thatcher in British politics. Their policies, values, and background differed greatly, but both transformed their country's politics. A review of Thatcher's formative experiences, public image, leadership style, and policy concerns helps explain how and why she occupies such a prominent position in British politics.

Preparation for Power

Margaret Hilda Roberts was born in a small town (Grantham) in central England. Her father, Alfred, owned and operated a local grocery store. The business prospered, but Margaret did not live in luxury. She lived, in fact, over the grocery store in a flat without indoor plumbing. Never did she forget this modest childhood. No. 10 Downing Street, the official London residence of the British prime minister, has living accommodations on the top floor above the various meeting and reception rooms on lower levels. While serving as prime minister, Thatcher often spoke of "living over the store." Perhaps she was trying to project a diligent, always on-duty attitude toward her responsibilities. She may also have been trying, at least subconsciously, to dignify her father's work by suggesting it was in essence little different from serving as prime minister.

Alfred Roberts was active in the Methodist church, serving as a lay preacher. More important for Thatcher's development, he was active in local politics. Before she was old enough to go to school, her father was a local councillor. Subsequently he become an alderman and eventually was selected town mayor. Margaret Roberts heard politics discussed at home. She saw political activity as both a service demanded of the capable and a source of status conferred by community admiration.

Roberts won a scholarship to a local private girls' school. Despite the prosperity of the grocery store, whether her father could have afforded to pay the school's tuition fees is questionable. Had it not been for her academic abilities, she might have been educated in a state-supported school. The scholarship was one of her early lessons that merit and hard work are rewarded. Needless to say, Roberts was quite good in her studies. She also performed well in field hockey, physical games being almost as central a component of the English girls' school program as it was for boys' schools.

Her academic success enabled her to go to Oxford University, a considerable accomplishment for a woman of her generation. She studied chemistry and subsequently became an industrial research chemist. But her studies failed to satisfy her. Immediately after receiving her degree, she told a friend from Grantham who also had gone to Oxford: "You know, I've simply got

FIGURE 2.1 Margaret Roberts at age nineteen (right) with her parents, Alfred and Beatrice, and sister Muriel (left). (*Source:* Central Office of Information, London.)

to read law. It's no good, chemistry is no good for politics, so I shall set about reading law."[1] So she began studying law. Having just completed her training for one career, she began preparing for another.

While she was at Oxford, she had helped in the campaign of a Conservative candidate for Parliament in the 1945 election. The very next election, the first following her graduation, she herself stood for Parliament. She was the youngest candidate in that election. When another general election followed only twenty months later, she again stood. Both times she lost. In her second campaign she reduced the incumbent's majority only slightly and lost by more than 12,300 votes. The only Conservative constituency parties willing to have a young woman as candidate were those where the party had such little chance of winning that few political hopefuls sought the candidacy. To have won under these circumstances would have been a considerable upset.

1. Hugo Young and Anne Sloman, *The Thatcher Phenomenon* (London: British Broadcasting Corporation, 1986), 18.

Aspiring politicians campaign in such constituencies for the sake of experience. They hope to demonstrate their abilities by reducing the dominant party's margin of victory. Doing so can be the ticket to selection as candidate in a winnable seat. That is not, however, how Thatcher's career developed. Although her campaigns had not been a political success, they were a personal one. Among the active local party members where she stood for election was the head of a family paint and chemical business located in the area, a Denis Thatcher. On election night of her second campaign they announced their engagement; two months later they were married.

For a typical woman of her generation, this might have been the end of a nascent political career, particularly when less than two years later the Thatchers had twins. This event, however, simply provided a preview of a key characteristic that would be associated with her as prime minister: determination. While she was in the hospital recovering from the births, she filled out the application for the bar exam. Four months later she took it and passed. The Thatchers could afford to hire help to care for the twins. Nevertheless, being called to bar while a young mother of two children less than a year old was another major achievement. Again Thatcher must have concluded that those who do not succeed are the ones who have not worked with sufficient diligence.

Election to Parliament

Even she could not do everything. Raising twin infants and launching a legal career left little time for the laborious search for a winnable parliamentary constituency. A person as success-driven as Thatcher saw little reason to contest a forlorn hope for a third time. Her absence from the campaign trail in 1955 did not mean, however, that she had given up her desire for a political career. She had sought to qualify for the bar not because she wanted to be a lawyer, but as a means of getting ahead in politics. So in 1959 she stood for Parliament again; the third try was successful. She had achieved her goal: she was a Member of the House of Commons. She was reelected for the Finchley constituency in eight subsequent elections, serving through the spring of 1992. She spent a third of a century in the lower house of Parliament.[2]

---

2. She had managed to be selected by an excellent constituency. In the previous election the Conservatives had won by nearly three thousand votes. Before being chosen by the Conservative constituency party in Finchley (a north London suburb), she had been turned down by a half dozen other constituency parties. Her initial victory in 1959 was her biggest success, capturing over sixteen thousand (29 percentage points) more votes than her main opponent. Never again did she enjoy such a margin. Redistricting early in the 1970s made her vulnerable. In October

FIGURE 2.2 Margaret Roberts, age twenty-six, as Conservative candidate for Dartford, October 13, 1951. (*Source:* Central Office of Information, London.)

1974 she won by fewer than four thousand votes, only 10 percentage points more than the second place candidate. In the next election in 1979, however, she doubled her majority and remained at about the same level in her remaining two reelection campaigns. See her maiden parliamentary speech, delivered in 1960, in Part II of this book.

This is an extraordinary record of achievement. Nonetheless, this record is not sufficiently distinctive to make Thatcher unique. The process making her an extraordinary figure began in 1975, when she was selected leader of the Conservative Party. How such a tradition-bound party as the Conservatives broke with precedent to become the first British party to be led by a woman requires comment.

A few years into her first parliament, she was given a junior position in the Ministry of Pensions and National Insurance. The appointment smacks of tokenism, since both of her immediate predecessors had also been women. She served in this post for only three years, because in 1964 the Labour Party was voted back into power. During the rest of the 1960s while the Conservatives remained in opposition, she spoke for her party in Parliament on a variety of topics. Since her assignment for the last couple years of this period was education, her appointment as Secretary of State for Education and Science following the Conservatives' electoral victory of 1970 was no surprise.

Although she held that position until the Conservatives were defeated in 1974, her tenure was not noted for any great accomplishments. The main thing for which she is remembered was hardly positive: the cutting of free milk for school children. A leading member of the Labour Party dubbed her "Thatcher the milk snatcher." This was good politics, but unfair. During the time that she was in charge, the budget for education as a percentage of the national income rose considerably.

Within eight months of becoming head of the Conservative Party in 1965, Edward Heath had led it into electoral defeat. His success in winning the subsequent election in 1970 was such a surprise to nearly everyone that it was regarded as an aberration, rather than a personal triumph. When he failed to deliver victory in either of the two elections held in 1974, he clearly had come to be perceived as a loser. To make matters worse, his personal shyness made him seem rude and aloof. Only rarely would he share a drink with fellow Conservatives in the smoking rooms of the Parliament building. When he endeavored to do so, he was quite ill-at-ease and unable to make small talk. Dislike soon grew to antipathy.

Election as Party Leader

Many Conservatives had made up their mind: anyone but Heath. But this does not explain why the "anyone" was Thatcher. Even among political insiders few lists of possible successors would have included her name. Her eventual triumph was due largely to Sir Keith Joseph and Airey Neave. Sir Keith was an ascetic, ivory tower intellectual who often seemed lacking in common sense. He came to reject the "metooism" involved in Heath's

FIGURE 2.3 The Thatcher family during the 1979 election campaign. From left to right, Denis, Mark, Margaret, Carol. (*Source:* British Information Services, New York.)

U-turn toward consensus, preferring instead the pure conservatism of economists Friedrich Hayek and Milton Friedman. In the summer of 1974, between Heath's two election losses, Thatcher helped Sir Keith set up the Centre for Policy Studies to pursue free market economics.[3] Sir Keith was the natural standard bearer of the right wing in any challenge to Heath's leadership. But he was forced to drop out of the race because he had made an ill-considered elitist remark in public that the high birth rate among the poor was diminishing the quality of the British population. He had the personality of a thinker rather than a doer. The Conservative dissidents sought another challenger, and ultimately, virtually in desperation, they came to Thatcher as something of a surrogate Sir Keith.

Despite the widespread animosity towards Heath, running against him

3. See her 1968 speech for this group in Part II of this book.

FIGURE 2.4 Edward Heath speaking after signing the treaty on Britain's entry into the European Community. (*Source:* British Information Services, New York.)

for the office of party leader was a high-risk gamble. The architect of Thatcher's success was Neave. During the time she had been a practicing lawyer, she and he had worked in the same law office. Once she joined him in Parliament, he was further impressed with her abilities. Neave had a distinguished war record, always worth a good deal in the Conservative Party, and possessed the effective organizational skills of a political "boss." He was just the person to direct her campaign.

The leadership election was contested by only one person other than Heath and Thatcher, an obscure Conservative who could expect little support. Tories whose public prominence was nearly equal to Heath's were prevented from becoming candidates because Heath demanded that they remain loyal to him as leader. To everyone's amazement, Thatcher received eleven votes more than Heath. This margin was insufficient under the party's rules for her to be elected. A second ballot would be needed for which new candidates were permitted to enter the race. Heath immediately withdrew from the contest, thus removing the constraint of personal loyalty from his followers. Four Conservatives of equal, if not greater, prominence to Thatcher entered the contest.

Had Thatcher's initial support merely been an anti-Heath vote, it would have ebbed on the second ballot. Instead her vote increased by more than 10 percent, and she won more votes than the other four candidates combined. Some Conservatives admired her courage in daring to challenge Heath and decided that that deserved to be rewarded. Although the depth of her commitment to Sir Keith's ideas was uncertain, some Conservatives voted for her on both ballots because of the alternative policy orientation linked to her. Thus her victory had elements of positive support in addition to a dislike of her predecessor.

Being elected leader of a major British party is a considerable achievement. More importantly, it means that one will become prime minister whenever one's party controls a majority of the seats in the House of Commons. When that occurred in the first general election following her selection as Conservative leader, Thatcher became the first female prime minister in British history in May 1979. She also was the first female chief executive in a major Western democracy, although not in the world, Indira Gandhi and Golda Meir having been prime ministers of India and Israel respectively. Perhaps the only thing that prevented her from fully savoring her triumph was the fact that her father, who had died several years earlier, was not alive to witness it.

Thatcher served as prime minister eleven and a half years, until November 1990. For many people the term "British prime minister" calls to mind Winston Churchill, the country's indomitable leader during World War II. Churchill served a total of less than nine years, and this was divided into two periods, one of somewhat more than five years and the other—after an interval of six years out of office—of about three and a half years. Thatcher's eleven and a half years were without a break. She is the longest serving British prime minister of the twentieth century. None of the great names of twentieth-century British politics was her equal in time running the country. She is, indeed, a unique figure in British politics.

Public Image

Longevity records can be compiled in various ways. Someone who dedicates himself to never offending anyone may be retained in politics for some time. This was not Thatcher's way. Reviewing the tenor of post–World War II British politics reveals the extent of her departure from the norm.

During the 1950s British politics became consensus politics. While Labour was in office from 1945 to 1951—the first time it held a majority of the seats in the House of Commons—it introduced many "socialist" measures, including government-run comprehensive health care, extensive social welfare programs, and ownership of major enterprises. When the Conservatives regained power, they returned the iron and steel industry to private owners, but left untouched the bulk of Labour's social and economic reforms. So similar did the policies of the two main parties appear that a leading news magazine coined the term "Butskell." This combined the names of Conservative Richard A. Butler and Labourite Hugh Gaitskell, two of the foremost politicians of the period. "Butskellism" implied that elections were simply a choice between one set of personalities or another. Policy outputs would vary little regardless of which party won.

Having rebuilt from the destruction and economic dislocations of World War II, Britain in the 1950s enjoyed considerable prosperity. As Prime Minister Harold Macmillan said in 1957, "most of our people have never had it so good." During the 1960s, however, economic problems began to develop.[4] Seeking to drive Labour from power, Thatcher's predecessor as leader of the Conservatives, Edward Heath, promised harsh medicine in the 1970 election campaign to make Britain competitive again. Once prime minister, however, Heath proved unwilling to make good his threat. Doing so would have required his government to defy various entrenched economic interests. Eschewing confrontational politics, he altered course back to the familiar consensus politics. This change in direction became widely known as a "U-turn." Despite, or because of, Heath's opting for consensus politics, the Conservatives lost the elections of 1974, and Labour returned to power.

Added to the country's economic problems in the 1970s was widespread labor unrest (the so-called British disease). Even more serious, international trade problems threatened to bankrupt the country.[5] Thatcher became

---

4. Opposition Labour party leader Harold Wilson retorted that, on the contrary, under Conservative rule the voters never had been "had so good." Little economic growth combined with increasing inflation to produce "stagflation." The retail price index and gross domestic product per capita had varied very similarly. Using 1963 as a base of 100, RPI had been 90 in 1959 as had been GDP/capita. And in 1965 the former was 108 and the latter 107. By 1970 a gap had developed, with figures of 135 and 118. This trend continued so that in 1978 GDP/capita was little more than a third greater than in 1963, while the RPI was more than three and a half times larger.

5. Nearly twenty-four million work days were lost to labor disputes in 1972. The number of strikes never fell below two thousand during any year in the decade of the 1970s and in some years was close to three thousand. In the twenty-one years from 1950 through 1970, Britain's balance of payments had been in deficit only seven years. The largest shortfall had been

FIGURE 2.5 Newly elected Conservative Party leader Margaret Thatcher with William Whitelaw, 1975. (*Source:* British Information Services, New York.)

Conservative leader in 1975 in the midst of this economic malaise. Like her predecessor, she, too, promised harsh medicine to restore Britain to economic health. When the election occurred in 1979, the electorate chose to be ruled by her party.

Thatcher began administering her promised harsh medicine. Businesses

---

£369,000,000 in 1951. In 1973 the deficit was £999,000,000, followed the next year by a catastrophic £3,591,000,000. The next two years with deficits of £1,843,000,000 and £1,137,000,000 were better only by comparison with the disaster of 1974.

were allowed to go bankrupt rather than be bailed out by government subsidies. Unemployment began to grow to levels that Britain had not known since the days of the world-wide depression in the 1930s. Not surprisingly, people began to complain. Observers, recalling Prime Minister Heath, anticipated another U-turn, a shift to the traditional consensus politics of attempting to soothe all ruffled feathers. Speaking to her party's annual mass gathering when she had been in office for less than a year and a half, she defended her policies. A play, rather well-known in Britain, about a woman accused of witchcraft, is entitled *The Lady's Not for Burning*. Punning on that title, Thatcher challenged the conference with the invitation: "You turn, if you want: the lady is not for turning." The cozy consensus of the past was not for her. She proclaimed, "I am a conviction politician. The Old Testament prophets did not say, 'Brothers, I want a consensus.'"[6]

What is surprising is that someone so willing to cultivate an abrasive political image was so successful. Analysts of American political behavior have noted that a key element in the political success of Ronald Reagan was the perception that he was a nice guy. Was he competent to be president? Could he distinguish reality from make-believe? Was he on the verge of senility? American voters did not seem to care: All that mattered was that he seemed like an agreeable person.

Margaret Thatcher most certainly was not perceived by anyone as a "nice guy." In fact, one scholar has argued that she was nearly the most unpopular British prime minister of the second half of the twentieth century. Gallup regularly asks British respondents whether they are satisfied or dissatisfied with the prime minister. During Thatcher's first term in office, the proportion satisfied ranged from just over half to only a quarter, averaging 39 percent satisfied. These numbers varied only slightly during her second term. With but one exception, this was the lowest level of satisfaction recorded for any prime minister back to 1945. The one exception was her predecessor as Conservative leader. During his one term as prime minister, Edward Heath never satisfied as many as half the respondents and averaged only 37 percent. Thatcher equalled his unpopularity during her final term in office. Her high for satisfaction was 47 percent (only two points higher than his maximum), and her low was only 23 percent (eight points below his minimum). Her average was the same as his—37 percent.[7]

---

6. Her speechwriter, Ronald Millar, intended for her to say, "The lady's not for turning." In the actual delivery of the speech, however, Thatcher used the full verb, rather than the contraction, thereby lessening the pun. Millar was upset and buried his head in his hands. But her change made no difference in the effectiveness of the phrase. Millar never expected the line to have as long a life as it did. See interview with Millar in *The Times*, May 7, 1993. The text of her speech appears in Part II of this book.

7. For Thatcher's unpopularity, see Anthony Messina, "Public Satisfaction with Post-war Prime Ministers," *British Politics Group Newsletter*, Winter 1992, 2–5. By contrast, the prime

A considerable contrast in the thinking of the British and American electorates can be seen by comparing Thatcher's image with that of her principal opponent during much of her time in office. Neil Kinnock led the Labour Party from 1983 to 1992. Public opinion pollsters often asked people what qualities they associated with the two leaders. Although the exact figures varied from one survey to another, the basic finding remained the same. Kinnock was regarded as a nice guy, exactly the kind of person with whom one would like to go out for a drink. Welsh male choruses are world renowned, and he is a Welshman who enjoys singing. He would be the "life of the party." The public also perceived him to be likeable, warm and friendly. They felt that he cared about people. Finally, they were certain that he was someone who listens to reason.

None of these characteristics was associated with Thatcher. Nevertheless, the British electorate put her in the office of prime minister three times in succession. What was her appeal? The public saw her as tough and determined, as strong and forceful. She was someone who would stick to principles. None of these things were thought to be true of Kinnock. So Thatcher, known as the "Iron Lady," was what the voters wanted as prime minister, not the pleasant, but probably ineffective, Kinnock.

The public's perceptions offered a fascinating reversal of gender stereotypes. It was the woman who was perceived to be strong, tough and the man who was regarded as warm, caring. This reversal was a considerable asset for Thatcher. Whether a woman associated with the traditional stereotypes could have risen to the top of British politics is questionable. This is not to say that Thatcher was perceived as lacking femininity in the traditional sense. She was not a British version of Golda Meir.[8]

Thatcher was a wife, a mother, a woman. While serving in the cabinet, before becoming prime minister, she continued to prepare breakfast for husband Denis. She once broke off an important briefing by a civil servant the day before a key cabinet meeting so that she go buy bacon before the stores closed. The civil servant objected and suggested that someone could be sent to make the purchase. Thatcher brushed this option aside with the comment that only she knew exactly the type of bacon Denis liked. In 1982 son Mark disappeared for six days while racing in a rally across the Sahara

---

minister with the highest average rating was Harold Wilson during his first term. He ranged from 48 to 66 percent satisfied with an average of 59 percent. The prime minister achieving the highest maximum was Harold Macmillan, who rose to 79 percent satisfied during his first term.

8. Many people had thought that if a woman of this generation were to become prime minister, it would be Labourite Shirley Williams. Many of the familiar gender stereotypes are attached to her image. For a variety of reasons, not just image, she never rose to the leadership of her party. By the time Mrs. Meir became prime minister of Israel she appear to be a dumpy, somewhat disheveled middle-aged woman. Apart from lacking any quasi-glamorous or stylish aura, she did not even project a motherly image.

Desert. Thatcher was distraught; she showed all the emotion and concern that one would expect of any mother. Although her role in the raising of her children had been limited (as is not uncommon for English parents of the Thatchers' class), she still appeared motherly. Thatcher is a complex person who manages to balance both softness and hardness. This mix and the ambivalence it produces in those who deal with her was nicely encapsulated by French President François Mitterrand. No fan of Thatcher, he observed that she had the eyes of Caligula, but she had the mouth of Marilyn Monroe.[9]

Some have thought that her gender might be a weakness, that because she was a woman she could be made to crack. At the very start of the 1979 election campaign Airey Neave, perhaps her closest political confidant, was killed by an Irish Republican Army bomb planted under his car. She knew that if she failed to lead the Conservatives to victory in election she would be replaced as leader.[10] Facing her greatest challenge, she had to contain her grief and go forward without the help of her most trusted aide. She managed to do so and won the election for the memory of Neave.

Leadership Style

Comments about public image might be dismissed as mere political froth. Such matters might be of some electoral importance, but they scarcely rise above the level of trivia. Of greater consequence is her leadership style. Examining that aspect of the Thatcher phenomenon demonstrates her uniqueness. Her leadership style clearly set her apart from her male predecessors as prime minister. Again, the contrast reverses gender stereotypes. Her style can be characterized as combative, argumentative, abrasive, and domineering.

In the American system, the president dominates the cabinet, which is little more than his hand-picked advisors. One of the stories about Abraham Lincoln concerns a cabinet meeting in which everyone voted against a

---

9. This is the commonly accepted version of Mitterrand's comment. Jacques Attali, who was his personal assistant at the time, records a different quote in his book *Verbatim*, a compilation of Mitterrand's public and private comments from 1981 to 1986. According to Attali, the French president said Thatcher had "eyes like Stalin and the voice of Marilyn Monroe." *The Times,* May 7, 1993. Whichever quotation is correct, the point about Thatcher's complex persona remains valid. For Thatcher's views on women's roles, see her 1982 speech, "Women in a Changing World," in Part II of this book.

10. "I'll only be given the chance to lose one," was her comment. Chris Ogden, *Maggie: An Intimate Portrait of a Woman in Power* (New York: Simon and Schuster, 1990), 146. The party had lost three of the four elections it contested while Edward Heath was leader. Thatcher believed that because she was a woman, one failure would be all that the party would permit her. See her *Downing Street Years,* 15.

particular action except Lincoln himself. He announced the vote with his being the only "aye," and said "the ayes have it." The British executive is supposed to operate differently, involving more collective decision making. The traditional practice of prime ministers had been to use cabinet discussion to ascertain the range of views and then try to formulate a position that could command the greatest support.

In contrast, Thatcher would begin discussing an issue by stating her position and then, explicitly or implicitly, dare anyone to challenge what she had said. In an interview granted a few months before she became prime minister, Thatcher revealed exactly how she would operate. She asserted:

> There are two ways of making a Cabinet. One way is to have in it people who represent all the different view points within the party. . . . The other way is to have in it only the people who want to go in the direction in which every instinct tells me we have to go. . . . We've got to go in an agreed and clear direction. As Prime Minister I couldn't waste time having any internal arguments.[11]

Since her views and mode of operation were well-known outside the cabinet, many people concluded that she wanted to be surrounded by yes-men. This view was mistaken. She respected those who were sufficiently brave to disagree with her. The only caveat was that the challenger had better have done his homework and know the facts because he would find that she was prepared and well-informed on the subject. Thatcher was something of a bully; she was perfectly willing to ride roughshod over the weak. She would not hesitate to cut to shreds, to reduce literally to tears, those who had the temerity to disagree with her without having adequately prepared for the discussion.

This domineering style is the product of great self-assurance. Sir William Pile, who was her top civil servant while she served as Secretary of State for Education and Science, once observed:

> She is the only person I know who I don't think I've ever heard say 'I wonder whether.' Most of us, at moments of uncertainty or when faced with a lot of conflicting circumstances and confusion of objectives, will say, 'Well, what's it all about? What should we do?. . . I wonder whether. . . ?' Now 'I wonder whether' was not a phrase that I ever heard on her tongue.

11. Kenneth Harris interviewed her for *The Observer* in February 1979. After being published in that form, the paper issued it as a pamphlet, *Margaret Thatcher Talks to The Observer* (no page numbers). Harris quotes from the interview in his biography *Thatcher* (Boston: Little, Brown, 1988), 77–80. Thatcher describes this style of rule in *Downing Street Years,* 560–61. According to a popular joke, Thatcher took her cabinet to the best restaurant in London. The waiter went to Thatcher first for her order, since she was the only woman in the group. She ordered the roast beef. "Very good, madam, a splendid choice. And what about the vegetables?" Thatcher responded, "Oh, they'll have the same thing as I'm having."

Thatcher herself has said, "I make up my mind about people in the first ten seconds and I very rarely change it."[12]

Such self-assurance and determination carried Thatcher a long way in British politics. The same characteristics also led to her downfall. The unshakable conviction that she was right, the difficulty of persuading her to consider other alternatives were seen in the conflict over the community charge, popularly known as the poll tax. She had sought a means of controlling local government spending. So long as this loophole, this drain on public finances, remained, she could see no way of reducing the share of the country's wealth the government consumed, despite her extensive efforts to cut waste and eliminate programs at the national level. As she saw the problem, voters always would elect profligate local politicians who promised them benefits at no personal cost. Given the structure of local property tax, many people paid no local taxes. The solution was to require everyone to pay. Then one would get new programs and additional spending only if one were willing to bear some of the cost. This cold splash of fiscal reality should rein in local government spending.

Although this was a logical approach to the problem, she made the mistake of enacting a statute that not only required everyone in a given area to pay, but to pay exactly the same amount. The millionaire would owe no more than the lowly paid worker. This so outraged many people's sense of fairness that the poll tax soon became widely hated. Demonstrations and near riots erupted in many places. Campaigns to refuse to pay the tax were organized. Eventually, many people were prosecuted and in some instances sent to prison for failure to pay. Through it all, Thatcher refused to budge. She was certain she had hit upon the correct remedy.[13] She did not care that the tax was making her unpopular. She never had been concerned with courting popularity. Unlike several successful American politicians, she would not pander to every wind of public opinion. She would rather be right than win.

The other element in her downfall, in which she also exhibited unbending conviction, was foreign affairs, specifically the European Community (EC). She had been as willing to hector the heads of government of the entire EC as she was to defy her domestic opponents. Her efforts had won a number of grudging concessions for Britain which helped make the country's membership in the EC less costly. Despite always fighting for Britain's interests, she had been willing to accept various steps toward a more integrated Europe, such

---

12. Pile in Young and Sloman, *Thatcher Phenomenon,* 25.

13. There were rebates for persons with low incomes, but they were less than 100 percent "so that everyone should contribute something, and therefore have something to lose from electing a spendthrift council. This principle of accountability underlay the whole reform." Thatcher, *Downing Street Years,* 648; see also 642–67.

as the Single European Act and Britain's entry into the Exchange Rate Mechanism, which tied its currency to that of the other members. Nigel Lawson, as Chancellor of the Exchequer, and Geoffrey Howe, as, first, foreign secretary and, latter, deputy prime minister, had been able to persuade her to accept these measures. Both eventually resigned from the cabinet because of her increasing skepticism and scarcely veiled hostility toward Europe. In his resignation speech Howe accused her of seeing a Europe "positively swarming with ill-intentioned people." He challenged her with the rhetorical inquiry, "What kind of vision is that?" This powerful critique from the usually mild-mannered Howe was the trigger for the leadership contest that drove her from power.[14] The determined self-assurance that had served her so well in the past had once again betrayed her.

These comments may seem to suggest that Thatcher lacks any sense of humor. It is true that she is recalled by those who knew her as a very serious child, and some of those who have worked with her as an adult have noted little frivolity. Perhaps those who have worked with her to improve her image have managed to loosen her style because she learned to tell a joke at her own expense. At the Conservative annual party conference in 1989 she was speaking about the need of opportunity for all, in particular to give people a chance for a middle-aged career change. With a straight face and a factual tone that heightened her comment's effectiveness she observed: "I was 52 when I became Prime Minister. I'd never been a Prime Minister before. But I adapted to the work. And I did so well that twice my employers have asked me to stay on."[15]

Thatcher's style can be summed up in the events at the end of her period in office. Michael Heseltine, a former member of her cabinet, had decided to challenge her for the position of party leader. Losing this election to him would require her to resign as prime minister since she no longer would have the support of the majority party in the House of Commons. On the day of the party balloting, she had to be in Paris for a European Community meeting. When her campaign organizer phoned her that evening, it was to impart the incredible news that she had failed to win a sufficient number of votes to be confirmed as leader. A second ballot would have to be held. She immediately charged out of the building where the British delegation was staying and gave an impromptu press conference on the steps, declaring that she would fight on to retain control of the party.

---

14. Thatcher confessed to have been "hurt and shocked" by Howe's speech. "It was cool, forensic, light at points, and poisonous. . . . Underneath the mask of composure, my emotions were turbulent. I had not the slightest doubt that the speech was deeply damaging to me." It was an act of "bile and treachery." See Thatcher, *Downing Street Years,* 838–40, and his critical review of her memoirs in the *Weekend Financial Times,* October 23–24, 1993, I, VII.

15. Ogden, *Maggie,* 260–61, claims that Queen Elizabeth teased Thatcher about her unwillingness to enter in to the spirit of the charades that the royals enjoy playing at informal gatherings.

When she returned to London the next day, her backers told her that she could not win and that if she insisted on contesting the second ballot she would receive even fewer votes than she had on the first one. The following morning she met the cabinet for its regularly scheduled session and announced that she was withdrawing from the leadership contest and would be resigning as prime minister. After all that had happened, she could not allow herself the luxury of spending a long weekend to pull herself together. That afternoon she had to respond to a motion of no confidence that the opposition Labour Party was proposing in the House of Commons. Normally when the opposition offers such a motion, the prime minister can count on the full support of a united party. Thatcher, however, had just failed to obtain the endorsement of her party legislators. How would they vote at the end of this major debate? To maintain a united partisan front, her speech would have to show no weakness even though she was a lame duck.

Interjections are normal during speeches in the House of Commons. Sometimes the person speaking will "give way" to allow another member to raise a point needing a response. Other times members simply shout remarks to ridicule or embarrass the person. Near the end of her speech, after Thatcher had already given way a few times, she yielded the floor so that a member could inquire whether, now that she no longer would be prime minister, she would continue her fight against the proposed central bank for the European Community. Before she could reply, another member shouted in typical British working class *patois,* "She going to be the gov'nor of it!" There was a split second of dead silence. Then, as the total incongruity of this idea registered, the House broke into uproarious laughter. Anyone else would have been so flustered and thrown off stride by these remarks that finishing the speech would have been impossible. Thatcher's response was: "What a good idea! I hadn't thought of that." She added that if she were to become the governor, she would not allow the bank to avoid being responsible to anyone, as it seemed to her was being proposed. Then striking a vibrant, defiant pose this embattled prime minister declared: "Now, where were we? I'm enjoying this, I'm enjoying this."[16]

To use a term that had been applied to an American politician more than a half century earlier, this was truly the happy warrior. Politics was her recreation, her reason for being. This was why she was able to drive herself to work with such determination for so many years and why her leadership style was so demanding and domineering.

To this point the comments have touched on image and style. But what can be said of substance? Was Thatcher merely consumed with the desire to be prime minister, or did she want to do something? Did she have goals to

---

16. See the text of this debate in Part II of this book. See also her description of the entire resignation crisis in *Downing Street Years,* 829–62.

accomplish, a vision to seek? While the content of her policies is examined more fully in other contributions to this book, the last portion of this chapter provides a few comments on this aspect of her uniqueness.

The Substance of Thatcherism

Any discussion of Thatcher's "programme" (to use the British spelling and, thereby, to suggest an integrated set of comprehensive policies) needs to begin with a caveat. Kenneth Harris has correctly pointed out that Thatcherism is more "a description of attitude rather than policies. It is [her] way of thinking that singles her out from her post-war political contemporaries, and why she has thus coined an 'ism' all of her own. Mrs Thatcher has always believed in simple truths."[17]

Nonetheless, the question can be raised of what it means in terms of substance to become an "ism." This, in turn, raises the fundamental question of leadership: how much difference can one person make, however strategically placed? Is will, determination, and the courage not to flinch from unpopularity sufficient to achieve anything? If not, then there is little excuse for confrontation. If an abrasive style and a tough image can achieve little, then emollient consensus should be preferred at least to make people feel relatively comfortable.

Two main streams can be identified in British conservatism. One is associated with the traditional patrician. This is the conservatism of social hierarchy and paternalism. Social differences require *noblesse oblige*. The resulting charity should help produce social harmony that bridges class differences and helps to unite the nation. Most Conservative leaders during the last century and a half have been of this type and outlook. The other stream is rooted in what could be called nineteenth-century or Adam Smith liberalism. This stream emphasizes the free market; the market, not the government, is to decide. Economic efficiency, opportunity, and competition are the central values. Those finding these values attractive are self-made people, the upwardly mobile, not those of aristocratic background. In short, this stream is the philosophy of the small grocery store owner—and his daughter.[18]

Without going into policy details, the substance of Thatcherism can be summarized under three headings. All three concern domestic politics because this is the arena in which her break with the prevailing consensus was most

---

17. Harris, *Thatcher,* 92.

18. For a more elaborate classification of the various streams of Conservatism, see "Varieties of Conservatism," Chapter 2, in Philip Norton and Arthur Aughey, *Conservatives and Conservatism* (London: Temple Smith, 1981). For her admiration of Adam Smith, see *Downing Street Years,* 291, 618, and her September 1975 speeches in the U.S. in Part II of this book.

distinctive. One is downsizing government. Although eliminating waste was an element in this effort, the main thrust was to seek greater efficiency. When Thatcher became prime minister, central government employed some 750,000 civil servants. Her policies managed to reduce the number by nearly 25 percent. When she left power, approximately 200,000 fewer civil servants were employed.

The second heading is privatization. This took two forms. A variety of governmental activities, usually relatively menial, were put out for competitive tendering. Instead of having government hire people to clean public buildings, for example, private janitorial services were allowed to bid for the contract to perform the work. The other form was of considerably greater importance and reversed about a quarter of a century of consensus. When the Conservatives returned to power in the 1950s following the Labour government's extensive nationalizing of private industries, they accepted the bulk of these measures. They returned both the iron and steel industry and road haulage to private ownership in 1953, but Labour renationalized iron and steel in 1967. Although Labour's left wing wanted to continue the acquisition of private enterprises, the party's leaders managed to fend them off.

Although some Conservatives objected to government ownership of business, party leaders gave little priority to the issue. During Heath's term as prime minister from 1970 to 1974, the Conservatives did not denationalize iron and steel again. Thus, no government-owned enterprise had been returned to the private sector for a quarter of a century when Thatcher became prime minister.[19] The issue of government ownership had been resolved, or so it seemed. The British state would own considerably more enterprises than in the United States, but the great bulk of all businesses would remain in private hands, and the balance between public and private ownership would alter only slightly. The issue no longer seemed worth fighting over.

Shortly after Thatcher became prime minister, however, the government announced that it would begin selling several enterprises. Not only did Thatcherites want to get the government out of business, but they sought to further the goal of a property-owning democracy. Compared with the United States, a much smaller proportion of the British population owned stocks. Selling government-owned enterprises through a share flotation would increase the proportion and, it was hoped, give more people a sense of a stake in the health of the economy. About three and a half dozen enterprises were sold while Thatcher was prime minister. This reduced the

---

19. The Heath government had begun "hiving-off," selling portions of some nationalized enterprises. For example, the Thomas Cook travel agency and the Carlisle state breweries were sold to private owners in 1973. These enterprises hardly represented what Labour called "the commanding heights of the economy."

number of government-owned enterprises by about 60 percent. Approximately 800,000 workers were shifted from the public to the private sector. Those who work in government enterprises are not considered to be civil servants, so this figure should not be confused with the ones mentioned for downsizing the government.

The third heading of substantive Thatcherism is trade union reform. Certain union features that Americans take for granted were not present in Britain. Democratic elections for union officers were rare. Once in office the top officers remained there for life; periodic elections to call them to account were not held. Almost never were secret ballots used to determine whether a strike should be called. The workers at a particular industry would be herded together in some large open space like a parking lot, and all those favoring a strike would raise their hand. Thus, intimidating the members was so easy that the leaders could call a strike wherever they wished.

On the eve of becoming prime minister, Thatcher set forth four goals that she particularly wanted to achieve in office. One of them was to alter "the balance of trade union law back to the ideals of trade unionism, and away from the power of the militants." Her government proceeded to pass legislation imposing many reforms on the unions. Equally important was her refusal to give in to the demands of those miners led by the far-left Arthur Scargill. As a result, the incidence of strikes dropped dramatically. During the early years of Thatcher's period in office (1982–86), working days lost due to strikes annually averaged well over four hundred per thousand employees, roughly four times the rate in the United States. At the close of her service (1987–91) the average had declined to little over one hundred per thousand, under twice the American rate.[20]

Thatcher's antiunion measures did not make her a typical pro-business conservative. She refused to bail out weak and inefficient enterprises with government subsidies, preferring to let them go bankrupt. Previous governments had tried to control inflation through an elaborate incomes policy. Such policies, some quasi-voluntary and others backed by legislation, attempted to set limits for pay increases. Invariably they failed. Thatcher imposed the burden of dealing with wage demands upon business. A firm was free to give employees whatever wage increase it felt that its profits permitted. If it ran into financial problems because it had conceded too much, it could expect no help from the government.

This section began with a quotation from one of her biographers that "Mrs Thatcher has always believed in simple truths." One of those is that "people have a moral responsibility which they must accept. Moral in the

---

20. Quotation from the pamphlet version of the Harris interview cited in note 11. For her privatization and trade union policies, see "The Thatcher Legacy," *The Economist,* October 2, 1993, 65–67, and *Downing Street Years,* 339–79, 676–87.

widest sense of the term. . . . Moral responsibility must be kept going. Moral responsibility will not keep going if the government steps in and takes all the decisions for you, decisions which you ought to make for yourself." She denounced elections in which each party seemed to bid for votes by promising more and more benefits. "*I'm* [emphasis in the original] not participating in that kind of competition." Her simple truth was self-reliance: "I'm not promising you anything except greater fruit from your own efforts." Greater fruit because she would limit the role of government and had as her "top priority the reduction of personal tax." A limited role for government "doesn't make for a weak government—don't make that mistake. If you've got the role of government clearly set out, then it means very strong government *in that role*" [emphasis in the original].[21]

Government had a duty to take on the trade unions and use its police power to whatever extent necessary. Union power had to be curtailed so that it no longer could dominate and coerce business. Once some equality in power between the two sides had been achieved, then free collective bargaining and the market, not the government, should determine wages and prices. Workers would have to recognize that unreasonable wage demands could force a company out of business and cost them their jobs. Employers would have to exhibit some backbone—confrontation, not consensus—and refuse to grant wage increases that were not justified by increased productivity. This was responsibility, not emollient, all around.

Thatcher, herself, embodied her message and did not try to dodge responsibility. Her willingness to face down Scargill, to opt for confrontation rather than consensus, is in keeping with both her image and her leadership style. What was not as obvious was that her determination was so strong that she was willing to accept the consequences of her policies. Seeking to transform the British economy into one in which everyone was personally responsible for his or her actions was a bitter experience. Unemployment soared to a level that had been thought to be politically intolerable. A country in which a half million unemployed had been the norm now saw the figure rise past three million. More people were out of work in Britain than during the great depression of the 1930s although the proportion of the workforce unemployed under Thatcher was not as great as it had been a half century earlier. If that were what was needed to teach the country simple truths, then so be it. In economic policy Thatcher broke dramatically with the consensus of the past. Her uniqueness was remarkable.

Conclusion

One could draw up a long list of Thatcher's accomplishments. Although

---

21. All quotes in the paragraph from the previously cited Harris interview pamphlet.

many of the items on that list would be of considerable importance, her most significant contribution to British life was her transformation of the power structure. In the early 1970s social and economic conflict in Britain had reached such a stage that students of British politics asked: Is Britain ungovernable? When Prime Minister Edward Heath called an election in February 1974 in what proved to be a vain attempt to respond to the challenge of the miners, he posed the question: "Who Governs?" It is incredible that the chief executive of a centuries-old, stable democracy should have to raise such a question. Yet it correctly encapsuled the basic question Britain had to face.

After a decade of Margaret Thatcher as prime minister, no one asks such questions anymore. They have become irrelevant to the study of British politics. Thatcher, though out of office, is too full of life to require an epitaph. But were one looking for a phrase to put on a monument, the most appropriate one would be: "She Made Britain Governable." When strikes occurred in the spring of 1993, *The Economist* commented that while Thatcher had not completely cured the British disease (i.e., industrial unrest), "the post-Thatcher strains of the virus are far too feeble to cause the sort of attack that used periodically to bring Britain to its knees."[22]

The question is: How enduring will be the changes produced by a decade of Thatcherism? An expert on British electoral behavior wrote at the start of Thatcher's third term that "the Conservatives owe their three election wins not to ideology but to much more pragmatic causes—their economic record, Mrs Thatcher's leadership, and the electoral system. . . . Much of Thatcherism will die with Thatcher. Its permanent legacy at the level of the mass public will be very limited."[23] That conclusion appears applicable even to the Conservative Party itself. The Tory manifesto for the 1992 general election referred to various accomplishments over the previous thirteen years, such as the reduction of taxes. But only once in fifty pages did the name Thatcher appear. The party committed itself to ensuring that Britain continued to enjoy the reduced level of payments to the European Community that Thatcher negotiated early in her service as prime minister. As far as the rest of the manifesto was concerned, it was as though Thatcher had never existed. On the other hand, the manifesto set forth various proposals for cutting back the role of government and indicated that the privatization of government-owned enterprises would continue. New legislation was promised that would help ensure that unions did not regain coercive power. Thatcher's values, if not her name, imbued the document.

---

22. "The British Disease, 1993," *The Economist,* April 3, 1993, 57–58.

23. Ivor Crewe, "Values: The Crusade that Failed, " in Dennis Kavanagh and Anthony Seldon, eds., *The Thatcher Effect: A Decade of Change* (Oxford: Clarendon Press, 1989), 250. *The Economist* noted on October 2, 1993, 65, that "the legacy of Margaret Thatcher resists calm appraisal."

Following a fourth successive defeat in 1992—a defeat that only a week before election day seemed impossible—the Labour opposition tried to regroup and redirect its efforts. While the moderates were likely to prevail, it is impossible to predict what sort of Labour Party with what electoral strategy would emerge. In any case, a Labour government with the power and will to reverse the thrust of Thatcher's privatization is inconceivable in the near future. Nor can one expect a non-Conservative government that would repeal most of the constraints imposed on the unions. Such a government might propose some new public services and benefits, but this would not be start of a new round of bloated bureaucracy. The funds simply are not available for major new initiatives.

The public may tell opinion pollsters that they prefer services to tax cuts.[24] But in the postmortem of the 1992 election results, one of the chief factors in Labour's defeat was said to be its proposed tax increase. Similarly, the Liberal Democrats, Britain's third party, stressed a modest tax hike with the revenues to be devoted entirely to improve education. They thought during the campaign that this proposal was winning considerable public acceptance. But they received a smaller share of the vote than they had in the previous election.

Leadership style in Britain has reverted to its pre-Thatcher nature. Under Prime Minister John Major less is seen of adversarial government, and decision making is becoming more collective. Consensus, not conviction, has come to rule British politics again. The crucial point, however, is that Britain is not in the process of reverting to the old consensus. As Labour tries to map out its future, Britain is groping toward a new consensus. And the content of that consensus will be greatly influenced by the major themes of the Thatcher decade. Margaret Thatcher may not have inculcated all her values into the British public, but she certainly did change the face of British politics.

---

24. For example, a Market and Opinion Research International poll in February 1992 found that 69 percent favored more spending on public services compared to only 26 percent preferring a tax cut in the government's financial plans for the coming year. Even among supporters of the Conservative Party nearly twice as many supported more spending over a tax cut.

3

Thatcher's Ideology:
Economic Cures for English Diseases

James E. Alt

Nothing is ever entirely new. Thatcherism is certainly a distinctive ideology, but has roots in a variety of traditions of Conservative Party thinking. It is a new blend of ideas rather than a new idea. It made a difference. No one today would take seriously the assertion heard frequently only a few years ago that Britain had become ungovernable. Thirty years ago, Britain was held up as a model of responsible government, and Thatcherism certainly helped make it governable again.[1] But few things are ever entirely successful. Even its warmest supporters give Thatcherism "two cheers" rather than three. Much of what was promised was not achieved, or accomplished only temporarily.[2] Without a doubt even some of the restored governability of the country is due to lowered public expectations of what government can produce as much as successful public performance.

To make this verdict of conditional congratulation live a little, this chapter will do five separate things. It will describe (1) what Thatcher's three

---

1. She did so by preventing, to some extent, the "potentially political" from becoming the "actually so" and reducing the number of tasks government was expected to perform, much as suggested in Anthony King, ed., *Why Is Britain Becoming Harder to Govern?* (London: BBC, 1976), 29.

2. Even within a single narrow area like economic policy, her warmest supporters, like Patrick Minford, acknowledge some errors while vocal critics, like Frank Hahn, admit Thatcherism did some good. See their chapters in Robert Skidelsky, ed., *Thatcherism* (Oxford: Blackwell, 1988), esp. 97 and 124. More generally, that only some aims were achieved is acknowledged by a supporter like Letwin, who emphasizes the moral message of Thatcherism, as well as an antagonist like Gamble, who sees it as the construction of a new hegemony. See Shirley Robinson Letwin, *The Anatomy of Thatcherism* (London: Fontana, 1992) and Andrew Gamble, *The Free Economy and the Strong State* (Durham, N.C.: Duke University Press, 1988).

basic goals were (with respect to public opinion, the economic playing field, and economic outcomes), (2) what Thatcherism replaced (the main themes of what is usually called the "postwar consensus"), (3) how things were when she took over (the extremes of 1978–1979), (4) what she wanted (with a little more detail on where Thatcherism came from), and what she did (eight areas of significant policy intervention) and (5) what happened as a result. Since the results are mixed, its academic author concludes by giving Thatcherism a summary report card: an evaluation of what it really was responsible for, where its contributions were greater and more durable, and where less.

Three Main Ideas of Thatcherism

All we need to get started is a picture, from Margaret Thatcher's point of view, of the English disease. It included an economy with high inflation and sluggish growth, overly powerful unions, a bloated government and public sector producing low investment, lack of incentives for individual initiative and opportunity, and excessive social welfare policy producing over-dependence on the state.

Her three main purposes, put simply, were first to generate a new public attitude toward the state and people's dependence on the state, which would itself require two things. First, the state was to have less involvement in crises and problem solving, and less responsibility for the economy as a whole, leading people to expect less from it, so there would be, in her words, "less government and more independence from it." Partly as a consequence, possibilities were to be expanded for people to have more self-reliance or opportunities in general, so there would be "more personal responsibility," as she said in a lecture to the Conservative Political Centre in October 1968. She must have observed the next decade with horror.[3]

Second, reforms would be instituted to change the economic playing field, including a new role and legal status for trade unions, significant privatization (sale back to the private sector of publicly owned industries) and deregulation, and a government role reduced to a form of indicative planning, monetary control, and law enforcement.

Third, there were to be significant changes in economic outcomes, notably reduced inflation, through monetary control, a restoration of sound fiscal policy, and reduced public borrowing. Whatever else, she did this last thing, wherein lies the greatest difference in outcomes between the Thatcher and Reagan years. Each of these, the transfer of responsibility from government

---

3. Every author presents this list differently but ends up in about the same place. See Gamble, *Free Economy*, Chapter 4, or Peter Riddell, *The Thatcher Era and Its Legacy* (Oxford: Blackwell, 1991), Chapter 1. See Thatcher's 1968 speech in Part II of this book.

to individual, the tilt of the market away from the power of combinations and government, and the restoration of soundness to economic policy, required, as we shall see, several different policy initiatives.

How It Was: The "Postwar Consensus"

What was dramatically different about Thatcherism? Not these goals themselves, though I think reduced state dependence and privatization were pretty much new elements in the British political discourse of the last half century. Some of the other goals, as we shall see, appear before Thatcher, but not all together. What was more dramatic was what was jettisoned: a broad set of social and economic ideas which both parties had largely come to share about economic goals and the role of government.[4] Within this "postwar consensus," governments of both parties had created a social blueprint for Britain including:

1. The economy: Here by broad agreement the government took responsibility for securing full employment, defined as requiring unemployment rates of less than two percent for nearly all the period from 1950 to 1975. There was a political preoccupation with economic growth, which nearly every government reiterated as its top priority. (By contrast, *in fact* maintaining the exchange value of the pound sterling on international markets was probably the most important single economic goal of all governments at least before 1974, even if at some price in economic growth, caused by recurrent balance of payments problems.) In sum, this was the age of Keynesianism (economic management through fine-tuning of fiscal policy) in Britain, from 1949 to 1976.

2. The role of trade unions: Trade unions grew in strength in the postwar years, organizing from 40 to 55 percent of employees, with particularly strong growth and militancy in the public sector. Moreover, from 1962 on, as successive governments experimented with policies to manage inflation by managing incomes, unions became consultatively directly involved in policy, in spite of the frequent inability of union leaders to deliver the conduct they promised on the part of their members.[5] This is the era of British "experiments in corporatism" from 1962 to 1979.

3. Expanding public ownership: In Britain this meant that not just utilities (like the supply of power and water as Americans are used to) were publicly owned, but there were also state-owned corporations trading in coal, steel, rail transport, natural gas (including retail sale of gas appliances),

---

4. See Peter Hall, *Governing the Economy* (New York: Oxford University Press, 1986), Chapter 3.

5. Samuel H. Beer, *Britain Against Itself* (New York: Norton, 1982).

telephones, airways, road transport, airports, docks, and oil. It also involved public housing: nearly a third of British housing units were in the public rental sector (referred to in Britain as "council houses" because they were managed by local councils) built and supported as policy, before Thatcher, by both parties.

4. Finally, the welfare state: The provision of health care was arranged through a National Health Service, under which general taxation financed health care delivery at no or low charges available to all. Along with this existed extensive social support policies, including child benefits, an allowance payable to all with dependent children.

How It Just Was: 1979 and the Winter of Discontent

How were the social and economic arrangements of the postwar consensus working out? Up to the mid-1960s and even into the 1970s, these underpinnings of the old order—a government taking responsibility for the economy, particularly employment, and managing it along Keynesian lines, with increased involvement in incomes policies by the unions, and increased public ownership of industry, with a strong commitment to social welfare policy—were seen by many American liberals[6] (and others) as natural outlines of a harmonious political economy involving elements of socialism and corporatism. By 1979, when Thatcher came to power, things were different.

The economy had become a sorry chronicle of inflation, unemployment, stagnation, and debt. Inflation stood at 10 percent, though down from its disastrous 25 percent level in 1975. The unemployment rate was 6 percent, up from 2.5 percent in 1974. Growth was sluggish: national income (real Gross Domestic Product [GDP] per capita) increased by 1.5 percent per annum from 1973 to 1979, half the average growth rate of 1960–1973. The public sector deficit, which had averaged less than 1 percent of GDP from 1960 to 1973, averaged over 4 percent from 1974 to 1979 (for an interesting comparison, that is a little worse than the average U.S. deficit from 1980 to 1989).[7] The only apparent bright spot was the exchange rate of the pound, floated since 1972 by international agreement, which had dropped below $1.20 but was now rising fast again.

The unions now organized about 55 percent of employees.[8] The years

---

6. Bernard D. Nossiter, *Britain: A Future that Works* (Boston: Houghton Mifflin, 1978).

7. British economic data are from O.E.C.D., *Historical Statistics,* various dates. Public sector deficit data are from the *National Institute Economic Review,* August 1991 (Britain), and Council of Economic Advisors, *Economic Report of the President,* 1991 (United States).

8. Department of Employment *Gazette* (London: HMSO, 1981).

FIGURE 3.1 Thatcher shopping in her Finchley constituency, October 26, 1979, to demonstrate her understanding of voters' worries about the economy. (*Source:* British Information Services, New York.)

1978–1979 will longest be remembered, I believe, for the "winter of discontent," a phrase describing a series of public sector strikes by municipal grave diggers, trash collectors, and hospital nurses leaving a trail of unpleasantness and bad feeling everywhere.[9] The year also saw the collapse of Labour's "social contract" with the unions as Chancellor of the Exchequer Healey asked for union cooperation in a third consecutive year of wage restraint below prevailing inflation rates, and failed to get it.

---

9. The episode is beautifully described in Peter Jenkins, *Mrs. Thatcher's Revolution* (Cambridge, Mass.: Harvard University Press, 1987), Chapter 1.

Public ownership had hit new heights by 1979. Labour had created a National Enterprise Board to invest selectively in industries. Rolls Royce (Aeroengine Division) and British Shipbuilders had been nationalized by the Conservative government in 1972. British Leyland (cars) in 1974 and North Sea Oil (1975) were all subsequently added by Labour to public enterprise. Increasingly these firms were showing losses. Government employment had risen by nearly half, from just over 14 percent of total employment in 1960 to over 21 percent in 1979,[10] amid growing concern among academics and journalists that government was "overloaded"—taking on too much and able to do too little.

Welfare policy was also on the move. Child benefit, an indexed, flat-rate system of family allowances, had arrived in 1977. The state earnings-related pension scheme (SERPS) had just been introduced in 1978. It was Labour's vision of the future, a pay-as-you-go tax-financed social security system, in the style of the U.S. system of the time. This seems ironic in retrospect, since it was introduced just as the U.S. went off its tax-financed scheme onto a sinking-fund based system.

The main point of this and the previous section, however, is that if one looked at 1962–1979 one would sometimes find it hard to know when the party in power changed. There were incomes policies in 1962 (under the Conservatives), 1966–1969 (under Labour), 1972–1974 (Conservatives again), and 1976–1979 (Labour again). Industrial relations reform failed in 1969 under Labour and again in 1972 under the Conservatives. Labour nationalized steel in 1966; the Conservatives nationalized Rolls Royce and Upper Clyde Shipbuilders in 1972; Labour added British Leyland in 1974. American readers can measure the difference between countries by imagining companies like Lockheed and Chrysler becoming state-owned industries in their times of trouble, rather than having loans guaranteed and being bailed out of debt.

Of course, there were still differences between the parties in Britain. In social policy the differences were most durable. Labour policy tended to be egalitarian, universal, and extensive: its accomplishments include comprehensive schools and the broadest entitlements to pensions and benefits. Conservative welfare policy, by contrast, remains means-tested and selective. Thus it is in this last area that the change to observe under Thatcher is least distinctive, since party policies had previously differed more. But in the other areas this is the English disease of the day: not just a failure of the economy but a failure of ideas, since both parties largely agreed on the recipe for failure.

---

10. See O.E.C.D., *Historical Statistics 1960–81* (Paris, 1983), Table 2.13.

What She Wanted and What She Did

Margaret Thatcher's Conservatives won the 1979 election. In 1983, hers became the first British government in a quarter century to be reelected after a full term in office (1959 was the previous occasion), and in 1987 her Conservatives were reelected again. The American press quickly picked up the implications of her victory in 1983: "Thatcher's Victory May Offer Lessons for '84 U.S. Election" headlined the *Wall Street Journal*. The key to that newspaper was *Thatcherism,* an economic-strategic package of fiscal and monetary austerity with tight restraint on government spending and borrowing aimed to curb inflation and reduce interest rates, able to overcome even the electoral burden of an unemployment rate that had more than doubled to 13 percent during her first term.[11] The broad goals were described above, but where did the ideas come from?

Journalistic treatments of Thatcherism as a set of ideas stress its *moral* underpinnings in themes of thrift, self-reliance, competition, and patriotism. That is certainly part of it, but all of these values have a long history in Conservative thought as ethical colorants for efficiency arguments against public assistance of various sorts. *Politically,* it is in step with some earlier Conservative acts, particularly from the years immediately after the 1951 election. Denationalization (as privatization used to be known), decontrol of prices and the end of rationing, introducing commercial television, and the abolition of resale price maintenance all displayed a pro-market emphasis on restoring competition in industry and commerce.[12]

Economically, Thatcherism is often described as a market-oriented monetarism. The basic economic ideas of the new approach *were* monetarist in the narrow sense that changes in the supply of money were seen as the proximate cause of inflation. These ideas had started to circulate among academics and fringe politicians in the 1960s, gained ground among journalists in the early 1970s, and found public expression in speeches and pamphlets by Sir Keith Joseph after the Conservatives' 1974 defeat. Joseph's ideas were formalized in the work of the Centre for Policy Studies and embraced by Margaret Thatcher, who became leader of the Conservative Party in a coup owing more to dissatisfaction with Heath after his losing battle with the miners and electoral defeat 1974 than warmth for Thatcher's central economic ideas. The monetarism was legitimized by Denis Healey's

---

11. The 1987 reelection, occurring in circumstances of rapid economic growth, falling unemployment, and lower inflation and interest rates, seemed no mystery at all.

12. Just what a "conservative" economic policy would look like is ambiguous. See James Alt, "New Wine in Old Bottles?" in Barry Cooper, Allan Kornberg, and William Mishler, eds., *The Resurgence of Conservatism in Anglo-American Democracies* (Durham, N.C.: Duke University Press, 1988).

period at the Treasury, which coincided with the rapid spread of monetarism in British administrative circles, particularly at the Bank of England.

But the most important feature of Thatcherism was its promise in the context of 1979: the specific intentions that Thatcher brought to office. Consider three broad areas of her policy proposals. One was a fiscal package. First, inflation was to be reduced. Inflation, seen as producing uncertainty harmful to investment, became the central target of policy. Economic growth was relegated to a long-run outcome of political reform while high employment was dropped completely. The macroeconomic stabilization role of government economic policy was to be reduced and de-emphasized. To achieve the inflation goal, secondly, money growth targets were explicitly tied to medium-term targets for public borrowing (this was the "Medium Term Financial Strategy").[13] Each year the government would publish four years' worth of forecasts for the budget deficit and promise to meet them as targets.

Third, public expenditures were to be cut in order to reduce public sector borrowing (in line with the medium-term strategy's requirements), promote efficiency, and avoid the need for higher taxes. Fourth, then, taxation was to be switched away from personal incomes and onto personal consumption spending (and subsequently oil profits), and reduced if possible. The basic rate of income tax was indeed almost immediately reduced by three percentage points (that is, about a 10 percent tax cut) to 30 percent (and ultimately further to 25 percent by 1987), and the top *marginal* rate was reduced from 83 (actually 98 on investment income) to 60 percent, and ultimately to 40 percent. However, this did not reduce total revenues, since the rate of value-added tax (VAT) was increased to 15 percent, eliminating the formerly high rate on luxuries. More recently corporate taxes have been cut and employers' national insurance charges reduced. So that was the fiscal package: inflation control, budget control, spending cuts, and tax shifts toward proportionality.

Clearly, second, Thatcher's aim was to replace the macro, demand-centered strategies of the postwar consensus with micro, supply-oriented regimes, creating new institutions to promote competition, the importance of market sentiment, and the efficiency of private enterprise. This was to be achieved through two broad policy thrusts, one relating to financial controls and the other to public ownership. Controls over bank lending and foreign exchange were to be eliminated where possible. This was mostly done by 1981, as the Bank of England abolished reserve requirements, special deposits, and foreign exchange controls, to support market determination

---

13. The mechanics are well summarized in Peter M. Jackson, "Economic Policy," in David Marsh and R. A. W. Rhodes, *Implementing Thatcherite Policies: Audit of an Era* (Buckingham: Open University Press, 1992), esp. 17–25.

of interest rates and the value of sterling.[14] Official government "guidance" on mortgage rates was eliminated between 1983 and 1986, and in July 1982 the government abolished all restrictions on hire purchase terms. (American readers really need to use imagination to capture the previous practice. The British government had for nearly half a century kept, varied, and regulated down payments and interest rates on consumer purchases. Compare that to the American case, recalling the public flap when George Bush mildly tried to "talk down" credit card rates, as an example of the degree of macromanagement in the old Britain.) These changes were accompanied by a variety of measures deregulating financial services as well.

Moreover, consistent with this, some publicly owned enterprises were to be sold off ("privatized"). Although this promise was introduced into the 1979 Conservative Manifesto almost as an afterthought, sales of publicly held assets from 1979–1980 through 1984–1985 totalled nearly £5,000,000,000, a substantial part of the cumulative reduction in public sector deficit achieved by the Thatcher government.[15] *Annual* asset sales for the next few years nearly matched this figure, as British Gas, British Aerospace, Airports, and Airways, British Telecom, some of British Steel, and more of BP and Britoil were sold off. Furthermore, the increase in asset sales was accompanied by aggressive pursuit of efficiency through reorganization and rationalization in public corporations. Capital spending cutbacks and labor force reductions in steel, coal, railways, airlines, and other state enterprises cumulatively reduced public corporation employment by 250,000 jobs, accompanying the 400,000 jobs sold back to the private sector. Finally, one could point to an "implicit" privatization as the government's role in exploiting North Sea Oil discoveries was strictly limited, in comparison with other countries like Norway where state involvement was much greater.[16] The privatization of housing was as aggressive as that of state enterprise. Public spending on housing in real terms was cut by over half between 1979 and 1985, and the proportion of owner-occupier households in Britain now exceeds 60 percent, an increase of about a fifth over the last decade alone. A fifth of all council houses, over 1,500,000 dwellings, were sold in a decade, bringing in £17,500,000,000, half the receipts of the privatization initiative, and government financial support shifted from subsidizing housing construction to housing benefit, a means-tested form of assistance for low-income renters.

---

14. See J. R. Sargent, "Deregulation, Debt, and Downturn in the UK Economy," *National Institute Economic Review*, August 1991, 75–87.

15. S. Brittan, "The Politics and Economics of Privatisation," *Political Quarterly* 55 (1984): 109–28, presents a balanced appraisal of the government's fiscal, economic, and ideological motives for pursuing privatization.

16. James Alt, "Crude Politics," *British Journal of Political Science* 17 (1987): 149–99.

With respect to pensions, Thatcher's government limited the growth of the basic state pension by indexing it to prices rather than the higher of prices or wages. This change, made in the Social Security Act of 1980, had by 1988 reduced a typical pension relative to the old scheme by over a sixth, saving £4,000,000,000 per annum. The Social Security Act of 1986 began the dismantling of SERPS by lowering benefits and encouraging (indeed subsidizing) private alternative savings schemes, particularly for younger workers with longer time to make contributions. By the end of 1990, four million people (three-fourths in their mid-thirties or younger) had already contracted out and set up personal pensions. This trend, projected thirty years further on, predicts a reduction of more than 50 percent in public pension expenditures.[17]

Finally, but by no means least important, in the area of unions, labor market, and industrial policy, legal reforms were promised which were intended to reduce the frequency of strikes and eliminate wage pressure as a source of inflation. The Thatcher years include a series of legal reforms (Employment Acts of 1980, 1982, 1988, and 1989; Trade Union Act of 1984; Wages Act of 1986) affecting the legal position of unions. Of course, many of the actual reforms had been Conservative Party policy for some time. On the whole, the legal changes were aimed not just to weaken unions politically, but also to produce incentives for discipline both among and within unions, by imposing responsibility and liability on them. Measures included among other things a legal ban on secondary picketing (forbidding a union not directly concerned in a dispute to support those actually involved by picketing), removal of union immunity to sequestration of funds by courts to pay fines imposed for violations of industrial relations law, including unofficial actions not expressly repudiated by the unions, and the mandating of periodic secret ballots to affirm strikes, elect leaders, and retain political affiliation of unions to the Labour Party, as well as banning all action to maintain and reaffirm closed shops.[18]

Generally, industrial intervention (for instance, bailing out failing firms, loan guarantees, incentive policies) was to be reduced, though there were

---

17. For details of retrenchment of social welfare policy under Thatcher, see Paul Pierson, *Dismantling the Welfare State?* (Cambridge: Cambridge University Press, 1994). Despite the gradual erosion of universal systems of unemployment insurance and child allowances, Pierson remarks, "the main structure of income maintenance remains intact after a decade of Thatcherism." In health care as well, limited tinkering with private insurance and competition within the structure of the National Health Service produced little fundamental change. Education reforms, generally designed to weaken local education authorities by introducing new elements of national curriculum and standard examinations and increasing individual schools' flexibility, are another matter, as Letwin's *Anatomy of Thatcherism,* Chapter 9, describes.

18. William Brown and Shushil Wadhwani, "The Economic Effects of Industrial Relations Legislation since 1979," *National Institute Economic Review,* February 1990, 57–70.

also some programs giving firms incentives to obtain financial and technical assistance to introduce technological innovation, as well as some official intervention to encourage contracts with British rather than foreign firms in high technology, and for a time there was even a Minister for Information Technology.

How Did It Turn Out?

It had ups and downs: perhaps the easiest and best way to understand the outcome is to think of the Thatcher era as not one whole, but divided into three parts by years. First, there was the early period, from 1979 to early 1982, when everything went wrong. Unemployment soared, targets were regularly and embarrassingly missed, inflation went up. Her critics were everywhere: her job approval ratings were spectacularly low, and politicians, journalists, and academics all joined a chorus calling for a change of direction. Of course, there is at the end of her first term one great success, her managing of the Falklands War with Argentina. In reality this success, along with the weakness of her opposition (the division between the centrist Social Democrats and left-wing Labour under Michael Foot) and the beginnings of an economic recovery were together just enough to secure her reelection. Nevertheless, it would be foolish to fail to record the Falklands victory to her credit: she saw her opportunity and took it.[19]

Then there was the middle period, from the Falklands War through 1988, when just about everything went right. There were seven straight years of real income growth greater than 2.5 percent per annum, inflation fell to just over 4 percent, the miners' strike collapsed and strikes generally fell off (though, or perhaps because, unemployment remained high), and the privatization campaign bounded ahead. In spite of Labour's new leadership and a more effective campaign by the opposition, Thatcher's reelection in 1987 seemed, and was, a foregone conclusion. The second reelection was so easy that it was hard to remember that the first had been no sure thing even after three years in office. The "Thatcher Revolution" was, if not complete, at least well on its way.

And then there is the end of her term, from late 1988 to the end of 1990, when all the trouble started up again. Unemployment finally fell, but growth staggered again. Inflation rose, strikes increased, and after the October 1987 Wall Street crash the market for privatized shares dropped, the property boom overheated, the recession hit. Obviously, I do not want to claim that these factors made her fall from the Conservative leadership

---

19. According to both Helmut Norpoth, *Confidence Regained* (Ann Arbor: University of Michigan Press, 1992), and Ivor Crewe, "Has the Electorate Become Thatcherite?" in Skidelsky, *Thatcherism,* 25–50, her statecraft was a significant element in the elections of 1983 and 1987.

inevitable. Others will describe the many specifics that belong in that story, but one should not forget the context. It happened not at the peak of her achievements, but two years beyond it, into a slide which was already creating doubts about the depths of the changes she had brought about.

So how big were the changes? Which were permanent and which transitory? How high a standard should we set? Let us not be unreasonable and ask for performance on a scale never seen before. A reasonable standard would define success as a restoration of outcomes to levels or values which were common or typical before the era of corporatism and consensus, that is, typical of the years before 1962. Even if we think of success in this modest way, on the macroeconomic side her promise was clearly greater than her performance.

Nevertheless, some things clearly did change. The proportion of employees organized into trade unions dropped sharply, from 53 percent in 1980 to 43 percent by 1985. This approximates a return to the position of the 1950s or so. With regard to strikes, there are now one-third as many as there were on average in 1970–1974, and the number of working days lost to strikes has fallen to the levels of the 1960s.[20] In a more general way, union leaders are no longer consulted, even ritualistically, over economic policy, and active union cooperation is not sought in policy implementation. This lack of a policy role, added to union unpopularity stemming from strikes in the winter of 1978–1979, has weakened the political position of the unions, and the political position of the Labour Party has weakened along with it.

I will have to leave it to professional economists to argue over whether the costs of excess expectations and overlending since 1988 outweigh earlier gains in investment and productivity.[21] The privatization campaign had one clear effect on the public: the proportion of households with experience of some share (stock) ownership rose from 7 percent to over 20 percent during the Thatcher years.[22] Even allowing for the general tendency of a boom to spread stock ownership (the corresponding proportion in the U.S. rose by half between 1982 and 1987, without any special privatization), this was a big change.

Aggregate investment itself was far more disappointing: gross fixed capital formation was 17.4 percent of GDP on average from 1980 to 1989, *down* from 19.4 percent from 1974 to 1979.[23] Even at the end, aggregate investment had only regained its earlier levels. More of it was private than before: the share of investment by public corporations fell as many were privatized, and the share of investment supplied by government fell steadily,

20. See Brown and Wadhwani, "Economic Effects," Tables 1 and 3.
21. Sargent presents the arguments on each side.
22. Christopher Johnson, *The Economy under Mrs. Thatcher, 1979–1990* (Harmondsworth: Penguin, 1991), 169.
23. O.E.C.D., *Historical Statistics, 1960–1990* (Paris, 1992).

at least until Thatcher's last two years. Aggregate investment in Britain was 30 percent public in 1980; it was 15 percent public in 1987–1990.[24] But in spite of this, there is no evidence that investment was any higher overall than before: private investment clearly did no more than replace cuts in public investment.

On the whole, if numbers do not lie, the macro indicators paint a mixed picture of Thatcher's tenure. It is well known that persistent unemployment was a standing problem of the Thatcher years, remaining above 10 percent until 1986–1987, and falling only just below seven percent at the end of her tenure. Were there compensating gains? To be fair, economic growth was restored to some extent. From 1982 to 1988 there were, as we remarked above, seven years of growth at rates exceeding 2.5 percent per annum, which is a return to the sort of overall performance last seen in the late 1950s. Even so, taken over her whole term, real growth was no more than average for postwar Britain. Inflation rose to 20 percent and fell to 4 percent, but was back to 10 percent by 1990.[25] On average, this performance was better than what went just before, but it is hard to see it as good either by the standards of other European economies or the United States. Britain has a chronic inflation problem, and there is no evidence that Thatcher ended it.

With respect to the restoration of sound finance, I think more or less all are agreed that the MTFS never really worked well.[26] In the early years, deficits were always larger than forecast and in the later years always smaller. The huge budget deficit of the 1970s *was* cured. Balanced budgets were restored, though largely through the proceeds of asset sales and cuts in public investment. Even if these are not recurring items in the future, the restoration of order to the public balance sheet should not be ignored.

By contrast, when looking for the promised spending cuts, there is not really much change to see. During the recession of 1979–1981 government consumption—spending on wages, salaries, and materials, not on transfer payments or capital—rose from 19.7 percent of GDP to 21.7 percent, partly at least because national income was falling as much as because spending was rising. Public consumption fell back to 19.4 percent of national income by 1989, but this is only just below where it began. Social security spending, on the other hand, rose across the period from 11.2 percent of GDP to 11.9 percent, more than offsetting the decline in consumption. When one considers that government consumption was 16 percent of national income and social security spending 7 percent in 1960,

24. Figures on the composition of British investment are from the Central Statistical Office, *Annual Abstract of Statistics* (London: HMSO, 1993), Tables 14.1–5.

25. A readable summary of developments is Johnson, *Economy under Mrs. Thatcher,* Chapter 2.

26. In fact, Johnson subtitles his chapter "the monetarist experiment that was never tried."

one can see how much further there was to go.[27] By absolutely the same token, government employment was 20 percent of the labor force in 1992, down from 22.4 percent in 1983, but still a third higher than in 1960, when government employed 15 percent of the British labor force. Public sector growth was at most arrested, not reversed.

Taxation under Thatcher tells much the same story. Public sector receipts from all sources were just under 40 percent of GDP in 1980; they were just under 40 percent of GDP in 1990 (accounting differences between sources are bigger than anyone's estimate of the change!), but they were *30* percent of GDP in 1960. For all the attention that various budget tax changes and declining marginal rates of tax got, the share of national income taken by income taxation was about the same (a little above 10 percent) at the beginning and at the end of her term. What promised, in her first five years, to be a significant shifting of the income tax burden from individuals to companies disappeared entirely in the next five years.[28] For all the promise, the structure of government revenues as a share of national income in total, and within this total taxation the relative size of the slices belonging to taxes on expenditures, personal incomes, and company incomes are indistinguishable in 1980 and 1990.

An Evaluation

So what does one make of this mixed record? How much was really achieved? How much was really unique to Britain and Thatcher? The last question is a good place to start. Above I remarked that she had problems early and late and good times in between. But her problems, both early and late, as many of her supporters point out, were problems with a world recession, not a uniquely British condition. The problem is, it was a world boom in between as well, evident in many countries' economies—but at least her government did not get in the way. Inflation was down, strikes were down, income tax rates were down in the 1980s pretty much everywhere, and under governments of very different partisan coloration, but Thatcher was a moving force in these global changes. The growth of the public sector, and more important the growing assumption that the public sector held the cure for whatever was ailing, needed arresting. She did that, and did much of it first.

In a way, though, even the successes (sounder finance, a more market-oriented economy, less role for government and unions) have not changed

---

27. O.E.C.D., *Historical Statistics 1960–1990* (Paris, 1992), Section 6.

28. Details of individual tax changes are set out in Johnson, *Economy under Mrs. Thatcher,* 111.

Inflation rate
 in per cent

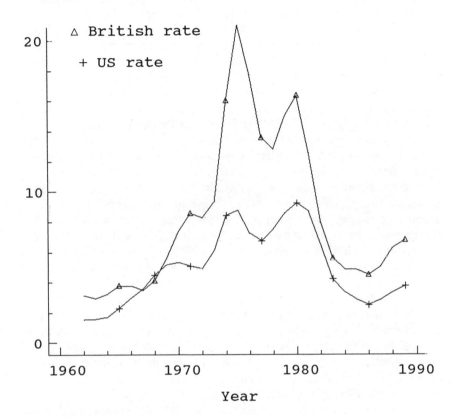

FIGURE 3.2 British and American inflation rates, three-year moving averages, 1962-1990. (*Source:* OECD.)

the fundamental position of the country very far. There is still a chronic prices problem. In the 1960s, it was easy to describe British inflation performance as the U.S. inflation rate plus two points. Now? As Figure 3.2 shows, Thatcher's average inflation performance was the U.S. rate plus two points, much as before. Moreover, in the 1980s the British inflation rate still followed the U.S. rate up and down: the British low of 3.5 percent in 1986 parallels the American low of 2.1 percent that year.[29] Thatcher never achieved sustained low inflation by other international standards.

29. The figure serves as yet another reminder of how exceptional (and exceptionally poor) was Britain's economic performance in the 1970s.

Overall price inflation in Britain is average for the European Community in the period: a little below average from 1982 to 1986 and above thereafter. This is a long-standing British problem, and it remains one. Maybe it is best to take Thatcher's own advice, though, and not hold the government itself responsible. The public probably take this view too, at least more than before. It will be even better when discussions of British economic policy routinely include considerations of developments outside the country.

Reforming the economic playing field was less clearly successful than winning elections. Labor market reforms were clearly necessary, and indications are that they have succeeded in reducing strikes. Equally clearly, the fact that inflation is still relatively high in Britain means not that further reforms are needed, but that unions are not—and maybe were not—the cause of Britain's inflation problem. A big part of the problem is that Thatcherism was far less effective in instilling competitive forces outside the labor market. Complaints about the pricing policies of newly privatized monopolies are many, and rare are the pieces of legislation mandating access. For example, the competing phone services do not connect to each other with consequences many Americans would find surprising. The faith that capitalism somehow produces virtue is naive. Yet Mrs. Thatcher herself is said to have complained about the consequences of some television licensing auctions.

Because the reforms were incomplete, Britain's long-term investment problems were not really solved. Much of the new investment generated by Thatcherism flowed abroad. Of course, the returns on that investment flowed into Britain. However, Thatcherism will clearly have succeeded when those with funds to invest find Britain a particularly attractive place in which to do so, without the added inducement of relatively high interest rates. To date there is not much sign of this having happened, but one does not turn a century-old problem around overnight. It was a start, though, and recession or not, it is hard to imagine many wanting to return to 1979.

Some day, hard times or maybe even some new issue will finally split the ruling Conservative coalition and restore two-or-more-party competition to Britain. One thing is sure: when this happens the partisan arguments over the economy will no longer be the same as before. Much has also been made elsewhere of how, in spite of winning elections, Thatcher never persuaded too much of the public to share her views.[30] She was nevertheless clearly more successful in persuading her principal opposition, the Labour Party, to change the central economic arguments of its electoral program away from the sort of issues which had dominated British politics for over half a century. Labour's October 1974 General Election Manifesto (at p. 30) put its traditional stance clearly: "our objective is to bring about a

---

30. Crewe presents convincing evidence on this point.

FIGURE 3.3 In the glitter of Christmas tree decorations, George Schultz, former Secretary of Treasury and Secretary of State, receives a warm welcome from Prime Minister Thatcher at 10 Downing Street. (*Source:* British Information Services, New York)

fundamental and irreversible shift in the balance of wealth and power in favour of working people and their families." Labour's April 1992 Manifesto (at p. 11) described the new central theme of its economic policy equally precisely: "Modern government has a strategic role, not to replace the market but to ensure that the market works properly. . . . It is the government's responsibility to create the conditions for enterprise to thrive." Apparently, when it comes to the politics of economic policy, all the parties now speak her language.

FIGURE 4.1 Thatcher greets the new U.S. Ambassador, Henry Catto, at 10 Downing Street, April 1989. (*Source:* British Information Services, New York.)

4

Margaret Thatcher and Foreign Policy

Alan J. Ward

In Britain, foreign and defense powers belong to the Crown and are exercised by Her Majesty's government. There is no formal constitution to require that these powers be shared with Parliament, nor is Parliament sufficiently independent as an institution to demand a significant role. The reality is that the government is selected from the majority in the House of Commons and uses party discipline to dictate policies to Parliament. In Britain, therefore, one can say with great certainty that national policies are those of a particular government.

Mrs. Thatcher dominated her government as few other prime ministers have done. When she came to power in 1979, her cabinet included party leaders representing a range of views in the Conservative Party, but she served as prime minister for almost twelve years, led the party to three election victories, and was able to weed out ministers who did not share her views. We should note, however, that foreign policy was extraordinarily complex during her period in office, and it was inevitable that the Foreign and Commonwealth Office, very capably led by Lord Carrington (1979–1982), Sir Geoffrey Howe (1983–1990), and Douglas Hurd (1990–1991), was able to act more independently than other departments. It will not be until confidential government records are released that we will know precisely how influential Thatcher was in foreign policy.

Mrs. Thatcher had no governmental experience in foreign affairs. Indeed, she had very little experience in government at all, but her basic instincts were well understood. When she became leader of the Conservative Party in 1975, for example, she attacked the process of détente, which was the prevailing foreign policy doctrine of the time. In doing so, she put the world on notice that there would be a new style of British foreign policy when the Conservatives returned to office. That occurred on May 3, 1979, when

Margaret Thatcher became prime minister, at a time of great international tension. The Iranian revolution had occurred in January that year, and in December the U.S.S.R. invaded Afghanistan, setting in motion a new phase of the Cold War and enhanced superpower tensions.

We should cast our minds back to the early 1970s to see what it was that Thatcher was rejecting. Détente was framed by President Richard Nixon and his national security adviser, Henry Kissinger. Peace, Kissinger argued, is a by-product of stability, which itself is produced when rivals learn to accept each other's legitimate interests. Stability depends upon mutual restraint, on the acceptance of military sufficiency, not military superiority, and on a balance of power, not a preponderance of power. West European foreign ministers, who have always been uncomfortable with America's tendency to interpret world politics as a conflict between the forces of light and darkness, instinctively respected Kissinger's view of the international system and the policies which followed from it: mutual deterrence coupled with a cautious willingness to negotiate with the U.S.S.R. on subjects of mutual interest, such as arms control and trade.

During the presidency of Gerald Ford, from 1973 to 1976, détente came under attack from conservatives in the United States, the so-called New Right, led by Ronald Reagan, who challenged Ford for the Republican presidential nomination in 1976. Détente, Reagan argued, was an amoral, no-win policy which treated the Soviet Union, what Reagan was to call "an evil empire," not as an enemy but as a partner. While the United States and its NATO partners practiced détente, Reagan argued, the Soviet Union was seeking military superiority and expanding its influence in the world by supporting Marxist regimes in Africa, Asia, and Latin America.

Margaret Thatcher was the spokeswoman of the New Right in British politics. She was described as a "conviction politician," which in her case meant opposing consensus politics in the domestic arena and the accommodationist policies of détente in the international arena. This made her a natural ally of Ronald Reagan when he came to the presidency in 1981, though it often put her at odds with the Foreign and Commonwealth Office, which found her unnecessarily confrontational in her dealings with the European Community (EC), the Commonwealth, and the U.S.S.R. Like Reagan, Thatcher ultimately did compromise on important issues, but she was able to argue that her early defense of principle made compromise possible later on terms which were acceptable to Britain.

Ronald Reagan did not become president until January 1981. Until then Mrs. Thatcher had to deal with President Jimmy Carter, who had a much more complex view of international affairs than his successor. Carter did not view the world in dichotomous terms, as an arena for a life-or-death struggle with communism. He was particularly sensitive, for example, to third world concerns and to violations of human rights, in the communist countries and elsewhere. But the fall of the Shah of Iran in January 1979, which was followed by the seizure of the American embassy and fifty-three hostages in November, together with the Soviet invasion of Afghanistan in December, shook Carter very badly. In January 1980, he announced what became known as "the Carter Doctrine," that any attempt by an outside force to gain control of the Persian Gulf would be viewed as a threat to United States's vital interests and would be repelled by any means necessary. He laid the groundwork for the renewal of the Cold War by increasing defense spending, authorizing the Rapid Deployment Force, and increasing the size of the U.S. Navy in the Indian Ocean. He also withdrew the SALT II treaty, which he had signed in 1978, from the U.S. Senate, initiated a grain embargo against the Soviet Union, and canceled U.S. participation in the 1980 Moscow Olympic Games. President Reagan accelerated these policies and dramatized them with Cold War rhetoric. Thatcher shared this world view, if not all its details, and it influenced much of her foreign policy. It also led to a period of unprecedented peacetime cooperation between the United States and Britain.

Views of Europe and Arms Control

Thatcher's foreign policy might best be reviewed by concentrating on the three interlocking circles of interests which Winston Churchill used to define British foreign policy after World War II: Europe, the Empire and Britain's global role, and the relationship with the United States. This typology was not altogether obsolete in 1979. We will begin with Europe.

Thatcher's European policies demonstrated a traditional British ambivalence towards Europe. On one hand, Britain has an aversion to Europe, a sense that it is set apart from the countries of the continent. On the other hand, Britain recognizes that its independence depends on a favorable distribution of power in Europe, and this requires a degree of participation in continental affairs. Sir William Nicoll reviews Thatcher's EC policy in another chapter, where it is clear that her policy exemplified this ambivalence, but so too did her defense policy, if to a lesser degree.

Thatcher was a good European in the sense that she recognized the importance of Europe to Britain's national security. The Soviet Union posed a deadly threat. It had a substantial superiority in conventional forces, and the Mutual and Balanced Force Reduction talks, which began in 1973, produced no tangible reductions until 1990, after the Warsaw Treaty Organization had collapsed. The U.S.S.R.'s decision to deploy 420 SS-20 intermediate-range nuclear ballistic missiles, two-thirds of them targeted on Western Europe, introduced a new element of insecurity in the late 1970s, and it followed for Thatcher that Britain had to increase its NATO commitment. The NATO powers had agreed in 1977 to raise defense spending by 3 percent per annum in real terms from 1979, and under Thatcher, Britain was almost alone in meeting that target. Between 1978–1979 and 1985–1986 its defense spending rose by 25 percent in real terms.

Britain also shared with its European NATO partners some concerns about America's commitment to Europe at a time when many in the United States Congress were questioning both the need for large numbers of American servicemen to be based in Europe, and the size of the Europeans' contribution to their own defense. Thatcher wanted U.S. forces to remain in Europe lest even a partial withdrawal should signal the beginning of America's disengagement. She was apprehensive that the major nuclear arms control talks were bilateral, involving only the U.S. and the U.S.S.R.: the Strategic Arms Limitation Talks (SALT), which led to the SALT I agreement in 1972 and SALT II in 1978, the Strategic Arms Reduction Talks (START), which led to the START Treaty of 1991, the U.S.-Soviet summit meetings in Geneva (1985), Reykjavik (1986), Washington (1987), and Moscow (1988), and the talks which led to the Intermediate-range Nuclear Forces Agreement of December 1987.

The European NATO members were consulted, of course, but they were sensitive to the fact that the Americans might compromise on European security. For example, there was great alarm in Western European capitals at the recklessness with which President Reagan accepted at the Reykjavik summit the principle of the phased elimination of all nuclear weapons, without regard to the fact that this would leave the Soviet Union with conventional weapons superiority in Europe. Similarly, the U.S. Strategic Defense Initiative (SDI) of March 1983, Reagan's decision to build a system to defend the continental U.S. from nuclear attack, was not welcomed in Europe. If the United States were really able to defend itself from a Soviet nuclear attack, why would it need to involve itself in the defense of Europe? It was also clear to the Europeans after the Reykjavik summit, which collapsed because of Reagan's intransigence on SDI, that arms control would be stalled as long as the U.S. and U.S.S.R. treated their positions on SDI as non-negotiable. Britain was the first NATO ally to agree to work on SDI research, but in March 1985 the British foreign secretary, Geoffrey Howe, called for SDI to be included in arms control.

The U.S. did act to reassure the European NATO members with respect to one particular Soviet threat, intermediate-range forces (INF), particularly the new Soviet SS-20 missiles, which the Europeans believed would alter the balance of nuclear forces in Europe by the mid-1980s. West German Chancellor Helmut Schmidt took the initiative in asking the U.S. to counter the SS-20 deployments by basing U.S. INF weapons in Europe, and in 1979 President Carter agreed to send ground-launched cruise and Pershing II

FIGURE 4.2 Group of Seven leaders meet in Tokyo, 1979. From left to right: Joe Clark (Canada), Jimmy Carter (U.S.), Masayoshi Ohira (Japan), Helmut Schmidt (West Germany), Valery Giscard d'Estaing (France), Margaret Thatcher (U.K.), and Giulio Andreotti (Italy). (*Source:* British Information Services, New York.)

missiles. In June 1980, the Thatcher government announced that 160 cruise missiles would be stationed at two U.S. air bases in England, Molesworth and Greenham Common. They arrived in November 1983.

The U.S. offered not to deploy its missiles if the U.S.S.R. would withdraw its SS-20s, but the Soviets rejected this "zero-option" plan because it equated the two sets of missiles. They regarded cruise and Pershing missiles as strategic weapons because they could reach the Soviet Union from Europe. The SS-20s, on the other hand, could not reach the U.S. The Soviets also insisted that the zero option must include British and French nuclear weapons, which were independently targeted on the U.S.S.R. That is to say, they wanted all missiles capable of reaching the U.S.S.R. to be withdrawn from Western Europe, but the British and French refused to surrender their weapons.

In deciding to reject the zero-option, the Soviet Union hoped that a newly aroused public in Western Europe would prevent governments from accepting the American missiles. The U.S., which was sending these weapons at the specific request of its European partners, found itself blamed by antinuclear activists for escalating the arms race. In Britain, for example, the Campaign for Nuclear Disarmament, which had been an important feature of the political scene in the 1950s, was revived. Some opponents of cruise missiles were unilateralists who believed that Britain should have nothing to do with nuclear weapons. Others, impressed by the extraordinary, and arguably insane, number of weapons in the arsenals of the nuclear powers, asked what additional deterrent the new American missiles might provide which British and French nuclear weapons, U.S. nuclear bombers based in England, U.S. submarine-launched weapons, and U.S. intercontinental missiles and bombers did not already provide, at less risk to European populations? Thatcher and her European partners resisted enormous popular pressures and accepted the missiles, which were not as unpopular as contemporary news coverage suggested. Conservative governments were returned to office in both the British and West German elections in 1983.

Nuclear disarmament talks were suspended by the U.S.S.R. after the cruise and Pershings were deployed in Europe in 1983, but they were resumed after Mikhail Gorbachev came to power. An INF agreement was signed by Reagan and Gorbachev at the Washington summit meeting in December 1987. British and French missiles were excluded from its terms, as were nuclear weapons with a range of less than five hundred kilometers.

Thatcher clearly worked closely with the European NATO members on these matters, and her friendship with Reagan allowed her to represent European interests to the United States in an effective way. But her nuclear weapons policy also illustrated Britain's tendency to distance itself from Europe. Thatcher insisted on maintaining a so-called "independent nuclear deterrent," but in fact Britain has been dependent on the United States for a delivery system for its nuclear forces most of the time since they were introduced in 1952. From 1952 to 1955 it used B-29 bombers acquired from the United States, before its own bombers were available. In 1962 President John F. Kennedy agreed to supply Polaris missiles for four British-built submarines, with Britain supplying the nuclear warheads. The last of the four submarines went into service in 1968, and well before Thatcher came to office it was recognized that the submarines and missiles had to be modernized, replaced, or abandoned during the 1990s. The U.S. was itself planning to phase Polaris out of service. In 1980 President Carter offered the Trident missile system as a replacement. The Thatcher government decided to build four new nuclear submarines armed with these missiles and British warheads at an officially estimated cost (in 1992) of approximately £10,500,000,000. Trident will therefore give Britain an independent nuclear capability until about 2020. The decision was presented to Parliament as a *fait accompli* and has been the subject of controversy ever since, with opponents arguing that Trident is both too costly and, in a post–Cold War era, unnecessary. The environmental group, Greenpeace, has estimated that total costs for

Trident, including operating costs and refits, will be £33,100,000,000 over a period of thirty years. The new submarines will maintain Britain's independent deterrent and its residual great power status, but the cost will be large, and the policy continues to tie Britain to the United States. Under Thatcher, therefore, Britain continued to maintain its distance from NATO and its attachment to the U.S. in nuclear weapons.

The French developed their nuclear weapons system alone. When President Kennedy offered him missiles on the same terms as those accepted by Britain in 1962, President Charles de Gaulle refused, arguing that Europe could not rely on the United States for its nuclear protection in the long-term. It was in large part because Britain had this close relationship with the U.S., and was therefore not truly a European country, that de Gaulle rejected the U.K.'s application to join the European Economic Community (EEC) in January 1963. It is ironical, therefore, given de Gaulle's criticism of Britain, that Thatcher's European policy was very close to his. For her, as for him, Europe is a group of sovereign states tied together by inter-governmental organizations such as NATO and the EC, which she insists is not, and should not be, a super-state. She despises the word "community" and the pooling of sovereignty which it suggests, and she had no interest in French and German plans for a European army.

Thatcher's defense policy in her first administration, from 1979 to 1983, was predicated on a threatening and expansionist Soviet Union. In her second administration, from 1983 to 1987, she dramatically reevaluated the Soviet Union after a major Foreign Office study of Eastern Europe challenged her assumptions. The U.S.S.R. was changing rapidly in this period. Leonid Brezhnev died in November 1982, and his two aging successors spent very short periods in office. Yuri Andropov died in 1984 and Konstantin Chernenko in 1985. The Foreign Office had concluded in 1983 that opportunities for change were opening up in the U.S.S.R., and the communist empire in Eastern Europe was weakening. Thatcher therefore set out to establish a new relationship with Eastern Europe. She was not alone, of course. West Germany had long practiced a policy of rapprochement with the East (*Ostpolitik*), and in January 1984 even President Reagan broke from his "evil empire" rhetoric of the past and described a new approach to the U.S.S.R., what he described as "a policy of credible deterrence, peaceful competition, and constructive cooperation."[1] Both Thatcher and Reagan argued that their newfound willingness was made possible by the fact that after a period of military expansion they were dealing from a position of strength.

In 1984 Thatcher visited Hungary, which was already well advanced in its

---

1. Ronald Reagan, "The U.S.-Soviet Relations," Washington, D.C.: U.S. Department of State, 1984, 3.

experiment with a mixed economy, "goulash communism." She went to
Moscow for Andropov's funeral in 1984, and that same year she invited the
Soviet minister for agriculture, Mikhail Gorbachev, to London for talks.
The Foreign Office had identified him as a new kind of leader, and he
thoroughly impressed Thatcher as someone with whom the West could
work. Gorbachev succeeded Chernenko as general secretary of the Communist party early in 1985, and although there was a brief hiatus in
September 1985, when Britain expelled thirty-one Soviet diplomats for
espionage, it was soon evident that the new leader was moving the U.S.S.R.
into a period of cooperation with the West. Thatcher made a very successful
visit to the Soviet Union in 1987, but by this time the relationship she was
cultivating with Gorbachev was being overtaken by events. First, his relationship with Reagan took priority over all others. Second, the forces which
Gorbachev liberated led unexpectedly to the collapse of the Soviet empire in
Eastern Europe in 1989, and then to the disintegration of the U.S.S.R. itself
in 1990 and 1991.

The movement leftwards in the British Labour Party in the 1970s and
early 1980s, particularly under the leadership of a unilateral disarmer,
Michael Foot, from 1980 to 1983, opened a huge gap between the two
major parties on issues of national defense and East-West relations. Whereas
the Conservatives were committed to raising British defense spending to a
little over 5 percent of GNP, Labour wanted to reduce it to the much lower
average of all NATO members, approximately 3.5 percent of GNP in 1981.
Whereas the Conservatives were committed to the renewal of Britain's
nuclear deterrent, Labour officially supported the elimination of nuclear
weapons from Britain. It was only after Gorbachev came to power that the
new Labour leader, Neil Kinnock, was able to finesse the nuclear weapons
issue by arguing that Labour's policy could be accommodated in the nuclear
disarmament process, which was making such rapid progress that unilateralism was obsolete. Thatcher, meanwhile, was claiming victory over
communism.

Britain's Global Role

The second of Britain's traditional foreign policy interests is its imperial,
or global, role. Although all the great British colonies had gone by 1979, the
residues of empire caused Thatcher enormous problems. The Labour government of Clement Attlee had begun to dismantle the empire by granting
independence to India and Pakistan in 1947 and Burma in 1948. In the late
1950s, the Conservative government of Harold Macmillan made the decision
to dismantle most of the rest. In 1967 the perennial balance of payments
crisis which preceded the discovery of North Sea oil led the Labour govern-

FIGURE 4.3 Thatcher visits an exhibition of Soviet craftsmanship in London, May 30, 1979. (*Source:* British Information Services, New York.)

ment of Harold Wilson to decide that Britain should no longer play a military role "east of Suez," in the Commonwealth country of Malaysia, for example. But there still remained some distant outposts of empire, and it fell to Thatcher in 1979 to defend or dismantle them.

Thatcher's first imperial problem was in Rhodesia. In 1965 the white minority regime of Prime Minister Ian Smith unilaterally declared that the colony of Rhodesia was independent (UDI). No other state recognized its independence, and the country was battered by United Nations economic sanctions. But it hung on with the aid of oil and other supplies traded largely through the Portuguese colony of Mozambique. In 1975 Portugal withdrew from Mozambique and Angola, leaving Rhodesia perilously exposed. Meanwhile, two tribally based nationalist groups, Robert Mugabe's ZANU and Joshua Nkomo's ZAPU, were combined into a single Patriotic Front, a guerilla movement which received support from outside the country. Smith recognized that Rhodesia had to move towards some form of black majority rule or suffer collapse. He therefore engineered a constitution in January 1979 which recognized universal suffrage but assigned the white minority, about one twelfth of the population, twenty-eight seats in the proposed one-hundred-seat legislature and the power to block amendments to certain clauses in the constitution.

In April 1979, Bishop Abel Muzorewa, whose party had won fifty-one of the black seats in the first elections, became prime minister, but the Patriotic Front rejected the settlement. The legitimacy of Muzorewa's government was further undermined when Thatcher joined the United States and Commonwealth states in refusing to recognize it. Thatcher's initial impulse had been to recognize Smith's settlement, which had ended white minority rule, but it had not ended the civil war. At the urging of the foreign secretary, Lord Carrington, and Commonwealth prime ministers, she invited the disputing parties to a conference in London. Between September 10 and December 15, 1979, a new settlement and cease-fire were agreed. The settlement provided that whites would have a guaranteed number of seats in the legislature, but not the power to block constitutional changes. Rhodesia ended its rebellion against the Crown, economic sanctions were withdrawn, and British colonial rule was formally restored for a brief period. Britain transferred sovereignty to the Republic of Zimbabwe in April 1980. Elections were won by Robert Mugabe, an avowed Marxist, who subsequently declared the country a one-party state. But the settlement averted a guerilla war which the Patriotic Front would undoubtedly have won with communist support, and a period of post-independence stability was achieved. Furthermore, Mugabe stopped well short of the worst excesses of Marxist rule elsewhere in Africa. The outcome might have been very much worse.

The Falklands War

In 1981 Britain quietly granted independence to Belize, in Central America, but Thatcher's next imperial crisis came in 1982 in the Falkland Islands. The Falklands were settled by Britain in 1832 although they were claimed earlier by Britain, France, and Spain. The islands cover an area of 4,700 square miles in the South Atlantic Ocean and are located eight thousand miles from Britain and about five hundred miles northeast of Cape Horn. They have a population of approximately eighteen hundred and an economy based on sheep and fishing. Argentina, as the successor state to Spain, had long disputed Britain's sovereignty over what it calls the Malvinas, but diplomatic efforts to resolve the dispute had failed. Thatcher's government recognized that the islands were indefensible in the long-term and proposed a policy which would cede them to Argentina, subject to a lease-back agreement which would return them to British control for a number of years. The islanders rejected this arrangement, claiming British sovereignty and the right of self-determination. There was also substantial parliamentary opposition, particularly in the Conservative Party, to forcing British citizens to accept Argentine sovereignty.

In 1981 and 1982, Britain made a number of decisions which, in hindsight, may have hastened the crisis. First, it closed a British research station on the island of South Georgia, a dependency of the Falklands eight hundred miles to the southeast. This left the island uninhabited, and the Falklands crisis actually began on March 19, 1982, when a group of Argentine scrap metal merchants appeared there to salvage equipment. Second, the British Defence White Paper of July 1981 announced that a British naval patrol vessel, HMS *Endurance,* would be withdrawn from the Falklands as an economy measure. Third, the British Nationality Act of 1981 denied British residency to millions of British colonial citizens, including the eighteen hundred Falklanders. This put them very clearly into the colonial category, an unpopular status with most members of the United Nations. Britain appeared to be signalling a lack of interest in the Falklands at precisely the time that the Argentine government, a repressive and unpopular military regime, was seeking ways to improve its popularity. On April 1, 1982, it suspended diplomatic negotiations with Britain, and on April 2 it invaded the Falklands, which was the one thing calculated to win it popular support at home.

Britain was certainly not prepared for a war in the South Atlantic. The Falklands were not vital to its economic or security interests, and its defense planning was based on the defense of Europe and the North Atlantic. Furthermore, the navy, which was absolutely essential to a long-distance military operation, was targeted for large cuts in the 1981 defense review. In addition to the obvious logistical problems of putting a military force in the South Atlantic, the severe southern winter was fast approaching which would make military operations virtually impossible. Time was not on Britain's side, but two circumstances were. First, Argentina had unquestionably invaded the Falklands, and Britain was within its rights in using Article 51 of the United Nations Charter, "the inherent right of individual or collective self-defense," to defend its sovereignty. Second, Argentina had been governed since 1976 by a military junta with an appalling records of human rights abuses. It was unlikely to win much international sympathy. Thatcher was therefore able to assert that both moral and legal principles were at stake. British territory, occupied by British citizens who had clearly indicated their desire to remain British, had been invaded by a brutal military dictatorship. In Parliament she said of the Falklanders, "They are few in number, but they have the right to live in peace, to choose their own way of life, and to determine that their allegiance is to the Crown."[2]

---

2. Alan Sked and Chris Cook, *Post-War Britain: A Political History,* 3d. ed. (London: Penguin, 1990), 400.

Thatcher took personal charge of Falklands policy within the government, and although Parliament met in an extraordinary Saturday session on April 3, and several times thereafter, its debates were used primarily to mobilize support for the war. Fundamental criticism of the government for having been woefully unprepared for the Argentine invasion was deflected on April 3 when Lord Carrington and his junior ministers accepted responsibility and resigned. Thatcher herself impressed Parliament and the public with clear statements of policy and decisive leadership.

Thatcher acted on many fronts. First, as early as April 1, she asked President Reagan to mediate the dispute. He assigned the task to Secretary of State Alexander Haig, whose "shuttle diplomacy" in the first two weeks of the crisis failed. Second, she took the issue to the United Nations Security Council, which condemned the Argentine aggression by a vote of ten to one in Resolution 502. Panama alone voted against, and the U.S.S.R., China, Poland, and Spain (whose own quarrel with Britain over the status of Gibraltar determined its vote) all abstained. The resolution called upon Argentina to withdraw before negotiations on a settlement should begin. Third, Britain secured the support of its fellow EC members for economic sanctions, including a ban on imports from Argentina and a ban on arms sales. Although this support wavered as attempts at a peaceful solution failed, the war was won before Britain could be handicapped by the irresolution of its European allies. The U.S. and many Commonwealth states also supported economic sanctions and a ban on arms sales. Fourth, the government decided on a full-scale military response. Fifth, the time that it took British forces to reach the South Atlantic offered a two- to three-week window of opportunity for negotiations. Thatcher was prepared to negotiate on the basis of Resolution 502, which required Argentina to withdraw, but General Leopoldo Fortunato Galtieri, the president of Argentina, refused to leave the islands before negotiations began.

The military campaign to liberate the Falklands was an amazing enterprise. It was a carefully calibrated limited war which avoided attacks on the Argentine mainland and risks of escalation. The only major threat to Britain's international support came when the Argentine Cruiser, *Belgrano,* was sunk by a British submarine, with the loss of more than three hundred of the crew. Britain was to lose four ships in the war, but with far fewer casualties.

The first elements of a naval task force started out from Britain on April 5. Forty-four British warships were involved in the war, as were a large number of merchant ships, including the great ocean liners, *Queen Elizabeth II* and *Canberra.* The force also included twenty-eight thousand military personnel, of whom ten thousand were land forces. The U.S. allowed Britain to use the facility it leased on the British-owned Ascension Island, about two thousand miles west of Angola, as a training, staging, and supply

FIGURE 4.4 Second Battalion Grenadier Guards on patrol on Mount Pleasant, Falkland Islands. (*Source:* Central Office of Information, London.)

base. Once the British forces were in position, the war went quickly. South Georgia was recaptured on April 25, with no casualties. The first British landing on the main island took place on May 14. Despite being outnumbered by two-to-one on the ground and lacking adequate air cover, British forces completed the liberation on June 14. About 250 British and 750 Argentine lives were lost in the campaign. Britain demonstrated that it could respond virtually alone to an attack on its sovereignty eight thousand miles away. The war led to the downfall of General Galtieri and the Argentine junta. It contributed very substantially, therefore, to the restoration of democracy in Argentina, but it also led to a major distortion of British defense priorities. It made Britain's withdrawal from the South Atlantic impossible, and very large sums of money had to be committed thereafter to defending the islands.

The after-effects of the war were predictable. After a period of poor economic performance at home, both the government and Mrs. Thatcher rose in the opinion polls. The war fostered a widespread jingoism which was sympathetic to Conservative values, and during the general election campaign of 1983 Thatcher used the war to good advantage. "We have regained the regard and admiration of other nations," she said. "We are seen today as people with integrity and resolve and the will to succeed. This is no small achievement." The Labour Party had no means of reply. Argentina had started the war, Mrs. Thatcher and the Conservative government had won it, and all but a small minority of the Labour Party in Parliament had supported it. The government went on to win the election. Dunleavy and Husbands estimate that the war was worth 17 percent of the Conservatives' vote. That is to say, but for the war, over one in three people voting Conservative would not have done so. Most of them would have supported Liberal or Social Democratic Party candidates.[3]

The war also demonstrated a major difference between American and British politics. Margaret Thatcher's personal popularity reached a peak of only 52 percent after the war whereas George Bush reached 90 percent in 1991 after the war with Iraq. This suggests what other data confirm, that Thatcher was never a particularly popular leader. She certainly accomplished a great deal by winning three successive elections, but her party won only 43.9 percent of the vote in the 1979 general election, 42.4 percent in 1983 after the Falklands War, and 42.3 percent in 1987. She never had a popular mandate.

Hong Kong, South Africa, and the Third World

Margaret Thatcher was prepared to take on Argentina in the South Atlantic, but she was not prepared to take on the People's Republic of China (PRC) in the South China Sea. Indeed, the resolution of the Hong Kong problem in 1984 illustrates far better than the Falklands War the limits of British power in the late twentieth century and Britain's determination to withdraw from a globalist policy.

Hong Kong Island and parts of the Kowloon Peninsula on the Chinese mainland were leased to Britain in perpetuity, in 1843 and 1860 respectively, but a number of other islands and the New Territories on the mainland, which are now included in the Hong Kong colony, were leased to Britain in 1898 for a period of only 99 years. These leases are due to expire in 1997, but without them to house its swelling population and supply much of its food, water, and power, the colony is simply not viable. The PRC announced that it would not renew the leases and set 1984 as the date for completion of

---

3. Patrick Dunleavy and Christopher T. Husbands, *British Democracy at the Crossroads* (London: George Allen and Unwin, 1985), 82, 154. For Thatcher's Falklands campaign, see *Downing Street Years,* Chapter 9.

negotiations on Britain's withdrawal from the whole colony. Britain had no choice but to withdraw as gracefully as it could. Mrs. Thatcher and Premier Zhao signed an agreement in December 1984 in which Britain agreed to surrender all its leases in 1997. In return, the PRC agreed to create a special administrative region in which Hong Kong would have considerable political autonomy. It also agreed to respect the capitalist economic system of Hong Kong and a convertible local currency for period of fifty years. The agreement was signed well before the 1989 massacre on Tiananmen Square.

In at least three respects, Britain's commitment to liberal principles has suffered badly in Hong Kong since the agreement was signed. First, the agreement permits pre-1997 residents of Hong Kong to retain both PRC and Overseas British citizenship, but the latter does not give the residents of colonies the right to migrate to Britain. Indeed, the government set a limit of 225,000 on the number of Hong Kong residents it will permit to relocate in Britain, a concession designed to encourage people in particularly important occupations to remain in Hong Kong until the transfer of sovereignty. But those in Hong Kong who cannot claim full British citizenship by birth or ancestry feel trapped as 1997 approaches. Wealthy Hong Kong residents may buy their way into Australia, Canada, and the United States legally by taking large sums of money to invest, but this avenue of escape is not available to the great majority.

Second, Hong Kong became the destination of tens of thousands of Vietnamese "boat people," but Britain regards most of them as economic refugees and refuses to allow them to settle as political refugees. It therefore agreed with the government of Vietnam that they should be forcibly returned to Vietnam, where there is to be no government retribution.

Third, Britain only opened one-third of the seats in the Hong Kong Legislative Council to election. The remaining seats were filled by the governor. Furthermore, no members of the United Democratic Party, which won sixteen of eighteen seats contested in the Legislative Council elections in 1991, received seats in the Governor's Executive Council. Under Thatcher, Britain had resisted demands for local self-government before 1997 in deference to the wishes of the PRC.[4] Hong Kong is still governed as a Crown Colony, with most powers of government exercised by a British governor, and that is how it will be transferred to the PRC.

Thatcher's government acted in the only way open to it in Hong Kong. China was entitled to refuse to renew the 1898 leases. Britain cannot absorb

---

4. Chris Patten, whom John Major appointed governor, seriously raised China's hackles in October 1992 when he proposed that twenty-nine of the sixty council seats be directly elected and an additional ten be chosen by elected local officials. Although the council is a fairly powerless body, China regarded this proposal as too much democracy. Patten also recommended that his Executive Council be selected from the majority in the Legislative Council. See als Thatcher, *Downing Street Years,* 259–62, 466, 487, 491–92.

millions of Hong Kong residents who might want to flee because terribly overcrowded Hong Kong cannot house tens of thousands of Vietnamese refugees. Britain cannot ignore the wishes of the PRC on the question of local self-government. Nonetheless, there are many in Parliament, including many Conservatives, who are very uncomfortable with what has been done. Britain is in the embarrassing position of having to justify its policies by saying, in effect, that we must trust the governments of China and Vietnam to keep their word.

South Africa ceased to be a British colony in 1910 and withdrew from the British Commonwealth when it became a republic in 1961, but it remained a residual imperial interest. Many in Britain have relatives in South Africa, and Britain is the largest foreign investor there. South Africa also consumed the attention of British Commonwealth meetings during Mrs. Thatcher's years in office, particularly after the South African Declaration of Emergency in July 1985. The position of every Commonwealth country—black and white, liberal and conservative, with the exception of Britain—was that economic sanctions should be used to bring down the apartheid system in South Africa. Thatcher stood alone in meetings of Commonwealth heads of government in arguing for fewer rather than more sanctions. In doing so, she was anxious to protect Britain's economic interests, of course. But there was also a strong element of moral principle in her policy and she stuck to her position with little regard to the sensibilities of her Commonwealth partners. Brian White observes, "Mrs. Thatcher usually contrived to be both abrasive and indifferent to Commonwealth opinion."[5] She simply did not believe that sanctions would hasten the political reforms already begun by President Botha. She believed that they would harm the South African economy, to the long-term detriment of black and white South Africans, and that this would lead to chaos and instability in the country.

Thatcher made no secret of her view that African and Asian members of the Commonwealth, some of them with reprehensible human and political rights records themselves, were engaging in "moral blackmail." She entertained President Botha in London in June 1984 and did nothing to prevent thirty-two Commonwealth states from boycotting the Commonwealth Games in Edinburgh in July 1986. Under pressure from the Foreign Office, which was itself responding to pressure from the Commonwealth, the EC, and the United Nations, Thatcher agreed to limited economic sanctions, including a ban on new investment, a ban on imports of iron, steel, and gold coins, and a ban on cooperation in nuclear and other technologies, but she resisted a total ban on economic activities and disinvestment of British assets. Quite soon after the release of African National Congress (ANC) leader Nelson

---

5. Brian P. White, "British Foreign Policy: Tradition and Change," in Roy C. Macridis, ed., *Foreign Policy in World Politics* (Englewood Cliffs, N.J.: Prentice Hall, 1992), 24.

Mandela from prison, Britain unilaterally lifted the UN ban on new investments.

Thatcher's policy on North-South relations was another issue on which Britain and its Commonwealth partners differed. There was widespread support in the United Nations and the Commonwealth for the Brandt Commission's 1980 conclusion that the developed countries, predominantly located in the northern hemisphere, had a responsibility to assist in the development of the developing countries, predominantly located in the southern hemisphere. During Thatcher's years in office Britain maintained an overseas aid program at approximately the level of her predecessors, about .04 percent of GNP. But Britain joined other developed countries in questioning the assumptions of the UN-endorsed New International Economic Order (NIEO) and the Brandt Report, both of which called for a radically altered, and redistributionist, international economic regime. John Vogler notes:

> The Thatcher government's approach to North-South issues may justly be regarded as an extension of its domestic economic philosophy: monetarism, a distaste for public spending and economic management, allied to a belief in the efficacy of market forces.[6]

Given this approach, there was no way by which the Commonwealth could become a cohesive force in North-South relations.

Ireland

One final foreign policy issue for Margaret Thatcher which grew out of Britain's imperial past was the Irish problem. In 1921 Ireland was partitioned into a twenty-six-county Southern Ireland—today's Irish Republic, which is 90 percent Catholic—and a six-county Northern Ireland, which is 60 percent Protestant. Northern Ireland remained a part of the United Kingdom but was assigned its own subordinate parliament. Almost all Northern Ireland Protestants now define themselves as Unionists, that is to say, as supporters of the Union with Britain. But most Northern Ireland Catholics vote for Irish Nationalist parties, either the Social and Democratic Labour Party or Sinn Fein, although for most of them a united Ireland is a very distant goal.

The present phase of sectarian conflict in Northern Ireland began in the mid-1960s when a civil rights movement was launched to demand equal

---

6. John Vogler, "Britain and North-South Relations," in Michael Smith, Steve Smith, and Brian White, *British Foreign Policy: Tradition, Change and Transformation* (London: Unwin Hyman, 1988), 198.

rights for the Nationalist minority. When the Northern Ireland government, under great pressure from Britain, made concessions to the Nationalist community, Unionist extremists exploded in violence directed against the minority. The British army was sent to restore order in 1969. The Irish Republican Army (IRA) took this opportunity to reopen the war against British authority which it had waged sporadically since 1921. In 1972 Britain abolished the Northern Ireland Parliament and imposed direct rule from Britain.

Since 1972, both Labour and Conservative governments have agreed on two basic policies to be followed in Northern Ireland. First, violence in Northern Ireland must be suppressed, whether it is directed against the Unionist or Nationalist communities. Second, some form of regional self-government must be established which has the support of both communities. To date, two efforts to establish a Northern Ireland Assembly have failed, and violence has continued, though at levels which the population of Northern Ireland can probably sustain indefinitely. For the past fifteen years the numbers of dead directly attributable to the conflict have averaged less than one hundred per annum in a population of one and a half million, a small fraction of the murder rate in most American cities.

Northern Ireland became an international issue for Mrs. Thatcher for two reasons. First, the United States came under great pressure from Irish-Americans to make Northern Ireland an issue in Anglo-American relations. Although the executive branch resisted this pressure, many members of Congress catered to IRA supporters in their districts by agitating for a British withdrawal. Second, and much more important, the government of the Irish Republic became embroiled in the conflict. A united Ireland is an important long-range goal of all Irish governments, and they have often spoken out on behalf of the Nationalist community in Northern Ireland. However, they have strongly opposed the use of Irish territory as a staging area and sanctuary for the IRA and have cooperated with British governments to apprehend and prosecute IRA members. They have also campaigned very hard to stop Irish-American support for the IRA.

The Conservative Party has traditionally been identified with Unionism in Northern Ireland, but it was the Conservative government of Edward Heath which abolished the Northern Ireland Parliament in 1972. Furthermore, in 1973 Heath determined that any future self-government must involve some form of power-sharing by the Unionist and Nationalist communities. Mrs. Thatcher disappointed Unionists by firmly embracing the consensus policies of her Labour and Conservative predecessors and cooperating with the Irish government on Northern Irish affairs. For example, police commanders from North and South met to discuss border security.

Progress was stalled during the winter of 1981–1982 when IRA prisoners at the Maze prison in Northern Ireland staged a hunger strike to demand

FIGURE 4.5 Thatcher laying a wreath by a plaque commemorating the deaths by an IRA bomb outside Harrods department store in London, December 17, 1983. (*Source:* British Information Services, New York.)

treatment as political prisoners rather than as criminals. Thatcher absolutely refused to be intimidated by an international campaign which was mounted in support of the hunger strikers. Ten of them died, including Bobby Sands, who was elected to the British Parliament during the strike, which lasted for 203 days. Thatcher nearly paid for her intransigence with her life on October 12, 1984, when an IRA bomb demolished part of the hotel in which she and other members of the government were staying during the Conservative Party annual conference in Brighton.

Progress was resumed in November 1983 when Thatcher and Irish Prime Minister Garret FitzGerald agreed to establish an Intergovernmental Council at ministerial level, which met approximately thirty times in the next sixteen months. In May 1983 FitzGerald had initiated a new process of consultation in Dublin, the New Ireland Forum, to which democratic political parties, churches, and interests groups from the whole of Ireland, North and South, were invited to discuss the constitutional future of the island. The motivation for the Forum was the fear, forcibly expressed by John Hume, leader of the largest Nationalist party, the Social Democratic and Labour Party, that Sinn Fein, the political wing of the IRA, would gain ground in the Nationalist community if a settlement were not achieved which recognized the rights and interests of the minority community. Unionist politicians from the North boycotted the Forum, but it was a useful airing of the issues. Its report, published in 1984, identified three frameworks for a possible constitutional settlement in Northern Ireland: a united Ireland as a unitary state, a united Ireland as a federal-confederal state, and joint British and Irish sovereignty in Northern Ireland. The report was completely unacceptable to Mrs. Thatcher, who rejected it peremptorily because it challenged British sovereignty. Garret FitzGerald described the manner of her rejection as "gratuitously offensive."[7]

Anglo-Irish relations appeared to be at an impasse, but in June 1985 at a meeting of the EC Council in Milan, FitzGerald was able to convince Thatcher of the urgency of situation and of the need to reassure the Nationalist community in Northern Ireland. Top civil servants got to work, and the result was the Anglo-Irish Agreement, signed at Hillsborough, Northern Ireland, on November 15, 1985. The Agreement recognized the constitutional *status quo* in Northern Ireland, and both parties accepted that there could be no change without the consent of the people of the province. However, it also recognized the existence of two distinct cultural communities in Northern Ireland and the right of the Irish Republic to make representations to Britain concerning the interests of the minority community. An Intergovernmental Conference was established, with a permanent secretariat in Belfast, in which the governments of Britain and Ireland would meet regularly to discuss human rights, fair employment practices, police and security issues, and other matters. Finally, the Agreement provided that matters falling within the purview of the Intergovernmental Conference might be transferred to a new Northern Ireland Assembly, were one to be established which enjoyed the confidence of both communities.

The Agreement appeared to compromise British sovereignty, and it thoroughly alienated the Unionist majority. However, until the end of her

7. William V. Shannon, "The Anglo-Irish Agreement," *Foreign Affairs* 64 (1985): 863. See also Thatcher, *Downing Street Years,* Chapter 14.

period in office, Thatcher remained loyal to her undertaking. There were frequent meetings of the Inter-governmental Conference, and her government never ceased to search for a power-sharing framework by which Northern Ireland could be returned to self-government. No long-term solution has yet appeared, but Sinn Fein has not grown further. Also, prospects for progress may have been enhanced in 1985 when Thatcher destroyed what had been the permanent Unionist veto on constitutional change in Northern Ireland. In 1974 the Unionists destroyed the first power-sharing assembly and executive with a general strike, but this tactic failed utterly to destroy the Anglo-Irish Agreement in 1985.

FIGURE 4.6 Thatcher visiting South Armagh, Northern Ireland, August 29, 1979. (*Source:* British Information Services, New York.)

Relations with the United States

The third of Britain's traditional overseas interests is its relationship with the United States, which is often referred to as the "special relationship." There is some doubt that this term has any significant meaning. Jorgen Rasmussen and James McCormick find no evidence in public opinion polls that British mass sentiment is particularly sympathetic to the United States.[8] Indeed, with the exception of the U.S. response to Iraq's 1990 invasion of Kuwait, the British public was very critical of U.S. policies during the Thatcher years, particularly its policies in Lebanon (1982) and Grenada (1983), and the retaliatory bombing of Libya (1986). However, political elites have frequently recognized the special character of the relationship between the two great English-speaking countries. The term appears to have been coined in 1945 by Churchill, himself the son of an Anglo-American marriage, after

---

8. Rasmussen and McCormick, "British Mass Perceptions of the Anglo-American Special Relationship," *Political Science Quarterly,* Fall 1993.

he and Franklin D. Roosevelt had been especially close during World War II. The sentiment it describes was widespread at elite levels in the early years of the century and during both world wars.

The quality of the Anglo-American relationship at any point in time can be debated, but there can be little doubt that it was particularly high during the period when Ronald Reagan and Margaret Thatcher were in power simultaneously. It can also be argued that this was the result primarily of a substantial coincidence of personal beliefs, not of a deep-seated national sentiment. Thatcher and Reagan agreed on a very conservative interpretation of East-West relations: that the U.S.S.R. was a monstrous empire, that détente was a smoke screen for Soviet expansion, that the invasion of Afghanistan in 1979 posed a special threat to the West, and that an appropriate response to Soviet behavior was a substantial increase in NATO military spending. They agreed that economic sanctions were a mistake in South Africa, and each worked hard to discourage or defeat them. In the United Nations, they agreed on an assertive defense of Western interests against communist and Afro-Asian criticisms of Western polices. Both countries withdrew from the UN Educational, Scientific, and Cultural Organization (UNESCO) in 1985 because of its Marxist bias, and both obstructed the progress of the New International Economic Order. Both sent ships to maintain oil shipping routes in the Persian Gulf during the Iran-Iraq war (1980–1988). They agreed, in their public pronouncements at least, on the need for a firm response to state-sponsored terrorism. Britain broke diplomatic relations with Libya in 1984, after a policewoman was killed and eleven demonstrators were injured by shots fired from inside the Libyan embassy in London. It also broke diplomatic relations with Syria in 1986 and with Iran in June 1987. Evidence generated by the Iran-Contra scandal in the United States suggests that Thatcher was more principled than Reagan in her policy towards terrorism, because the United States secretly traded arms to Iran for the release of American hostages in Lebanon. Thatcher would not deal.

The U.S. and Britain were more supportive of each other's policies than were other countries during the Thatcher-Reagan years. In the Middle-East, for example, Britain endorsed the stationing of U.S. troops in Lebanon in 1982. It was the only European country to support the U.S. reprisal raid against Libya in April 1986, following a terrorist attack on U.S. troops in Germany. The aircraft which attacked Libya flew from British airfields via the Bay of Biscay and the Straits of Gibraltar in order to avoid continental air space. British support in the early days of Iraq's invasion of Kuwait was also critical in enabling the U.S. to mobilize the international force which liberated Kuwait in 1991. In the first few days of the crisis, Thatcher, who was fortuitously in the U.S., met with President Bush in Aspen, Colorado, and Washington, D.C., and she chided the European states for their slow

FIGURE 4.7 President George Bush visiting Thatcher in London. (*Source:* British Information Services, New York.)

response to the crisis.[9] Britain made a much larger contribution to the war effort than any other state but the U.S. Thatcher was also absolutely

9. See Thatcher's speech to Parliament on the Libya strike and her address to the Aspen conference in Part II of this book.

unwavering in her support for the deployment of U.S. cruise and Pershing II nuclear missiles in Europe.

On the American side, there was very substantial support for Britain during the Falklands War, at some risk to America's standing in Latin America. The U.S. also ratified a treaty with Britain in July 1986 which permitted the extradition of IRA fugitives from the U.S. and denied them the right to claim political immunity. It continued to support Britain's so-called independent nuclear force, although those weapons clearly complicated bilateral arms control negotiations with the U.S.S.R.

There were sufficient disagreements between the two countries, however, to indicate that Thatcher cannot be accused of having slavishly followed the United States. For example, she would only support modest economic sanctions against Poland following the introduction of martial law there in 1982, and she would not support the U.S. embargo of oil pipeline equipment exports to the Soviet Union. European states, which had spent the 1970s establishing valuable trade links with the U.S.S.R., were not inclined to cut them off on instructions from the U.S., and certainly not while the U.S. continued to export grain to the U.S.S.R. When the United States ordered British subsidiaries of American companies to suspend sales of pipeline equipment, Thatcher instructed them to fulfill their contracts, and the U.S. was forced to withdraw its objections within a few months.

Mrs. Thatcher expressed her strong displeasure when the United States invaded the British Commonwealth island of Grenada in October 1983 without informing Britain. She never joined Reagan in undermining the Soviet position in Afghanistan, Angola, and Nicaragua, although Britain did make arms sales to anticommunist authoritarian regimes, such as Argentina (before the Falklands War) and Chile. Her government also expressed reservations about the SDI and the zero option INF proposal because she feared that both opened the possibility that the U.S. might disengage from Europe. In many ways, Thatcher's conception of the special relationship was that she had exceptional access to President Reagan through which to speak her mind.

Fall from Power and Conclusions

Her policy towards the EC contributed substantially to the circumstances which led to Thatcher's resignation in November 1990. In a withering attack on the prime minister before a packed House of Commons, her former deputy prime minister, chancellor of the exchequer, and foreign secretary, Sir Geoffrey Howe, denounced her policy as obstructionist and damaging to the national interest. Howe's action led members of the Conservative Party to conclude that Thatcher was vulnerable to a challenge, and Michael Heseltine decided to run against her in the annual election for party leader. He had been her minister of defence until his controversial resignation in 1986, when he sought to have Westland Helicopters sold to a European consortium rather than to the American company Sikorsky in order to strengthen a European defense industry. Thatcher opted for the American company, on free market grounds. Although Thatcher led Heseltine on the first ballot, it was by an insufficient margin for re-election under party rules. Fearing defeat, she withdrew and threw her support to her foreign secretary, John Major, who defeated Heseltine on the second ballot.

It is ironic that foreign policy did so much to bring Thatcher down because her foreign policy appeared to have been successful. During her term in office, the Cold War ended in the total defeat of communism in Europe and decline everywhere else. Capitalism even penetrated the People's Republic of China. Britain continued its withdrawal from empire and is much stronger for having done so. The war in the Falklands was a temporary aberration, forced on Britain by Argentina. But there will be, in time, an accommodation which will permit Britain to withdraw from the islands, and this will be hastened if Argentina can stabilize as a democracy. In South Africa, apartheid was dismantled without the draconian economic sanctions which Thatcher had always resisted, and the way was opened for negotiations on the future of the country. Even in the North-South debate, countries which have the potential for development and have accepted the conservative economic policies of Mrs. Thatcher, which are also those of the World Bank, are beginning to show gains.

What historians will have to determine is the degree to which Thatcher's policies actually contributed to all these ends. How much did she really have to do with the collapse of the Soviet Empire, for example? It was certainly fortuitous that a cohort of aged Soviet leaders left the scene in the first half of the 1980s and that Gorbachev won the succession stakes. He understood that centralized communism had failed, that the Soviet economy was headed towards ruin, and that Soviet foreign and defense policies had contributed to national bankruptcy. What Carter, Reagan, and Thatcher did at a critical time of Soviet self-evaluation was to convey that the West still had the will to continue the Cold War indefinitely. Once this message had been digested in the Kremlin, Reagan and Thatcher followed it up by demonstrating that they were prepared to negotiate an easing of tensions. But it was Mikhail Gorbachev who actually ended the Cold War, whereas others in his position might have acted differently. It was he, for example, who made such sweeping concessions in nuclear weaponry that the United States, with Thatcher urging caution from the wings, had no choice but to accept.

The fact that the Soviet Union almost unilaterally ended the Cold War and released Eastern Europe from the Soviet empire meant that some important issues of British defense policy virtually disappeared from the domestic political scene. The debate over Britain's nuclear weapons, which was largely about whether they would embroil Britain in an American war, ceased to have any urgency. Britain is still committed to building Trident submarines, and there is considerable debate about their cost and utility, but even the Trident's critics no longer feel that the system will endanger Britain.

The enormous change in South Africa similarly defused economic sanctions as an issue in British politics. Once again, Thatcher's role in political change is not immediately apparent. Did her obstructionism provide a cushion of time which Botha and De Klerk used to lead white South Africans to accept constitutional change peacefully, or did she slow down a process of change which more severe sanctions might have hastened? Historians will have to supply the answer.

One thing is already clear, however. The three interlocking sets of interests which have been used as a framework for reviewing Thatcher's foreign policy in this chapter will have no utility for future governments. During Thatcher's term of office, and despite her own hesitation, Britain moved beyond the point of no return in its EC membership. It cannot stay out of Europe now. It was because Thatcher was seen to be undermining Britain's ability to participate in shaping Europe's future that the Conservative Party rejected her policy in 1990. Britain's relationship with Europe is therefore growing stronger, but not so its relationship with the Commonwealth. As an institution, the Commonwealth has grown steadily weaker since Britain joined the EC in 1972 and abandoned the Commonwealth trading system. Thatcher's staunch opposition to a united Commonwealth position on economic sanctions against South Africa helped to redefine the organization. Britain will no doubt remain a member and will continue to be a link between some developed and some developing countries, but the old ties which bound Britain to its former dependencies have been substantially weakened. Furthermore, with the solution of the Rhodesia problem and substantial progress being made in South Africa, Britain is now free of its association with policies which at times caused virtually the entire Third World to be ranged against it.

Britain's relationship with the United States must also change. The Cold War has ended, and the simple, dichotomized view of the world which attracted Thatcher and Reagan to each other, and which required the United States to provide a military umbrella for Europe, now has no meaning. The New World Order of which President George Bush spoke is not an order at all. The world is a very chaotic place. With no simple model to unite them, the United States and Britain are likely to go very different ways. They are also likely to talk less of a special relationship, unless by that term is meant the friendship of two countries with a shared history and shared culture. There is no reason for that to change.

5

Lady Thatcher and the Cold War

Trevor Salmon and William Macnair

Dux femina facti —Virgil, *Aeneid*

It is possible that Lady Thatcher will be remembered as much for her stand on the Cold War as for the economic policies of her three administrations or her personal achievements as the politician who held the office of British prime minister for longer than anyone in one and one-half centuries. There was nothing about Mrs. Thatcher as the newly elected leader of the opposition, however, that could have given anybody a glimpse of that future reputation. Closer examination of her record in foreign and defence policy, moreover, presents a more complex and interesting picture than the conventional portrait of the "Iron Lady."

Mrs. Thatcher is a chemist by education, a lawyer by training, and a politician by instinct. She had no experience or knowledge of foreign affairs when elected leader of the Conservative Party in 1975. Her platform and appeal was in economic and domestic issues, such as trade union reform, and her experience in government was as a junior minister in the Ministry of Pensions and in the cabinet with responsibility for education. In his biography, Hugo Young reports that in foreign affairs "her ignorance . . . was startling."[1] However, Mrs. Thatcher was practical in mastering a brief, and her instincts and self-confidence overcame the handicap of lack of knowledge. In Britain, the prime minister, as head of government, takes a prominent role in foreign affairs. As leader of the opposition she had to confront Prime Ministers Harold Wilson and James Callaghan, both experienced in foreign questions

---

1. Hugo Young, *One of Us* (London: Macmillan, 1991), 168–70. This book was released in the U.S. under the title *The Iron Lady* and is referred to by the American title elsewhere in this work.

and backed by such formidable figures as Denis Healey, Labour Defence Minister from 1964 to 1970 and later Chancellor of the Exchequer.

Continuity in Defence and Foreign Policy

Between 1975 and 1979, Margaret Thatcher prepared herself for office and laid the foundations of her reputation. Conservative leaders in Britain have historically "wrapped themselves in the flag," identifying defence and patriotism as core values of the party and ones that particularly attract working-class support. As discussed below, this stance is more rhetorical than representative of major practical differences between the three main political parties. British defence and foreign policy since the Second World War is remarkable for its continuity and stability rather than radical changes associated with new governments. Her image with voters was undoubtedly helped by the Soviet epithet of "Iron Lady" which she earned by a series of speeches, particularly that of January 1976: "They [the Soviets] put guns before butter, while we put just about everything before guns. They know they are a superpower in only one sense—the military sense. They are a failure in human and economic terms."[2] Mrs. Thatcher signalled her determination to hold by what she said when she dismissed Reginald Maudling, her shadow foreign secretary. He had attempted to remonstrate with her over the policy implications of such rhetoric, but typically she wished to make clear that she meant what she said.

The Conservative election manifesto for the 1979 British election and associated policy papers, "The Right Approach" and "The Resolute Approach," contained clear endorsements of NATO, traditional British defence policy including the independent nuclear deterrent, concern about the Soviet Intermediate-range Nuclear Forces (INF), and commitments to conventional enhancement. However, the campaign was scarcely fought on any of these issues. Indeed, Conservative policy rather than rhetoric was not dissimilar to Labour's under Callaghan, Healey, and David Owen (incumbent Labour foreign secretary in 1979), none of whom would yield to Thatcher in patriotism. Gallup found that under 2 percent of the electorate claimed to have been influenced by the defence issue in the 1979 election.[3]

There had been a long continuity in British defence and foreign policy in practice if not in theory and rhetoric. The British decision to become a nuclear power was undertaken by Clement Attlee's Labour government. It had been Callaghan and Chancellor Helmut Schmidt of the German Social Democratic Party who had sounded the clarion on the Soviet deployment

---

2. Ibid., 170. See text of speech in Part II of this volume.
3. *Gallup Political Index,* no. 226, London, 1979.

of SS-20 missiles, Callaghan who had adopted the Chevaline programme for updating the Polaris missiles (which were the mainstay of the British independent deterrent) and who had negotiated with President Jimmy Carter the British purchase of the C-4 Trident at Guadeloupe in January 1979.[4] Perhaps most revealing was that the NATO goal of an annual increase in defence expenditure in the region of 3 percent in real terms had been agreed to by Labour government in 1977 and confirmed by the Social Democratic Party–Liberal Party alliance and Conservative government in 1981.

British statesmen since 1945 had tended to see the United Kingdom's role as the bridge between the United States and the European nations. Ernest Bevin, foreign secretary in the Attlee government, had been the sponsor of the Brussels Treaty of 1948 and the establishment of NATO. Sir Anthony Eden had found the way forward after the collapse of the European Defence Community, the threat of the American "agonizing reappraisal," and European concern over German rearmament relaunching the Western and European Union. Serious debate and policy differences tended to be over the balance of Atlanticism and Europeanism. They were not about the fundamental thrust of policy, and the threat from the Soviet Union and the need for NATO to counter it were certainly not questioned.

The European-Atlanticist debate was not, and is not, simply a left-right issue. Denis Healey and David Owen were from the same wing of the Labour Party, sharing many basic assumptions. But they diverged in their positions on the weight to be accorded in the balance, as did, for example, senior Conservative politicians, such as Sir Geoffrey Howe and Michael Heseltine. Margaret Thatcher proved to be Atlanticist, as the Libyan bombing episode showed. However, her attitudes were much more consistent with the British consensus than either she or her opponents were in general prepared to admit.

After the defeat of the Labour Party in the 1979 general election, a change occurred in the British political landscape. Overtly socialist elements and tendencies had managed to establish control in important sections of the Labour Party machine, and an avowed unilateralist and member of the Campaign for Nuclear Disarmament (CND) was elected as Labour Party leader and hence leader of the opposition. European politics in general was polarized at the time by the collapse of detente after the invasion of Afghanistan in December 1979 and the impending deployment of ground-launched cruise and Pershing II missiles in accordance with the Twin-Track decision. The changes in the Labour position made Mrs. Thatcher appear to be the staunch upholder of NATO (or mindless Cold Warrior),

---

4. For Lord Callaghan's account of the Trident negotiations, see James Callaghan, *Time and Chance* (Glasgow: Collins, 1987), 552–58.

	% increase (+) or decrease (−) over previous year	% GDP allocated to defence
1980	+ 8.1	5.0
1981	− 5.7	5.0
1982	+12.8	5.3
1983	+ 1.8	5.5
1984	+ 5.2	5.5
1985	− 1.2	5.2
1986	− 1.8	4.9
1987	− 0.7	4.7
1988	− 3.6	4.1
1989	+ 1.7	3.7
1990	− 2.8	4.1

FIGURE 5.1 Patterns of British Defence Expenditure, 1980-1990. (*Source:* International Institute for Strategic Studies, *Military Balance* [1980–1981 to 1992–1993].)

but that was really more because the Labour Party had moved away from the postwar consensus than because she had established a radical new position. As it was to turn out, Labour was to suffer electorally from their shift, and it was an important factor in the split in the Labour Party that resulted in the formation of the Social Democratic Party. In 1983 and 1987 the Labour Party fought general elections on a unilateralist platform and suffered two of their greatest electoral defeats ever.[5] They had left the people behind them.

Therefore, as far as the Cold War is concerned, Mrs. Thatcher was important mainly because of her articulation of a mood and trend in British and international politics, rather than of any radical change. However, certain of her contributions had a more direct bearing on foreign affairs, at least inasmuch as they reinforced and illustrated her reputation as strong on defence, a resolute anti-socialist and patriot, a British de Gaulle.

Weapons Modernization and Spending Cuts

For both President Ronald Reagan and Mrs. Thatcher, the rhetoric of their opposition to the threat from the Soviet Union required both nuclear

---

5. Jones quotes the ADIU Report as finding that "42% of those defecting from the Labour Party to other parties in 1983 gave defence as their reason for doing so." Vide Peter Jones, "The Politics of Defence Under Thatcher," in Peter Byrd, ed., *British Defence Policy: Thatcher and Beyond* (Hemel, Hempstead: Philip Allen, 1991), 124.

% of GDP

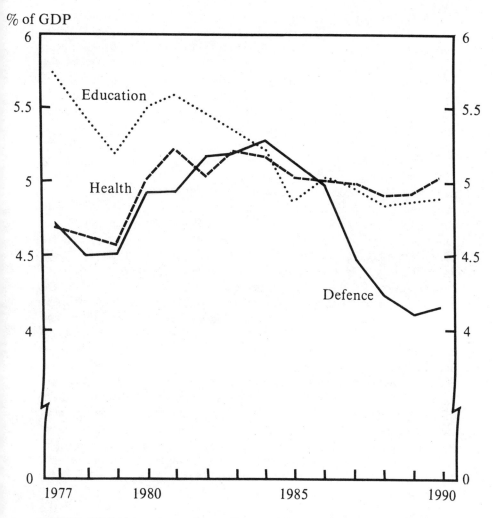

FIGURE 5.2 British government spending on defence, health, and education as a percent of Gross Domestic Product (CSO National Accounts definitions). (*Source: Defence Statistics 1992 Edition* [London: HMSO, 1992].)

and conventional rearmament. Both gained from the caricatures vigorously promoted by their opponents. At least in the British case, the actual increase in defence spending was relatively modest, as David Greenwood has shown. (See Figures 5.1 and 5.2.)[6]

6. David Greenwood, ibid., Chapter 2, "Expenditure Management."

The rhetoric of defence collided early with the foremost priority of the Thatcherite agenda, the control of public spending. At the beginning of the 1980s, Mrs. Thatcher's first defence secretary, Francis Pym, fought unsuccessfully against the treasury and lost, in spite of the chiefs of staff exercising their right of direct access to the prime minister to plead their case. Pym was replaced by John Nott, who then did his best to cut the defence budget to the resources given him. Nott undertook this task against the context of the second Cold War and the continuing drain of Northern Ireland and other residual commitments upon the British forces. He recognized that those defence commitments were, as had been the case with British obligations since the Second World War, greater than any likely level of resources to cover them. Slivers off a modernization here or a procurement programme there would no longer bridge the gap. Nott concluded that the conventional forces of the Royal Navy contributed least to the defence of the central front in Europe, to which the greatest part of the Army and Royal Air Force were devoted. It was regarded as the "front line." The Royal Navy's surface fleet was, therefore, to be cut.

The Nott review was the most intellectually honest attempt to solve the central riddle in British defence policy since Denis Healey's effort in 1966–1967. Whilst Mrs. Thatcher could hold down public expenditure and Nott could promise to cut back the Navy, neither could control external events. The Falklands War exposed the muddle in the glory and is discussed in more detail below. The war led to Nott's departure and to a reprieve for the Royal Navy's surface fleet. His replacement, Michael Heseltine, proposed to solve the "commitment/resources" riddle by an essentially bogus search for better management of existing resources, rather than by a reduction of commitments or a real increase in defence expenditure. Indeed nearly all the gains achieved by his new systems were offset by the cost push of procurement, where price rises consistently outstripped the general level of inflation, let alone the optimistic economic forecasts of the treasury on which government spending plans were based.

In political terms, Heseline's period of office is remembered by the controversial implementation of the 1979 NATO Twin-Track decision, symbolized in the United Kingdom by the construction of the infrastructure necessary for introducing the American Tomahawk Ground-Launched Cruise Missiles (GLCMs) at RAF Greenham Common. While the Ministry of Defence had clear title and powers within the fence along the borders of Greenham Common, no legal authority existed directly outside that fence to prevent the encampment of women's groups which were determined to challenge the missile deployment by physical obstruction, demonstration, and publicity designed to raise the public's awareness of the topic. Large reinforcements of the "Peace Campers" were organized for well-publicized demonstrations, which were confronted in the summer of 1983 by unarmed infantry battalions deployed within the wire by the Secretary of State.[7] Heseltine took on the challenge to a battle for the hearts and minds of the British electorate (and in the wider world media, which devoted a lot of attention to Greenham Common). By concentrating on the wider issue of the independent nuclear deterrent, the nature of the Soviet Union, and Labour's policy and links with CND, Heseltine managed to mobilize public opinion against his opponents, even if he did not always convince public opinion on the narrower issue of the GLCMs.

The Trident missile programme was to replace the existing independent nuclear deterrent based on Polaris. It was particularly identified with Mrs. Thatcher, although it was a logical extension of the Nassau agreement of Prime Minister Harold Macmillan with President John F. Kennedy in 1962. The decision had been foreshadowed and the initial negotiations made by the previous Labour government. Domestically, Mrs. Thatcher's achievement was to win the argument with the electorate against the opposition parties, in spite of the cost estimated at £10,000,000,000 and the increase in theoretical destructiveness by a factor of three or four. Internationally, Britain and France managed to avoid the inclusion of either national nuclear force in the INF or Strategic Arms Reduction Treaty (START) talks.

Apart from her government's specific practical measures in defence, the 3 percent expenditure increase, the Twin-Track decision, and the Trident discussed above, Mrs. Thatcher's record is most important in the Cold War for her demonstration that liberal democratic politicians could take tough and timely military decisions without losing their electoral support. Two episodes are particularly significant for her reputation: the Falklands War and the raid on Tripoli in 1986.

Falklands War

Ironically one of the most significant mistakes that triggered the Argentine invasion of the British colony in the South Atlantic was a product of Thatcher's priority of seeking to control of public expenditure, which in turn led to Pym's and Nott's review in defence expenditure discussed above. As part of the savings, the Navy was forced to find, and in the teeth of Foreign Office objections, the polar patrol vessel HMS *Endurance* was scheduled for withdrawal. It appeared that certain key blue-water capabilities

---

7. The motives of many, if not most, of the demonstrators were very mixed. The official position of the Campaign for Nuclear Disarmament (CND), to which the "Peace Campers" were loosely affiliated, was unilateral disarmament. However, in discussion equal concern was expressed about the Soviet SS-20s, and the Twin-Track decision was not universally rejected. In truth, most of the "reinforcement" demonstrators seemed concerned principally to "do something" rather than sharing the more polarized views of their sisters in the camps.

were to be cut back as well, such as carriers and assault ships.[8] Buenos Aires perceived that Britain, while unable to make the concessions sought by the Junta because of the strength of the Falklands lobby in the U.K., no longer had the stomach to reverse an Argentine *fait accompli*.[9] However, once the invasion of the Falklands Islands took place on April 2, 1982, Mrs. Thatcher rose to the occasion, whatever her own responsibility for provoking the original attack.

After the traumatic first confrontation with the House of Commons on Saturday, April 3, 1982, Mrs. Thatcher played the resolute and decisive war leader. She formed a "War Cabinet" of Nott, Pym (who had replaced Lord Carrington after his resignation as foreign secretary in the wake of the invasion), William Whitelaw (the deputy prime minister), and Cecil Parkinson (the Conservative Party chairman). She was able to hold together support for the delicate balance in policy between the diplomatic moves in the United Nations, the European Community, and the Commonwealth, on the one hand, and the sending of the task force on the other. During the diplomatic negotiations that followed the invasion—for example, the shuttle by U.S. Secretary of State Alexander Haig—she was able to enlist American support and portray the Argentineans as the party that was refusing to negotiate. Her appearance on the steps of 10 Downing Street after the recapture of South Georgia—when she proclaimed "Rejoice, just rejoice!"— was her public face of confident command. The swift decision making in the original dispatch of the task force was matched by the change in the rules of engagement to allow the sinking of the Argentinean cruiser *Belgrano* by the nuclear submarine HMS *Conqueror*.[10]

In the wider context of the Cold War, the Falklands allowed Mrs. Thatcher to demonstrate that a liberal democracy could make swift and effective diplomatic and military decisions and manage a war with overwhelming popular support. The war also proved that professional European armed forces were more than a match for a conscript army, even, as in the case of ground forces, where they were similarly equipped, badly outnumbered, and strapped with the disadvantages of being the attacker.[11]

---

8. Byrd points out that the changes in perceptions as a result of the Falklands War had little long term effect on the plan laid out in *The Way Ahead*, Nott's plan of 1981. See Byrd, *British Defence Policy*, 32–33.

9. For a full discussion of the political signals sent by Britain and the diplomatic history before the Falklands War, see Max Hastings and Simon Jenkins, *The Battle for the Falklands* (London: Michael Joseph. 1983), Chapters 1 and 2, and Lawrence Freedman and Virginia Gamba-Stonehouse, *Signals of War: The Falklands Conflict of 1982* (London: Faber and Faber, 1990), Chapters 1–7.

10. Young, *One of Us,* 258–83, has an excellent portrait of Mrs. Thatcher as war leader.

11. For an Argentinean conclusion of the performance of British troops, vide Informe Oficial del Ejercito Argentino, *Conflicto Malvinas* (Buenos Aires: Instituto Geografico Militar, 1983), 1: 177: "Todo esto . . . se unio a otro aspecto que, en justicia, debe tenerse en cuenta: la capacidad

FIGURE 5.3 Prime Minister Thatcher makes her first appearance at the Conservative Party Conference, October 10, 1979. Joining in the applause are (left) Minister of Defence Francis Pym and (right) Foreign Secretary Lord Carrington. (*Source:* British Information Services, New York.)

The British conduct of the war was most closely studied by Soviet military intelligence. Most of all, the victory confirmed the prime minister's instincts and her belief in herself and the rightness of her cause.[12] The war also gave a major lift to Britain's international reputation.

Thatcher's Image and Reputation

The aid and comfort that Mrs. Thatcher provided to President Reagan at the time of the Tripoli raid in 1986 strengthened her "Iron Lady" reputation. While no other European state was prepared to allow its air

---

de los mandos tacticos ingleses, y el valor y adiestramiento de sus tropas." For a skeptical analysis of the Falklands War from a nonbelligerent source, see Thomas Noetzel, *Die Revolution der Konservativen* (Hamburg: Junius, 1987), 56–69.

12. Young, *One of Us,* 280–81: "The nation had the resolution to do what had to be done, to do what it knew was right. We fought to show that aggression does not pay and that the robber cannot be allowed to get away with the swag. We fought with support of so many throughout the world. . . . Yet we also fought alone." Mrs. Thatcher here speaks in the Gaullist manner, identifying herself with the nation.

space to be used by the U.S. in the way that Britain did, she demonstrated that she could take unpopular decisions, that she was consistent (having spoken out frequently in favour of international action against terrorism), and that she was a good ally to the U.S.

Reputation and emotional responses to Thatcher and what she stood for in defence and foreign affairs are easier to illustrate than quantify. Hugo Young described how she enjoyed and cultivated the officers of the armed forces and "right-thinking" diplomats, such as Charles Powell, her foreign policy adviser, Sir Crispin Tickell, former British UN ambassador, and Sir Anthony Parsons, ambassador to the United Nations at the time of the Falklands War. In return, officers and other ranks in general admired the prime minister and her patriotism, believing that she was the best military leader since Winston Churchill, an opinion certainly shared by herself. It is true that she contributed to the high morale and self-confidence enjoyed by the armed forces between 1979 and the "Options for Change" exercise cutting the size of the forces after the end of the Cold War.

It will probably always be difficult to gauge the extent to which this emotional reaction to Mrs. Thatcher was also felt among her opponents overseas—for example, whether her reputation contributed to the collapse of confidence within the Soviet ruling class, as is sometimes now claimed. It would be a mistake, however, to exaggerate the importance of anything British, or even Western, in such a long-term and deep-seated process. What is clear is that deterrence, to be effective, requires credibility. Credibility includes the assurance that the political mechanism is capable of making the appropriate decision. In that sense at least, Thatcher's reputation contributed to the British and wider Western interest in the final stages of the Cold War. She was certainly better known internationally than any other British politician since the Second World War.

Atlantic Relations

Mrs. Thatcher's relationship with the U.S. spanned the administrations of Presidents Carter, Reagan, and Bush. There was neither ideological nor personal rapport between Carter and Thatcher, and the overlap was less than a year. It is instructive to note the continuity, remarked on above, working in the "special relationship." Thatcher assumed from her predecessor the three key themes already agreed with Carter: conventional force enhancement, the Twin-Track decision, and the purchase of Trident. The invasion of Afghanistan in December 1979 removed the divergence over detente by shocking the U.S. administration into stiffer diplomatic sanctions and language than had been seen or heard for years. This invasion ushered in the "Second Cold War."

FIGURE 5.4 Thatcher greets General John Galvin, Supreme Allied Commander, Europe. (*Source:* British Information Services, New York.)

The eight years of the Reagan presidency saw a strong link forged between both heads of government at the personal and ideological levels. Reagan's support during the Falklands War went beyond the technical aid through "Wideawake," the U.S. base on the Ascension Islands (which were, after all, a British possession), and the provision of munitions such as the Sidewinder missile. The link survived the trial of the Grenada invasion, when Reagan ordered the operation without consulting or informing the British government of an action in a Commonwealth state of which Queen Elizabeth was still the sovereign. After the damaging muddle over the promotion and then withdrawal of the neutron bomb during the Carter years, Thatcher's links with Reagan helped secure better links between the American and European pillars of the alliance during the various difficult disarmament talks throughout the 1980s, particularly the INF negotiations.

The GLCM deployment and the Tripoli raid were clear demonstrations of British commitment to the relationship with the United States.

Although President George Bush had been Reagan's vice-president, his administration signalled an early shift in emphasis in European policy from the relationship with Britain to relations with Germany, and in global policy from Europe to the Pacific. Inter-governmental relations were cordial without the warmth of the previous partnership. Events after the end of the Cold War are beyond the scope of this chapter, but it is significant that the 1990–1991 Gulf crisis showed the continuity and durability of the relationship between the U.S. and U.K. It also illustrated the limitations of the conventional improvements in the British forces during the Cold War years. British divisions had to borrow artillery support from U.S. corps. The 1 (BR) Corps in Germany had been effectively stripped of every serious combat, combat support, and combat service support asset, and it still had to rely on reservists. In spite of the NATO requirement to hold thirty days of stocks in theatre, the corps proved to be short of artillery, which had to be procured. The RAF lacked a modern stand-off capability to attack airfields.[13]

Approach to the Soviet Union

Thatcher's period of office spanned the final years of Leonid Brezhnev, the brief episodes of Yuri Andropov and Constantine Chernyenko, the advent of Mikhail Gorbachev, and the end of the Cold War. As has been seen, Thatcher established her reputation as a Cold Warrior partly through the attentions of the Soviet media. In her first year of office, the Soviet invasion of Afghanistan renewed the Cold War and dealt a heavy blow to the detente she had denounced. The Polish crisis of 1980 showed the tensions within the socialist states and foreshadowed the later collapse of the system. At the time, the imposition of martial law in Poland only heightened the sense of insecurity in the West. As Margaret Thatcher was to warn later, "there is no more insecure time in the life of an Empire than when it is facing the devolution of its power, no more dangerous time in the life of a religion (Communism being after all a secular religion) than when it has lost its inner faith but retains its outer power."[14]

That outer power had become almost entirely military. Gorbachev's and others' revelations of the scale of economic, social and environmental

---

13. For a fuller discussion of this analysis, see Greenwood, "Expenditure Management," 40–41.

14. Speech made by Margaret Thatcher at the Lord Mayor's Banquet Guildhall in Lawrence Freedman, ed., *Europe Transformed: Documents on the End of the Cold War* (London: Tri-Service Press, 1990), 359, quoting the librarian of the United States Congress.

FIGURE 5.5 Thatcher greets General Wolfgang Altenberg, Chairman of the NATO Military Committee. (*Source:* British Information Services, New York.)

disasters within the Soviet Union and the socialist states and the speed of their political collapse should not lead to the conclusion that the actual outcome was the only possible result of the power struggles within the Communist Party of the Soviet Union (CPSU). The wings of the CPSU were not clear cut in organization, personalities, or aims. Though Gorbachev withdrew from Afghanistan and made other changes, the force modernization programme continued, and the central pillars of Soviet society—the party, the armed forces, and the KGB—were largely unaffected. Christopher Andrew and Oleg Gordievsky have painted a horrifying picture of paranoia and incompetence at the centre of power in the years of Soviet decline, the last appearance of which was at the coup of August 1991.[15]

Margaret Thatcher's greatest contribution to the end of the Cold War was her prompt and public decision to back Gorbachev when he came to power and to reverse all her previous rhetoric. The successful stick of rearmament in the 1980s was to be followed by economic assistance and detente. Gorbachev had visited London in December 1984, one of his first visits to a Western state and the occasion of Thatcher's famous remark: "I like Mr. Gorbachev; we can do business together."[16] It was precisely because Thatcher, more than any other politician except Reagan, was associated with strong anticommunism that her commitment was most striking in terms of public opinion. It was made from a position of political security in that she would face no challenge from the right wing of her party. Her position was of great importance in persuading Reagan to modify his position as well. Gorbachev reciprocated.[17]

Conclusion

In the analysis of Mrs. Thatcher's contribution to the successful conclusion of the Cold War, we can contrast the relatively small practical changes in defence and foreign policy with the rhetoric with which she was so closely associated. The continuity is more striking than the innovation. The 3 percent annual increases in conventional defence improvements did not outstrip the cost constraints of the existing defence programme and were in theory to be matched by every NATO member. GLCM deployment was ultimately agreed by every NATO state involved, even, for example, the Netherlands. The Trident programme, though controversial, was in fact a continuation of existing British policy.[18]

Her success, like President Reagan's, was political. Her rhetoric was backed up by the demonstrational effects of the Falklands War and Tripoli. She and Reagan had the capacity to deliver public support for defence

---

15. Christopher Andrew and Oleg Gordievsky, *KGB: The Inside Story of Its Foreign Operations from Lenin to Gorbachev* (London: Scepter, 1991), particularly 534–605. The farcical but frightening history of Operation Ryan, the KGB's efforts to detect the signs of a nonexistent plot to mount a surprise nuclear attack by the U.S. and the U.K. on the U.S.S.R., is a telling illustration of a ruling class in decline.

16. For a good account of Mrs. Thatcher's thinking and the Gorbachev visit, see Young, *One of Us*, 389–96.

17. Andrew and Gordievsky, *KGB*, 607, for Gorbachev's reaction to his visit. Mrs. Thatcher's visit to Moscow before the 1987 British general election was widely held to contribute to her success and could not have been such a media triumph without Gorbachev's active approval.

18. An excellent overview of Thatcher's Foreign and Defence policy can be found in William Wallace, "Britische Aussen- und Verteidigungspolitik: Thatcherismus und die Folgen," Politik und Zeitgeschichte, 1991, 28: 37–46.

FIGURE 5.6 The Big Three—Joseph Stalin, Franklin D. Roosevelt, and Winston S. Churchill—and their advisers at the Teheran Conference, November 1943. (*Source:* George C. Marshall Library, Lexington, Virginia.)

policies which were affordable to the West, but the matching of which would be ruinous to the Soviet Union. She and Reagan together represented a mood and a trend in Western policy that contributed to the rise of the reformers in the CPSU. This promoted despair in the ruling class, pessimism toward the policies of Brezhnev, and encouragement for Gorbachev.

"My last guiding principle concerns the most fundamental issue, the European countries' role in defence. Europe must continue to maintain a sure defence through NATO. There can be no question of relaxing our efforts, even though it means taking difficult decisions and meeting heavy costs. . . . Above all, at a time of change and uncertainty in the Soviet Union and Eastern Europe, we must preserve Europe's unity and resolve, so that whatever may happen, our defence is sure. . . . Let us never forget that our way of life, our vision, and all that we hope to achieve are secured not by the rightness of our cause but by the strength of our defence. On this we must never falter, never fail."[19]

---

19. Quoted from Thatcher's speech to the College of Europe, Bruges, September 20, 1988; text in Part II of this book.

FIGURE 6.1 French leaders Henri Giraud and Charles de Gaulle meet at the Casablanca Conference with Franklin D. Roosevelt and Winston S. Churchill, January 1943. (*Source:* George C. Marshall Library, Lexington, Virginia.)

6

Thatcher and the Unification of Europe

Sir William Nicoll

One could simply say "She was against it."[1] But there is more to it than that. Mrs. Thatcher is of the generation which was in its teens during the Second World War. One does not have to be a jingoist to take pride in the memory of how Britain stood alone from June 1940 until a year later when Hitler turned his murderous intentions towards the Soviet Union. Thatcher's hero is Winston Churchill, our great war leader. It was, he said, the British lion that roared, but he gave it its tongue. In a television interview she gave in November 1991, Thatcher recalled, with justified pride, that it was the chimes of Big Ben that rang out across Europe in the dark days.

Her generation has not lost its recollection of the wartime alliance epitomized by the Churchill-Roosevelt bond, when the two countries fought under a single command, in which the United States inevitably took the lead. To her generation, and under the inspiration of Churchill, it seemed that the Anglo-American cooperation which had won the war was the natural instrument to secure the peace and promote progress in the postwar world. This was, in fact, one of the reasons which had made it impossible for British governments of whatever political persuasion to "join Europe," as the phrase has it, when their neighbours began their postwar reconstruction and reorganization.

Thatcher's predecessors in Labour administrations before 1979 were by no stretch of the imagination pro-Europeans, although they proclaimed that theirs was the party of Europe.[2] Thatcher was the champion of change in

---

1. Kenneth Harris, *Thatcher* (London: Fontana Collins, 1989), 52. Nicholas Ridley, *My Style of Government* (London: Hutchinson, 1991), 136.

2. Notably in the letter which the General Secretary of the Labour Party sent to all constituency agents after the June 1975 referendum.

most of her political agenda. She once said that consensus is what you do when you cannot agree. She detested fudge and empty compromise. This marked a break with the domestic tradition of "Butskellism," the bipartisan handling of affairs. Towards Europe, the European Community (EC), there is, if I may be allowed to invent the word, "Thatchcallism." Despite party rhetoric, there is not much difference in the basis of the European policies of James (now Lord) Callaghan, and his successor, Mrs. (now Lady) Thatcher.

The early years of British membership were marked by reservations about the policies and purposes of the organization. It had never been demonstrated that Europe was a path to British prosperity. No serious official cost-benefit analysis was ever published. It was usually said that there was no other recourse and that the political gains would be significant. This was the notion propounded by Heath: that Britain would lead and would obtain its purposes through the strength which Europe would give it. The only major attempt to estimate the actual outcome in quantitative terms was that of Douglas (now Lord) Jay who, both as a member of the Wilson government and after he was removed from it, showed that economically the results would be negative. This was one of the reasons why Harold Wilson decided to get rid of him.

Thatcher's Views on Europe

Mrs. Thatcher did not come to power on a pro-European platform. She came to European affairs without previous involvement in them at a time when they were in the doldrums. Europe was suffering from its combination of inflation and stagnation, and the EC seemed almost irrelevant to the real conditions of the populations. There had been two major developments in the years immediately before: the direct elections to the European Parliament and the setting up of the European Monetary System (EMS) of tied exchange rates. Britain had, in fact, delayed the former when the necessary legislation foundered in the House of Commons, where Thatcher led the opposition to the use of a proportional representation system. Britain, although invited to participate in the formulation of the EMS, had withdrawn, fearing that it would restrict national freedom to protect sterling, which seemed likely to become a world currency again with the exploitation of North Sea oil.

Her early exposure to the doings of the EC must have been distasteful. As an intelligent woman, a scientist, and a lawyer, she must have been put off by the rodomontade of the European vocabulary, with its talk of union, solidarity, and European identity. It was obvious to her (and no doubt also to all the orators) that throughout Europe political recognition attached to the thing the people call the government, the thing they vote for, the thing they call to account—or try to—when things go wrong. A brief study of what the EC was doing would have revealed that it was not much, but that it was not even doing that very well. Its member states were slow to enact the measures they had decided upon. Even when they had enacted them, they sometimes did not apply them, which brought them before the European Court of Justice. The Commission, whose functions few in Britain or elsewhere understood, was fertile in making proposals, but there was something amiss somewhere, because at one time there were eight hundred proposals lying around with nothing being done about them.

Costs of EC Membership

There was one EC matter, however, which needed urgent British attention in 1979. It was the cost of membership. Britain and Germany were alone in paying into the Community budget more than they took out. For Britain this was a matter of some £2,000,000,000 a year. This had not been seriously addressed in the Wilsonian renegotiations of 1974–1975 or by his successor, James Callaghan, who had been the negotiator for British entry and could scarcely acknowledge that he had left it untouched.[3]

This then was the origin of the long running dispute about "my money" and the "*juste retour.*" The British case was simple and almost unanswerable: they wanted to reduce the cost of belonging to the EC. Most of the responses they were given were irrelevant, such as that the budgetary outturn is not the only barometer of benefit (Belgian contribution). But it was not explained what the other benefits were. Britain would be made rich by oil revenue (French observation), but this had nothing to do with the matter under discussion. The British should change their trade patterns and buy more goods free of import charge from Europe (commission proposition), but it was not explained how governments were to play a role in trading decisions or in changing consumer preferences. Finally, the principle of *juste retour* was inimical to the structure of EC finance which is that spending lies where it falls—an easy rule to argue if you were a net beneficiary.

After long years of argument, at times heated, a solution was found which relieved the U.K. of part of the burden, while leaving it a substantial net contributor.[4] Along the road, Mrs. Thatcher crossed swords with all her colleagues, with the Commission[5] and with the European Parliament,

---

3. As Foreign Secretary, Mr. Callaghan had negotiated an adjustment mechanism which never adjusted.

4. Hugo Young, *One of Us* (London: Pan, 1990), 183–91, 381–88.

5. Hugo Young and Anne Sloman, *The Thatcher Phenomenon* (London: BBC, 1986), 111–14.

which tried to overturn an agreement and which she dismissed as "contemptible." So far as she herself was concerned, all this simply gave her stomach for the fight.

She and her advisers had correctly diagnosed the root trouble: the Common Agricultural Policy (CAP) was being used to produce food which the Europeans themselves did not want and which, when thrown onto world markets at subsidized prices, disrupted them and the livelihood of farmers in other countries. But the other member states were slow to agree to any changes in the policy or in the financing of it. In 1982 the British tried hard to obtain reform. A farm price package was going through which would be grotesquely expensive, as it proved. The British opposed. The prevailing rule was that unanimity was needed for a decision. Indeed it was the issue of farm prices which in 1964–1965 had provoked the famous crisis, from which the Six emerged with a nominal agreement on future behaviour. It was actually a disagreement (the Luxembourg compromise), but they turned it back into an agreement by accepting that they would decide matters consensually, even where the treaty said that they should vote. But in 1982 and at the suggestion of the Commission, a majority of the member states decided that farm prices that year should be settled by vote. Much casuistry was devoted to explaining why this was justified in the circumstances. The real explanation was a good deal simpler. Britain was fighting a war in the Falklands. With some effort it had obtained EC support for economic measures against Argentina,[6] but the support was fragile. Normally the British would have mounted a diplomatic offensive against the EC farm vote, but they could not afford to do so in the circumstances. It left a nasty taste, especially when member states began to resile from the Falklands measures, too late to do any damage to the British cause.

In all the other member states, governments were socially conscious and believed in legislation to underpin the rights as well as the obligations of working people. Social policy had been born in Bismarck's Germany, and the welfare state was established throughout Europe. Most of the member states were in favor of Community social policy, partly because they believed that it was right, partly because they wanted their partners to level up with them, and partly because they could use EC uniformity as a domestic reason for not acceding to new spending proposals. Mrs. Thatcher had devoted a considerable part of her redoubtable energies to transforming the landscape in Britain by reducing the power and influence of the trade unions. She was not prepared to allow socialism to come back in by the back door or, as she once said, making a pun on the name of the French President of the Commission, himself a Socialist, "by the back Delors."

In the financial sphere, the EC could give her two grounds for concern.

---

6. *The Falklands War* (Sphere, 1982), 117–18.

First, there was a doctrine that the Community must be in the business of incremental budgeting, as evidence of the continuing expansion of European integration. This was usually accompanied by reminders that it was not a case of new expenditure, but of the transfer of expenditure from national budgets. This, however, does not wash. Most of the new spending schemes were for co-financing and were expressly stated to involve additional expenditure.[7]

Monetary Union and Bruges Speech

More importantly, there was another perceived threat to the conduct of British financial policy: the pressure for monetary union. The vision of a monetary union goes back a long way in the Community although there is nothing about it in the original treaties. It was endorsed by nine member states at the Paris Summit of 1972, and 1980 was set as the date. This deadline slid later into the 1980s, which was also missed. The EMS, suggested by Lord Jenkins when he was president of the Commission but worked out in 1979 by the advisers of Chancellor Helmut Schmidt and President Valery Giscard d'Estaing, was a new start. But especially in its early days it fell far short of a monetary union. A fresh impetus was given to the task by the separate decision of 1985 to proceed to a Single Market by 1993. The reasoning is that in a single trading space there is an unavoidable need for a single currency, ergo a monetary union. This issue was skirted round in the Single European Act of 1986, which says something like this in code language: "Some would have liked to begin the move towards an Economic and Monetary Union. But others did not want to at this stage, so let us put down a marker to come back to it." And they did, despite British objections, by convening an intergovernmental conference in 1991, which is the way in which the treaty is amended.

Why were the British under Mrs. Thatcher unwilling to accept monetary union and have remained so? For the answer we turn to Mrs. Thatcher's European political testament, the speech which she delivered at the College of Europe in Bruges, in Flanders, Belgium in September 1988. This is a big occasion in the European calendar. It marks the beginning of the new year in the postgraduate college, where young people from all over the world with a European interest gather to take courses in law, economics, or administration. The ceremony includes speeches of welcome from the

---

7. The Commission and the British government fought a series of skirmishes in 1992 over the question—which remained unresolved—whether the funds which Britain obtained under Community spending programs were used for additional expenditure, or simply replaced scheduled national expenditure.

Flanders government, an address by the Rector of the College, usually devoted to the work of the European who is to be recalled in the name given to the class of that year, and the speech by the visiting dignitary. The great and the good are assembled for what is usually an eloquent pro-European speech, in which the honoured guest recalls and demonstrates his or her commitment to a unified Europe and sends out a call for greater effort in the noble cause.

With Mrs. Thatcher it was not quite like that. The keynote of her remarks was her definition of what was meant by the EC. To her it consisted of the willing cooperation of independent sovereign states.

Willing. Not enough for a true blue European. Willingness is pre-supposed and needs, according to him, to be reinforced by the acceptance of legal obligations, which cannot be departed from, even if the willingness were to go. *Co-operation.* Decidedly not. Co-operation in the technical European sense is a thing governments do to each other. It is not what governments do within the EC, where in the form of the Council to which they belong they compose an institution. You cannot co-operate with yourself. *Independent.* Not when they are acting in the framework of the treaties. They are not then independent of each other but are part of a greater whole. *Sovereign.* Again not in the framework of the EC. Sovereign means on top and no EC member is on top. In the much used expression the member states have pooled their sovereignty in the terms of the treaties and accordingly can no longer exercise it on their own behalf. *States.* This is de Gaulle language. According to both the EEC Treaty and the Treaty on European Union (Maastricht) the thing is supposed to be in the act of becoming an ever closer union of the peoples of Europe, which is what the member states signed up for when they joined. In fact, if they ever looked back to the statement which began it all on 8 May 1950 when Foreign Minister Robert Schuman launched the Coal and Steel Plan, they would find that he described it as a step towards a Federation of Europe.[8]

Mrs. Thatcher was saying at Bruges that she was more or less content with the structure of the EC more or less as it was, although she had ideas about how to improve its working. She was ruling out any future development which might diminish the authority of the member states' governments. She was thereby opposing, on behalf of the British Parliament, any increase in the governing power of the European Parliament. She was setting her face against a federation. Much is said by her opponents, including British Conservative members of the European Parliament, about the virtues of a federation, which according to dictionary definitions is a system of government in which power is shared among different authorities. They miss the point. The essence of a federation of states is that the federal authority can

---

8. See text of this speech in Part II of this book.

act without the participation of, and if necessary despite the national or state authorities. Mrs. Thatcher was also ruling out a monetary union because it would deprive national authorities of the power to manage the national economy in accordance with their political judgments. It would replace the latter by some other authority whose accountability is meager because priority is given to its independence over its democratic control. If federalism is bad, then to a lover of British parliamentarianism this is even worse.

Conclusion

I conclude by summoning other witnesses of Mrs. Thatcher's conduct of European affairs. The first is Sir Michael Butler, who was Britain's ambassador to the EC from 1979 to 1985 and one of her close advisers. In a piece which he contributed to the London *Times* of November 28, 1991, he said that he admired her, but must now add his voice to the chorus of criticism. He continues: "From the beginning . . . she showed a deep-seated prejudice against the European Community." This prejudice overrode the reasonable positions she took in EC discussions, and "she had more than a tendency, a downright habit, of forgetting the concessions she had herself made . . . or of blaming them on her advisers," among them, no doubt, the luckless Butler. After winning her third election in 1987, "her prejudices seemed to gain ground."

I now call my other witness. This is Sir Bernard Ingham, her faithful press secretary, whom she once called the best press secretary in the world. In his book, *Kill the Messenger,* he gives a different balance sheet.

> Mrs. Thatcher did more than the rest put together to advance [progress]. There was no future for the European Community with its unfair method of financing. . . . It took the Prime Minister five years . . . to secure justice. . . . She then applied herself to the reform of the profligate Common Agricultural Policy. . . . By dint of persistence and well informed argument she secured reforms. . . . She warmly espoused the cause of a single internal market by 1993. . . . She sought to develop the Community politically, economically and monetarily on flexible pragmatic lines.

Finally, I cite Mrs. Thatcher herself on Europe. In the television interview which she gave at the end of 1991, after her devastating intervention in the House of Commons debate on Europe, she quoted her favorite Briton, Winston Churchill: "Whatever happened to the British lion of whom Winston said it was his privilege to give the roar? And Winston said in 1953, 'We will be with Europe but not of it, and when they ask us why, we will say we dwell in our own land.'" There is no possible doubt that Mrs. Thatcher will be remembered as a great prime minister of Britain.

Was she a great European as well? The conventional judgment is that she fought hard for what she wanted for Britain, but was needlessly antagonistic towards other European leaders and that her tireless campaign for her money distracted the Community for five years from the tasks it might otherwise have pursued in a changing world. Lord Soames, a member of her first Cabinet and a veteran pro-European, felicitously described her European views as those of an agnostic who continues to go to Church.

It is in fact sometimes difficult to know what the issues are in the internal British debate about its relations with Europe. There is now no question of Britain leaving the Community, as there was in the days when Labour was anti-European. But what does Britain want from Europe? Mainly that it should not do some of the things that some others want it to do. Mrs. Thatcher's nationalistic Bruges speech of September 1988 is squarely in the mainstream of the policy of her party. Consider the admirable continuity of the following sentiments, spread over twenty years:

> Like any other treaty, the Treaty of Rome commits its signatories to support agreed aims; but the commitment represents the voluntary undertaking of a sovereign state to observe policies which it has helped to form.
> —White paper on membership of the Community, 1972 (Heath Government)

> Union is not a commitment to a federal system or to the progressive erosion of national sovereignty. In our view, union amounts to the development of an ever-closer framework of co-operation between the sovereign states of the Community in all areas where this co-operation can be shown to be useful. . . . It does not entail the creation of any new institutions or increase in the formal powers of existing ones.
> —Douglas Hurd, in the European Parliament, 1981

> The active and willing co-operation of independent sovereign states.
> —Baroness Thatcher, Bruges, 1988

> It is the nation states of the Community that remain the fundamental political units in Europe.
> —John Major, London, September 1992

Ostensibly, Mrs. Thatcher fell when her erstwhile lieutenant, Sir Geoffrey Howe (now Lord Howe) told a tense House of Commons of the damage she was doing to British interests by her blanket rejection of all proposals for the further development of the Community. This was the occasion, but not the whole cause. She had become an electoral liability in a country which was signalling a new double blip recession, and in which the poll tax associated with her pledge to get rid of the inequities and iniquities of the rating system (of local property tax) had provoked intense hostility, as well as being tax-ineffective.

But her going opened up a new schism in the Conservative party. Her successor, Mr. John Major, negotiated in December 1991 a treaty—which Britain really did not want at all—which gave Britain an opt-out from the monetary union and the single currency, and excluded Britain from the alleged social engineering represented by the Social Chapter of the Maastricht Treaty. A year later in Edinburgh, in another feat of negotiation, he obtained statements, agreed by all the other leaders and by the Commission, to the effect that the powers of the Community are the exception, and the powers of the member states are the rule. But his message is that Britain must be at the heart of Europe, and this is achieved by ratifying the new treaty. Mrs. Thatcher was not interested in being at the heart of Europe. She certainly approved of the Single Market, which opened up prospects for British exports and for investment in Britain, and she at one point, but not for long, regarded the European Community as the corrective to Soviet communism, but she was not prepared to see Britain become just another middle-ranking European country, merged into something else. Working from her base in the House of Lords, Lady Thatcher's attempted unsuccessfully to hinder ratificationof the Maastricht Treaty in 1993, and she seeks to lay the basis for a continuing restraint on any European leanings.

So was she a great European when she was in control? As her helper, Lord Howe has an interest in looking at the positive achievements of their work.[9] But objectively, they are impressive enough.

The budget is fairer than it was. As all four big EC countries find themselves becoming net creditors, there is diminishing enthusiasm for higher spending. There is also the acceptance of the principle of a more equitable distribution in favour of the poorer member states.[10]

Britain's bugbear, the Common Agricultural Policy, is at last being substantially cut back. This was agreed all round in 1992. Sadly, American intransigence and French elections combined to put the future in doubt again.

The Single Market, which Thatcher's Britain eagerly championed, is a reality. This is almost the only positive contribution of British statesmanship to Community progress in the period of British membership. It became

---

9. Young, *One of Us,* 388.

10. Technically Britain is now a poorer member after the devaluation of the pound sterling in September 1992. But Britain is not asking to benefit from the "cohesion" money which the other poorer member states are to receive.

FIGURE 6.2 Thatcher addressing the Twenty-eighth Annual Session of the North Atlantic Assembly, London. (*Source:* British Information Services, New York.)

part of the Single European Act of 1987. Britain had nothing of similar weight to offer to the Treaty on European Union of 1991.

More widely, a European should not be judged only by what he or she does for the European Community. Nobody could dispute Mrs. Thatcher's support and leadership in the Atlantic Alliance, without which Europe would not exist. She faced the Evil Empire, deplored the weakening of the Western European resolve, demanded the freedom of the Soviet satellites, and was THE Iron Lady of the West.

She also transformed the geography of Europe. Her agreement with President Mitterrand on the construction—so often stalled and shelved—of the Channel Tunnel will be a physical reminder of her resolve and her unrelenting drive for efficiency. If it were ever to have a distinctive name, hers would be a strong candidate.

7

The Fall of the Iron Lady, 1990

Lewis G. John

The fall of Margaret Thatcher in November 1990 as leader of the Conservative Party and consequently as prime minister has been variously and extravagantly depicted as "the most extraordinary event in the history of British democratic politics," "the most remarkable period in the peacetime politics of the twentieth century," and "a human tragedy as well as an essay in British constitutional practice."[1]

The events leading up to her resignation on November 22 were chronicled and analyzed in exacting detail in the newspapers and periodicals of the day, as well as in numerous books and articles which appeared in print in the year following that resignation. Although a full and balanced assessment must await the perspective provided by the passage of time and the accounts and memoirs of all those most directly involved, it is my purpose here to outline the major factors or "plot lines" accounting for her demise, the actions of the primary cast of characters involved in the drama, and a very brief chronology of her last days in office.

Hugo Young wrote in *The Guardian* of Friday, November 23, 1990, the day following Margaret Thatcher's resignation, the following:

> She died as she had lived, in battle. It was a quite extraordinary end, but it was in keeping with everything important that had gone before. There was a continuity, not only in the texture of these events but in the circumstances of her long life and swift demise. Just as her triumphs were often rooted in her zest for combat, her refusal to listen to advice and her unwillingness to admit that she

---

1. First quote in Bruce Anderson, *John Major: The Making of the Prime Minister* (London: Fourth Estate, 1991), 98. Second in Alan Watkins, *A Conservative Coup: The Fall of Margaret Thatcher* (London: Duckworth, 1991), 27. Third in "One Short Year Later," *The Economist*, November 23, 1991, 99.

could be wrong, so were these the sources of her last predicament. Until yesterday, when all three habits were finally broken.

It is a shocking way to go. Having lost no vote either in the Commons or in the country, she was yet disposed of by the unaccountable will of fewer than 400 politicians. There has been nothing like it in the democratic era: no verdict apparently so perverse and unprovoked delivered by a governing party against a leader upon whom it had fawned and under whom it had grown fat for so many years. Many Conservatives will be thunderstruck by what they accomplished yesterday; some, even among those who did the deed, will be ashamed. For the first time in her prime ministership she provoked, while not requesting it, the human sympathy reserved for a helpless creature at bay.[2]

Plot Lines in the Drama

There are many and varied plot lines which can be identified in the drama in which this powerful leader and world figure, who had been head of her party for fifteen years, prime minister for eleven and a half, and winner of three national elections, was deposed in a bloodless (though certainly not tearless) coup by a relatively small number of her own parliamentary party colleagues who had given her a substantial majority of the votes on the first ballot for party leader. I shall concentrate on five different yet intertwined themes of significant dimensions.

The first major theme, or plot line, centered on Margaret Thatcher's management of the economy, and more specifically, on inflation. Following the deep recession of the early 1980s, the economy recovered strongly to a buoyant state in the mid-1980s, but there was a widening trade gap which reached a deficit of £19,000,000,000, or 4 percent of Gross Domestic Product (GDP) by 1989.[3] Policy options to deal with the deficit were a contributing factor to the collapse of the pound and a resurgence of inflation. The rate of inflation had fallen to as low as 3.3 percent early in 1988, but then it began a remorseless climb back to a level of just under 11 percent during the fall of 1990. Markets were nervous, and home owners felt the pinch of increased mortgage costs as inflation compounded and exacerbated all of the government's other problems. The "economic miracle" of 1987 had been transcended by the combined weight of inflation, the trade deficit, rising unemployment, and recession. Bruce Anderson suggests that "bad economics brought her in peril." It is his contention that Thatcher

2. Hugo Young, "The Thatcher Years," *The Guardian,* November 23, 1990, 21. For her own account of the events surrounding her resignation, see her final chapter in *Downing Street Years.* On "listening," see 560–61. See other memoirs in the bibliography of this book.

3. Bill Jones, "Thatcher and After," in Jones, ed., *Politics UK* (New York: Philip Allan, 1991), 593.

would have survived the leadership challenge had inflation been under control.[4]

The second major contributing factor turned on the question of European integration and the deep disagreement over Britain's future in Europe. It was closely linked with the issues of inflation and economic management, given the controversy over full British membership in the European Monetary System (EMS) and later the prospects of a single European currency and central bank. Especially since Nigel Lawson's resignation as Chancellor of the Exchequer in October 1989, the question of Europe had threatened to divide the Conservative Party "as damagingly as the Corn Laws in 1846 or Free Trade in 1903."[5] Britain became increasingly isolated among members of the European Community (EC) as Thatcher railed against the loss of sovereignty. It was her attack on European federalism ("No! No! No!") in the House of Commons on October 30, 1990, that was decisive for Sir Geoffrey Howe in his decision to resign from the cabinet.

The third plot line involved the "hideously unpopular" community charge, or poll tax as it was commonly known. This head tax, a uniform flat fee per individual regardless of circumstances, stoked the fires of discontent and rebellion throughout the country. It was a tax which grew more out of her own character than it did out of reason. Reason, as expressed by the Treasury and Chancellor Nigel Lawson, said that it would be unjust, unworkable, and insupportably expensive. Sticking blindly with a commitment dating from 1974, however, Thatcher insisted it must go forward, and she was able to enlist the support of enough compliant ministers for it to be instituted.

The fourth plot line involved her personal and leadership style about which so much has been written. "As a leader," Young observed, "she developed abrasiveness into an art form. She despised, above all, consensus: the goal of most other leaders, but not her."[6] With her, the style *was* the woman and with it came eventually a steady disintegration of trust within her cabinet. She fought with colleagues over not just the management of the economy, the poll tax, and Britain's future in Europe, but her whole approach to the business of governing. Her cavalier ways and occasionally imperious disregard for the views and sensitivities of others have been chronicled in excruciating detail.

All of these factors led to what can be identified as the fifth and last major plot line, the dimming electoral prospects for the Conservative Party and its survival instinct, a force not even she could defy. Public opinion polls and by-election defeats suggested that an election was about to be lost

---

4. Anderson, *John Major,* 157.
5. Jones, "Thatcher and After," 588.
6. Young, "The Thatcher Years," 22.

and power surrendered to the other side. The polls further suggested that the Tories would move back into the lead with someone else at the helm. In her statement to the cabinet on the morning of her resignation, she declared, "I have concluded that the unity of the party and the prospects of victory at a general election would be better served if I stood down to enable cabinet colleagues to enter the ballot."[7] The polls and the collective wisdom of her fellow Tory Members of Parliament (MPs) affirmed the correctness of this judgment. In the end, it was her cabinet colleagues and junior ministers, persuaded that hers was a lost cause and faced with their own loss of office within a party seemingly headed toward electoral suicide, who were finally able to convince her.

Resignation Denouement

These five plot lines were all prominent and intertwined in the months and days leading up to the November 22 resignation. There had been at least eighteen months of rising tension in all of these troublesome areas prior to the resignation denouement. In his devastating speech to the Commons of November 13, Sir Geoffrey Howe, who had sustained a succession of both public and private humiliations at the hands of Mrs. Thatcher over a period of years, revealed that as Foreign Secretary, he and then-Chancellor of the Exchequer Nigel Lawson had threatened to resign as early as June of 1989, ahead of the Madrid European Summit.

These two proponents of increased integration within the EC had insisted that she break through the "incredibility barrier" about Britain and the Exchange Rate Mechanism (ERM) and specify the detailed conditions for membership in the ERM rather than rely on vague, indefinite statements about joining "when the time is right." She was to specify four conditions which were outlined in the first stage of the Delors Report. Soon afterwards, Thatcher took what can be seen as her revenge upon Sir Geoffrey in the cabinet reshuffle of July 24, 1989. This once again pushed Howe to the verge of resignation by moving him from his powerful foreign office post to the position of Leader of the House of Commons and, upon his request, the ill-defined role of deputy prime minister.

By the time of the Conservative Party conference at Blackpool in October 1989, the government's credibility in economic affairs was being severely strained. As the Commons returned, Lawson was clearly at odds with Sir Alan Walters, the prime minister's personal economic adviser, over

---

7. Quoted in Robin Oakley and Philip Webster, "Bravura End for Thatcher Era," *The Times,* November 23, 1990, 1. See also their *Times* article on the same day, 24: "How the Cabinet Assassins Struck."

FIGURE 7.1 Geoffrey Howe. (*Source:* British Information Services, New York.)

the EMS. Lawson gave the prime minister an ultimatum. On October 26, she called his bluff, and he resigned. On December 5, Sir Anthony Meyer, as a 'stalking horse' candidate in the first challenge to Mrs. Thatcher since 1975, persuaded sixty Conservative MPs either to vote for him or to abstain. Anger over the poll tax, always closely identified with Thatcher, came to a head on March 31, 1990, with a bloody riot in London, though the local government elections on May 3 helped to steady her ship of state for a short period.

Cabinet differences over Europe kept providing political shocks. On July 14, Nicholas Ridley, who was the trade and industry secretary and (much more significantly) one of Thatcher's last remaining cabinet soul mates, was forced to resign after his anti-German views were published in an interview with the *Spectator*. This matter opened for all to see the internal divisions within the Conservative Party on the issue of Europe and raised new questions about the prime minister's continued party leadership. As Nicholas Baldwin has observed, Mrs. Thatcher, by failing to dismiss Ridley immediately, stimulated speculation that he had only dared to articulate publicly what the prime minister thought privately.[8]

With the Labour Party enjoying a double-digit lead in the polls for most of the year, the October 1990 Conservative Party conference in Bournemouth reflected the deep divisions within the party and a general malaise despite an outward appearance of enthusiasm and confidence. Just before the conference, under continuing pressure from Chancellor John Major and Foreign Secretary Douglas Hurd, Mrs. Thatcher had accepted the inevitable by announcing that Britain would join the EMS exchange rate mechanism. That announcement, coupled with a simultaneous interest rate reduction of one point, contributed to a certain euphoric atmosphere at the conference, and Thatcher's speech was greeted with an extended and enthusiastic ovation.

---

8. Nicholas D. J. Baldwin, "The Demise of the Prime Minister," *British Politics Group Newsletter* No. 64 (Spring 1991): 5.

Ministers, however, received only muted ovations, while potential rival and former cabinet member Michael Heseltine was well received at a packed fringe meeting on the subject of Europe. Geoffrey Howe also publicly questioned the government's European policy when he framed the issue in this way: "The next European train is about to leave, for a still undefined destination, but certainly in the direction of some form of EMU. Shall Britain be in the driver's cab this time or in the rear carriage?"[9]

On October 18, the Conservatives lost badly in the Eastbourne by-election, which had been made necessary by the IRA's murder of Ian Gow in July. On a swing of over 20 percent, a Conservative majority of almost 17,000 was turned into a seat for the Liberal Democrats by a majority of over 4,500. *The Guardian* observed that the Eastbourne result "struck in the bleakest of times and made it even bleaker." The Tories attempted to rationalize the defeat on the basis of localized conditions involving an unattractive candidate, complacency, and "moral blackmail of the electors" through a misguided campaign strategy of implying that a vote against the Conservative candidate would be giving "aid and comfort to terrorism."[10] But party morale was further and deeply shaken.

In late October, Thatcher was outmaneuvered by other EC heads of government at the Rome European Summit. She was alone and isolated in opposition to the broad endorsement given by the other eleven EC partners to rapid progress toward monetary and political union. She returned to give her robust performance on October 30 in the House of Commons, denouncing the Delors vision of the EC and the EMU as "federalism by the back door." She emphasized that Britain would reject the imposition of a single European currency, and she declared that Britain, in her view, had already surrendered enough powers to Europe. Her vision was one of "willing cooperation between independent sovereign states." It is significant that her prepared statement, agreed to by the cabinet, was generally positive and well reasoned, but her anger was evident in uncompromising and anti-European rhetoric in some of her responses to questions.[11] In any event, this speech, together with her stance in Rome, prompted Sir Geoffrey Howe's resignation from the government on November 1.

Shortly thereafter, Michael Heseltine, who had been Minister of Defence before dramatically resigning in a row with Mrs. Thatcher over the Westland helicopter affair in 1986, joined the battle by issuing an open letter to his constituency party chairman. He criticized Thatcher's style of government, writing that a democratic party leader must "pay proper regard to the myriad of opinions and, indeed, prejudices that go to make up its support."

---

9. Ibid. EMU stands for European Monetary Union.
10. *Guardian* quote ibid., 6. Final quotes in Watkins, *Conservative Coup,* 141.
11. Jones, "Thatcher and After," 589.

FIGURE 7.2 Michael Heseltine. (*Source:* British Information Services, New York.)

He emphasized a partnership with Europe: "We Tories . . . know we must reach for the world of tomorrow, which is with our partners in Europe."[12]

On November 12, Thatcher warned her opponents that she would "fight [her] corner robustly," but the very next day, Howe delivered his fateful resignation speech in the House of Commons. In quietly delivered but bitterly devastating remarks, the naturally loyal and highly respected Sir Geoffrey (once described by Denis Healey as having the aggressiveness of a "dead sheep") attacked the prime minister's uncompromising stand toward Europe and accused her of subverting cabinet policies. Her vision, he said, was of "a Continent that is teeming with ill-intentioned people scheming, in her words 'to extinguish democracy,' to dissolve our national identities, to lead us through the back door into a federal Europe. . . . The tragedy is . . . that her perceived attitude towards Europe is running increasingly serious risks for the future of our nation." He spoke of the conflict of loyalty he felt to her and to what he perceived as the true interest of the country. He concluded that he no longer believed it possible "to resolve that conflict from within this Government."[13]

The speech echoed much of what Nigel Lawson had said when he resigned a year earlier, and it was also to set off Heseltine's challenge for the leadership. As *The Independent* observed in an article the next day:

> The force of the attack lay in the breadth and the directness of the accusations made by the former deputy prime minister—one of the chief architects of Thatcherism—against his leader, and in the measured manner in which this naturally loyal and patently suffering man delivered a fundamental critique, linking for all time the offensive style and the ill-considered and self-indulgent substance of Mrs. Thatcher's rule.[14]

In terms of issues, the poll tax was splitting the Conservative rank-and-

---

12. Quoted in Watkins, *Conservative Coup,* 148.

13. Geoffrey Howe, Resignation Statement in House of Commons, November 13, 1990.

14. Quoted in Baldwin, "Demise of the Prime Minister," 7.

file most decisively, while it was Europe which most threatened the unity of the cabinet. Howe, Lawson, and Heseltine—the three individuals vividly referred to by *The Economist* as the disillusioned "rebel barons of her reign"[15]—had much the same views on Europe and the poll tax, and all three were bitterly critical of Thatcher's cavalier ways with her cabinet. It is impossible in any analysis of the individuals most involved in the prime minister's downfall, however, to neglect the central role played by Mrs. Thatcher herself. It was she who was basically responsible for creating an environment of electoral vulnerability and whose attitude toward the party leadership contest led her, once challenged, to run a poor, totally disorganized campaign.

Leadership Contest

On November 6, a week prior to Sir Geoffrey's resignation speech and following discussions she had with Cranley Onslow, who as chairman of the 1922 Committee of backbenchers was responsible for organizing any party leadership election, it had been announced that this annual process was to be moved up by two weeks; any challengers would have to declare themselves by November 15. This strategy was apparently an attempt to pull the rug out from under any momentum to challenge the leadership, as well as an effort to emphasize her prominence as a world leader unconcerned with the internal details of the Conservative Party. It was undermined, however, both by the results of the Bradford North by-election of November 8, in which Labour convincingly retained its seat with the Conservatives forced into an embarrassing third-place-finish behind the Liberal Democrats, and by Howe's speech.

Howe had concluded his speech on November 13 by inviting his fellow Conservative MPs "to consider their own response to the tragic conflict of loyalties with which I have myself wrestled for perhaps too long." With the gauntlet thus laid down, the battle was truly joined, and Heseltine was forced to decide whether to challenge or to forego his leadership aspirations. He announced on November 14, one day before the deadline, that he was standing against the prime minister for party leader and thus head of government. After Howe's speech, Heseltine had said to some friends, "Well, I've got to go, haven't I?" They had agreed, though some had told him he would lose if he did.[16]

In his statement, Heseltine declared that there would be an immediate and fundamental review of the poll tax under his leadership. Further, he

---

15. "The Fall of Thatcher," *The Economist*, March 9, 1991, 21.
16. Ibid., 22.

said, "I am persuaded that I would now have a better prospect than Mrs. Thatcher of leading the Conservatives to a fourth electoral victory and prevent the ultimate calamity of a Labour government." Opinion poll results seemed to support that assertion. Six polls published in the Sunday, November 18, newspapers showed striking agreement that Conservatives under Thatcher were behind Labour by margins ranging from two to fifteen percentage points, but would be ahead under Heseltine's leadership by margins ranging from one to ten points; the projected swings were between six and ten points.[17]

The first ballot was scheduled for Tuesday, November 20, a day when Thatcher would be in Paris for a thirty-five-nation Conference on Security and Cooperation in Europe (CSCE). To say that she underestimated the opposition which had built up against her would be a gross understatement. She did almost no personal campaigning. The efforts to support her were lackluster and disorganized, and her staff failed to keep her adequately informed. As rival groups within the party exchanged unreliable declarations of loyalty in the lobbies and tea rooms of Westminster, her campaign team was mocking the very idea that she would have anything less than an easy victory on the first ballot. A close adviser, Norman Tebbit, is said to have described any challenge against her as "suicide" for that challenger. Reflecting that complacency, her team failed to canvass some key MPs; her nominal campaign manager, former defense minister George Younger, was not much in evidence.[18]

Too late, the Thatcher camp realized that a Heseltine bandwagon had been picking up speed. A low-key campaign had been planned, but in a *Times* interview of November 19, Thatcher overreacted, accusing Heseltine of being little better than a socialist and an economic interventionist who would "jeopardise all I have struggled to achieve."[19] By contrast, he avoided personal attacks, spoke much about party unity, explained his policies with "statesmanlike aplomb," and continually reminded MPs that the polls suggested that he would now be a better vote-winner than the prime minister.

In projecting the vote on the first ballot, the Thatcher campaign staff significantly overestimated her support. In contrast, the "Parliament" program on ITV astutely projected a result of 192 to 140, with the remaining MPs identified as abstainers or unable to be identified. Although both votes were underestimated, the projected margin of victory for Thatcher coincided precisely with the first ballot result. In the view of Bruce Anderson,

---

17. Quote in Baldwin, "Demise of the Prime Minister," 7. Polling data in Watkins, *Conservative Coup,* 182.

18. "Pulled Down," *The Economist,* November 24, 1990, 30.

19. Watkins, *Conservative Coup,* 186.

134

FIGURE 7.3 Margaret Thatcher with George Younger in Dundee, Scotland, May 1975. (*Source:* British Information Services, New York.)

the fact that "a television programme could perform more efficiently than the Thatcher campaign is conclusive evidence of that campaign's incompetence."[20]

The announcement of the result of the first ballot vote of Conservative Party MPs came at 6:30 on that Tuesday evening to what was described as scenes of pandemonium in the Commons committee corridor: Thatcher, 204 votes (she had been told by her campaign staff that she could expect a minimum of 238); Heseltine, 152 votes; abstentions, 16. The outcome was a clear majority for the prime minister, but not sufficient to satisfy the complex rules of her own party. The candidate with an absolute majority wins on the second ballot but not necessarily on the first. A surplus majority of 15 percent of the total electorate, or 56 votes of the 372 Conservative MPs at the time, was also necessary. Thatcher's margin over Heseltine was only 52, four short of the necessary 15 percent. In Paris, she stunned many senior colleagues by declaring, within minutes of the announcement, her intention to fight on by contesting the second ballot. A majestic appearance at a ball in Versailles that night, however, turned out to be "her last dance on the international stage" as prime minister.[21]

On Wednesday morning, as she was concluding her business in Paris, the news on the home front was gloomy. A clear majority of cabinet ministers was now against her pressing on, while there were equally clear signs of some of her supporters shifting to Heseltine. Admittedly another shift was also taking place of first-round Heseltine voters who had really wanted another candidate and who were steeling themselves to return to Thatcher in the second ballot. But senior Tories thought the net flow was heavily in Heseltine's favor.

Mrs. Thatcher arrived back at Downing Street for a lunchtime council of war. Among those who came to give advice were Lord Whitelaw, the deputy leader; Tim Renton, the chief whip; Cranley Onslow, whose backbenchers' 1922 Committee officers were now deeply split; and Kenneth Baker, the party chairman. Thatcher noted that the campaigning had been poor on the first ballot, and said she felt that, with a better campaign, she could win on the second. No one at that stage told her not to stand. John Wakeham, her energy secretary, offered to run her campaign. She summed up her mood with a defiant battle cry outside Number 10: "I fight on, I fight to win." But starker advice came that evening as Thatcher, in meetings arranged by Wakeham and her parliamentary private secretary Peter Morrison, interviewed the cabinet ministers individually in her Commons room. According to one eyewitness, they were lined up "like naughty schoolboys outside her study" as they waited for their interviews. She opened each

---

20. Anderson, *John Major,* 109.
21. "The Long Good-Bye," *The Economist,* November 24, 1990, 30.

conversation with a short homily on how she had won three elections in a row, how she had overwhelming support in the party throughout the country, how she had not lost a motion of censure or vote of no-confidence, and how she was backed by the majority of MPs in the first ballot. Yet "in this funny old world, my future as prime minister is cast in doubt. What do you think?"[22]

One by one, most of the ministers pledged their personal support if she insisted on fighting on, but the majority told her they thought she would be beaten if she did so. The same grim message had also come from back-benchers and junior ministers as conveyed by the chief whip. Some of her most fervent supporters urged her to fight on, but some of her closest and most loyal friends told her she was putting herself through a personal and political torture that would only end in defeat. The other consideration was a growing anger among ministers who felt that if she did fight on, she would hand over the mantle of party leadership to an "ideologically opposed corporatist," in the person of Heseltine. If she stood down, he could still be stopped by a "unity candidate," such as Douglas Hurd, the foreign secretary. That may have been the crucial argument.

Between 8:00 and 9:00 that evening she returned to Downing Street to discuss the situation with her husband Denis. Whatever her inner turmoil, she then turned her attention during the next four hours to working on her speech for a no-confidence debate in the House of Commons, which had been called by the Labour Party opposition and was scheduled for the next day. At sometime around midnight, a group of five right-wing junior ministers saw her to try to convince her to fight on. They talked about numbers, but numbers no longer mattered; by that time, her demeanor indicated that she too had lost hope. The conversations with her cabinet colleagues had shaken her resolve, especially the strong negative comments of Kenneth Clarke and Malcolm Rifkin. But perhaps of even greater impact were the views of passionately loyal junior ministers, such as Alan Clark. The message of their comments was that she must stand for the second ballot, but, of course, she would lose.[23] In any event, sometime during the course of that long evening, she decided to throw in the towel.

Resignation

Early the next morning, November 22, the Queen was informed of Thatcher's decision to resign, and an audience was arranged. A cabinet

22. "Pulled Down," 29–30.
23. Philip Norton, Speech at 1991 American Political Science Association conference, as reported in "That Was the Year That Was," *British Politics Group Newsletter* No. 66 (Winter 1991): 2–3.

FIGURE 7.4 Douglas Hurd. (*Source:* British Information Services, New York.)

meeting began at 9:00 A.M., which was scheduled an hour earlier than usual for the convenience of those wishing to attend a memorial service for Elizabeth Douglas-Home in Westminster Abbey. Thatcher read out her resignation statement. Following brief tributes by James Mackay and Cecil Parkinson (with several colleagues in tears), discussion proceeded on the day's agenda, the main item of which was the reinforcement of British troops in the Gulf. Shortly after the meeting, which was concluded within an hour with a minimum of discussion, she departed for the Palace, repeating her refrain of the previous day, "It's a funny old world."

Following her resignation, she marched into Parliament that afternoon and, in best Thatcher fashion, gave a forceful, bravura defense of her administration in the no-confidence debate. As *The Guardian* reported in bold headlines, "Dying swan gives Commons a command performance." The article began: "Nothing became Margaret Thatcher's prime ministership as her leaving of it. The last big performance was a command one, a dying aria that played to a packed House." A *Guardian* editorial entitled "Another closing, another show" commented that the "day was one of living theatre and of evident personal tragedy. . . . She began transmutation, as she spoke, in the roseate role of elder statesman and Dulwich icon; a card, a folk legend, someone to tell the grandchildren about. She managed, for herself, to turn complete disaster into a kind of triumph " Another observer, Bruce Anderson, has similarly noted that it was

characteristic of her that she should face trauma with triumph, and choose the moment of her downfall to deliver her greatest parliamentary performance. . . . In her last speech as Prime Minister, she had brushed aside transient adversity, brushed aside even her own resignation to assert herself once again as a talismanic world-historical figure.[24]

---

24. *The Guardian,* November 23, 1990, 1. See also "Another Closing, Another Show," *The Guardian,* November 23, 1990, 18. Anderson, *John Major,* 156. See text of her November 22 speech in Part II of this book.

Public reaction to the prime minister's downfall was wide-ranging and varied, just as it had been to her presence in Number Ten. It ran the entire emotional gambit from shock and dismay and from sympathy and shame to jubilation and celebration. What had been virtually unthinkable in the days leading up to the ballot had become reality.

By resigning as leader, Margaret Thatcher had resolved an agonizing and frustrating dilemma for her supporters and had effectively stymied Michael Heseltine's ambition of becoming prime minister. On November 27, five days after she announced her resignation, John Major became Conservative Party leader on the second ballot and thereby assumed the governmental reins of command, as prime minister. During that five-day period, despite her publicly proclaimed intention to refrain from endorsing any candidate, Thatcher had been instrumental in helping to derail the Heseltine bandwagon and in having her own "unity candidate" in the person of her Chancellor of the Exchequer succeed her.

Post-Resignation Debate

Debate over the manner of Margaret Thatcher's demise continues. In regard to the circumstances of her fall from power, there is still speculation concerning plots, coups, and conspiracies. The question therefore—one raised prominently by Thatcher herself—is to what extent her resignation can be said to have been the result of a concerted coup or conspiracy on the part of her trusted ministerial colleagues in the government.

In the months following her ouster, there was widespread talk that she regarded many members of the Conservative government as "plotters" who acted deliberately and in concert to pull her down. *The Economist,* in an article subtitled "Was it, or was it not a plot?", reported that she had told the Soviet ambassador to Britain at a private meeting that she had been ousted from power by a "constitutional coup" organized by Tim Renton, her former chief whip. John Wakeham has said that "she will to her dying day think it was a plot." Others have singled out Norman Lamont, who is said to have led a cabal of Treasury ministers and other individuals who decided in advance that she had to be replaced by Major and who pushed her into resigning.[25]

A book written by Alan Watkins, a political columnist for *The Observer,* focuses specifically on her fall and is titled *A Conservative Coup.* The publishers, Duckworth Press, promoted the book on the ground that Watkins had uncovered some 'hitherto-unsuspected skulduggery." Watkins's

---

25. Report to Soviet ambassador in "The Fall of Thatcher," 21. Wakeham quote in Watkins, *Conservative Coup,* 213.

FIGURE 7.5 John Major. (*Source:* British Information Services, New York.)

alleged "initial plot" amounts in essence to a meeting held between John Wakeham, Agriculture Minister John Gummer, and Education Secretary Kenneth Clarke. According to Watkins, this meeting, which took place *prior to* the first ballot, resulted in an agreement that she was not going to win outright on that ballot, that she would split the party if she stood for a second round, and that therefore she had to be persuaded to step down quietly.[26]

Whether this meeting really changed anything is, of course, open to question. There were many such informal meetings as the one described by Watkins which also reached the conclusion that she must go. They include the well publicized one at the Catherine Place home of Tristan Garrel-

---

26. See the review article of Watkins's book: "One Short Year Later," *The Economist*, November 23, 1991, 99.

Jones after the results of the first ballot were in. The reported outcomes of many of these meetings—that she should not stand again—became the conventional wisdom, and their importance was in the role they played as catalysts, not conspiracy. The most conspiratorial interpretation would have Wakeham as campaign chairman orchestrating events—in particular the face-to-face meetings between Thatcher and her senior ministers—in order to force her to give up. Clarke and Gummer were certainly among those who told her, when asked, that she should. One could also add to this scenario the speculation that the conspirators actually misled her and pushed her into resigning by giving her bogus information and engineering her resignation at a time when she could have fought and won.

Watkins in fact concludes that Margaret Thatcher "was disposed of by means of a coup" whereas "Mr. Major became Prime Minister through a conspiracy . . . defined as 'the agreement of two or more persons to effect any unlawful purpose.'" He offers little evidence for the latter assertion, beyond the fact that party rules were not strictly followed in their requirement for holding a third ballot. Major fell two votes short of an absolute majority on the second ballot, but both Michael Heseltine and Douglas Hurd immediately conceded defeat and withdrew their candidacies. Even given our affinity for conspiracy theories, the evidence surrounding the circumstances of Thatcher's resignation falls far short of permitting any such conspiratorial interpretation. *The Economist*'s investigation of the "whodunnit, why, whether they planned it together" concludes that her fall "may have involved disloyalty, but not conspiracy." Bruce Anderson observes that the conspiracy theory "has only one problem: an entire lack of evidence."[27]

More realistic is its description as a coup, in the dictionary sense of "successful stroke" or "a sudden, successful move or action . . . master stroke." The most plausible interpretation of events seems to be that scores of Conservative MPs simply decided that her continued leadership would lose the election for their party, and the cabinet ministers merely picked up on what the backbenchers were doing and advised her accordingly. Their advice to her probably reflected accurately a surge of support away from Thatcher to Heseltine by MPs who were fearful for their seats if she stayed in office and who felt that they had paid their debts to her on the first ballot.

Conclusion

What was of ultimate significance, then, in the demise of Margaret Thatcher was the survival instinct of the Conservative Party. With somewhat

---

27. Watkins, *Conservative Coup*, 200. *Economist* investigation in "The Fall of Thatcher," 21. Anderson, *John Major*, 99.

FIGURE 7.6 The Prince and Princess of Wales at 10 Downing Street, with Prime Minister Thatcher, her husband Denis, and cellist Mstislav Rostropovich, his daughter Elena, and his wife Galina Vishnevskaya (right). (*Source:* British Information Services, New York.)

brutal and unsentimental swiftness, in contrast with the more usual pomp and circumstance, the reins of power were transferred to a leader who was considered to have the best chance of ensuring that the Conservatives would remain the party of government. As Nicholas Baldwin reminds us, the one overriding factor in the politics of Great Britain that must not be ignored is that the country is governed by and through political parties. A leader must have the confidence and support of the party. In this transfer of power, it was the party rather than any individual—even such an individual as Margaret Thatcher—that ultimately prevailed in its quest for survival.[28]

And so the reign of Margaret Thatcher as prime minister suddenly and dramatically ended eleven years, six months, and twenty-three days after it had begun. As she was relegated to the back benches in the House of Commons (and, as some critics would have it, to an attempt to become a back-seat driver for Major), the Thatcher era was indeed over. She continues as an important and sometimes defiant figure in the House of Lords and on the world stage, however. The legacy of Thatcherism remains very much alive in terms of her profound impact on British society and on both the substance and the style of British politics.

---

28. Baldwin, "Demise of the Prime Minister," 8.

FIGURE 8.1 Denis and Margaret Thatcher at 10 Downing Street. (*Source:* British Information Services, New York.)

8

The Historical Margaret Thatcher

James E. Cronin

It is difficult to believe that Margaret Thatcher is no longer prime minister. The habit of command came so naturally to her that it is almost impossible to imagine her without legions at her back and even harder to conceive of her successors— John Major for the moment—having at their disposal roughly the same power. Apparently Mrs. Thatcher has herself had trouble reconciling her exaggerated sense of self with her diminished political stature. That trouble manifests itself variously, depending on the moment: coming out in September 1992 as a resounding "I told you so" when the British government was forced to cut loose from the European Monetary System (EMS) and allow the pound to be devalued. Since Thatcher is unlikely to return to power, however, her interventions in the future are likely to center primarily upon the interpretation of her legacy. Having worked so hard and so successfully to control the world around her, Thatcher (and her supporters) will now fight to control history.

She is right to be concerned with her legacy. Though Thatcher dominated British politics and political discourse for over a decade, the tendency to forget is strong. Rival politicians, even among the Tories, are happy to have her gone and do not want to be reminded of how completely she controlled their fates. Officials are likewise relieved that she is no longer their boss. Thatcher was, after all, an abrasive presence who fit awkwardly into the chummy world of politics and elite journalism. Academics, moreover, have in a curious way abetted the self-interested forgetfulness of politicians, bureaucrats, and journalists. Scholars responded to Thatcher's election and to her early, ideologically aggressive initiatives with great fascination, and spent some years explaining this apparently novel political phenomenon that many chose to call "Thatcherism." Just what distinguished "Thatcherism" was much debated, but implicit in all the arguments about its meaning was a strong sense that it was new and that it made a difference. That sense has begun to fade in subsequent discussions, however, and the danger now would seem to be a tendency to underestimate its, and her, impact.[1]

Any effort to assess the impact of politicians, and of parties and governments, turns largely on the choice of standards and starting points. That is particularly difficult in the case of Thatcher because she herself had such strong views on both issues. She came to office claiming that the nation was in desperate shape, that Labour's inability to control the unions made them incapable of controlling inflation and hence the economy and, more important, that the impasse had incapacitated government itself. The Conservatives argued as well that taxes and spending were excessive and in no small way responsible for the nation's economic plight. She pledged therefore to roll back the frontiers of the state and to restore to individuals the power that they had supposedly lost to government.[2] Thatcher also declared an ideological war against socialism, even in its relatively benign "Labourist" manifestation. These claims and objectives, if taken literally and simply, would seem to have committed Thatcher and her colleagues to a very high standard.

No government can reasonably expect to translate its vision directly into programs, and when the vision involves an ideological transformation, as Thatcher's did, the gap between objectives and results will likely be wider still. Perhaps the only government in modern times whose achievements even remotely approximated its hopes and plans was the Labour government of 1945–1950. It is possible as well to count the Conservative governments of the 1950s a relative success, but largely because they promised little and so were held to low standards of judgment and because they had the good fortune to preside over a sustained period of growth. Otherwise, postwar governments were beset by growing claims upon the state, particularly in terms of economic management, and a diminished capacity to satisfy them.

To what standard, then, should Thatcher and her government be held? Should she be judged against the impressive achievements of the first Attlee government? Should Thatcher's successive cabinets be measured against her own, obviously exaggerated, rhetoric? Or should she and they be compared to their most recent predecessors, those notably ineffective governments that held office from 1964 to 1979? There are strong arguments in favor of the latter, for it was those governments that created, or allowed

---

1. The scholarly assessments of Thatcherism are just beginning to emerge. For a preliminary list and evaluation, see Lisanne Radice, "The Thatcher Legacy," *Parliamentary Affairs* 45 (July 1992): 441–44.

2. See especially Barbara Waine, *The Rhetoric of Independence: The Ideology and Practice of Social Policy in Britain* (Oxford: Berg, 1991).

to emerge, those developments in the economy, in taxes and spending, in industrial relations and in policy making generally that constituted the trend line inherited by Thatcher. It was these trends that she had first to comprehend and confront, then to deflect or push further ahead. Thatcher did not write upon a blank slate, nor did she accede to power in a situation that allowed her great flexibility. Understanding that context is critical to arriving at a fair assessment of Thatcher's legacy.

There are also arguments in favor of taking an even longer view in assessing the achievement of Margaret Thatcher. Thatcher staked a claim, more forcefully and credibly than most politicians, to genuine novelty, to having made a decisive break with tradition and to having ushered in a new brand of Toryism and a new style of ideologically committed politician. To judge these claims requires a much broader perspective. It requires, to be precise, an effort to find parallels and anticipations, if such exist, in a much longer history of modern politics and modern Conservative politics in particular. Reaching even a provisional verdict on the historical significance of Margaret Thatcher thus demands that her achievement be measured first against the performance of the politicians and governments that preceded her, going back at least to 1964 and preferably to 1951, and second, some effort to determine whether there were significant precursors to Thatcherism in modern British political history.

Thatcher and Her Predecessors

It is perhaps best to begin where Thatcher herself had to begin—at her accession to the Tory leadership in the aftermath of Edward Heath's two defeats in the elections of 1974. The closeness of the votes in 1974 belied the magnitude of the Tory debacle, for it had been preceded by four years of Conservative government that seemed to have failed on all counts. It had failed to produce the economic growth it had promised. When its initial thrust toward free-market policies encountered resistance, it had backed off (Heath's famous U-Turn); and when its efforts to tame the unions conjured up the inevitable resistance, the government was unable to prevail. Its call for a election that would serve to strengthen its hand against the unions was itself a desperate move, whose failure was an appropriate capstone to four very bad years.

Thatcher's emergence as a politician of commitment and conviction, then, owed at least something to the circumstances of her victory over Heath in the leadership contest of 1975. Thatcher's claim to leadership was premised on her firm resolve not to repeat the previous Conservative government and, even more important, not to be perceived as Heath had been seen. Her antipathy to the welfare state and Keynesian policies of

demand management and her attachment to free-market policies had
somewhat deeper roots. As early as 1968, Mrs. Thatcher had spoken of her
belief that "the great mistake of the last few years has been for the
government to provide or to legislate for almost everything. . . . What we
need now is a far greater degree of personal responsibility and decision, far
more independence from the government, and a comparative reduction in
the role of government."[3] Still, Thatcher had not primarily distinguished
herself as an ideologue, and it is thus not surprising that, prior to her taking
office, it was widely assumed that Keith Joseph was the source of her ideas.
It is also important to remember that the international retreat from Keynesianism and from the commitment to extensive and increasing social provision
was just beginning in the mid-1970s. At that point it was still possible to
understand both the current economic difficulties and the looming "fiscal
crisis of the state" as temporary problems stemming from the collapse of
the Bretton Woods system and the rise in commodity prices, especial oil.
The ideological thrust of Thatcherism before 1979 remained relatively
weak; her criticism of the Labour government was more pragmatic than
theoretical. And if there was a central theme to her evolving critique, it had
less to do with the virtues of the market than with the seemingly manifest
evils of trade union power. Similarly, Thatcher's attack on the state was
based less upon the theoretical argument for private provision than upon a
straightforward claim that it cost too much and led to excessive taxation.

The record of the Labour government of 1974–1979 must surely have
reinforced the lessons that Thatcher had learned first from Heath. Labour
itself began the retreat from Keynes and the welfare state in 1976 by
coming to terms with the International Monetary Fund (IMF), cutting
back its spending plans and jettisoning its program to stimulate growth
through state intervention in industry. James Callaghan's address to the
Labour party conference of that year made the retreat explicit. By the late
1970s, therefore, it had become obvious that the repertoire of policies
available to government could not do the job and that their intellectual
underpinnings provided no means even of explaining the persistence of
inflation and stagnation. What the difficulties of the Labour government
also made obvious were the liabilities of its ties with the unions and the way
its preference for corporatist bargaining not only failed to strengthen, but
instead notably weakened, the state's capacity for action.[4] To Thatcher,

3. Speech to the Conservative Political Centre, October 10, 1968, quoted in D. Coates and J.
Hillard, eds., *The Economic Decline of Modern Britain: The Debate between Left and Right*
(Brighton: Harvester, 1986), 64–65. See the text of this speech in Part II of this book.
4. It would appear that the government's relations with the unions and the failure of its
industrial relations policies constituted the most salient issue in the election of 1979. See Helmut
Norpoth, *Confidence Regained: Economics, Mrs. Thatcher, and the British Voter* (Ann Arbor:
University of Michigan, 1991), 67–91.

FIGURE 8.2 Unveiling in the House of Commons Members' Lobby of a memorial statue to former Prime Minister Clement Attlee (1945–1951) in the presence of former Prime Ministers (left to right) James Callaghan (1978–1979), Harold Wilson (1964–1970, 1974–1978), Margaret Thatcher (1979–1990), and Edward Heath (1970–1974), November 12, 1979. (*Source:* British Information Services, New York.)

therefore, the connections between excessive government intervention in the economy, growing expenditure and rising taxes, and Labour's apparent inability to govern were clearly revealed. Not surprisingly, she concluded that a government that made itself responsible for less and was responsive to fewer interests of all sorts would be potentially much stronger, freer to carry out its will and more capable of dealing with those things that were legitimately within the purview of government.

The education of Margaret Thatcher was thus only partly theoretical. It was a very practical thing: she had seen and understood what it was that had caused first Heath and then Labour to fail, or to appear to have failed. Most important, the insights she took away from these experiences would prove extremely valuable when she took office in 1979. That was because the first fruits of Conservative economic policies were so very bitter. Within two years of taking office, Mrs. Thatcher found herself presiding over the worst recession of the postwar era and under severe pressure to do something about it. It is difficult to say how much responsibility Thatcher should bear for the slowdown. The roots were in large part international, and the consequences were by no means limited to Britain. Still, it is likely that the Conservatives' severely deflationary fiscal policies made the slump deeper and more destructive of manufacturing than it might otherwise have been. The government's fiscal stance, moreover, was undoubtedly exacerbated by monetary policy and by the upward trend in the value of the pound.[5] The recession was particularly disconcerting because there were no obvious remedies within the theoretical arsenal available to Thatcher. She had, after all, come to power proclaiming that the old Keynesian remedies were not working; she could hardly revert to them so soon after taking office. In general, her government was committed to the view that the state could do little to influence economic performance. They could create the preconditions for growth, but little more, and even that required a break with past practice—a break whose consequences, it was admitted, might well be adverse in the short run.

The question of whether to "turn," therefore, was the central issue of Thatcher's first term. In the end she did not, largely because of her reading of the fate of her predecessors in government who had changed course. What Thatcher also did remarkably well was to shift expectations about the proper role, and likely impact, of government. Her survival in office depended to a great extent on convincing the electorate that the economy was beyond the control of government and that state action to solve the crisis would probably make matters worse. In that effort she had on her side the dismal record of twenty years of interventionist and growth-

5. John Toye, "Britain, the United States and the World Debt Crisis," in Jonathan Michie, ed., *The Economic Legacy, 1979–1992* (London: Academic Press, 1992), 13–15.

oriented politics, initiated by Harold Macmillan, pushed to new heights by Harold Wilson and continued under Edward Heath and the Labour government of 1974–1979. So Thatcher worked assiduously to limit the government's responsibility for ensuring economic performance.

What she did commit herself and her government to, however, was reducing inflation. In 1979, voters apparently trusted Labour more than the Tories on their ability to control prices. This was due in part to the record, and memory, of Edward Heath; it owed something as well to the fact that inflation had begun to moderate in the last years of the Labour government. But Thatcher chose to fix her sights narrowly upon taming inflation, rather than generating growth, and remained firm. Her resolve on the issue was crucial, for in fact the initial result of her policies was a sharp jump in inflation rates. She was committed to carrying out the terms of a prior pay award to civil servants; and her first budget shifted much of the tax burden from income taxes to Value Added Tax (VAT), thus increasing prices in the shops. By 1981, moreover, the signs of recession were everywhere, and there was pressure to relent and to allow a loosening of fiscal policy. Instead, Thatcher turned the screws and at least temporarily worsened the slowdown. But inflation also began to respond, and by 1983 it was seen to be under government control.

The economic record of Thatcher's first term was hardly a success, and the unemployment it created was a major liability in the election of 1983. Nevertheless, Thatcher had by 1983 altered the terms of economic discourse. By claiming that growth was beyond the capacity of government to engineer and that Britain's economic decline was the product of too much government, the Conservatives escaped from under the burden that had bedeviled previous governments. By fixing upon one key indicator, inflation, and managing to control that, they were able to claim a genuine victory on an admittedly more limited goal. Of course, this strategy only succeeded because of the disarray in the Labour party, the formation of the Social Democratic Party and the resulting split in the opposition vote, and because of Thatcher's great good fortune in the Falklands. Nonetheless, the shift took hold, and Thatcher won reelection. In so doing she succeeded in "breaking the mold" in a way that David Owen and his colleagues never could.

By her second term, therefore, Thatcher had freed government, or her government at least, from the major constraint that had dictated policy: the need to preside by the next election over a period of good times. That did not mean that the performance of the economy no longer mattered to her or to the electorate. Indeed, Thatcher was quite happy to reap the happy electoral results of the mid-1980s boom in 1987 and to attribute it to her policies. Only a fool would have done otherwise. But what Thatcher also did during her second, and even into the third, term was to intensify the ideological character of her regime and to carry the war against socialism into whole new arenas of public policy. Rather than drift toward the center, as seems so often the pattern as governments grow more accustomed to power and the perquisites of office, Thatcher's government became more, not less, marked by "the politics of conviction." The attack on the unions, for example, was pressed much further than anyone could have predicted. So, too, was privatization, which began opportunistically as a ploy to lure council tenants away from their attachments to Labour by allowing them to purchase their homes, built at public expense, at a tremendous discount. But privatization proceeded much further, toward the dismantling of nationalized industries and the contracting out of services long associated with the public sector. Whatever the effect in terms of efficiency, the short-term impact on the budget was extremely beneficial and helped to finance tax cuts to the middle and upper classes. The more long-term political consequence was to reduce the potential leverage which any future government, Tory or Labour, could exert over the economy. The Tories under Thatcher even went so far as to reshape government itself, targeting at first the spending policies of local government, then challenging the very existence of the Greater London Council (GLC), threatening the prerogatives of the local education authorities, and finally introducing the poll tax.[6] By the middle of Thatcher's third term, the government moved toward restructuring the Health Service, albeit with great care and constant assurances that its integrity would be preserved, and drastically reorganizing the finances of local government by means of the "poll tax."

Taken together, the Thatcherite program was more ambitious and creative than anything on offer since 1945. It was, however, unlike the program proposed and ultimately implemented by Labour in several key respects. First, it was evolved more than planned. Labour's program had been debated extensively for years, and the question of reform was at the top of the political agenda for all parties in the two years prior to the election. Labour's victory, then, could legitimately be construed as a mandate for its implementation. Thatcher's program, while ideologically quite consistent, was not worked out in great detail before 1979. Her election, in consequence, could be read as a decisive repudiation of the past but not as a guide to the future. Nevertheless, Thatcher displayed a tremendous sense of what was possible and what was not, and she responded much more deftly than other politicians to the opportunities that presented themselves. She quickly sized up the depth of Labour's post-1979 crisis and

---

6. See Jim Bulpitt, *Territory and Power in the United Kingdom* (Manchester: Manchester University Press, 1983), 200–224; Bulpitt, "The Discipline of the New Democracy: Mrs. Thatcher's Domestic Statecraft," *Political Studies* 34 (March 1986): 19–39.

pressed forward with proposals that reflected her free-market outlook and did not wait upon the development of public opinion. It is not surprising that surveys done after a decade of Thatcher's rule showed that her "crusade" to transform public attitudes had largely failed. There is no doubt that Thatcher aimed at a "cultural revolution," but her policies did not depend upon it succeeding.[7]

The most obvious contrast between Labour's program in 1945 and Thatcher's various initiatives was, of course, the vastly different roles the two sides assigned to the state in British society. On a deeper level, however, the Thatcher governments and the Labour governments of 1945–1951 shared a common desire to restructure the relationship between state and society. In this they both differed from the normal pattern in which governments take for granted the shape of the administrative machine and seek to change policies, hoping thereby to improve economic outcomes or to address particular social problems. Thatcher saw beyond specific policies to the question of the state itself. She understood, for example, that if the state's ability to extract revenues was diminished, so would the scope for intervention; that once taxes were lowered, a reforming administration would confront the task not merely of crafting new policies but of raising funds to pay for them; that if the nationalized industries were back in private hands, there could be no debate about how to run them; that if there were no GLC, there would be one less forum within which her policies could be criticized. The Tories under Thatcher grasped, in other words, that questions of state structure and capacity—what one author has called the "infrastructural," as opposed to the "despotic," power of the state—must take precedence over issues of policy.[8]

Few previous governments understood this as clearly as did Thatcher, and none acted upon it so resolutely. Both Wilson and Heath sensed that economic modernization was being hindered by the traditional character of British central administration, but neither managed to implement any serious package of reforms. The Labour ministers who came to power in 1945 were, in a curious sense, more like Thatcher in this respect. They knew that they were not merely changing policies, but making commitments for the long term and putting in place the institutions and the funding necessary to make them real. Labour's great advantage in this effort was the legacy of the Second World War. The war had required an enormous mobilization of resources that had, in turn, demanded a revamped state machinery to direct it. Normal procedures had been bypassed, the normal

7. Ivor Crewe, "Values: The Crusade that Failed," in Dennis Kavanagh and Anthony Seldon, eds., *The Thatcher Effect* (Oxford: Clarendon, 1989), 239–50.

8. The distinction is made by Michael Mann in "The Autonomous Power of the State: Its Origins, Mechanisms and Results," *European Journal of Sociology* 25 (1984): 185–213.

constraints on the scope of activity lifted, and a set of policy-making tools put into the hands of the state that could be used to run the economy. Labour was determined in 1945 not to give up any of those tools and, arguing that the nation's economic problems would be as dire after the war as during it, opted to continue the wartime style and structure of policy making into peacetime. The transition to a peacetime style of government was thus much delayed. Labour sought throughout the 1940s to create institutions and establish practices that would ensure a continued strong role for government in the postwar economy and make it possible for the state to live up to the commitments taken on at the end of the war. To be sure, Labour could have done better. It could, for example, have been more resolute in establishing an apparatus for planning; and it could have been made more thoroughgoing changes in the key departments of state, the Treasury and the Foreign Office in particular. Nevertheless, Labour had good reason to believe in 1951 that it had left behind an administrative machine reasonably well-adapted to carrying out the task of managing the postwar, Keynesian welfare state.[9]

Thatcher also had good reason to believe in 1990 that she was leaving behind a state that had settled into a new, but much more limited, role. Her successor was much less of an ideologue than Thatcher, but he showed no signs of wanting to tamper fundamentally with the pattern of state-society relations imposed under Thatcher. His most innovative idea—the "Citizens Charter"—involved a more open and friendly government, but not a more active one. And when in the spring of 1992 it seemed likely that voters would repudiate Major and turn finally to Labour, he reverted to the thoroughly "Thatcherite" issue of taxation to win re-election. The transformation wrought by Thatcher was thus, if not permanent, nevertheless structural and as such likely to last for some time. It might well be argued that it constituted the most profound reshaping of the relationship between the state and society since the 1940s, even if its aim was to reverse the terms and destroy the institutional framework of the postwar settlement.

These structural changes are easily missed or misunderstood. For one thing, they are not captured well by the quantitative data on taxes and spending. The total tax burden did not decrease under Thatcher, and spending did continue to increase, at least through the mid-1980s. But scholars who take comfort from such numbers and conclude from them that the impact of Thatcher was less than one might expect from her rhetoric would seem to be missing the more telling qualitative shifts. On taxes, for example, Thatcher reversed a long-term trend toward a greater reliance on direct and progressive taxation and less reliance upon indirect

---

9. For more detail, see James E. Cronin, *The Politics of State Expansion: War, State and Society in Twentieth-Century Britain* (London: Routledge, 1991), chapters 8–9.

and, in most instances, regressive taxation. Virtually her first fiscal decision was to dramatically lower income tax rates, especially at the top, and to make up the revenue by a major increase in VAT, an indirect tax imposed without regard to ability to pay, and by a lesser increase in National Insurance contributions, a levy whose incidence ceases at higher levels of income. Subsequent tax changes involved further reductions in both the top rates and in what is called the standard rate of income tax. Tax thresholds for those on the bottom were not raised along with inflation, however, making the impact of income tax itself less progressive than it might have been. Thatcher's final fiscal innovation was the poll tax, surely the most regressive proposal proferred since the debate over protection early in the century. The poll tax was designed to replace the local rates which were, if flawed, nevertheless an attempt to assess local tax burdens in some relation to wealth, or at least wealth as measured by real property. Discontent over the poll tax was, of course, a key factor in Mrs. Thatcher's fall from grace, and her successors promised to abandon it. They will not, however, revert to the older, putatively more progressive, system but instead raise VAT still further. The preference for indirect, regressive taxes remains a more or less permanent, and politically extremely potent, legacy of the Thatcher era.

Nor is it the case that Thatcher failed to have an impact on the brute, quantitative facts of taxation and expenditure. A study concludes "that under a Labour, or Heath-style Tory government the level of public expenditure would have risen significantly faster and that higher taxes would have been required to finance this growth."[10] As a result of Thatcher's policies, Britain is now among the least taxed of European nations, and the government spends relatively less of the national income than do the governments of its neighbors and competitors in Europe. Need, on the other hand, has increased, as unemployment has become a more or less permanent feature of the economic landscape, and poverty has increased visibly. In keeping the totals roughly constant, therefore, Thatcher achieved a marked break in the established trends of taxation and expenditure.

Thatcher's goal of pushing back the boundaries of the state was thus more than mere rhetoric. It was a consistent, ideologically inspired effort to transform the structure and logic of British politics. Why, then, have scholarly commentators been so skeptical? One clear reason is that, while seeking to cut back on benefits and to shed responsibility for growth and welfare, Thatcher displayed a considerable fondness for making use of the "despotic" powers of the state. The obsession with leaks and secrecy, the coddling and relatively lavish support of the police, the unflinching resolve

---

10. Bob Rowthorn, "Government Spending and Taxation in the Thatcher Era," in Michie, *Economic Legacy*, 261–93.

to let Irish prisoners die in jail, the harsh treatment of strikers, the tough talk on defense and the resolution manifest in the Falklands crisis—these are surely as much a part of Thatcher's impact as her stance toward the economy and state provision. Indeed, during the first Thatcher government much of the interest in her regime centered on the "authoritarian populism" that seemed so central to her ideological project.[11] The question, however, is whether these two sides of Thatcher are in contradiction or are better seen as complementary.

Again, the key to understanding Thatcher is placing her administration in the context of a series of governments most remembered for their mistakes and failures. Particularly memorable in this regard were the efforts of Wilson, Heath, and Callaghan to deal with the unions. The question of just how to handle the trade unions has been at or near the top of the agenda of virtually all postwar governments. But what was once seen as a successful means of managing this relationship has in recent years been perceived as a record of failure and folly. The change is reflected in the writings of academic commentators as well as in the more lurid accounts of journalists and the contentious claims of rival politicians. Thus academics seeking to make sense of the postwar pattern of relationships between the unions and the state evolved the notion of "corporatism" as a means of describing the system in which well-organized unions, big companies or employers' organizations, and an expanded state utilizing Keynesian techniques of economic management bargained over policy. Unions, it was argued in this view, had acquired a legitimacy unknown before the Second World War and were now properly seen and treated as an "estate of the realm," regularly consulted and intimately involved in the details of policy making.[12] For some time it was assumed that this system worked: it seemed responsible for muting industrial conflict, generating consensus on domestic policy, and fostering the conditions for growth. It seemed also appropriate to associate corporatism with an enlarged and powerful state. The very links the state had forged with the two sides of industry appeared to have increased its leverage over matters economic and industrial; and its aspiration to superintending growth was evidence of a much expanded view of the role of the state in society.

What was less obvious so long as the system was working and the economy booming was how much it also compromised the authority and independence of the state. The practice of "corporatist" bargaining severely

---

11. See the essays gathered together in Stuart Hall, *The Hard Road to Renewal: Thatcherism and the Crisis of the Left* (London: Verso, 1988).

12. The "corporatist" rendition of twentieth-century British history has been most forcefully articulated by Keith Middlemas, first in his *Politics in Industrial Society* (London: Andre Deutsch, 1979) and then in more detail in his three-volume study, *Power, Competition and the State* (London: Macmillan, 1986–91).

limited the policy options open to government, for it gave to both business and the unions effective veto power over policies that would impact one or the other side adversely. Moreover, the sorts of policies that emerged from such bargaining depended for their effectiveness on the state's partners in planning. On incomes policy, for example, the state at various times relied upon the unions or employers' organizations to get their members to go along with essentially voluntary restraints on prices and wages. But they had little ability to police the actions of their constituents and no authority to compel compliance, and so they found themselves exhorting their members to cooperate and seeing those requests ignored or defied. Government therefore found itself committed to a system that constrained its choices and that was unable to deliver on the narrow range of policies that could elicit agreement. It was a system that, in fact, weakened the state and invited contempt.

Thatcher, therefore, had a strong incentive for opting out of the "corporatist" arrangements and traditions bequeathed to her by previous governments. And she understood intuitively that doing so would free up and strengthen the authority of her government. Just as the largely successful effort to escape responsibility for economic growth made the Thatcher governments less vulnerable to criticism over the performance of the economy, so detaching themselves from institutions designed to develop and implement an economic policy aimed at growth likewise distanced Conservatives from the legacy of past failures and allowed them a new lever of freedom in policy making. It led, in consequence, to a state that appeared more competent, more authoritative, a state in which "confidence" appeared to have been "regained."[13] At the heart of Thatcher's economic and industrial policies, therefore, was a desire for a stronger state with a more limited social and economic agenda. There is no contradiction between that objective and a broader willingness to augment and flaunt the state's "despotic" powers.

Thatcher and Modern British Politics

By at least two of the three standards against which it seems fair to assess Thatcher's impact, then, her achievement stands out clearly. She broke sharply with the policies and with the governing style of the Labour and Tory governments of the late 1960s and 1970s. Her attention to the structure of state-society relations was particular novel, if not in rhetoric then certainly in practice. In comparison with the aims and achievements

---

13. The phrase comes from the title of Helmut Norpoth's thoughtful book, *Confidence Regained: Economics, Mrs. Thatcher, and the British Voter.*

FIGURE 8.3 During the 1979 election campaign, Thatcher promises a "clean sweep" of the opposition and the old corporatist traditions. (*Source:* British Information Services, New York.)

of a longer run of postwar governments, the Thatcher governments also look distinctive. The only government with a comparably broad agenda was that of 1945; the only government that remained so steadfast in the effort to implement its program was again that of 1945. But what about the longer term? Was the Thatcher impact wholly unprecedented? And, more specifically, has she created a new kind of conservatism, a new Tory party for the late twentieth century?

On this standard, it can be argued, Thatcher was perhaps less innovative and less "revolutionary."[14] There is, for example, a remarkable similarity between the turn toward the market undertaken by Thatcher and the slightly more protracted, but equally if not more effective, trend toward laissez-faire in the years 1820 to 1846. In that quarter century a succession of governments, mostly Tory, effectively restructured the links between the

---

14. Much of the evidence summarized in this and subsequent paragraphs is presented at greater length in Cronin, *Politics of State Expansion,* especially chapters 2, 3, and 6.

state and society. The two key moments were the passage of the New Poor Law and the abolition of the Corn Laws, but they were merely part of a broader effort to remove from the government any responsibility for ensuring welfare by provisioning the populace, either through controlling the grain trade or subsidizing wages. At the same time, there was a reform of the banking system and a determined effort to reduce the national debt. Not only were the specific reforms of the early nineteenth century similar in thrust and intention to those of Thatcher many years later; their implementation was also similarly heavy handed. The New Poor Law, for example, was draconian in its operation, even if its aim was to create a free and mobile labor market and reduce the state's involvement in social provision. The intensification of policing during the same years likewise finds its echoes in Thatcher's preference for law and order.

The final act of these reforms, the repeal of the Corn Laws, severely divided the Tories and led ultimately to the rise of a new conservatism. Late-nineteenth-century Conservatives thus looked and sounded different from their predecessors: Disraeli denounced Peel for selling out agriculture and elaborated a set of fiscal policies designed to give preference to landed interests. He also adopted a rhetoric of "one-nation" paternalism, implying a much increased concern with the welfare of the working class; and the new Tory party was unabashedly imperialist. The image crafted by Disraeli has stuck, and commentators ever since have persisted in attributing a paternalist bias to the modern Conservative Party. If by that is meant simply a tendency to be led by men of inherited wealth, often from landed backgrounds, it would not be unreasonable. But if it is meant as an accurate description of Conservative policies or of the party's bases of support, it is greatly oversimplified. Even during Disraeli's time, for example, the Conservatives did not dissent fundamentally from the Gladstonian ideal of limited government and fiscal prudence. The consensus on limited government and low taxes began to shift slowly in the late nineteenth century, but the change was most evident within Liberalism, while the Unionists under Lord Salisbury's leadership resisted efforts—associated most clearly with Joseph Chamberlain—to move toward a policy of social reform. The Conservatives finally moved toward a more interventionist and expansive stance after 1900, but mainly in the interests of the empire, defense, and the manufacturers who were joining the party's ranks in increasing numbers. The Unionists' conversion to protection, moreover, was characteristically and transparently regressive. The preference for taxing food rather than wealth looked back to the Corn Laws and forward to Thatcher's decision to remove taxes on income and impose greater burdens on consumption by raising VAT. It was not part of a credible plan for social reform, and as such it was rejected by voters in four separate elections (1905, twice in 1910, and in 1922).

Nor was there much evidence of Tory paternalism during the interwar slump. If ever there were a time that called out for state intervention on behalf of the poor and those out of work, it was the 1930s. If ever there were a moment when the Conservatives' "one-nation" rhetoric ought to have led to policy innovations, it was that prolonged period of economic stagnation. Instead, the Conservatives remained opposed to even the most modest schemes aimed at reflation, and they pinned their fortunes as a party to fiscal orthodoxy and the resistance to socialism. The reasons behind this stance are not hard to find. The Conservatives had only recently re-emerged as a unified party. That fragile unity was constructed in opposition to progressive taxation and the expanded, interventionist state that had emerged from the war and that, so long as Lloyd George held power, was unlikely to be dismantled. The Tories' subsequent electoral domination was thus premised on a politics of retrenchment, underpinned by widespread middle-class fears of the power of an organized and politicized labor movement.[15] The party's success, moreover, demonstrated to its leaders that slow growth and high unemployment were liabilities, but not insuperable obstacles to reelection. That lesson was forgotten by a generation of postwar Conservatives, but rediscovered by Mrs. Thatcher and her supporters.

It is a mistake, therefore, to speak of the Thatcher phenomenon as if it represented a decisive break with Conservative tradition. It is true, of course, that Thatcher's personal background was more plebeian than that of previous Conservative leaders. Her origins were distinctly petit bourgeois, and she was disdainful of old wealth and the "gentlemanly" values and life-style that normally accompanied it. She was and remains more openly enthusiastic about the virtues of enterprise and the worthiness of entrepreneurs. But her preference for free-market solutions to social problems, her distaste for collectivism, and her antipathy to progressive taxation are deeply rooted in the history and traditions of the Conservative Party. They go back well into the last century, as her evident belief in "Victorian values" suggests, and are firmly grounded in the electoral realities of the twentieth century.

The Thatcher legacy looks very different, then, depending upon whether one adopts a short-term or a long-term view. In the short term—that is, when compared with the record of British governments since 1970—Thatcher represented a major break. She took the relatively recent past as her guide and resolved to do just the opposite, and she was remarkably faithful to that goal. In so doing, she herself set a new standard in terms of

---

15. Ross McKibbin, "Class and Conventional Wisdom: The Conservative Party and the 'Public' in Inter-war Britain," in *Ideologies of Class: Social Relations in Britain, 1880-1950* (Oxford: Clarendon, 1990), 259–93.

what is expected of government, of Tory government in particular, a standard which might well be the downfall of her successors. Her governments' record also stands out against the pattern of rule common since 1951, when the Conservatives chose not to tamper greatly with the outlines of the postwar order left in place by Labour. While scholars and journalists have often overstated the extent of consensus that prevailed in the era of "Butskellism," they are right to contrast the Conservatism of Butler, Eden, and Macmillan (and, of course, the later Churchill) with that of Keith Joseph and Margaret Thatcher. During the 1950s, Conservatives opted to work within the framework created by Labour, while Thatcher set out to destroy it and proceeded in practice to carry out a truly self-conscious effort to turn back the clock to the period before the war. But, of course, the Tories who came back to office in 1951 had no mandate to revert to the politics of prewar and every reason to avoid even the appearance of wanting to do so. The war had brought a major change in public attitudes that even an ideologue such as Thatcher would have been powerless to resist. To put it slightly differently, Thatcher was able to succeed with her ideologically based agenda after 1979 because she was swimming with the tide of public opinion.

Unlike other politicians, Thatcher sought to turn a swing in public opinion into a "cultural revolution." Still, the values she sought to instill were not new, and the shift in public discourse that she sought to engineer was largely a move back to the rhetorical certainties of a simpler age. Her goal, in this sense, was to recapture for the Conservatives a certain stance toward politics, the market and the role of government—an essentially negative stance of resistance to the state, to progressive taxes, to collective provision, and to economic management. This stance had served the Tories well for most of the previous century, and it was certainly reasonable to argue, as Mrs. Thatcher implicitly did, that its abandonment in the 1950s and 1960s had paved the way for the ignominious failures of Edward Heath. The Thatcher governments deserve respect for having aimed at a genuinely structural change in the links between state and society and in the scope and boundaries of politics. The relationship they envisioned, however, was neither new nor innovative; nor was it meant to be productive of better policies. It was a formula for lowering expectations and evading responsibility. And to a considerable extent Thatcher and her supporters have succeeded in what can best be described as a "restoration." If only the project had been a more worthy one.

FIGURE 8.4 Margaret Thatcher. (*Source:* British Information Services, New York.)

PART TWO

Speeches by and Interviews with Margaret Thatcher

9

Admission of the Press to
Meetings of Local Authorities

Maiden Speech in the House of Commons, February 5, 1960

This is a maiden speech, but I know that the constituency of Finchley, which I have the honour to represent, would not wish me to do other than come straight to the point and address myself to the matter before the House. I cannot do better than begin by stating the objects of the bill in the words used by Mr. Arthur Henderson when he introduced the bill which became the Local Authorities (Admission of the Press to Meetings) Act, 1908, which was also a Private Member's Measure. He specified the object and purpose as that of guarding the rights of members of the public by enabling the fullest information to be obtained for them in regard to the actions of their representatives upon local authorities.

It is appropriate at this stage to mention that the public does not have a right of admission, either at common law or by statute, to the meetings of the local authorities. Members of the public are compelled, therefore, to rely upon the local press for information on what their elected representatives are doing. The original measure was brought as a result of a case in which the representatives of a particular paper were excluded from a particular meeting.

The public has the right, in the first instance, to know what its elected representatives are doing. That right extends in a number of directions. I do not know whether hon. Members generally appreciate the total amount of money spent by local authorities.... Less than half is raised by ratepayers' money, and the first purpose in admitting the press is that we may know how those moneys are being spent.

In the second place, I quote from the report of the Franks Committee: "Publicity is the greatest and most effective check against any arbitrary action." That is one of the fundamental rights of the subject. Further, publicity stimulates the interest of local persons in local government. That is also very important. But if there is a case for publicity, there is also a case for a certain amount of private conference when personal matters are being discussed and when questions are in a preliminary stage. It is in trying to find a point of balance between these two aspects—the public right of knowledge and the necessity on occasion for private conference—that the difficulty arises. . . .

Having got the press in to these meetings, or having entitled them to be in, there must inevitably be occasions, such as personal circumstances coming under discussion, matters preliminary to legal proceedings, matters with regard to the acquisition of land, or such matters which would inevitably come up, when the press were entitled to be present, unless some effective provision was made to exclude the press on these occasions.

My second point, therefore, is: having got the press in, upon what grounds is a local authority entitled to exclude it? There must inevitably be some occasions. . . . I suggest most earnestly that when the press is excluded, it must be because of some particular reason arising from the proceedings of the local authority at the time, and there must be very good reason for the exclusion. The reason for excluding the press is that publicity of the matter to be discussed would be prejudicial to the public interest.

There are two prongs to this clause. Publicity would be prejudicial for two main groups of reasons. The first group is where the matters under discussion are of a confidential nature. They may relate to personal circumstances of individual electors. They may relate to a confidential communication from a government department asking local authorities for their opinion on a subject which the minister would not like to be discussed in open session until he is a good deal further on and has received the views of local authorities.

There is another group of subjects which perhaps could not be strictly termed confidential, but where it would be clearly prejudicial to the public interest to discuss them in open session. They may relate to staff matters, to legal proceedings, to contracts, the discussion of which tender to accept and other such matters. On this prong the press has to be excluded for a special reason which would need to be stated in the resolution for exclusion. Where the matter is confidential, it would not need to be specified further in the resolution for exclusion. Where it was for a special reason, that reason would need to be specified in broad general terms in the resolution for exclusion. This subsection is effective and wide enough in its drafting to cover all occasions upon which a local authority could possibly have good grounds for going into private session. Those are the two main operative clauses of the bill.

My third point relates to documents. I understand that there is a very wide variation in practise between the number of documents which different local authorities give to the press. I do not know how many hon. Members have tried to obtain information about a local authority of which they are not a member, but happen to be a ratepayer. One sometimes goes to a council meeting without any idea of what is to be discussed. One sits there for about fifteen minutes, and all one hears is numbers being counted up to about twenty and starting all over again. Unless the press, which is to report to the public, has some idea from the documents before it what is to be discussed, the business of allowing the press in becomes wholly abortive. Therefore, Clause 1 (3, b) makes provision for a limited number of documents to be supplied to the press at its request in advance of the meeting. It specifies that the agenda must be supplied to the press if it so requests and is prepared to pay for it.

Agendas vary very much. Some are couched in terms which do not betray for one moment the subject which is to be discussed. One sees such items as "To discuss the proposal of Mr. Smith" and "To receive the recommendation of Mr. Jones." As distinct from the supporting accompanying documents, the agenda itself is usually a comparatively brief document. I have, therefore, thought fit to put into the subsection a provision that the agenda shall be supplied to the press together with such further statement or particulars as are necessary to convey to an outside person the nature of the subject to be discussed. Therefore, the press must have some idea from the documents what is the true subject to be discussed at meetings to which its representatives are entitled to be admitted.

If the whole agenda was supplied, it might include some things which would be likely to be taken when the press was excluded. The corporation, acting through its proper officer, to whom it would have to give instructions, is entitled to exclude from the agenda matters which are likely to be taken in camera so that no confidential matters will leak out by that process. Another provision in the clause is that the corporation may, if it thinks fit—not must—include supporting committee reports or documents, but it would have to exercise its mind to include them. The press would not be able to demand such documents as of right.

Fourthly, I have been approached and asked about the question of qualified privilege for local councillors and the people who serve on local authorities. I have been approached by people who suggest that the privilege should be made absolute. I could not possibly accede to that, as I think that absolute privilege should be given very rarely indeed. However, there is a consequential provision in the bill which means that where qualified privilege at present exists for statements made by people serving on local authorities, that qualified privilege shall not cease to exist merely because the press is present. That retains the present position and removes one of the reasons why people can object to the press being present, because unless there were a consequential provision, it might serve to remove the qualified privilege.

Fifthly, I understand from various sources that my proposals are under some criticism because they contain no sanctions or penalties upon local authorities. I should therefore like to state briefly what I am advised the position is when any statute is breached. There are general sanctions available at law for this purpose. Where a public right is infringed, as it would be in the event of the bill becoming law and local authorities wrongfully excluding the press, any person can apply to either the Attorney-General or the Solicitor-General for what is known as a relator action.... When that is done, the courts can adjudicate on whether that exclusion was legal or illegal.... I submit that those sanctions that are available by the ordinary law are sufficient to enable this measure to be enforced....

I hope it is evident from what I have said that we are trying very hard to put into the form of legislation a code of practise that will safeguard the rights of the public.... It is not, therefore, only a matter of bringing the 1908 Act up to date. Because of the abuse of the law, there is a case for safeguarding the rights of the citizen. I hope that hon. Members will think fit to give this bill a second reading and to consider that the paramount function of this distinguished House is to safeguard civil liberties rather than to think that administrative convenience should take first place in law.... I should like to thank the House for its very kind indulgence to a new Member.[1]

---

1. By tradition, a member's maiden speech is not interrupted by other members.

10

What's Wrong with Politics?

Speech to the Conservative Political Centre Meeting in Connection with the Party Conference at Blackpool, October 10, 1968

Criticism of politics is no new thing. Literature abounds with it. In Shakespeare we find the comment of King Lear:

> Get thee glass eyes;
> And, like a scurvy politician, seem
> To see the things thou dost not.

Richard Sheridan, reputed to have made one of the greatest speeches the House of Commons has ever heard (it lasted five hours and forty minutes), commented that "conscience has no more to do with gallantry than it has with politics." Anatole France was perhaps the most scathing: "I am not so devoid of all talents as to occupy myself with politics."

Nor have political leaders escaped criticism:

> Disraeli unites the maximum of Parliamentary cleverness with the minimum of statesmanlike capacity. No one ever dreams to have him lead. He belongs not to the bees but to the wasps and the butterflies of public life. He can sting and sparkle but he cannot work. His place in the arena is marked and ticketed for ever

This from the Controller of the Stationery Office, in 1853, quoted in the *Statesman* by Henry Taylor. There is no need to remind you how utterly wrong that judgment was.

There are even some things that have improved over the years. Bribery and corruption, which have now gone, used to be rampant. The votes of electors were purchased at a high price. The famous Lord Shaftesbury, when he was Lord Ashley, spent £15,600 on successfully winning Dorset in 1831. It is interesting to note that £12,000 of this went to public houses and inns for the refreshment of the people. And this when gin was a penny a glass! Some forty years before, Lord Penrhyn spent £50,000 on his campaign—and then lost!

But we can't dismiss the present criticism as easily as that. The dissatisfaction with politics runs too deep both here and abroad. People have come to doubt the future of the democratic system and its institutions. They distrust the politicians and have little faith in the future.

Why the Present Distrust?

Let us try to assess how and why we have reached this pass. What is the explanation? Broadly speaking, I think we have not yet assimilated many of the changes that have come about in the past thirty to forty years.

First, I don't think we realise sufficiently how new our present democratic system is. We still have comparatively little experience of the effect of the universal franchise which didn't come until 1928. And the first election in this country which was fought on the principle of one person, one vote was in 1950. So we are still in the early stages of dealing with the problems and opportunities presented by everyone having a vote.

Secondly, this and other factors have led to a different party political structure. There is now little room for independent members, and the controversies which formerly took place outside the parties on the large number of measures now have to take place inside. There is, and has to be, room for a variety of opinions on certain topics within the broad general principles on which each party is based.

Thirdly, from the party political structure has risen the detailed programme which is placed before the electorate. Return to power on such a programme has led to a new doctrine that the party in power has a mandate to carry out everything in its manifesto. I myself doubt whether the voters really are endorsing each and every particular when they return a government to power.

This modern practise of an election programme had, I believe, influenced the attitudes of some electors; all too often one is now asked, "What are you going to do for me?" implying that the programme is a series of promises in return for votes. All this has led to a curious relationship between elector and elected. If the elector suspects the politician of making promises simply to get his vote, he despises him, but if the promises are not forthcoming, he may reject him. I believe that parties and elections are about more than rival lists of miscellaneous promises. Indeed, if they were not, democracy would scarcely be worth preserving.

Fourthly, the extensive and all-pervading development of the welfare state is also comparatively new, not only here but in other countries as well. You will recollect that one of the four great freedoms in President Roosevelt's wartime declaration was "freedom from want." Since then in the Western world there has been a series of measures designed to give greater security. I think it would be true to say that there is no longer a struggle to achieve a basic security. Further, we have a complete new generation whose whole life has been lived against the background of the welfare state. These developments must have had a great effect on the outlook and approach of our people even if we cannot yet assess it properly.

Fifthly, one of the effects of the rapid spread of higher education has been to equip people to criticise and question almost everything. Some of them seem to have stopped there instead of going on to the next stage which is to arrive at new beliefs or to reaffirm old ones. You will perhaps remember seeing in the press the report that the student leader Daniel Cohn-Bendit has been awarded a degree on the result of his past work. His examiners said that he had posed a series of most intelligent questions. Significant? I would have been happier had he also found a series of intelligent answers.

Sixthly, we have far more information about events than ever before, and since the advent of television, news is presented much more vividly. It is much more difficult to ignore situations which you have seen on film with your eyes than if you had merely read about them, perhaps skimming the page rather hurriedly. Television is not merely one extra means of communication; it is a medium which, because of the way it presents things, is radically influencing the judgments we have to make about events and about people, including politicians.

Seventhly, our innate international idealism has received many nasty shocks. Many of our people long to believe that if representatives of all nations get together dispassionately to discuss burning international problems, providence and goodwill will guide them to wise and just conclusions, and peace and international law and order will thereby be secured. But in practise a number of nations vote not according to right or wrong, even when it is a clear case to us, but according to their national expediencies. And some of the speeches and propaganda to explain blatant actions would make the angels weep as well as the electorate.

All of these things are a partial explanation of the disillusion and disbelief we encounter today. The changes have been tremendous, and I am not surprised that the whole system is under cross-examination. I welcome healthy skepticism and questioning. It is our job continually to retest old assumptions and to seek new ideas. But we must not try to find one unalterable answer that will solve all our problems, for none can exist. You may know the story of the soldier of fortune who once asked the Sphinx to reveal the divine wisdom of the ages in one sentence, and the Sphinx said: "Don't expect too much." In that spirit and against the background I have sketched, let us try to analyse what has gone wrong.

The Great Mistake—Too Much Government

I believe that the great mistake of the last few years has been for the government to provide or to legislate for almost everything. Part of this policy has its roots in the plans for reconstruction in the postwar period when governments assumed all kinds of new obligations. The policies may have been warranted at the time, but they have gone far further than was intended or is advisable. During our own early and middle period of government we were concerned to set the framework in which people could achieve their own standards for themselves, subject always to a basic standard.

But it has often seemed to me that from the early 1960s the emphasis in politics shifted. At about that time "growth" became the key political word. If resources grew by X percent per annum, this would provide the extra money needed for the government to make further provision. The doctrine found favour at the time, and we had a bit of a contest between the parties about the highest possible growth rate—four percent or more. But the result was that for the time being the emphasis in political debate ceased to be about people and became about economics. Plans were made to achieve a 4 percent growth rate. Then came the present government with a bigger plan and socialist ideas about its implementation. That is to say, if people didn't conform to the plan, they had to be compelled to; hence compulsion on prices and incomes policy, and with it the totally unacceptable notion that the government shall have the power to fix which wages and salaries should increase.

We started off with a wish on the part of the people for more government intervention in certain spheres. This was met. But there came a time when the amount of intervention got so great that it could no longer be exercised in practise by government, but only by more and more officials and bureaucrats. Now it is difficult, if not impossible, for people to get at the official making the decision. And so paradoxically, although the degree of intervention is greater, the government has become more and more remote from the people. The present result of the democratic process has therefore been an increasing authoritarianism.

During July the *Daily Telegraph* published a rather interesting poll which showed how people were reacting against this rule of impersonal authority. The question was: "In your opinion or not do people like yourselves have enough say or not" in the way the government runs the country (68 percent not enough), the services provided by the nationalised industries (67 percent not enough), the way local authorities handle things (64 percent not enough—note this rather high figure; people don't like remote local authorities any more than they like remote governments).

Recently more and more feature articles have been written and speeches made about involving people more closely with decisions of the government and enabling them to participate in some of those decisions. But the way to get personal involvement and participation is not for people to take part in more and more government decisions, but to make the government reduce the area of decision over which it presides and consequently leave the private citizen to "participate," if that be the fashionable word, by making more of his own decisions. What we need now is a far greater degree of personal responsibility and decision, far more independence from the government, and a comparative reduction in the role of government. These beliefs have important implications for policy.

Prices and Incomes

First prices and incomes policy. The most effective prices policy has not come by controlling prices by the government, through the Prices and Incomes Board, but through the Conservative way of seeing that competition flourishes. There have been far more price cuts in the supermarkets than in the nationalised industries. This shows the difference between the government doing the job itself and the government creating the conditions under which prices will be kept down through effective competition.

On the incomes side, there seemed to be some confusion in the minds of the electorate about where the parties stood. This was not surprising in the early days because a number of speeches and documents from both sides of the House showed a certain similarity. For example, here are four separate quotations—two from the Labour Government and two from our period of office. They are almost indistinguishable.

1. "Increases in the general level of wage rates must be related to increased productivity due to increased efficiency and effort." (White Paper on Employment Policy, 1944)

2. "It is essential therefore that there should be no further general increase in the level of personal incomes without at least a corresponding increase in the volume of production." (Sir Stafford Cripps, 1948)

3. "The Government's policy is to promote a faster rate of economic growth.... But the policy will be in jeopardy if money incomes rise faster than the volume of national production." (Para. 1 of Incomes Policy, *The Next Step,* Cmnd 1626, February 1962)

4. "...the major objectives of national policy must be...to raise productivity and efficiency so that real national output can increase and so keep increases in wages, salaries and other forms of income in line with this increase." (Schedule 2, Prices and Incomes Act, 1966)

All of these quotes express general economic propositions, but the policies which flowed from those propositions were very different. We rejected from the outset the use of compulsion. This was absolutely right. The role of the government is not to control each and every salary that is paid. It has no means of measuring the correct amount. Moreover, having to secure the state's approval before one increases the pay of an employee is repugnant to most of us.

There is another aspect of the way in which incomes policy is now operated to which I must draw attention. We now put so much emphasis on the control of incomes that we have too little regard for the essential role of government, which is the control of money supply and management of demand. Greater attention to this role and less to the outward detailed control would have achieved more for the economy. It would mean, of course, that the government had to exercise itself some of the discipline on expenditure it is so anxious to impose on others. It would mean that expenditure in the vast public sector would not have to be greater than the amount which could be financed out of taxation plus genuine saving. For a number of years some expenditure has been financed by what amounts to printing the money.

There is nothing *laissez-faire* or old-fashioned about the views I have expressed. It is a modern view of the role the government should play now, arising from the mistakes of the past, the results of which we are experiencing today.

Tax and the Social Services

The second policy implication concerns taxation and the social services. It is no accident that the Conservative Party has been one which has reduced the rates of taxation. The decisions have not been a haphazard set of expediencies, or merely economic decisions to meet the needs of the moment. They have stemmed from the real belief that government intervention and control tends to reduce the role of the individual, his importance, and the desirability that he should be primarily responsible for his own future. When it comes to the development of the social services, the policy must mean that people should be encouraged, if necessary, by taxation incentives to make increasing provision for themselves out of their own resources. The basic standard through the state would remain as a foundation for extra private provision. Such a policy would have the advantage that the government could concentrate on providing things which the citizen can't. Hospitals are one specific example.

The other day I came across a quotation which you will find difficult to place.

> Such a plan as this was bound to be drastic and to express nothing less than a new pattern ... (for the hospitals of this country). ... Now that we have it, we

must see that it lives. As I have said before, it is a plan which has hands and feet. It walks and it works. It is not a static conception stated once and for all but something which is intended to live and to be dynamic.... My Ministry will constantly be carrying this review forward so that there will always be ten years work definitely project ahead. (*Hansard*, 4th June 1962, Col. 153)

No, it doesn't come from Harold Wilson. It is not about our enormous overall plan, but a very limited plan in a small area in which the government could make a distinctive contribution. It was Enoch Powell introducing his ten-year hospital plan in the House of Commons on 4th June 1962.

Independence from the State

To return to the personal theme, if we accept the need for increasing responsibility for self and family, it means that we must stop approaching things in an atmosphere of restriction. There is nothing wrong in people wanting larger incomes. It would seem a worthy objective for men and women to wish to raise the standard of living for their families and to give them greater opportunities than they themselves had. I wish more people would do it. We would then have fewer saying, "the state must do it." What is wrong is that people should want more without giving anything in return. The condition precedent to high wages and high salaries is hard work. This is a quite different and much more stimulating approach than one of keeping down incomes.

Doubtless there will be accusers that we are only interested in more money. This just is not so. Money is not an end in itself. It enables one to live the kind of life of one's own choosing. Some will prefer to put a large amount to raising material standards; others will pursue music, the arts, the cultures; others will use their money to help those here and overseas about whose needs they feel strongly. And do not let us underestimate the amount of hard earned cash that this nation gives voluntarily to worthy causes. The point is that even the Good Samaritan had to have the money to help; otherwise he too would have had to pass on the other side.

In choice of way of life, J. S. Mill's views are as relevant as ever.

The only freedom which deserves the name is that of pursuing our own good in our own way so long as we do not deprive others of theirs, or impede their efforts to obtain it.... Mankind are greater gainers by suffering each other to live as seems good to themselves than by compelling each to live as seems good to the rest.

These policies have one further important implication. Together they succeed at the same time in giving people a measure of independence from the state, and who wants a people dependent on the state and turning to the state for their every need? Also they succeed in drawing power away from

governments and diffusing it more widely among people and non-govern-
mented institutions.

The Problem of Size

The second mistake politics have made at present is in some ways related
to the first one. We have become bewitched with the idea of size. As a result,
people no longer feel important in the scheme of things. They have the
impression that everything has become so big, so organised, so standardised
and governmentalised that there is no room for the individual, his talents,
his requirements or his wishes. He no longer counts.

It is not difficult to see how this feeling has come about. In industry the
merits of size have been extolled for some years now, and too little attention
given to its demerits. Size brings great problems. One of the most important
is the problem of making and communicating decisions. The task of decision
tends to be concentrated at the top, and fewer people get used to weighing
up a problem, taking a decision, sticking to it and carrying the consequences.
The buck is passed. But even after a decision has been made, there is the
problem of communicating it to those who have to carry it out in such a way
that it is understood, and they are made to feel a part of the team. In a
large-scale organisation, whether government, local government or industry,
failure to do this can lead to large-scale mistakes, large-scale confusion, and
large-scale resentment. These problems can and must be overcome, but all
too often they are not.

Government Agencies and the Public

The third mistake is that people feel they don't count when they try to get
something done through government agencies. Consider our relations with
government departments. We start as a birth certificate; attract a maternity
grant; give rise to a tax allowance and possibly a family allowance; receive a
national health number when registered with a doctor; go to one or more
schools where educational records are kept; apply for an educational grant;
get a job; start paying national insurance and tax; take out a television and a
driving license; buy a house with a mortgage; pay rates; buy a few premium
bonds; take out life assurance; purchase some shares; get married; start the
whole thing over again; receive a pension and become a death certificate and
death grant, and the subject of a file in the Estate Duty Office! Every one of
these incidents will require a form or give rise to some questions, or be
recorded in some local or national government office. The amount of
information collected in the various departments must be fabulous. Small
wonder that life really does seem like "one damned form after another."

A good deal of this form-filling will have to continue, but I think it is time to reassert a right to privacy. Ministers will have to look at this aspect in deciding how to administer their policies. There is a tendency on the part of some politicians to suggest that with the advent of computers all this information should be centralised and stored on magnetic tape. They argue that this would be time-saving and more efficient. Possibly it would; but other and more important things would be at stake. There would be produced for the first time a personal dossier about each person, on which everything would be recorded. In my view, this would place far too much power in the hands of the state over the individual. In the USA there is a Congressional enquiry sitting on this very point because politicians there have recognized the far-reaching dangers of such a record.

Fourthly, I believe that there is too great a reliance on statistical forecasts; too little on judgment. We all know the old one about lies, damned lies and statistics, and I do not wish to condemn statistics out of hand. Those who prepare them are well aware of their limitations. Those who use them are not so scrupulous.... The truth is that statistical results do not displace the need for judgment; they increase it. The figures can be no better than the assumptions on which they are based, and these could vary greatly. In addition, the unknown factor which by its very nature is incapable of evaluation may well be the determining one.

The Party Political System

Fifthly, we have not yet appreciated or used fully the virtues of our party political system. The essential characteristic of the British constitutional system is not that there is an alternative personality, but that there is an alternative policy and a whole alternative government ready to take office. As a result, we have always had an opposition to act as a focus of criticism against the government. We have therefore not suffered the fate of countries which have had a "consensus" or central government, without an official opposition. This was one of the causes of trouble in Germany. Nor do we have the American system, which, as far as presidential campaigns go, appears to have become almost completely one of personalities.

There are dangers in consensus; it could be an attempt to satisfy people holding no particular views about anything. It seems more important to have a philosophy and policy which, because they are good, appeal to sufficient people to secure a majority.

A short time ago when speaking to a university audience and stressing the theme of second responsibility and independence, a young undergraduate came to me and said: "I had no idea there was such a clear alternative." He found the idea challenging and infinitely more effective than one in which

FIGURE 10.1 Thatcher speaks at the Lord Mayor's Banquet in the Gildhall, London, November 12, 1979. Lord Mayor Sir Peter Gadsden is seated beside her. (*Source:* British Information Services, New York.)

everyone virtually expects their MP or the government to solve their problems. The Conservative creed has never offered a life of ease without effort. Democracy is not for such people. Self-government is for those men and women who have learned to govern themselves. No great party can survive except on the basis of firm beliefs about what it wants to do. It is not enough to have reluctant support. We want people's enthusiasm as well.

11

Changes in World Affairs

To a Meeting of Chelsea Constituency Association,
July 26, 1975

Already this year, we have seen remarkable changes in world affairs. Here in Britain the question of our membership of the European Community has been clearly and dramatically settled. The policies we have pursued over the past years have been overwhelmingly supported by the British people. Membership is no longer an issue. The argument is over, and we are established as full partners, accepting the comradeship of our fellow Europeans. Now it is up to us to make our contribution to a new Europe.

But it is a dangerous world that we live in. Freedom has taken a major battering over the last few months. Close to home in Portugal the first faint flickers of democracy are being snuffed out by Communist reaction. Further East the island of Cyprus is torn by communal strife. Next door Middle Eastern neighbours struggle to achieve a just and lasting settlement.

Meanwhile, the world's most formidable navy, not America's, not Britain's, but Russia's, relentlessly extends its power from the Mediterranean to the Indian Ocean. Only this spring the Soviet fleets displayed their awesome new potential to strike at the world's shipping lanes in the largest navel manoeuvres ever staged. Yet this is the moment the Labour government has chosen to start pulling the Royal Navy out of the Mediterranean and to ditch the Simonstown Agreement. In South East Asia the loss of South Vietnam and Cambodia was a major setback for the free world. Who can tell where it will end?

To remain free we must stay strong and alert. In purely economic terms a united Western Europe is as powerful as the Soviet Union. But in military terms we are much weaker. The Soviet Union now spends twenty percent more each year than the United States on military research and development, twenty-five percent more on weapons and equipment, sixty percent more on strategic nuclear forces. Then there is the Soviet Navy, now a global force. It has more nuclear submarines than the rest of the world's navies put together. It has more surface ships than could possibly be needed to protect the Soviet Union's own coast and merchant shipping. Can anyone truly describe this as a defensive weapon?

In the light of these facts, it is clear that the safety of Europe can only be secured within the Western Alliance. America remains by far the most powerful element in that alliance. Only two months ago, President Ford specially visited Europe to emphasise that America's interest in our security is undiminished. Perhaps this was the most important declaration of recent months. He renewed American pledges that United States troops would not be reduced in Europe except in response to real concessions by the Warsaw Pact. Nothing could be more important and nothing will curb Russian opportunism more surely than the knowledge that America stands at Europe's side. Together we can preserve freedom for us all.

But during the past few months freedom has come under heavy attack. Those who protested against American involvement in Vietnam and Cambodia have since overlooked and even managed to ignore the open savagery of the Khmer Rouge. Where are the protest marchers now? These events are tragic for the peoples of Vietnam and Cambodia. There was a feeling here in Europe, as in Asia, that the parties and people of the United States might be falling into a mood of isolationism. Many feared a withdrawal of the most powerful democracy from the centre of world affairs. Fortunately, this has not happened, but the less willing and able we Europeans become to carry our share of the common burden, the less willing the Americans will be to man the defences with us.

An isolationist Britain would encourage an isolationist America. The Conservative Party rejects any such course. We took Britain into Europe; Conservatives more than anyone else kept Britain in Europe during the Referendum. In joining as full partners in the European Community, we did not, and we shall not, turn our back on the Atlantic world. It was one of the greatest Conservative leaders—Winston Churchill—who cemented our alliance with America. It is just as much our duty to help keep America in Europe as it is to help Europe maintain its close links with America.

The Atlantic Alliance is the formal expression of the common interest of the nations of Free Europe and North America. NATO, a part of it, was formed and is maintained to counter any threat of Soviet expansion. Of course, we want a world in which our relations with the Soviet Union are based upon peace and trust, as they ought to be with every country. But if we have not yet got that world, and plainly we have not, then merely saying so, merely pretending that we have, is as foolish as it is dangerous. This is the background to the Summit Conference on European Security and Co-operation which meets at Helsinki next week.

Detente sounds a fine word. And, to the extent that there really has been a relaxation in international tension, it is a fine thing. But the fact remains that throughout this decade of detente, the armed forces of the Soviet Union have increased, are increasing, and show no signs of diminishing. Mr. Brezhnev, in a speech in June 1972, made a statement on detente which is quoted in virtually every Soviet speech or article on the subject. He said that peaceful co-existence "in no way implies the possibility of relaxing the ideological struggle. On the contrary, we must be prepared for this struggle to be intensified and become an even sharper form of confrontation between the systems." Within the last month the two Soviet leaders specially concerned with Communism in the West, Messrs. Suslov and Ponomarev, have reasserted the same point, if anything, more strongly. There can be little doubt that if a leading Western statesman made an equivalent statement, he would be bitterly condemned by the Soviets as an enemy of detente in Europe.

On our side we long for a *real* detente. We demand only that it is a *reality*, a reality which Russia supports in actions as well as words. We in this country allow full and free expression for the point of view of the Soviet Union and its supporters here. But they have ruthlessly trampled on the ideals of the West in every country where it is in their power to do so.

Czechoslovakia in 1968 showed that the Soviets are prepared not only to destroy liberty, but also to crush systematically any brand of Communism which differs from their own. They are in principle arrayed against everything for which we stand. So when the Soviet leaders jail a writer, or a priest, or a doctor or a worker, for the crime of speaking freely, it is not only for humanitarian reasons that we should be concerned. For these acts reveal a country that is afraid of truth and liberty; it dare not allow its people to enjoy the freedoms we take for granted, and a nation that denies those freedoms to its own people will have few scruples in denying them to others.

If detente is to progress, then it ought to mean that the Soviet authorities relax their ruthless opposition to all forms and expressions of dissent. And as we talk of these things, we naturally think of Alexander Solzhenitsyn and the other writers, thinkers, and scientists who have fearlessly expressed their belief in freedom. They are not politicians or diplomats. But they have gained a deep understanding of the real attitudes and intentions of the Soviet ruling clique. And that understanding has taught them that the only way to obtain real concessions is by standing firm. Indeed, the whole history of negotiation with the Soviet Union teaches us that if you do something they want without insisting on something in return, the Soviets do not regard it as a kindness to be reciprocated, but as a weakness to be exploited.

There is a lot of fashionable nonsense talked about how we misunderstand Communism, misrepresent Communism, see Communists under every bed. An attempt is being made, its seems, to create an atmosphere where truth and common sense on these matters are actively discouraged. I believe the people of this country understand better the truth of the matter than those who try to mislead them.

We must work for a real relaxation of tension, but in our negotiations with the Eastern bloc we must not accept words or gestures as a substitute for genuine detente. No flood of words emanating from a summit conference will mean anything unless it is accompanied by some positive action by which the Soviet leaders show that their ingrained attitudes are really beginning to change. That is why we so strongly support all those European and American spokesmen who have insisted that no serious advance toward a stable peace can be made unless some progress at least is seen in the free movement of people and ideas. We in Europe have always been specially concerned that an accord with the Soviets should involve some progress in this direction. We would like them to read our books and newspapers just as we can read theirs. We would like them to visit our countries just as we can go to theirs. We will be alert not to miss the moment when the Soviets turn to genuine detente. But until that is achieved, we must quietly determine to maintain Western military strength at a level adequate to deter any aggression.

At this very moment we are all watching with apprehension the events in Portugal where a Communist clique is trying to manoeuvre its way to power. Indeed, recent press reports suggest that the Portuguese Communist Party, which seems to regard twelve percent of the popular vote as an entitlement to absolute power, is being subsidised by the Soviet Union. We must hope and work for the triumph of those moderate elements which yet survive in Portuguese politics. A democracy in which only left-wing parties are allowed is not a democracy at all.

How then should we approach the urgent need to relax tension in the world? We must be firm in our desire for real detente, provided it is real. We must work hard for disarmament, provided it is genuine and balanced. But let us accept no proposals which would tip the balance of power still further against the West. The power of NATO is already at its lowest safe limit. And it is worth drawing the attention of some of our more gullible disarmers to the fact that if we reduce our conventional forces further, then should hostilities break out, there would be no effective middle course between surrender or the early use of nuclear weapons.

We should, of course, be prepared to give and take, but not to give something for nothing. We want neither confrontation nor unilateral concessions. Serious and solid negotiation is the only way to real detente and lasting peace. In this dangerous world we must never allow the momentum of reconciliation to slacken. Let us recognize that we in the West have a common interest and a common purpose: the pursuit and preservation of liberty. That is the basis of our unity and determination. Without that unity we should be weak. With it we can be strong—strong to preserve a peace that will endure.

FIGURE 12.1 Margaret and Denis Thatcher in the garden at 10 Downing Street, London. (*Source:* British Information Services, New York.)

12

Britain's Economic Problems:
Roots and Solutions

*Speeches Delivered in the United States,
September 15–16, 1975*

Let the Children Grow Tall[1]

Vermont Royster wrote that: "Britain today offers a textbook case on how to ruin a country." I do take some consolation that there is only one vowel sound difference between "ruin" and "run" a country. That small vowel sound is "I." However, the rather morbid and fatalistic tone of much of what is written about Britain by commentators on both sides of the Atlantic is misplaced.

I think most outside observers have not noticed that amidst our well-published difficulties a new debate is beginning —or perhaps I should say an old debate is being renewed—about the proper role of government, the welfare state and the attitudes on which it rests. May I stress that the attitudes are extremely important. Of course, many of the issues at stake have been debated on countless occasions in the last century or two, and some are as old as philosophy itself. But, the welfare state in Britain is now at least thirty years old. So after a long period in which it was unquestionably accepted by the whole society, we can now do more than discuss its strengths and weaknesses in the hackneyed, abstract language of moral and political principles. We can depart from theory and actually look at the

---

1. This was the title of a speech, a lengthy extract of which follows, delivered to the Institute for Economic Studies, New York, September 15, 1975.

evidence and see how it has worked and what effect it has had on the economy. We ought now to assess it before we decide what to go on and do next.

Consensus on Welfare State

The debate is centered on what I shall term, for want of a better phrase, the "progressive consensus." Things that are called progressive are not always progressive in practise. But, of course, some of them are—and the progressive consensus is the doctrine that the state should be active on many fronts in promoting equality in the provision of social welfare and in the redistribution of wealth and income. That philosophy is well-expressed in a quotation well-known in my country about social justice—and again I pause for a moment to point out that if you ever see a word with "social" in front of it, I think you ought to analyse it fairly carefully and see precisely what it means. One of the reasons I think we have got some things a little bit not-quite-straight is that we have not always been precise with our use of language. If you are going to think straight, you must talk straight and be very precise with the way you use your words.

There is a quotation on social justice. It is: "Because market forces tend toward growing inequality in incomes and property, massive redistribution is necessary if political freedom and other civilized values are to be preserved. So it should be the aim of the democratic state to re-share these rewards—to socialize the national income if you like to call it that. There can be no doubt that by far the most effective method has proved to be the instrument of public finance, and in particular progressive direct taxation and centrally financed public services."

Now, that is the end of the quotation on social justice. It so happens that it was written in 1962 by a former Labour cabinet minister. However, I am not particularly interested in party politics tonight. For such views are held in varying degrees in all our political parties, in schools and universities, and amongst social commentators generally. It is interesting that they are now being questioned right across the same broad spectrum.

It is not that our people are suddenly reverting to the ideals of total *laissez faire*, or rejecting the social advances of recent decades. It is rather that they are reviving a sober and constructive interest in the noble ideals of personal responsibility, because in some respects the concepts of social responsibility have turned sour in the practise, and we are making an attempt to identify and eliminate errors and fallacies to consolidate and retrench before advancing further.

It is in that constructive spirit, and as a former Secretary of State for Education and Science myself, that I am speaking. I shall try and concentrate on three broad issues, particularly in view of that quotation which I read to you a short time ago which has some very strange phrases in it. The three issues are: One, what are the facts about the distribution of wealth and incomes? Two, to what extent is greater equality desired in Britain today? Three, has the economy been strengthened by the promotion of more equality and the extension of the welfare state?

Distribution of Wealth and Income

Now, what I have to say involves quite a number of statistics because with a measure of scientific training and a period spent at the Revenue Bar and dealing with treasury matters, one has tried to adduce a mass of evidence. But I will try and put the statistic in as human a way as I can. So, let me start with the fact. All of you in either science or law, and the wiser ones in politics, say one first must find the facts.

Most people say that the distribution of the incomes and wealth in Britain is highly inequitable, that it has changed little, despite the steps taken by government to even it out. From there, it is only a short step to two complementary arguments: either that redistribution would greatly swell the incomes of the average man, or that the wealth of the rich is sufficient to finance the substantial extension of the role of the state. I think both are conducive, but neither of them are attitudes which I think we would particularly wish to encourage in the modern state.

Fortunately, a major study has just been published by the newly created Standing Royal Commission on the Distribution of Income and Wealth. It gives the first proper statistical picture of the changes that have taken place in Britain between the last war and the year 1972–73, the latest year for which figures are available. May I quickly tell the findings because these are the facts on the distributions of income and wealth. Let us start with income, and, of course, the relevant income is income-after-taxes. We find that in 1972 income-after-taxes in Britain was divided roughly as follows— at the upper end of the scale, the top one percent of income earners got four percent of income, four times the average. If you take the top ten percent, they had twice the average, and if you take the bottom ten percent, a bit under half the average. Now, if you look at it from half the average income at the bottom to four times the average income at the top, it is not really a very wide range of income. It is not dramatic by any set of rules. Indeed, research has shown that the distribution of income in Britain is surprisingly similar to that of Poland, which is a rather shattering conclusion to reach!

That is where we were in 1972. So let us have a look at the changes. Over the previous forty or so years, you find that, taking account of taxes, the share of taxable wealth of the top one percent of earners, which used to be twelve percent, is now four percent. So it has come down over forty years from about twelve percent to about four percent. And, the share of the taxable income of the poor has not increased to so great an extent. But, nonetheless, they are markedly better off in relative as well as in absolute terms than they were before the war. By 1972, the tax-free benefits in cash and kind added about half to the pre-tax income of a typical household in the bottom ten percent. For poor families with many dependents, the gain could be nearer 100 percent. Today the figures would probably be higher still. Now, those are the income figures. They show quite considerable changes over forty years. But at the moment in Great Britain, the range of income is not unduly wide.

Let us turn quickly to have a look at wealth. Of course, capital assets have been more unevenly spread than income in Britain, as in most other countries. For this reason they have been the chief target of egalitarian critics. In Britain, it is almost an undisputed truth that ten percent of the population owns eighty or ninety percent of all assets. But, in fact, that is not so. The Royal Commission has now set up the figures. You find that ten percent of the population over eighteen own less than half of personal wealth, when state pension rights are counted as an asset, as they should be. As you will appreciate, even these figures are rather misleading, since wealth is normally unevenly distributed between husbands and wives, old and young. If these distorting factors could be properly allowed for, the picture might well look still less extreme.

As with income, there have been big changes over the years. On a narrow definition of wealth which excludes pension rights, the top one percent of the population owned: personal wealth of sixty-nine percent in 1911; personal wealth of fifty percent in 1938; personal wealth of thirty-eight percent in 1960; and personal wealth of twenty-eight percent in 1972 (or 16.5 percent if pension rights are included in wealth holdings). So the facts about economic inequality (as opposed to the myths) are these: the rich are getting poorer and the poor are getting richer. This is due both to market forces and the actions of government through the tax system. And it is no longer the case that taking further money from the rich will make a significant difference to the wealth of the bulk of the population. Nor will taxing them more heavily pay for much more government spending. Finally, one notes that it would do little to diffuse economic power more widely. It is already largely in the hands of government and labour unions.

Is More Equality Desired?

So much for the facts of economic inequality in Britain. Now, let me look at the second question: To what extent is more equality desired in Great

Britain today? These statistical myths lead directly to the claim that there is a widespread sense of resentment and injustice over the current degree of inequality in our society and great enthusiasm for its elimination. This political judgment is closely linked in many commentators' eyes with the quite separate proposition that class divisions in Britain are severe and reinforced by economic inequality.

My own experience in politics has always made me doubt that argument. Now, fortunately, more work has been done. We have had a massive survey of political and economic groups reported in July 1975. This is what it showed: "... little spontaneous demand for the redistribution of earnings across broad occupational categories and the suggestion that any such redistribution would in itself provide no solution to any problems of pressure-on-pay. Neither is it necessary to allay any general feelings of injustice in society.... It may be little consolation to the government in present circumstances that the chief requirement for maintaining general satisfaction with incomes and earnings is steady economic growth... rather than massive redistribution.... This point is a crucial one to be met by those who suggest that any problem we have is one of distribution rather than of resources of growth."

Despite the evidence of what ordinary people actually want, there remains in Britain a powerful and vocal lobby pressing for greater equality—in some cases even, it would seem, for total equality. One tries to analyze what it is that impels them to do so? Of course, one important pressure is undoubtedly the ordinary desire to help our fellow man. But often the reasons boil down to an undistinguished combination of envy and what might be termed "Bourgeois Guilt."

Envy is clearly at work in the case of the egalitarian who resents the gap between himself and those who are better off, while conveniently forgetting his own obligations to those poorer than himself. Bourgeois guilt is that well-known sense of guilt and self-criticism that affects people, not only the very rich, when looking the other way, at the position of those poorer than themselves. It is not for me as an individual to criticize or ridicule their doubts and worries. But as a politician, I must criticize the attempts of such people to impose on others a program of impoverishment through the medium of the state. That brings happiness to no one except to those who impose it. In a free society, they can give away as much as they want to, to whom they want to. If they believe in pooling their possessions with others in a commune, they are welcome to do so.

The point of this section is that it has been shown that there is a far less general desire for equality, as opposed to equity, in Britain today, than is often claimed. The facts about equality are that people don't appear to want further distribution. They are more interested in growth and new resources of wealth.

Economic Effects of Pursuing Equality

Now, I can turn to the third section—a vital one—called, "Is socializing national income good for the economy?" The promotion of greater equality goes hand-in-hand with the extension of the welfare state and state control over people's lives. Universal and usually free social services necessarily transfer benefits-in-kind and cash from the richer to the poorer members of the community. Taken together, they define rather well the process of "socializing the national income" which occurs in my first quotation. How far has it strengthened our economy?

The public sector has been a large part of the British economy since the early post-war years. Despite the statistical fog which surrounds all international comparisons, it is clear that the government's share in GNP has been consistently one of the highest of the OECD countries. And for at least twenty years it has risen faster in the UK than elsewhere. Today the state controls in various ways well over half of our national income. In fact, this year about fifty-six percent of the gross national product is controlled and spent by the state.

Now, of course, the tax-bill has risen sharply, particularly for the private citizen. In the later '50s and '60s, the increase in tax and social security payments in effect knocked about one percent off the gross of private spending each year. The massive transfer of resources from the private to the public sector—and correspondingly to that an enormous increase in taxation—is what has been probably one of the major sources of inflation.

Let me take a typical wage earner, a man and wife with two children, with industrial earnings. Typically, you find that since 1963—not very long ago—the state has increased its take from the average salary from a negligible five percent to about twenty-five percent today. But, of course, you can imagine what has happened. The wage earner has said, "I want to keep my net tax income intact." This sentiment has been quite a strong factor in his demanding more wages and salaries, as replacement for what has been taken away in taxation. So they press their employers for ever-higher wage increases, and this has led to a relentless acceleration of cost and price increases, from two percent per annum in the mid-1930s to twenty-five percent today. And so, of course, they have also pressed not only for increased pay, but for increased growth, sometimes financed by inflationary policies. Of course, it is one thing to have increased government expenditures when you have genuine increased growth. It is quite another thing to go on increasing government spending when you have no growth.

There are many who regard this desire for private spending as irrational, selfish, and unworthy. After all, they say, the taxes have financed a substantial growth in the provision of public goods. Any economist will tell one that this is a part of increasing living standards. Unfortunately, any experienced politician or detached observer can also now see that in practise people attach peculiar importance to using their own money to buy what they want when they want. Moreover, they cannot relate the tax-man's apparently arbitrary and growing take to the services it finances. These services they regard as one's absolute right, a kind of manna from heaven. We will come to the end of that time. They are not manna from heaven.

I know you will find that this has a familiar sound to some of the problems that you have to deal with now. So, that is how the average person has reacted to what is called "socializing the national income." He expects the benefits to come from somewhere, but he is not prepared to pay increased taxes (and remember I said in Britain the government controls fifty-six percent of the expenditure of the gross national product). One consequence is a very heavy taxation on companies. In turn, company profits have steadily been reduced and they have had to pay increased corporation taxes.

The inexorable acceleration of wages, partly in response to overtaxation, has naturally resulted in a wage-price spiral—a spiral with a twist in it. For various reasons, business cannot raise prices far enough or quickly enough to preserve its profits when wage increases are large and accelerating. So, profits have fallen for many years on any measure—before tax, after tax, as share in national income or as a rate of return on capital. Since retained profits are the principal source of funds for investment and profit levels, the main incentive, capital expenditure in private industry, has faltered more and more. The upswings have got shorter and the downswings deeper and longer with succeeding cycles of activity. Manufacturing investment next year—1976—is likely to be little higher in real terms than it was ten years before. It appears, as a natural consequence, that our underlying rate of economic growth has stopped improving after thirty years of modest but perceptible acceleration.

The situation has not been made any easier recently by the curious belief that profits are rather evil and of little economic significance. Both the present and previous governments have therefore had little choice but to pursue price and profit controls as part of their counter-inflationary policies. The levels of profit emerging from these controls were selected with insufficient regard for their effects on capital spending, employment, or growth, and they have bitten hard. Our economy has thus been pushed into a loss of profit and therefore an investment recession at a time when the world economy was in serious downturn. Now the damage has been done. The situation can only be put to rights if considerable price rises can be made and accepted by labour without any response in the form of wage increases. It is a pretty challenging "IF."

Two decades of declining profits naturally mean that the saver who invests in equity shares has had a raw deal. The real rate of return has recently been negative even before tax, let alone when changes in the capital value of investments are allowed for. However, government has made the position worse by taking powers to restrain dividends further—in the name of fairness and equity, one should note! The case for doing so was simple. Unless profit distribution is restrained, how, it was asked, could one expect unions and workers to acquiesce in a program of wage restraint?

It is bad enough that this seductive little trade-off is based on a very unjust bargain. Savers and retired people have already suffered severely from the costs of accelerating inflation which they have done nothing to cause. Why should they make yet further sacrifices to induce those who have already gained so much at their expense to desist for a while? What is at stake is more than a painful injustice. Negative real profits and dividend control must, if sustained for any period, have a corrosive effect on the life insurance and pensions institutions. They are put in a position in which it becomes more and more difficult to plan and guarantee the flow of future income which they have promised their beneficiaries. Private employers for their part find themselves faced with a sudden need to make enormous payments into their pension funds even to maintain their existing pension obligations in money terms. I am not suggesting for a moment that these great institutions are dying or dead. But they have a nasty fight on their hands.

Some of the problems I have talked about combine together to create further subtle distortions of the marketplace which are not immediately evident. The first is an unbalanced competition for savings. The process works like this. The government increases its spending to fulfill its commitments to extend its activities. The wage earner begins to revolt against the consequent rising tax burden. His resentment leads to higher wages, and lower profits, lower corporate taxes, and ultimately slower growth. It also deters the government from raising taxes in line with spending. So the government has a growing deficit and then has to borrow growing sums of money, assuming, of course, that it does not resort to the printing press. In doing so, it competes with the private company and the home-buyer in the savings market. The private company finds it increasingly impossible to bid for funds, since its profits are depressed. The housebuyer may still be able to do so, but even then he is probably subsidised by the savers who lend him the money. At the end of the day, a public spending bill which exceeds the taxable capacity of the economy sucks away money which should be spent on investment in industry or private housing.

The second distortion is an unbalanced competition for labour. As wealth increases, spending patterns switch from industrial products toward services in all economies. This will affect the pattern of employment and competition for labour between the private and government sectors. Public sector employment in Britain has steadily grown at a substantial rate for more than a decade—about one percent per annum—while the overall working population has contracted. The net effect has been to reduce the pool of labour available to private employers. So when the economy entered its last major upswing, in 1972-73, labour shortages were encountered unexpectedly soon. Although the leap in production was as large and sudden as any we have experienced, employment in industry scarcely increased at all. Many of the missing workers had in effect been absorbed by government during the previous period of slack business activity. The importance of this cannot be understated, particularly for a trading economy like ours. The private sector creates the goods and services we need both to export to pay for our imports and the revenue to finance public services. So one must not over-load it. Every man switched away from industry and into government will reduce the productive sector and increase the burden on it at the same time.

One other effect that I would like to refer to in Great Britain about the incentive effect of taxation is that it has been particularly damaging on middle and upper management. The level of taxation has been such that it has not been possible for us to pay our management as much as they could get in other countries in net taxed income. For example, a British employer wanting to promote his manager in terms of post-tax salary from 8,000 per annum to a top job and 12,000 per annum, would have to give him an extra 15,000 per annum! This sort of increase is more than most firms can think of at the best of times. Thus, rewarding skill or hard work has become almost prohibitive. The whole country therefore loses much of the benefit of competition in the labour market.

If you look across to the continent, you will find that other countries may be able to pay their managers less, but they nonetheless provide a much higher net taxed income. The result has been, if British companies put top management in Europe or elsewhere on French salaries or French levels, they cannot get them back. We cannot pay a big enough gross salary. Accordingly, losses of highly trained manpower through emigration are becoming more serious despite the depressed state of the world economy.

These have been the economic effects of pursuing far too much equality. I think we have very much come to the end of the road. In fact, we find that the persistent expansion of the role of the state and the relentless pursuit of equality have caused, and are causing, damage to our economy in a variety of ways. It is not the sole cause of what some have termed the "British Sickness," but it is a major one.

Lessons from the Past

What lessons have we learned from the past thirty years?

First, the pursuit of equality is a mirage. What is more desirable and more practisable than the pursuit of equality is the pursuit of equality of opportunity. And opportunity means nothing unless it includes the right to be unequal. And the freedom to be different.

One of the reasons why we value individuals is not because they are all the same, but because they are all different. I believe you have a saying in the Middle West, "Don't cut down the tall poppies—let them rather grow taller." I would say: "Let the children grow tall—and some grow taller than others, if they have it in them to do so." We must build a society in which each citizen can develop his full potential both for his own benefit and for the community as a whole; in which originality, skill, energy, and thrift are rewarded; in which we encourage rather than restrict the variety and richness of human nature. . . .

Nothing that I am saying should in any way be seen as a diminution of our recognized responsibilities to those people who, through physical, mental or social handicaps, suffer disadvantages. Rather, it is a consciousness that unless we have incentive and opportunity, we shall not have the resources to do as much as we want to do. Having been a Secretary of State for Education, I am the first to understand that.

Second, we must strike a proper balance between the growing demands and powers of the state and the vital role of private enterprise. For private enterprise is by far the best method of harnessing the energy and ambition of the individual to increasing the wealth of the nation; for pioneering new products and technologies; for holding down prices to the mechanism of competition; and, above all, for widening the range of choice of goods and services and jobs. Government must therefore limit its activities where its scope and scale harms profits, investment, innovation and future growth. It must temper what may be socially desirable with what is economically reasonable.

Third, we must measure the consequences of the economic and political demands of some of our people. We must have regard for the effect of those demands on our political and social framework. We must devote ourselves to a greater understanding and more realistic pursuit of true justice and liberty and the maintenance of the free institutions on which these values depend. . . .

Tragically, we are a nation that lived beyond our means. . . . For thirty-five years we have been going on, expanding our expenditures. All of a sudden, we are quite surprised when reality arrives. We are now up against reality. And that is always the best time for politicians to get some of their views across. It is also a situation that neither the politicians nor the people can ignore. It is a time to take active steps to put things right. I think that reality has arrived for us. . . .

What Has Happened to a Proud Nation?[2]

Wherever I travel in the world, one thing is obvious: there is a wealth of goodwill towards Great Britain. Our friends are willing to help us surmount our problems. Somehow they recognize that in Britain democracy is on trial and that if Britain were to break, a well-nigh mortal blow would be struck against the whole Western ideal.

Whatever our present shortcomings in the eyes of the world, we still stand for those fundamental freedoms which are the breath of life to nations who believe in human dignity; for a just and impartial rule of law without which there can be no freedom, no certainty, no security; and for a stubborn independent character which would capitulate to neither man nor nation nor alien creed.

What then has happened to this proud nation? We are beset by problems, some common to other countries, some of our own making. For too long we have played the soft options. They lead where we Conservatives always said they would lead—to inflation at twenty-five percent; to unemployment over one million; to a lower standard of living; to a lesser standard of living. Let me update some of the sentiments of a famous American: You cannot pay yourself more money unless you do more work. You cannot print more money unless you produce more goods. You cannot have more jobs unless you have more investment. You cannot have more investment unless you have more savings. You cannot have more savings unless you keep faith with the saver. You cannot keep faith with the saver unless you have sound money. You cannot have sound money if you spend beyond your means. But you can't increase your means unless you increase your effort. And there we are back where we started.

Perhaps these things can be summed up with the phrase: "You cannot have self-government unless you have learned self-discipline." If we ignore these truths, if we encourage people to talk of "free" services and of government expenditure as if neither really affects their own pockets, but only other people's, then it will be a long time before we really beat inflation and start to create more wealth instead of redistributing what we already have. Some of these lessons, I fear, have got lost in Britain. But the underlying sense of the British people is sound. These fundamental truths strike a chord which we cannot fail to hear. We have been brought face to face with today's realities, and we must act now, if we are to keep pace with tomorrow's world.

My party's policies would, of course, be different from those of the present government, and at home I am continually critical of some of the

---

2. What follows are remarks made to the Pilgrims of the U.S., New York, September 16, 1975.

things they do. But the ability, inventiveness, and determination of our people are just as much there today as they were in the past. You can count on them for the future. There is too a new determination—that the will of the commonsense majority shall prevail, as it prevailed in the recent referendum [to join the European Community]. We are an eleventh hour nation. But the eleventh hour has struck. There is yet time to prepare for the morrow.

Progress Through Interdependence[3]

In 1976 we shall be commemorating two bicentenaries—the bicentenary of the Declaration of Independence and the bicentenary of the publication of the *Inquiry into the Nature and Causes of the Wealth of Nations* by Adam Smith. This remarkable Scottish philosopher set out in over a thousand pages the first systematic description of the economic process. It was widely acclaimed and read throughout the literate world. Its influence was profound. Adam Smith in fact heralded the end of the strait-jacket of feudalism and released all the innate energy of private initiative and enterprise which enabled wealth to be created on a scale never before contemplated.

Economists and Politicians

Now, in my view, it is significant that the chairs of economics at the Scottish universities are still known as chairs of political economy, for there is a profound difference between political economy and economics, of which a practising politician should become very aware. Much of the teaching of economics in the Western world has become divorced from practical politics. As a result, much economic writing, though academically respectable, seems to the politician to have little relevance to the problems he has to solve. Economic dissertations have become more and more theoretical, more and more mathematical, and to the politician less and less

---

3. The following discussion is taken from the third of her September speeches in the U.S. A paper with this title was printed in London in the autumn of 1975.

human. This has the unfortunate result that many politicians in formulating policy have failed to take into account the underlying realities of economics.

I welcome... the opportunity to explore some of the difficult problems faced by politicians as they grapple with the very complex problems in the realms of national and international financial and economic policy. These problems tend to be associated with ironing out the extremes of the business cycle. Politicians would dearly like there to be a steady upward sloping line of economic activity, but attempts to intervene in the cycle to smooth out the peaks and troughs have not been very successful. Between them politicians seem to have a propensity for getting the timing wrong, and sometimes reinforce the trend they are trying to eliminate. But when political intervention does not produce the desired results, the reaction is to impose still further controls which slow up enterprise and lead to greater inefficiency in the system. The ultimate result of this process is the corporate state, with its restriction on human liberty, absence of choice, and suppression of alternative forms of government, coupled with an actual lowering of the material standard of living.

But if the politician tends not to achieve the results he or the people he represents desire, because he neglects economic realities, some economists have shown similar lack of understanding of politics by suggesting that they (the economists) know all the answers, implying that it is the incompetence of politicians which produces the problems. But the realities of the world are such that we must always consider the political consequences of proposed economic solutions. Otherwise, the economists will not achieve their desired results either. This is not just an academic point. It is one that is at the heart of political economy today. In the economic sphere it has resulted in growing frustrations for both the people (because of the disincentives to be enterprising and responsible), and politicians because their efforts have not borne the results they expected.

Keynesian Economics

There are, I believe, some economic, physical, and also moral laws which just cannot be repealed even by the most authoritarian regimes. Since the late 1930s, we in the Western world have especially relied on one great economist—Lord Keynes—for his insights into economic affairs to guide on policy matters, particularly in regard to high levels of unemployment. He did his main thinking in the 1930s when the depression in North America and Europe was at its height. To some extent the *General Theory*, published in 1936, reflects this situation. Certainly it answered the critics of the day who saw the imminent demise of capitalism as certain.

One wonders what Keynes would have advised concerning the control of inflation, if he had been alive today. A look at his writings other than the *General Theory* may give us some clues; I suggest that the answer is not what some of his latterday disciples are advising. Certainly his advice would have been to balance budgets over longer time periods than one year, but balance them is the key phrase. I do not believe he would have advocated running a continuous and growing borrowing requirement year in, year out. He recognized that a stable value of currency was as essential to the survival of capitalism as oxygen is to life.

Perhaps one quotation from his early writings, *The Economic Consequences of the Peace*, will illustrate what I mean: "There is no subtler, no surer means of overturning the existing basis of society than to debauch the currency. The process engages all the hidden forces of economic law on the side of destruction, and does it in a manner which not one man in a million is able to diagnose." The Nobel Laureate, Friedrich Hayek, wrote recently: "I have good reason to believe that he [Keynes] would have disapproved of what his followers did in the post-war period. If he had not died so soon, he would have become one of the leaders in the fight against inflation."

In the United States the authorities have succeeded in bringing the inflation rate down to levels which might be described as tolerable. This has been done at some cost, but it has been done. In the United Kingdom we have not had this degree of success. It has taken us a long time to come to realize as a nation that unless we elevate the reduction of inflation to a first priority in policy, moral values, our social and political institutions, and the very fabric of our society will fall apart.

Meanwhile, we have a rate of inflation (twenty-five percent per annum) which has become quite intolerable to live with for ordinary decent people to whom thrift and hard work are virtues. We also have an official unemployment rate which, for us, is high: one and a quarter million, or four percent of the work force, is unemployed. And at the same time we have no real growth. But this is a situation in which the old fashioned Keynesian remedy of priming the pump will not work, for the pump has already been primed. The economy is bearing its maximum degree of public expenditure consistent with a democratic way of life. The percentage of our gross national product being absorbed by the public sector is between fifty percent and sixty percent.

It is not surprising therefore that people are saying "get government out of our hair," and complain that government takes too much of their incomes for what is now called the "social wage." This is the estimated annual value of the services provided out of public funds for each individual. They would rather have a little less public service and more freedom of choice on how they spend the money they earn. Perhaps universal subsidies are the best example of something many would prefer to do without; selective subsidies would be less costly and better. I have a lot of sympathy with them, because the public sector is not known for its efficiency in producing goods and services, or for producing exactly those goods and services which people most want.

Dangers of Inflation

Absence of growth, rising unemployment, and a rapid inflation are the outward signs of our malaise. Inwardly we have the doubt and uncertainty they cause. Inflation is a pernicious evil capable of destroying any society built on a value system where freedom is paramount. No democracy has survived a rate of inflation consistently higher than twenty percent. When money can no longer be counted on to act as a store of value, savings and investment are undermined, the basis of contracts is distorted, and the professional and middle class citizen, the backbone of all societies, is disaffected.

We saw the result of this process in Germany in the interwar period and indeed see it in some Latin American republics today. We know the danger of letting inflation get out of hand, yet the prospect of world economic recovery brings with it the possibility of increasing inflation. The next inflation will be extremely difficult to control, and the Western world may well experience super inflation unless we are single-minded in fighting it. Now is the time, not only to take action to contain this threat, but to warn the man in the street what may happen next time around.

Yet none of the tools for fighting it which economists offer us can work unless there is the political will to use them, and public opinion understands what is at stake if we fail. One problem is that a nation pursuing what should be an effective anti-inflationary policy may have its objective frustrated by the policies of other countries. Professor Robert Triffen has pointed out recently one way in which this can operate: A large part of monetary credit expansion escapes "national sovereignty" controls. In the eight European countries reporting external liabilities and assets of banks in domestic and foreign currencies, "controlled" domestic money supply rose by about two-thirds in the short space of four years (1970-1973), but Euro-currencies' liabilities tripled, and the combined total nearly doubled.

Psychologists tell us that inflation is partly (some say wholly) a question of social psychology. They argue that if we can contain expectations concerning income and living standards, the problem will be overcome. But in the past these expectations have been fostered by politicians and transmitted by the mass media all over the world. The result is that people have come to believe that things will go on getting better without any extra effort on their part, and it is this attitude that has led to increasing inflation.

Global Economic Interdependence

It is unlikely that any one country can solve either the problem of inflation or any other problems which affect us, for we live in an increasingly interdependent world, and what happens in Western Europe, Russia, or the Middle East affects life in the United States, just as what happens in the U.S. affects us in the United Kingdom.... The time has come to consider whether we have the institutions with the right terms of reference and structures to take us into the age of interdependence. Take for instance the post-war monetary structure set up at the Bretton Woods in the late 1940s. This worked well until the end of the 1960s. However, its structure and procedures could not survive unscathed the strains imposed by persistent payments surpluses or deficits of some countries. (Incidentally, Lord Keynes predicted its demise in 1946 on the basis of lack of discipline in this very respect.) Discussions on a new agreement have been postponed as new challenges to the system have arisen. This has resulted in a number of *ad hoc* arrangements which so far, at any rate, have kept the system going, but if, as I believe, new threats are on the horizon, reform becomes a matter of increasing urgency.... It may be doubted whether GATT and the institutions associated with trading systems are flexible enough to deal with the problems which are inevitable as the world grows more interdependent. In all this welter of activity, I believe that we are in danger of losing sight of the basic principles and that a restatement of these is now overdue.

On the analogy of the *Declaration of Independence*, which has had such an effect on the development of thought throughout the world, this might take the form of a Declaration of Interdependence, incorporating certain basic "self-evident" truths. The states which signed the *Declaration of Independence* in 1776 have all made great progress. I believe we can do the same. This concept of interdependence is, of course, not all that new. Our mutual defence system based on the North Atlantic Alliance is a living example of it. International trade theory is based on it. World trade on its present scale is a tribute to its virtue. The reaction of people to natural disasters all over the world with their spontaneous response offering help and goodwill is a testimony of its value. However, interdependence is always under threat. There are forces at work which snatch at every opportunity to stress the virtues of self-sufficiency and isolationism. The nature of these forces is such that calls for isolationist policies appear as a natural first reaction to any crisis. An even more natural second reaction sets in when generosity and unselfishness are followed by rebuffs. But at best an isolationist policy has only short-term political and economic advantages.

Let me make it clear that I am not questioning patriotism. On the contrary, it is one of the strong and important emotions which must be cultivated. There is, however, a world of difference between patriotism and nationalism. During the Second World War, patriotism was channelled into constructive use; yet the interdependence of the allies was self-evident. During that period the convoy was a feature of our daily lives in Europe, and it seems to me to provide an excellent illustration of interdependence in practise. Each individual ship has a purpose—to get to its destination—which it can best achieve only in concerted action. Yet each ship can only play its part if it is in good working order and keeping a certain distance from its neighbour. This is the strength of the convoy.

Nowhere is this concept more important today than in the realm of international financial and economic relations. During the last two years it would have been easy for a number of nations to have resorted to beggar-my-neighbour policies in order to defend their reserve positions following the four-fold rise in oil prices. The governor of the Bank of England, speaking a year ago, commented that the vast capital flows being generated by the oil price rise would alter the whole manner in which the international monetary system operates. He warned that for the United Kingdom and other countries it would "make it increasingly subject to hazard" and "inevitably constrain our policies." His conclusion, with which I concur, was that there will be need for "continuous and intense co-operation abroad."

In the face of the new strains, the temptation was to try to intrude upon the market system and its silent way of sorting things out. Many voices were raised suggesting that Adam Smith had been dead for two hundred years, and intervention in the system was the only appropriate action. But the market system proved its stability.

Firstly, forces of the market place operated BY THEMSELVES to bring about natural re-adjustments. For instance, oversupply of liquid capital placed by OPEC countries in the world banking system contributed to the decline of short-term interest rates, thus encouraging OPEC investment into longer-term assets. Market forces helped to stabilize oil prices and stimulated a serious search for alternative energy sources and for more efficient use of present energy supplies, which will help to solve the longer-term problems.

Secondly, the principle of international co-operation—interdepend-ence—was adhered to. Governments of deficit and surplus countries set up special facilities to recycle oil revenues. Members of the major international financial institutions—IMF, OECD, and the Common Market—all agreed to mutual support systems. OPEC countries and the developed nations demonstrated their interdependence with the developing countries, particu-larly the most seriously affected, by making grants or loans. The market system plus international co-operation and mutual help mitigate the worst effects of the crisis. . . .

A "Declaration of Interdependence" would enable both the new and the older nation states to set out some basic principles which may help to form the basis for solving international economic problems. Such a declaration should include statements that:

(1) Nations have an obligation to help each other when there are adverse effects from the cycle of economic life, or from crop failure or natural disaster.

(2) Trade between nations should be as liberal as possible and based on the principle of fair competition.

(3) Any system of financial relations between countries should encourage the flow of economic resources—not restrict it.

(4) Nations should cultivate the habit of consultations before taking actions which can have a far-reaching effect on the lives and well-being of other people.

(5) International law and other obligations be respected as the basis for international economic and political relations.

A Declaration of Interdependence incorporating such principles would help to do two things:

(1) Consolidate the gains the world has achieved since World War II in the process of economic liberalisation and economic welfare.

(2) Help to resolve the growing conflict that governments find between their external obligations and their internal ones—a conflict that is very real, and on which we often have to reach an acceptable compromise.

The forces making for disruption of the international economic order are powerful. Its preservation and improvement remains our best hope of solving the problems of inflation and poverty which beset us. I believe that a public affirmation of faith in the basic principles of international co-operation and interdependence can play a useful part in our attempts to hand on to our children a world which offers security and a way of life based on principles of obligation and responsibility.

13

Conservative Party Conference

Address Delivered in Blackpool,
October 10, 1975

The first Conservative Party conference I ever attended was in 1946, and I came to it as an undergraduate respresenting Oxford University Conservative Association (I know our Cambridge supporters will not mind). That conference was held in this very hall, and the platform then seemed a long way away, and I had no thought of joining the lofty and distinguished people sitting up there. But our party is the party of equality of opportunity, as you can see.

I know you will understand the humility I feel at following in the footsteps of great men like our leader in that year, Winston Churchill, a man called by destiny to raise the name of Britain to supreme heights in the history of the free world; in the footsteps of Anthony Eden, who set us the goal of a property-owning democracy—a goal we still pursue today; of Harold Macmillan, whose leadership brought so many ambitions within the grasp of every citizen, of Alec Douglas-Home, whose career of selfless public service earned the affection and admiration of us all; and of Edward Heath, who successfully led the party to victory in 1970 and brilliantly led the nation into Europe in 1973.

During my lifetime all the leaders of the Conservative Party have served as prime minister, and I hope the habit will continue. Our leaders have been different men with different qualities and different styles, but they all had one thing in common: each met the challenge of his time.

Now, what is the challenge of our time? I believe there are two: to overcome the country's economic and financial problems, and to regain our confidence in Britain and ourselves.

The economic challenge has been debated at length this week in this hall. Last week it gave rise to the usual scenes of cordial brotherly strife. Day after day the comrades called one another far from comradely names and occasionally, when they remembered, they called us names too. Some of them, for example, suggested that I criticized Britain when I was overseas. They are wrong. It was not Britain I was criticizing, it was socialism, and I will go on criticizing socialism and opposing socialism because it is bad for Britain. Britain and socialism are not the same thing, and as long as I have health and strength, they never will be.

Labour Government Record

Whatever could I say about Britain that is half as damaging as what this Labour government has done to our country? Let us look at the record. It is the Labour government that has caused prices to rise at a record rate of twenty-six percent a year. They told us the Social Contract would solve everything, but now everyone can see that the so-called contract was a fraud—a fraud for which the people of this country have had to pay a very high price. It is the Labour government whose past policies are forcing unemployment higher than it need ever have been. Thousands more men and women are losing their jobs every day, and there are going to be men and women, many of them youngsters straight out of school, who will be without a job this winter because Socialist ministers spent last year attacking us instead of attacking inflation.

It is the Labour government that brought the level of production below that of the three-day week in 1974. We have really got a three-day week now, only it takes five days to do it. It is the Labour government that has brought us record peacetime taxation. They have the usual Socialist disease: they have run out of other people's money. It is the Labour government that has pushed public spending to record levels. How have they done it? By borrowing and borrowing. Never in the field of human credit has so much been owed.

Dangers of Socialism

Serious as the economic challenge is, the political and moral challenge is just as grave and perhaps even more so, because economic problems never start with economics. They have much deeper roots in human nature and roots in politics, and they do not finish at economics either. Labour's failure to cope, to look at the nation's problems from the viewpoint of the whole nation, and not just one section of it, has led to a loss of confidence, and to a sense of helplessness; and with it goes a feeling that Parliament, which ought to be in charge, is not in charge, and that the actions and decisions are taken elsewhere.

It goes even deeper than that, to the voices that seem anxious not to overcome our economic difficulties, but to exploit them, to destroy the free enterprise society and put a Marxist system in its place. Today those voices form a sizeable chorus in the parliamentary Labour Party, a chorus which, aided and abetted by the many constituency Labour parties, seems to be growing in numbers. Mind you, anyone who says this openly is promptly accused of seeing "reds under the beds," but look who is seeing them now. On his own admission, Mr. Wilson has at last discovered that his own party is infiltrated by extreme left-wingers or, to use his own words, it is infested with them. When even Mr. Wilson gets scared about their success in capturing key positions in the Labour Party, should not the rest of us be? Should not the rest of us ask him, "Where have you been while all this has been going on, and what are you doing about it?" The answer is nothing. I sometimes think the Labour Party is like a pub where the mild is running out. If someone does not do something soon, all that is left will be bitter, and all that is bitter will be left.

Whenever I visit Communist countries, their politicians never hesitate to boast about their achievements. They know them all by heart; they reel off the facts and figures, claiming this is the rich harvest of the Communist system. Yet they are not prosperous as we in the West are prosperous, and they are not free as we in the West are free. Our capitalist system produces a far higher standard of prosperity and happiness because it believes in incentive and opportunity, and because it is founded on human dignity and freedom. Even the Russians have to go to a capitalist country—America— to buy enough wheat to feed their people, and that after more than fifty years of a state-controlled economy. Yet they boast incessantly, while we, who have so much more to boast about, forever criticize and decry. Is it not time we spoke up for our way of life? After all, no Western nation has to build a wall round itself to keep its people in.

So let us have no truck with those who say the free enterprise system has failed. What we face today is not a crisis of capitalism but of socialism. No country can flourish if its economic and social life is dominated by nationalisation and state control. The cause of our shortcomings does not, therefore, lie in private enterprise. Our problem is not that we have too little socialism. It is that we have too much. If only the Labour Party in this country would act like Social Democrats in West Germany. If only they would stop trying to prove their socialist virility by relentlessly nationalising one industry after another.

Of course, a halt to further state control will not on its own restore our belief in ourselves, because something else is happening to this country. We are witnessing a deliberate attack on our values, a deliberate attack on those who wish to promote merit and excellence, a deliberate attack on our heritage and our great past. And there are those who gnaw away at our national self-respect, rewriting British history as centuries of unrelieved gloom, oppression, and failure—as days of hopelessness, not days of hope. And others, under the shelter of our education system, are ruthlessly attacking the minds of the young. Everyone who believes in freedom must be appalled at the tactics employed by the far left in the systematic destruction of the North London Polytechnic—blatant tactics of intimidation designed to undermine the fundamental beliefs and values of every student, tactics pursued by people who are the first to insist on their own civil rights while seeking to deny them to the rest of us.

We must not be bullied or brainwashed out of our beliefs. No wonder so many of our people, some of the best and the brightest, are depressed and talking of emigrating. Even so, I think they are wrong. They are giving up too soon. Many of the things we hold dear are threatened as never before, but none has yet been lost, so stay here, stay and help us defeat socialism so that the Britain you have known may be the Britain your children will know.

Challenges

These are the two great challenges of our time—the moral and political challenge, and the economic challenge. They have to be faced together, and we have to master them both.

What are our chances of success? It depends on what kind of people we are. What kind of people are we? We are the people that in the past made Great Britain the workshop of the world, the people who persuaded others to buy British, not by begging them to do so but because it was best. We are a people who have received more Nobel prizes than any other nation except America, and head for head we have done better than America, twice as well in fact. We are the people who, among other things, invented the computer, the refrigerator, the electric motor, the stethoscope, rayon, the steam turbine, stainless steel, the tank, television, penicillin, radar, the jet engine, hovercraft, float glass and carbon fibres, *et cetera*—and the best half of Concorde.

We export more of what we produce than either West Germany, France, Japan, or the United States, and well over ninety percent of these exports come from private enterprise. It is a triumph for the private sector and all who work in it, and let us say so loud and clear. With achievements like that who can doubt that Britain can have a great future, and what our friends abroad want to know is whether that future is going to happen.

Well, how can we Conservatives make it happen? Many of the details have already been dealt with in the Conference debates. But policies and programmes should not just be a list of unrelated items. They are part of a total vision of the kind of life we want for our country and our children. Let me give you my vision: a man's right to work as he will, to spend what he earns, to own property, to have the state as servant and not as master—these are the British inheritance. They are the essence of a free country, and on that freedom all our other freedoms depend.

But we want a free economy, not only because it guarantees our liberties, but also because it is the best way of creating wealth and prosperity for the whole country. And it is this prosperity alone which can give us the resources for better services for the community, better services for those in need.

By their attack on private enterprise, this Labour government has made certain that there will be next to nothing available for improvements in our social services over the next few years. We must get private enterprise back on the road to recovery, not merely to give people more of their own money to spend as they choose, but to have more money to help the old and the sick and the handicapped. And the way to recovery is through profits, good profits today leading to high investment, leading to well-paid jobs, leading to a better standard of living tomorrow. No profits mean no investment, and that means a dying industry geared to yesterday's world, and that means fewer jobs tomorrow. Other nations have recognized that for years now, and because they have recognized it, they are going ahead faster than we are; and the gap between us will continue to increase unless we change our ways. The trouble here is that for years the Labour Party has made people feel that profits are guilty unless proven innocent. When I visit factories and companies, I do not find that those who actually work in them are against profits. On the contrary, they want to work for a prosperous concern, a concern with a future—their future.

Governments must learn to leave these companies with enough of their own profits to produce the goods and jobs for tomorrow. If the Socialists will not, or cannot, there will be no profit-making industry left to support the losses caused by fresh bouts of nationalisation. If anyone should murmur that I am preaching *laissez-faire,* let me say I am not arguing, and have never argued, that all we have to do is to let the economy run by itself. I believe that, just as each of us has an obligation to make the best of his talents, so governments have an obligation to create the framework within which we can do so—not only individual people, but individual firms and particularly small firms. If they concentrated on doing that, they would do a lot better than they are doing now. Some of the small firms will stay small, but others will expand and become the great companies of the future. The Labour government has pursued a disastrous vendetta against small businesses and the self-employed. We will reverse its damaging policies.

Nowhere is this more important than in agriculture, one of our most successful industries, made up almost entirely of small businesses. We live in a world in which food is no longer cheap or plentiful. Everything we cannot produce here must be imported at a high price. Yet the government could not have destroyed the confidence of the industry more effectively if they had tried deliberately to do so with their formula of empty promises and penal taxation.

So today what is the picture? Depressed profits, low investment, no incentive, and, overshadowing everything, government spending, spending, spending far beyond the taxpayers' means.

To recover, to get from where we are to where we want to be—and I admit we would rather not be here—will take time. "Economic policy," wrote Maynard Keynes, "should not be a matter of tearing up by the roots but of slowly training a plant to grow in a different direction." It will take time to reduce public spending, to rebuild profits and incentives, and to benefit from the investments which must be made. But the sooner that time starts, the better it will be for Britain's unemployed and for Britain as a whole.

One of the reasons why this Labour government has incurred more unemployment than any Conservative government since the war is because they have concentrated too much on distributing what we have and too little on seeing that we have more. We Conservatives hate unemployment. We hate the idea of men and women not being able to use their abilities. We deplore the waste of natural resources and the deep affront to people's dignity from being out of work through no fault of their own. It is ironic that we should be accused of wanting unemployment to solve our economic problems by the very government which has produced a record post-war unemployment and is expecting more. The record of Mr. Wilson and his colleagues on this is unparalleled in the history of political hypocrisy. We are now seeing the full consequences of nearly twenty months of Labour government. They have done the wrong things at the wrong time in the wrong way, and they have been a disaster for this country.

Freedom to Choose

Now let me turn to something I spoke about in America. Some Socialists seem to believe that people should be numbers in a state computer. We believe they should be individuals. We are all unequal. No one, thank heavens, is quite like anyone else, however much the Socialists may pretend otherwise. We believe that everyone has the right to be unequal. But to us, every human being is equally important. Engineers, miners, manual workers, shop assistants, farmworkers, postmen, housewives—these are the essential foundations of our society, and without them there would be no nation. But there are others with special gifts who should also have their chance, because if the adventurers who strike out in new directions in science, technology, medicine, commerce, and industry are hobbled, there can be no advance. The spirit of envy can destroy; it can never build. Everyone must be allowed to develop the abilities he knows he has within him, and she knows she has within her, in the way they choose.

Freedom to choose is something we take for granted until it is in danger of being taken away. Socialist governments set out perpetually to restrict the area of choice, and Conservative governments to increase it. We believe that you become a responsible citizen by making decisions for yourself, not by having them made for you. But they are made for you by Labour all right!

Take education. Our education system used to serve us well. A child from an ordinary family, as I was, could use it as a ladder, as an advancement, but the Socialists, better at demolition rather than reconstruction, are destroying many good grammar schools. Now this has nothing to do with private education. It is opportunity and excellence in our state schools that are being diminished under socialism. Naturally enough, parents do not like this, but in a socialist society parents should be seen and not heard.

Another denial of choice is being applied to health. The private sector helps to keep some of our best doctors here and so available part-time to the National Health Service. It also helps to bring in more money for the general health of the nation. But under Labour, private medicine is being squeezed out, and the result will be to add to the burden of the National Health Service without adding one penny to its income.

Let me make this absolutely clear: when we return to power we shall reverse Mrs. Castle's stupid and spiteful attack on hospital pay beds. We Conservatives do not accept that because some people have no choice, no one should have it. Every family should have the right to spend their money, after tax, as they wish, and not as the government dictates. Let us extend choice, extend the will to choose, and the chance to choose.

Trade Unions

I want to come now to the argument which Mr. Wilson is trying to put across to the country: namely, that the Labour Party is the natural party of government because it is the only one that the trade unions will accept. From what I saw on television last week, the Labour Party did not look like a party of government at all, let alone a natural one.

But let us examine the argument, because it is important. If we are told that a Conservative government could not govern because certain extreme leaders would not let it, then general elections are a mockery, we have arrived at the one-party state, and a parliamentary democracy in this country will have perished. The democracy for which our fathers fought and died is not to be laid to rest as lightly as that.

When the next Conservative government comes to power, many trade unionists will have put it there. Millions of them vote for us at every election. I want to say this to them and to all of our supporters in industry: go out and join in the work of your unions; go to their meetings and stay to the end, and learn the union rules as well as the far left knows them. Remember that if parliamentary democracy dies, free trade unions die with it.

Rule of Law

I come last to what many would put first, the rule of law. The first people to uphold the law should be governments, and it is tragic that the Socialist government, to its lasting shame, should have lost its nerve and shed its principles over the People's Republic of Clay Cross, and that a group of the Labour Party should have tried to turn the Shrewsbury pickets into martyrs. On both occasions the law was broken, and on one violence was done. No decent society can live like that, and no responsible party should condone it. The first duty of government is to uphold the law, and if it tries to bob, weave, and duck round that duty when it is inconvenient, the governed will do exactly the same thing, and then nothing will be safe, not home, not liberty, not life itself.

There is one part of this country where, tragically, defiance of the law is costing life day after day. In Northern Ireland our troops have the dangerous and thankless task of trying to keep the peace and hold a balance. We are proud of the way they have discharged their duty. This party is pledged to support the unity of the United Kingdom, to preserve that unity, and to protect the people, Catholic and Protestant alike. We believe our armed forces must remain until a genuine peace is made. Our thoughts are with them and our pride is with them, too.

I have spoken of the challenges which face us here in Britain—the challenge to recover economically and the challenge to recover our belief in ourselves, and I have shown our potential for recovery. I have dealt with some aspects of our strength and approach, and I have tried to tell you something of my personal vision and my belief in the standards on which

FIGURE 13.1 Queen Elizabeth II with Margaret Thatcher and five other former prime ministers. Left to right are: James Callaghan, Alec Douglas-Home, Thatcher, Harold Macmillan, the Queen, Harold Wilson, and Edward Heath. (*Source:* British Information Services, New York.)

this nation was greatly built, on which it greatly thrived, and from which in recent years it has greatly fallen away. I believe we are coming to yet another turning point in our long history. We can go on as we have been going and continue down, or we can stop and with a decisive act of will say "Enough."

Let all of us here today, and others far beyond this hall who believe in our cause, make that act of will. Let us proclaim our faith in a new and better future for our party and our people; let us resolve to heal the wounds of a divided nation, and let that act of healing be a prelude to a lasting victory.

FIGURE 14.1 Margaret and Denis Thatcher at Chequers. (*Source:* British Information Services, New York.)

14

War of Words

*Speech to the Finchley Constituency,
January 31, 1976*

Ladies and Gentlemen, I stand before you tonight in my green chiffon evening gown, my face softly made up, my fair hair gently waved. The Iron Lady of the Western World! Me? A Cold War Warrior?

Well, yes, if that is how *they* wish to interpret my defence of values and freedoms fundamental to our way of life. And by *they*, I mean that somewhat strange alliance between the comrades of the Russian Defence Ministry and our own Defence Minister. They are welcome to call me what they like if they believe we should ignore the build-up of Russian military strength, that we should not disturb their dreams of detente by worrying over the Communist presence in Angola. But I happen to believe that what is at stake, both in this country and in the world, *is* important and *is* crucial to our future.

We are waging a battle on many fronts. We must not forget the guns and missiles aimed at us, but we must not let them blind us to the much more insidious war of words which is going on. It is not just a matter of hurling insults, where he who hurls loudest, hurls last. That is the final resort of the man who has already lost the argument and the first of the man who knows he has no case. No, this is not such a war. The war is a true war of words, where meanings get lost in a mist of revolutionary fantasy, where accuracy is slipped quietly under the carpet, and where truth is twisted and bent to suit the latest propagandist line. That is what we are up against. And we have to fight it if only because we find it totally offensive to our notions of freedom and truth.

To illustrate what I mean, let us take that last sentence. It contains in its two words which, together, are among the most abused in the language of the struggle: freedom and fight. To the Marxist—the man who, we must never forget, believes in total state domination of every aspect of people's lives—a freedom fighter is one who helps to bring about Marxism, a system which denies basic freedoms. In other words, that so-called freedom fighter is a man who helps to destroy freedom. Such is the corruption of the language they use, necessary in their eyes because they know freedom is an appealing word.

The men of the Khmer Rouge, whose first act on "liberating," as they put it, Cambodia last year, was brutally to drive a large part of the population out of the capital Phnom Penh. Yet they were called "freedom fighters." The men who tried to reverse the clear wishes of the people of Portugal, as expressed through the ballot box, in Marxist vocabulary they were "freedom fighters," too. This surely must have been one of the most blatant attempts at subversion we have seen in recent times. But the fallacies of the present propaganda war came nearer to home than this.

The Word "Public"

Let us look at another word being just as subtly corrupted in the litany of the left. The word is "Public." We use it many times a day. It is with us all the time because we are the public. All of us. Yet it has become devalued and distorted. Only when followed by the words "house" or "bar," do we instantly recognize its purpose. But when it is followed by the word "ownership"—"Public Ownership"—it has come to mean something totally different. We *own* the mines. We *own* the railways. We *own* the Post Office. But when it comes down to it, *we* don't really own anything. "Public ownership" should mean that you and I own something, that we have some say in how it is run, that it is accountable to us. But the fact is that the words "public ownership" have come to mean the very, *very* private world of decisions taken behind closed doors, and of accountability to no one. Yet what a cosy and democratic sounding word it is. How *good* for us all public ownership is presented as being. What a glimpse of socialist heaven it offers.

The Socialists tell us that there are massive profits in this particular industry, and they should not go to the shareholders, but that the public should reap the benefits. Benefits? What benefits? When you take into public ownership a profitable industry, the profits soon disappear. The goose that laid the golden eggs goes broody. State geese are not great layers. The steel industry was nationalised some years ago in the public interest. Yet the only interest now left to the public is in witnessing the depressing spectacle of their money going down the drain at a rate of a million pounds a day.

Socialists then shift the ground for taking industries into "public ownership." They then tell us that some industries cannot survive any longer unless they are taken into public ownership, allegedly to protect the public from the effects of their collapse. It all sounds so cosy, so democratic. But is it true? No, of course it is not. The moment ownership passes into the name of the public is the moment the public ceases to get what it wants. And it is invariably the moment when the public starts to pay: pays to take the industry over, pays the losses, pays for the inefficiencies in higher prices.

Outside many pits in the country is a notice which says: "Managed on behalf of the people." But will the people ever get to know who was responsible for the massive losses sustained since the mining industry was nationalised in 1947? If these are public industries, then surely the public has a right to know, the more so because they are monopoly industries. In fact, publicly owned authorities are usually the most private imaginable. We need to revise our vocabulary and call something public only when ordinary members of the public are in actual control.

The fact is the British public more truly own firms like Marks & Spencer and others, than they do any of our nationalised industries. Some of them directly own shares in Marks & Spencer. This gives them the right to ask questions about its management, its successes, its failures, and if they are not satisfied, they can sell their shares and invest their money elsewhere. Many more have an indirect share in it through pension funds at their own work. The managers of these funds are paid to ask the very questions which keep the company on its toes. And millions of us use the option every year of voting with our feet on the success of St. Michael. We can choose whether to buy there or somewhere else. That is *real* public ownership. And if the public ceased to benefit, then Marks & Spencer would cease to exist. What is it, then, that keeps them going? It is their incentive to satisfy their customers, you and me, the public.

Despite what the Socialists would have you think, theirs is not an unusual story. It is reflected in thousands of firms throughout the land—successful firms, proving by their results that today's crisis is not one of free enterprise, but one caused by socialism. Despite the handicaps imposed upon them, the taxation, the restrictions, they are still managing to give the public what it wants.

Alas, the same could not always be said of some of the nationalised industry services, as shown by the complaints received daily of rising costs and falling standards. Accountability to the public goes when its name is put to an enterprise, and because there can be no competition to a state monopoly, incentive to efficiency goes too. These are the fallacies in the use of the word "public." We must not let them get away with the deceptions and the half-truths which swarm around their dogma. Whenever we see the word "public," we must question it. Which public? Theirs or ours? How is it for the public? How does the public benefit? What choice does the public have?

Choice and Ownership

Choice is crucial in this. Where there is no feasible alternative to the existing state monopoly, we must make sure it is run genuinely for the public. But where choice is possible, we *must* guarantee choice is available. When a man moves his family into a council house, we must make sure he has the chance of buying it. The ambition to own the roof over your head is a totally natural one and, judging by the way the present Cabinet indulges in it, a pretty strong instinct it is, too.

Why then do these so-called socialists work so actively to prevent home ownership among the very people they traditionally regard as their supporters? The answer is that if you give the ambitious man in the council house the chance to buy it, you lose control over him. A socialist system which has penetrated so far in its control over people that it can dictate the colour of their front doors, is a system which will never let go control of the whole house. People might paint their doors a different colour, for a start.

We have always been the party of home ownership. Home ownership not only means security for the individual, it also means security and continuity for society as well: security because people who work hard to buy their own homes have learned the responsibility of property and have a respect for other people's property as well—continuity because the ownership of a house is not just for one generation. Its value is in more ways than one passed to the next, and the next. The only way for the majority of the public to have any real say in where they live and how they live is by extending home ownership. When we came to power in 1951, home ownership was only twenty-nine percent. In 1964 it was forty-five percent. By the time we had left office in 1974, it was fifty-two percent. With our policies the figure will go even higher. Housing policy shows that the Conservative way really does work for the public, in the true sense of the word.

When parents send their children to school, and I am talking about local authority schools, not fee paying schools, we must also see that some choice is available. In no field has the exclusion of the public been so severe as in the schools they nominally own, in whose name they are nominally run. . . . Nobody wants to see a school shut down, no more than they want to see a firm put out of business. That is why from the start we must make them more responsive to parents' wishes. That is why there must be choice of the type of education our children are given. Some children flower quickly in

FIGURE 14.2 Prime Minister Winston S. Churchill and Lord Louis Mountbatten at the Casablanca Conference, January 1943. (*Source:* George C. Marshall Library, Lexington, Virginia.)

the atmosphere of what is called the "progressive classroom." Others need the more organised structure of the traditional system. But parents should not be *told* which their children are going to get, and denied any choice at all.

We believe people are not mere cyphers to be ordered this way and that, into this job or that, into this house or that, their children sent to this school or that. Socialists believe *people* are not to be trusted with choice—I suppose because we might learn to use it, and enjoy it. And then where would it all end? Socialism is the denial of choice, the denial of choice for ordinary people in their everyday lives. There is a will in Britain to work and build up the future for our children. But Socialists don't trust the people. Churchill did. We do.

15

Interviews in the United States

September 14, 1977

Press Conference at the British Embassy

QUESTION: You already hold a position which is uncommon in the Western world. I wonder if you can tell us something about a woman holding the position of party leader in Britain, some of the things which you have found are difficulties, some of the advantages you receive perhaps as a woman.

THATCHER: I really haven't found any difficulties. I'm not the first woman leader of a party except in the Western world. But someone's got to be first, and after somebody's been first, there'll probably be a number of people following after. Now I'm honestly often asked this question, and the slightly flippant answer is to say I don't know what it's like, I can't compare what it's like with being a man leader because I've never had both experi ences. But I think some of you men are much more conscious of it than I am. I'll tell you something else you do. You say sometimes to a woman that she's got the mind of a man and you think it's a compliment. I don't necessarily. I think a good mind doesn't belong either to one sex or another, and I am what I am because of being the kind of personality. It doesn't really matter whether that personality is grafted on to being a man or a woman. But if I might just fly a little flag, it was Rudyard Kipling who said the female of the species is more deadly than the male, and I trust you'll keep that in mind.

QUESTION: Helsinki Agreements?

THATCHER: You're talking about human rights, in fact. If you look at the

Helsinki Agreements—human rights—I believe in them, of course, universally. What I am saying is the essence of a free society, and I will go on preaching the beliefs, ideologies, philosophies, and benefits of a free society, hoping that other peoples in the world will want them and will secure them within their own countries. That is a matter for them. When it comes to human rights beyond the Iron Curtain and in Europe, the particular difference there, if I might say so, is that those who negotiated under the Helsinki Agreement deliberately put those human rights in issue in the treaty to bargain with, to gain other advantages, so you actually have them brought into issue in a particular treaty. Otherwise, they are part of our general belief in a free society. It is part of our moral commitment. I believe passionately in a free society. It produces vast economic benefits, but that is not its greatest advantage. It produces the only society in the world which in fact honours and respects human dignity. And I am amazed that when you get other countries with different creeds, Communist creeds pounding out their propaganda, that we are ever shy in proclaiming what we believe about our countries and the infinitely superior benefits that it confers on both their people and their standard of living. That is part of my belief; it is inseparable from me. The whole of the free society is a moral commitment to choice and individual men and women and their families, their right to choice, and their right to be considered. Nothing will separate me from that.

Interview on the Today Show, NBC

RALPH ABERNATHY: I assume there's no doubt in your mind that your party will win.

THATCHER: Really, there isn't, no. But I know just exactly what happens at runup to elections, and it must be very irritating, I think, sometimes for viewers. Everyone expresses, and there can only be one winner. So you've got to work jolly hard at it.

ABERNATHY: I must confess that if I had to rank various groups in the world according to their reputation for male chauvinism, the Conservative Party of Britain would be near the top of the list.

THATCHER: Oh, I think you must have got us wrong.

ABERNATHY: Can you explain briefly how your party could overcome that attitude enough two and one-half years ago to elect you leader?

THATCHER: Well, you know, ours is the longest surviving party in British politics, and I reckon it'll survive longer than any other party. But, you know, that was said when Disraeli was made prime minister. It was an unusual choice. But the Conservative survived, really, because it's constantly prepared to change and adapt to new circumstances. We believe that you take old, traditional values, the very best values we've got, and you use them to adapt to new circumstances. And that, I think, is what's happened. And I don't find it at all surprising that they'd choose a woman leader.

ABERNATHY: If or when you become prime minister, would you feel you had to do or not to do anything in particular because you're a woman?

THATCHER: Well, you know, I wouldn't, but then I've been in what you would call men's jobs. I've been in scientific research, I've been in law, and I've been a Member of Parliament for eighteen years. And, of course, there aren't enough women in Parliament, so each of us is rather conspicuous. But never, in any of those times, have I ever thought, "Now, I must be tougher than I would be, merely to prove that a woman can do it." I've always thought, "What's the problem? What's the analysis? How can we find a way through?" And I've never been anything other than a woman, so I don't know how to think any other way.

ABERNATHY: But this—exactly this matter of toughness is exactly what I wanted to ask you about. For instance, any reason to think that you might feel it necessary to take a particularly hard line toward any settlement in Northern Ireland?

THATCHER: Oh, no, no. The views that I have about Northern Ireland come from looking at the situation, but not because I'm a woman. Mind you, I have seen the faces of women there, I've seen the suffering on them. And I must say, as an ordinary human being, I find it very strange indeed that after eight or nine years' suffering there, the people themselves haven't come together to say, "Enough. We'll now work together," and get a settlement.

ABERNATHY: President Carter recently issued a statement about Northern Ireland, the first American president ever to do that, I think. Was that resented at all in Britain, his interference?

THATCHER: Look, we were very, very pleased indeed that he made a statement that money should not go to the IRA. Because every time it goes there, what you're doing is helping people to pursue their cause by armed means And that's vented on innocent men, women, and children. So we're very pleased about that. And, naturally, we're always pleased when we get new investment in Ulster or in Britain. And, of course, Ford has very recently put a very big new investment in Britain. There's one very cheerful thing about Northern Ireland: the industrial relations are excellent. So there's always something good.

ABERNATHY: Let me ask you about some of Britain's other problems, besides Northern Ireland. First, attitudes toward work. I have the general impression that from top management down in your country there's a kind of disinterest in hard work.

THATCHER: No. No, there isn't at all. There's a great will to work, there's a great talent to work. After all, we can produce some of the most advanced technology, we can produce some of the best businesses. But there's no incentive to work in the tax system. We're the most heavily taxed nation in the world, when you think of the proportion that goes out of your wage packet. And, you know, if you feel you're working too hard for the government and not hard enough for your own family, and however hard you work, more goes to the government than to your own family, then you're not going to make as much effort as there is within you to make. So, the whole of our programme in the Conservative Party is to go towards an incentive, enterprising society so that we really can use the vitality that's there.

TOM BROKAW: Mrs. Thatcher, as you know, a lot of people think that regardless of what happens politically in your country, the fate of it depends on the labor unions. Should you become prime minister, do you think that there will be a need for a fundamental change in the labor laws of Great Britain?

THATCHER: Fundamental change, no. We tried that once before. When we came into power just after 1970, we said that the labour laws are the only ones that really date from the beginning of this century; they must be updated. That change was not accepted. And I think we have to go very, very much more slowly now. If there is a particular change that has to be made, then it will have to be made; but no general change. You know, for thirteen years, 1951 to '64, we got on very well indeed with the trade unions. More and more of their members are voting for us, more and more of them are believing in the things that we believe in. And I don't anticipate trouble with the trade unions when we get into power. Many of them will think, "Thank goodness, there's a government who believes that the task of trade unions is to look after their members, and leave the politics to the politicians."

BROKAW: But, Mrs. Thatcher, after all, the Labour Party is the party of the trade unions, and it has been having enormous problems. Now, why wouldn't the Conservatives have problems, even though you have some accommodation now?

THATCHER: If what you are saying is that you are bound to get problems after an incomes policy, of course you are. Every time you come out of an incomes policy—and I've been through four—you get problems. But we're no less likely to solve them than the Labour Party. And if any trade union leader ever said that they would not work with a Conservative government, what they would be saying is that they would not work and accept the people's verdict in a parliamentary democracy. They've never said they'll never do it, because that would be the end of democracy in Britain; nor would their members allow them to do it. We shall be all right. Let there be no doubt about that.

ABERNATHY: I'm sure you've thought about priorities. If you were asked to form a government in Britain, what would be the first thing that you would try to do?

THATCHER: The main thing is we really must introduce incentives into our society. Our problem is that our economy hasn't grown. Yours has; you have incentives, you have a climate of success. You can feel it when you come over here. And you've got ordinary people who can really build up a little bit of capital from their earnings. That's marvelous. We would like to have it.

FIGURE 16.1 Denis and Margaret Thatcher at the Youth for Europe rally, June 2, 1979. (*Source:* British Information Services, New York.)

16

The Ideal of European Freedom

*Speech at the Youth for Europe Rally in Birmingham,
June 2, 1979, Five Days Before the First Elections
to the European Parliament*

Next week 180 million free people of nine different free countries will go
to the polls in freedom to elect one free parliament to represent them all.
They will do so in a Western Europe which for the first time in its history is
composed entirely of democratic governments. How we all welcomed Portugal and Spain into the democratic European family. The new assembly will
be the first multi-national, multi-lingual parliament ever to be elected in the
long story of man's continuing struggle for peace and freedom... and marks
a crucial milestone in Europe's journey. . . .

The Socialists may be divided in this country, but the Communists and
Socialists are well organised elsewhere. Wherever there is a representative
assembly, Conservatives and those who share our beliefs in a free society
must fight with that zeal and dedication which, too often in the past, has
been the prerogative of the left. Whenever a representative assembly is being
elected, those who believe in democracy have a duty to cast their vote. We
are asking not only for a massive turn-out of voters, but for a massive
Conservative vote. Conservative principles do not change when we cross the
Channel. There must be a golden threat of consistency running through our
policies for Britain and our policies for the European Community.

During our own election campaign, we argued for reduced public
spending, lower taxation, more effective competition, and a relentless war
on bureaucracy. We shall pursue these same objectives in Europe. During
this European election, we argue for reduced spending on the Common

Agricultural Policy, a lower net budget contribution from Britain (indeed we could do with some of the money that we pay to the European budget to reduce income tax here) nearer to European levels; and we argue strenuously against the unnecessary deluge of detailed directives. But above all we stressed in the general election and we stress now the overriding need to preserve and defend the ideal and the reality of freedom.

We may ponder for a moment what that ideal of European freedom means to us. Just after the War, when most of Europe lay in ruins, Winston Churchill spoke at Zurich of what he called "the European family." He taught us that we must provide that family "with a structure under which it can dwell in peace, in safety, and in freedom." Other declarations have spelt out the philosophy of freedom in the most compelling terms—the American Declaration of Independence, the United Nations Declaration of Human Rights, and the Roosevelt Declaration of Four Freedoms.

These earlier declarations proclaimed the freedoms which we in this country have long taken for granted. But they said nothing about the economic structure necessary to put them into practise. There can be no freedom without a free enterprise economy. Every free country in the world is a free enterprise country. That is a truth which some have been slow to accept. Indeed, there are those who attack free enterprise, while formally proclaiming political freedom. In so doing they are preaching the virtue of liberty, while plotting the downfall of the very economic organisation which is its foundation.

Unlike those earlier declarations, the Treaty of Rome says little about the *ideal* of freedom, but defines at length the economic structures necessary to sustain it. It is a treaty based on free and fair competition in trade, on the free movement of people, goods, and capital across traditional frontiers. It is a treaty between peoples who have no time for hate, but only for living together in liberty, mutual cooperation, and security. Above all, it is a treaty which gives to the young people of Western Europe the opportunity to live in peace with one another, an opportunity which was denied to previous generations. That is why we in the Conservative Party reaffirm our commitment to the European ideal before two thousand young Europeans.

We believe in a free Europe, but not in a standardised Europe. The intellectual and material richness of Europe lies in its variety. Diminish that variety within the member states, and you impoverish the whole Community. We in Britain came late into membership and have been slow to find our role within it. Next week's elections give us a chance to find a new role and to give a fresh impetus to Conservative influence in the Community as a whole. European in ideal though we are, we shall nevertheless argue tenaciously for our national interests when these are at stake. We are not alone in that. But we shall do so as whole-hearted supporters of the Community and as resolute champions of the European ideal.

In politics it is the half-hearted who lose. It is those with conviction who carry the day. In Europe, as in Britain, the Conservative Party is the party of conviction. We are convinced that it is in the interests of Britain as well as Europe that our partnership should succeed. We insist that the institutions of the European Community are managed so that they increase the liberty of the individual throughout our continent. These institutions must not be permitted to dwindle into bureaucracy. Whenever they fail to enlarge freedom, the institutions should be criticized and the balance restored.

But the real battle will come to your generation and to those who come after, in years which my generation will not see. In the preamble to the Treaty of Rome, the founder members affirmed their commitment to eliminate the barriers within the Community. I can think of no more exciting prospect for the youth of Europe than to be able, as you will, to move freely without a passport from one member state to another or to acquire a qualification or a skill which will enable you to work anywhere within the Community.

Just as we have insisted in our own elections on the need to strengthen our defence forces, so our European ideal insists on the capacity of the Community countries, together with our other NATO allies, to defend our way of life against any military threat from outside. Communism never sleeps, never changes its objectives. Nor must we. Our first duty to freedom is to defend our own. Let no one be under any misunderstanding about the inflexible resolve of Her Majesty"s Government to strengthen our defences and to play our full part in the defence of a free Europe.

The population of the nine member states is as large as that of the Soviet Union. Add Greece and the two other applicant countries which we hope soon to welcome as full members, and the Community will exceed three hundred million free people. There is no need for Europeans to quake before any threat from the Soviet colossus. One of my wisest predecessors, Lord Salisbury, made the point very clearly a hundred years ago: "If we mean to escape misery and dishonour, we must trust to no consciousness of a righteous cause, to no moral influence, to no fancied restraints of civilisation.... We must trust to our power of self-defence, and to no other earthly aid."

Today Europe is still divided by opposing concepts of human rights in the western and eastern halves of our continent. So long as men and women are persecuted or imprisoned for their political beliefs, for daring to assert the right of every individual to dispute the official line; so long as people are denied the right to worship as they wish, freely and openly; so long as constraints are imposed on where people may go, what they may read and what they may say; so long as dissent, the inborn right of every human being and the cherished legacy of our European individualism, is regarded as treason or betrayal; so long as the Berlin Wall and the fortified frontiers

FIGURE 16.2 General and Mrs. George C. Marshall with Prime Minister Winston S. Churchill at 10 Downing Street, June 1953. (*Source:* George C. Marshall Library.)

divide East from West, the European ideal, the European values which we cherish will never be secure.

None of us can practise isolation or neutralism and hope to live in safety. Only if we pool our resources and share in each other's strength will free Europe survive. Only if we speak together can we expect the world to heed the voice of Europe. The new directly elected European Parliament will be one expression of that voice. Let us ensure that the voice of freedom speaks with firmness and courage and imagination to a troubled world.

Europe has been the seed-bed for all our ideas of freedom and liberty under the law. It is the storehouse of Christian belief. In the words of Goethe: "Resolute, now claim your hour, For the throng may quail and drift; For the noble soul has power To compass all if wise and swift."

17

Conservative Party Conference

Address in Brighton, October 10, 1980

At our party conference last year I said that the task in which the government were engaged—to change the national attitude of mind—was the most challenging to face any British Administration since the war. Challenge is exhilarating. This week we Conservatives have been taking stock, discussing the achievements, the setbacks, and the work that lies ahead as we enter our second parliamentary year. Our debates have been stimulating and our debates have been constructive. This week has demonstrated that we are a party united in purpose, strategy, and resolve. And we actually like one another.

When I am asked for a detailed forecast of what will happen in the coming months or years, I remember Sam Goldwyn's advice: "Never prophesy, especially about the future." (Interruption from the floor.) Never mind, it is wet outside. I expect that they wanted to come in. You cannot blame them; it is always better where the Tories are. And you—and perhaps they—will be looking to me this afternoon for an indication of how the government sees the task before us and why we are tackling it the way we are. Before I begin, let me get one thing out of the way.

This week at Brighton we have heard a good deal about last week at Blackpool. I will have a little more to say about that strange assembly later, but for the moment I want to say just this. Because of what happened at that conference, there has been, behind all our deliberations this week, a heightened awareness that now, more than ever, our Conservative government must succeed. We just must, because now there is even more at stake than some realized.

Steps Toward Britain's Recovery

There are many things to be done to set this nation on the road to recovery, and I do not mean economic recovery alone, but a new independence of spirit and zest for achievement. It is sometimes said that because of our past we, as a people, expect too much and set our sights too high. That is not the way I see it. Rather it seems to me that throughout my life in politics our ambitions have steadily shrunk. Our response to disappointment has not been to lengthen our stride but to shorten the distance to be covered. But with confidence in ourselves and in our future, what a nation we could be.

In its first seventeen months this government have laid the foundations for recovery. We have undertaken a heavy load of legislation, a load we do not intend to repeat because we do not share the Socialist fantasy that achievement is measured by the number of laws you pass. But there was a formidable barricade of obstacles that we had to sweep aside. For a start, in his first budget Geoffrey Howe began to restore incentives to stimulate the abilities and inventive genius of our people. Prosperity comes not from grand conferences of economists but by countless acts of personal self-confidence and self-reliance.

Under Geoffrey's stewardship Britain has repaid $3,600 million of international debt, debt which had been run up by our predecessors. And we paid quite a lot of it before it was due. In the past twelve months Geoffrey has abolished exchange controls over which British governments have dithered for decades. Our great enterprises are now free to seek opportunities overseas. This will help to secure our living standards long after North Sea oil has run out. This government thinks about the future. We have made the first crucial changes in trade union law to remove the worst abuses of the closed shop, to restrict picketing to the place of work of the parties in dispute, and to encourage secret ballots.

Jim Prior has carried all these measures through with the support of the vast majority of trade union members. Keith Joseph, David Howell, John Nott, and Norman Fowler have begun to break down the monopoly powers of nationalisation. Thanks to them, British Aerospace will soon be open to private investment. The monopoly of the Post Office and British Telecommunications is being diminished. The barriers to private nationalised industries and public utilities can be investigated by the Monopolies Commission—a long overdue reform.

Free competition in road passenger transport promises travellers a better deal. Michael Heseltine has given millions—yes, millions—of council tenants the right to by their own homes. It was Anthony Eden who chose for us the goal of "a property-owning democracy." But for all the time that I have been in public affairs, that has been beyond the reach of so many, who were denied the right to the most basic ownership of all—the homes in which they live. They wanted to buy. Many could afford to buy. But they happened to live under the jurisdiction of a Socialist council, which would not sell and did not believe in the independence that comes with ownership. Now Michael Heseltine has given them the chance to turn a dream into reality. And all this and a lot more in seventeen months. The left continues to refer with relish to the death of capitalism. Well, if this is the death of capitalism, I must say that it has quite a way to go.

Inflation and Unemployment

But all this will avail us little unless we achieve our prime economic objective—the defeat of inflation. Inflation destroys nations and societies as surely as invading armies do. Inflation is the parent of unemployment. It is the unseen robber of those who have saved. No policy which puts at risk the defeat of inflation—however great its short-term attraction—can be right. Our policy for the defeat of inflation is, in fact, traditional. It existed long before Sterling M3 embellished the *Bank of England Quarterly Bulletin,* or "monetarism" became a convenient term of political invective. But some people talk as if control of the money supply was a revolutionary policy. Yet it was an essential condition for the recovery of much of continental Europe. Those countries knew what was required for economic stability. Previously, they had lived through rampant inflation; they knew that it led to suitcase money, massive unemployment and the breakdown of society itself. They determined never to go that way again. Today, after many years of monetary self-discipline, they have stable, prosperous economies better able than ours to withstand the buffeting of world recession.

So at international conferences to discuss economic affairs, many of my fellow heads of government find our policies not strange, unusual, or revolutionary, but normal, sound, and honest. And that is what they are. Their only question is: "Has Britain the courage and resolve to sustain the discipline for long enough to break through to success?" Yes, we have, and we shall. This government are determined to stay with the policy and see it through to its conclusion. That is what marks this administration as one of the truly radical ministries of post-war Britain. Inflation is falling and should continue to fall.

Meanwhile, we are not heedless of the hardships and worries that accompany the conquest of inflation. Foremost among these is unemployment. Today our country has more than two million unemployed. Now you can try to soften that figure in a dozen ways. You can point out—and it is quite legitimate to do so—that two million today does not mean what it meant in the 1930s; that the percentage of unemployment is much less now than it was then. You can add that today many more married women go out to work. You can stress that because of the high birthrate in the early 1960s, there is an unusually large number of school leavers this year looking for work and that the same will be true for the next two years. You can emphasise that about a quarter of a million people find new jobs each month and therefore go off the employment register. And you can recall that there are nearly twenty-five million people in jobs compared with only about eighteen million in the 1930s. You can point out that the Labour Party conveniently overlooks the fact that of the two million unemployed for which they blame us, nearly a million and a half were bequeathed by their government.

But when all that has been said, the fact remains that the level of unemployment in our country today is a human tragedy. Let me make it clear beyond doubt. I am profoundly concerned about unemployment. Human dignity and self respect are undermined when men and women are condemned to idleness. The waste of a country's most precious assets—the talent and energy of its people—makes it the bounden duty of government to seek a real and lasting cure. If I could press a button and genuinely solve the unemployment problem, do you think that I would not press that button this instant? Does anyone imagine that there is the smallest political gain in letting this unemployment continue, or that there is some obscure economic religion which demands this unemployment as part of this ritual? This government are pursuing the only policy which gives any hope of bringing our people back to real and lasting employment. It is no coincidence that those countries, of which I spoke earlier, which have had lower rates of inflation, have also had lower levels of unemployment.

Excessive Public Spending

I know that there is another real worry affecting many of our people. Although they accept that our policies are right, they feel deeply that the burden of carrying them out is falling much more heavily on the private than on the public sector. They say that the public sector is enjoying advantages, but the private sector is taking the knocks, and at the same time maintaining those in the public sector with better pay and pensions than they enjoy.

I share this concern and understand the resentment. That is why I and my colleagues say that to add to public spending takes away the very money and resources that industry needs to stay in business, let alone to expand. Higher public spending, far from curing unemployment, can be the very vehicle that loses jobs and causes bankruptcies in trade and commerce. That is why we warned local authorities that since rates are frequently the biggest tax that industry now faces, increases in them can cripple local businesses. Councils must, therefore, learn to cut costs in the same way that companies have to.

That is why I stress that if those who work in public authorities take for themselves large pay increases, they leave less to be spent on equipment and new buildings. That in turn deprives the private sector of the orders it needs, especially some of those industries in the hard pressed regions. Those in the public sector have a duty to those in the private sector not to take out so much in pay that they cause others' unemployment. That is why we point out that every time high wage settlements in nationalised monopolies lead to higher charges for telephones, electricity, coal, and water, they can drive companies out of business and cost other people their jobs.

If spending money like water was the answer to our country's problems, we would have no problems right now. If ever a nation has spent, spent, spent, and spent again, ours has. Today that dream is over. All of that money has got us nowhere, but it still has to come from somewhere. Those who urge us to relax the squeeze, to spend yet more money indiscriminately in the belief that it will help the unemployed and the small businessman, are not being kind or compassionate or caring. They are not the friends of the unemployed or the small business. They are asking us to do again the very thing that caused the problems in the first place. We have made this point repeatedly.

I am accused of lecturing or preaching about this. I suppose it is a critic's way of saying, "Well, we know it is true, but we have to carp at something." I do not care about that. But I do care about the future of free enterprise, the jobs and exports it provides, and the independence it brings to our people. Independence? Yes, but let us be clear what we mean by that. Independence does not mean contracting out of all relationships with others. A nation can be free, but it will not stay free for long if it has no friends and no alliances. Above all, it will not stay free if it cannot pay its own way in the world. By the same token, an individual needs to be part of a community and to feel that he is part of it. There is more to this than the chance to earn a living for himself and his family, essential though it is.

No U-Turn in Government Policies

Of course, our vision and our aims go far beyond the complex arguments of economics, but unless we get the economy right, we shall deny our people the opportunity to share that vision and to see beyond the narrow horizons of economic necessity. Without a healthy economy, we cannot have a healthy society. Without a healthy society, the economy will not stay healthy for long. But it is not the state that creates a healthy society. When the state grows too powerful, people feel that they count for less and less. The state drains society, not only of its wealth but of initiative, of energy, the will to improve and innovate as well as to preserve what is best. Our aim is to let people feel that they count for more and more. If we cannot trust the deepest instincts of our people, we should not be in politics at all. Some aspects of our present society really do offend those instincts.

Decent people do want to do a proper job at work, not to be restrained or intimidated from giving value for money. They believe that honesty should be respected, not derided. They see crime and violence as a threat not just to society but to their own orderly way of life. They want to be allowed to bring up their children in these beliefs, without the fear that their efforts will be daily frustrated in the name of progress or free expression. Indeed, that is what family life is all about.

There is not a generation gap in a happy and united family. People yearn to be able to rely on some generally accepted standards. Without them you have not got a society at all, you have purposeless anarchy. A healthy society is not created by its institutions, either. Great schools and universities do not make a great nation any more than great armies do. Only a great nation can create and involve great institutions—of learning, of healing, of scientific advance. And a great nation is the voluntary creation of its people—a people composed of men and women whose pride in themselves is founded on the knowledge of what they can give to a community of which they in turn can be proud.

If our people feel that they are part of a great nation, and they are prepared to will the means to keep it great, a great nation we shall be, and shall remain. So, what can stop us from achieving this? What then stands in our way? The prospect of another winter of discontent? I suppose it might. But I prefer to believe that certain lessons have been learnt from experience, that we are coming, slowly, painfully, to an autumn of understanding. And I hope that it will be followed by a winter of common sense. If it is not, we shall not be diverted from our course.

To those waiting with bated breath for that favourite media catchphrase, the "U" turn, I have only one thing to say. "You turn if you want to. The lady's not for turning." I say that not only to you but to our friends overseas and also to those who are not our friends. In foreign affairs we have pursued our national interest robustly while remaining alive to the needs and interests of others. We have acted where our predecessors dithered, and here I pay tribute to Lord Carrington. When I think of our much-travelled Foreign Secretary, I am reminded of the advert about "the peer that reaches those foreign parts that other peers cannot reach."

Foreign and Defence Policy

Long before we came into office, and therefore long before the invasion of Afghanistan, I was pointing to the threat from the East. I was accused of scaremongering. But events have more than justified my words. Soviet Marxism is ideologically, politically, and morally bankrupt. But militarily the Soviet Union is a powerful and growing threat. Yet it was Mr. Kosygin who said "No peace loving country, no person of integrity, should remain indifferent when an aggressor holds human life and world opinion in insolent contempt." We agree. The British government are not indifferent to the occupation of Afghanistan. We shall not allow it to be forgotten. Unless and until the Soviet troops are withdrawn, other nations are bound to wonder which of them may be next. Of course, there are those who say that by speaking out we are complicating East-West relations, that we are endangering detente. But the real danger would lie in keeping silent. Detente is indivisible, and it is a two-way process.

The Soviet Union cannot conduct wars by proxy in South-East Asia and Africa, foment trouble in the Middle East and Caribbean, invade neighbouring countries, and still expect to conduct business as usual. Unless detente is pursued by both sides, it can be pursued by neither, and it is a delusion to suppose otherwise. That is the message we shall be delivering loud and clear at the meeting of the European Security Conference in Madrid in the weeks immediately ahead.

But we shall also be reminding the other parties in Madrid that the Helsinki Accord was supposed to promote the freer movement of people and ideas. The Soviet government's response so far has been a campaign of repression worse than any since Stalin's day. It had been hoped that Helsinki would open gates across Europe. In fact, the guards today are better armed and the walls are no lower. But behind those walls the human spirit is unvanquished. The workers of Poland in their millions have signalled their determination to participate in the shaping of their destiny. We salute them. Marxists claim that the capitalist system is in crisis. But the Polish workers have shown that it is the Communist system that is in crisis. The Polish people should be left to work out their own future without external interference.

At every party conference, and every November in Parliament, we used to face difficult decisions over Rhodesia and over sanctions. But no longer. Since we last met, the success at Lancaster House, and thereafter in Salisbury—a success won in the face of all the odds—has created new respect for Britain. It has given fresh hope to those grappling with the terrible problems of Southern Africa. It has given the Commonwealth new strength and unity. Now it is for the new nation, Zimbabwe, to build her own future with the support of all those who believe that democracy has a place in Africa, and we wish her well. We showed over Rhodesia that the hallmarks of Tory policy are, as they have always been, realism and resolve. Not for us the disastrous fantasies of unilateral disarmament, of withdrawal from NATO, of abandoning Northern Ireland.

The irresponsibility of the left on defence increases as the dangers which we face loom larger. We, for our part, under Francis Pym's brilliant leadership, have chosen a defence policy which potential foes will respect. We are acquiring, with the co-operation of the United States government, the Trident missile system. This will ensure the credibility of our strategic deterrent until the end of the century and beyond, and it was very important for the reputation of Britain abroad that we should keep our independent nuclear deterrent as well as for our citizens here. We have agreed to the stationing of cruise missiles in this country. The unilateralists object, but the recent willingness of the Soviet government to open a new round of arms control negotiations shows the wisdom of our firmness. We intend to maintain and, where possible, to improve our conventional forces so as to pull our weight in the alliance. We have no wish to seek a free ride at the expense of our allies. We will play our full part. In Europe we have shown that it is possible to combine a vigorous defence of our own interests with a deep commitment to the ideas and to the ideals of the Community.

The last government were well aware that Britain's budget contribution was grossly unfair. They failed to do anything about it. We negotiated a satisfactory arrangement which will give us and our partners time to tackle the underlying issues. We have resolved the difficulties of New Zealand's lamb trade with the Community in a way which protects the interests of the farmers in New Zealand while giving our own farmers and our own housewives an excellent deal, and Peter Walker deserves to be congratulated on his success. Now he is two-thirds on his way to success in making important progress towards agreement on a common fisheries policy. That is very important to our people. There are many, many people whose livelihoods depend on it. We face many other problems in the Community, but I am confident that they too will yield to the firm yet fair approach which has already proved so much more effective than the previous government's five years of procrastination.

With each day it becomes clearer that in the wider world we face darkening horizons, and the war between Iran and Iraq is the latest symptom of a deeper malady. Europe and North America are centres of stability in an increasingly anxious world. The Community and the Alliance are the guarantee to other countries that democracy and freedom of choice are still possible. They stand for order and the rule of law in an age when disorder and lawlessness are ever more widespread. The British government intend to stand by both these great institutions, the Community and NATO. We will not betray them.

Conclusion

The restoration of Britain's place in the world and of the West's confidence in its own destiny are two aspects of the same process. No doubt there will be unexpected twists in the road, but with wisdom and resolution, we can reach our goal. I believe we will show the wisdom and you may be certain that we will show the resolution. In his warm hearted and generous speech, Peter Thorneycroft said that when people are called upon to lead great nations, they must look into the hearts and minds of the people whom they seek to govern. I would add that those who seek to govern must in turn be willing to allow their hearts and minds to lie open to the people.

I have tried to set before you some of my most deeply held convictions and beliefs. This party, which I am privileged to serve, and this government, which I am proud to lead, are engaged in the massive task of restoring confidence and stability to our people. I have always known that the task was vital. Since last week it has become even more vital than ever. We close our conference in the aftermath of that sinister Utopia unveiled at Blackpool. Let Labour's Orwellian nightmare of the left be the spur for us to dedicate with a new urgency our every ounce of energy and moral strength to rebuild the fortunes of this free nation. If we were to fail, that freedom could be imperilled. So let us resist the blandishments of the faint hearts; let us ignore the howls and threats of the extremists; let us stand together and do our duty, and we shall not fail.

FIGURE 18.1 Margaret Thatcher. (*Source:* British Information Services, New York.)

18

The Virtue of the Individual
and the Nation

Speech at St. Lawrence Jewry,
Ash Wednesday, March 4, 1981

Part I: Introduction

Today is Ash Wednesday, the day when traditionally Christians begin a period of thoughtfulness about their relationship with God and how they are trying to serve Him here on Earth. It is therefore fitting that on this occasion we consider some of the things which have made our nation flourish in the past and some of the challenges we face today. My theme will be that the virtue of the nation is only as great as the virtue of the individuals who compose it.

Two years ago in this church, I spoke as both a Christian and a politician about how I found my religious convictions affecting the way I approached the responsibility of government. Since then I have been, as it were, called to higher service! My approach to my present responsibilities remains the same as it was then, and I am indeed thankful that I was brought up in a Christian family and learned the message of the Christian faith. I want to consider some of the characteristics of our way of life which have stood our people in such good stead in times past.

John Newton preached a sermon exactly two hundred years ago in a city church only a step away from this one. In the course of it he said: "Though the occasion will require me to take some notice of our public affairs, I mean not to amuse you with what is usually called a political discourse." I too will endeavour to keep to this self-denying ordinance.

Part II: Man as a Moral Being and the Nation

The concept of the nation is at the heart of the Old Testament Judaism and one which those who wrote the New Testament accepted. But there is an even more fundamental idea which is also common to both: the idea of personal moral responsibility. It is to individuals that the Ten Commandments are addressed. In the statements, "honour thy father and thy mother," "thou shalt not steal," "thou shalt not bear false witness," and so on, the "thou" to whom these resounding imperatives are addressed is you and me. In the same way, the New Testament is preoccupied with the individual, with his need for forgiveness and for the divine strength which comes to those who sincerely accept it.

Of course, we can deduce from the teachings of the Bible principles of public as well as private morality. But in the last resort, all these principles refer back to the individual in his relationships to others. We must always beware of supposing that somehow we can get rid of our own moral duties by handing them over to the community, that somehow we can get rid of our own guilt by talking about "national" or "social" guilt. We are called on to repent our own sins, not each others' sins.

So each person is all-important in the Christian view of life and the universe. But human beings have social needs as well. So it is that in the course of history, the family, the neighbourhood, and the nation come into being. All these communities have certain things in common. However they grew up, they are held together by mutual dependence, by the experience which their members have in common, by common customs and belief. They all need rules to enable them to live together harmoniously, and the rules must be backed by some kind of authority, however gently and subtly exercised. The nation is but an enlarged family. Because of its traditions and the mutual love and loyalty which bind its members together, it should ideally need little enforcement to maintain its life. But alas, because of man's imperfection, evil is ever present, and the innocent must be protected from its ravages.

So the first and, in a sense, the most important point I have to make to you is this: we must never think of individual freedom and the social good as being opposed to each other; we must never suppose that where personal liberty is strong, society will be weak and impoverished, or that where the nation is strong the individual will necessarily be in shackles. The wealth of nations, the defence of national freedom, and the well-being of society—all these depend on the faith and exertions of men and women. It is an old and simple truth, but it is sometimes forgotten in political debate.

But what of the common beliefs and habits which hold this British nation of ours together? There was, of course, a time when the Christian religion was the only permitted form of worship in our land. Today we live in what is called a "plural society," one in which many different traditions of belief exist alongside each other and also alongside other more recent fashions— those of total disbelief or even nihilism. No doubt we have absorbed much from other systems of belief and contributed much to them. The change, however, has also brought its dilemmas, not least for the legislator. We now have to concern ourselves not only with how Christians should behave towards each other within the framework of the nation, but with how they should seek to organise the nation's life in a way that is fair and tolerant towards those who do not accept the Christian message. What I am suggesting to you, however, is that even though there are considerable religious minorities in Britain, most people would accept that we have a national way of life and that it is founded on Biblical principles.

Part III: The Values of This Nation

As we emerged from the twilight of medieval times, which for many life was characterised by tyranny, injustice, and cruelty, so we became what one historian has described as "the people of a book and that book was the Bible" (J. R. Green). What he meant, I think, was that this nation adopted, albeit gradually, a system of government and a way of living together which reflected the values implicit in that Book. We acknowledged as a nation that God was the source of our strength and that the teachings of Christ applied to our national as well as our personal life. There was, however, a considerable gap between the precept and the practise. Even when men had become free to speak for themselves, to invent, to experiment, and to lay the foundations of what became known as the Industrial Revolution, considerable blotches remained on the canvas of our national life.

It took the vision and patience of men like Lord Shaftesbury and William Wilberforce to convince Parliament that it was inconsistent for a nation whose life was based on Christ's teachings, to countenance slave labour, children and women working in the mines, and criminals locked up in degrading conditions. These leaders were motivated first and foremost by their Christian beliefs. It is also significant that most of the great philanthropists who set up schools and hospitals did so because they saw this as part of their Christian service for the people of the nation. Indeed, something of that same vision can be seen today. Wherever there are refugees or suffering or poverty in the world, there you find Christians working to relieve pain, to provide comfort, hope, and practical help.

The spirit of our nation also includes some clear convictions about such things as fair play which we regard as almost a religion in itself, and bullying which we loathe. Perhaps Kipling put it best in one of his poems called "Norman and Saxon," set in A.D. 1100: "My son," said the Norman Baron,

"I am dying, and you will be heir To all the broad acres in England that
William gave me for my share When we conquered the Saxon at Hastings,
and a nice little handful it is. But before you go over to rule it I want you to
understand this: The Saxon is not like us Normans. His manners are not so
polite. But he never means anything serious till he talks about justice and
right. When he stands like an ox in the furrow with his sullen set eyes on
your own, and Grumbles, 'This isn't fair dealing,' my son, leave the Saxon
Alone."

This sense of fair play is based on the acceptance by the majority in the
nation of some moral absolutes which underpin our social and commercial
relationships. In other words, we believe that just as there are physical laws
which we break at our peril, so there are moral laws which, if we flout them,
will lead to personal and national decline. If we as a nation had accepted, for
instance, that violence, stealing, and deception were plausible activities, then
our moral fibre would soon have disintegrated.

There is one other characteristic of our nation which is, I think, worth
mentioning: we have always had a sense that work is not only a necessity; it
is a duty, and indeed a virtue. It is an expression of our dependence on each
other. Work is not merely a way of receiving a pay packet, but a means
whereby everyone in the community benefits, and society is enriched.
Creating wealth must be seen as a Christian obligation if we are to fulfil our
role as stewards of the resources and talents the Creator has provided for us.

These characteristics of our nation, the acknowledgement of the Almighty,
a sense of tolerance, an acknowledgement of moral absolutes, and a positive
view of work, have sustained us in the past. Today they are being challenged.
Although we are still able to live on the spiritual capital passed down to us,
it is self-deceiving to think we can do so forever. Each generation must
renew its spiritual assets if the integrity of the nation is to survive. Today, in
spite of the work of the churches, I suspect that only a minority acknowledge
the authority of God in their lives. Perhaps that is why we have turned to the
state to do so many things which in the past were the prerogative of the
family: why crimes of violence are increasing, and a few people are even
suggesting that murder can be justified on the grounds that it is political, a
view which must be abhorrent to Christians. Furthermore, the respect for
private and public property seems to be diminishing, and outside this city we
can no longer assume that a man's word is always his bond.

Ethics and Economics

In terms of ethics and national economics, I should like also to refer to
what I believe is an evil, namely, sustained inflation. For over thirty years
the value of our currency has been eroding. It is an insidious evil because its

effects are slow to be seen and relatively painless in the short run. Yet it has a morally debilitating influence on all aspects of our national life. It reduces the value of savings; it undermines financial agreements; it stimulates hostility between workers and employers over matters of pay; it encourages debt; and it diminishes the prospects of jobs. This is why I put its demise at the top of my list of economic priorities. It is, in my view, a moral issue, not just an economic one.

The second and equally great human and economic problem is the level of unemployment, which has been rising for over two decades and is still rising. I cannot conceal that of all difficulties I face, unemployment concerns me most of all. Leaving aside world recession and the details of economic policies necessary to defeat inflation (which would be the subject of a political discourse), what can we as individuals do to help? For none of us can opt out of the community in which we live. Whether we do something or nothing, our actions will affect it.

First, those who are in work fully accept their duty to provide for those who cannot find work. Second, if we are employers, we can try to take on as many young people as possible, to give them experience of the world of work. There are a number of schemes available for this purpose, and I must say that employers are responding splendidly. They, too, know how depressing it must be for a young person to feel that he is not needed and cannot find a niche for himself. Third, we could perhaps buy more British-made goods; not everything British made, because there are jobs in exports, too, and we expect others to buy our goods. But we could help our people by buying more "home-made" products. Fourth, we can recognize that if at a time when output is not rising we ourselves demand more pay, it can only come from the pockets of others, and it will reduce the amount they can spend on other goods. That kind of pay claim can price your own job out of existence, or cause someone else to lose his job. And that responsibility cannot be shirked; it is a *personal* responsibility. And it is a *moral* responsibility.

Another factor which affects us at present arises in part from the first and second. It is a sense of pessimism brought on because of the frustration of not seeming to have a national purpose. When this happens to a nation, groups within it tend to work toward their more limited goals, often at the expense of others. This pessimism is expressed in two ways. There are those who want to destroy our society for their own purposes—the terrorists and other extremists that we all too frequently see in action these days. Then there are those who adopt a philosophy of "eat, drink, and be merry for tomorrow we die." That can result in the grasping of wealth for its own sake and the pursuit of selfish pleasure.

If I am right, we need to establish in the minds of young and old alike a national purpose which has real meaning for them. It must include the defence of the values which we believe to be of vital importance. Unless the spirit of the nation which has hitherto sustained us is renewed, our national way of life will perish. Who is to undertake this task? Throughout history it has always been the few who took the lead, a few who see visions and dream dreams. There were the prophets in the Old Testament, the Apostles in the New, and the reformers in both church and state. I well remember hearing a sermon after the Battle of Britain in which this was said about the few pilots to whom so many owed so much. John Stuart Mill once said that "one person with a belief is a social power equal to ninety-nine who have only interests." If we as a nation fail to produce such people, then I am afraid the spirit of the nation which has hitherto sustained us will slowly die.

Part IV: How These Values Are Sustained

What then are the institutional means by which these values can be revived, for ideas and sentiments need institutions if they are to survive and be effective. Because we are talking primarily of the values bequeathed to us by a predominantly Christian culture, we must think first of the role of the church. The church, thought of as the bishops, clergy, and laity organised for public worship, has clear duties of its own: to preach the gospel of Christ, to celebrate the sacraments, and to give comfort and counsel to men and women struggling with the trials and dilemmas of life.

Politicians must respect and accept its authority in these spheres. In our own country the state pays homage to the church in many ways. The Queen is Supreme Governor of the Church of England and Protector of the Church of Scotland. These arrangements may seem to many to be anti- quated, but they express the state's fundamental respect for the Christian religion. I hope we shall never see here what we have seen in other countries: temporal governments trying to usurp the role of spiritual leadership which properly belongs to the church. That is a recipe for state tyranny as well as the corruption of religion. The church, on the other hand, can never resign altogether from what are called temporal matters. It has always rightly claimed to set before us the moral standards by which our public affairs should be conducted.

But I hope you will forgive me for stating what I think these days needs to be pointed out, namely the difference between defining standards and descending into the political arena to take sides on those practical issues over which many good and honest Christians sincerely disagree. This, surely, can only weaken the influence and independence of the church whose members ideally should help shape the thinking of all political parties. Bernard Shaw, in the preface to "Androcles and the Lion," makes the breath-taking statement, "Christ was a first-class political economist." But it was Christ himself who said of those who were too pre-occupied with material things: "Seek ye first the kingdom of God and his righteousness, and all these things shall be added unto you." I wonder if some people are not demanding that "things be added unto them" *before* they seek the kingdom of God, indeed, regardless of whether they seek it or not.

As for the role of the state (what the Bible calls "the things that are Caesar's"), I have never concealed my own philosophy. I believe it is a philosophy which rests on Christian assumptions, though I fully recognize that some Christians would have a different view. To me the wisdom of statesmanship consists of: knowing the limits within which government can and ought to act for the good of the individuals who make up society; respecting those limits; ensuring that the laws to which the people are subject shall be just and consistent with the public conscience; making certain that those laws are firmly and fairly enforced; making the nation strong for the defence of its way of life against potential aggression; and maintaining an honest currency.

Only governments can carry out these functions, and in these spheres government must be strong. But every one of these objects depends for its achievement on the faith and the work of the individuals. The state cannot create wealth. That depends on the exertions of countless people motivated not only by the wholesome desire to provide for themselves and their families, but also by a passion for excellence and a genuine spirit of public service.

The state cannot generate compassion. It can and must provide a "safety net" for those who, through no fault of their own, are unable to cope on their own. There is need for far more generosity in our national life, but generosity is born in the hearts of men and women. It cannot be manufactured by politicians, and assuredly it will not flourish if politicians foster the illusion that the exercise of compassion can be left to officials. And so, I repeat, it is on the individual that the health of both church and state depends.

Perhaps we have lost the idea that is inherent in Christ's parable of the talents. The steward who simply did not use the resources entrusted to him was roundly condemned. The two who used them to produce more wealth were congratulated and given more. To put up with the mediocre, to flinch from the challenge, to mutter "the government ought to be doing something about it," is not the way to rekindle the spirit of the nation.

V: Conclusion

And so what should we conclude about the relationship between the individual and the nation? I make no secret of my wish that everyone should be proud of belonging to this country. We have a past which, by any standard, is impressive; much in our present life and culture, too, commands great respect. We have as a nation a sense of perspective and a sense of humour; our scholars win international acclaim; our armed forces are renowned for their bravery and restraint; and our industries, in spite of economic recession, continue to do well in the markets of the world.

I want us to be proud of our nation for another reason. In the comity of nations, only a minority have a system of government which can be described as democratic. In these, economic and cultural life flourish because of the freedom their people enjoy. But a democratic system of government cannot be transferred to other nations simply by setting up imitations of our institutions. We have realized this all too clearly in recent times. For democracy to work, it requires what Montesquieu described as a special quality in the people: virtue and, I would add, understanding. I believe this quality of virtue to be that derived from the Biblical principles on which this nation and the United States, among others, are founded. I want this nation to continue to be heard in the world and for the leaders of other countries to know that our strength comes from shared convictions as to what is right and wrong, and that we value these convictions enough to defend them.

Let me sum up. I believe the spirit of this nation is a Christian one. The values which sustain our way of life have by no means disappeared, but they are in danger of being undermined. I believe we are able to generate the will and purpose to revive and maintain them. John Newton put it elegantly in the sermon to which I earlier referred: "Though the Island of Great Britain exhibits but a small spot upon a map of the globe, it makes a splendid appearance in the history of mankind, and for a long space of time has been signally under the protection of God and a seat of peace, liberty, and truth." I pray we may continue to receive such blessing and retain such qualities.

19

Women in a Changing World

First Dame Margery Corbett Ashby
Memorial Lecture, July 26, 1982

The life and work of Dame Margery spanned almost a century, from her birth in April 1882, to her death last year. Rarely has a century so exemplified Disraeli's maxim that in a progressive country change is constant. Dame Margery, who was instrumental in bringing about so much change, was herself born into a world of change. It was a world of *political* change, where not only *women* were deprived. It is obvious that the issue of women's right to vote arises only when *people's* right to vote has been established, or at least is on the agenda. For most of human history it has been absent. In 1882, only thirty-three percent of men had the right to vote. Two years later the Reform Bill doubled that percentage, extending civil rights to an extra two million men.

It was a world of *educational* change. Elementary education had just been made compulsory by an Act of 1880. Schools and colleges for women were springing up. Newham College, Cambridge, where Dame Margery was to take a degree in classics, had been founded in 1871. It was a world of *scientific and religious* change. In 1882, Charles Darwin, whose theory of evolution had challenged many accepted beliefs, disturbed many faiths and brought about a radical change in all human thought, was buried in Westminster Abbey, to the disgust of many churchmen. Some years earlier, Bishop Samuel Wilberforce of Oxford, in his arguments with the Darwinians, had shown the typically Victorian chivalrous attitude to women. He said that he could accept that his grandfather might have been descended from an ape, but not his grandmother.

It was a world of *social* change, much of it generated by the numerous voluntary organisations founded at that time. Their names read like a roll-call of human compassion: the National Society for the Prevention of Cruelty to Children founded in 1884, the St. John Ambulance Association in 1877, the Soldiers, Sailors, and Airmen's Families Association in 1885, the Church Army in 1890, and many, many more.

It was a world in which we were just beginning to see the first glimmer of change in the *professional status of women,* for example in nursing and in medicine. Elizabeth Garret Anderson had qualified in 1865. The suffragettes did not fight for the right of women to work because so many women of that generation had of necessity to go out to work. Indeed, Shaftesbury had commented adversely on that trend when he said: "Domestic life and domestic discipline must soon be at an end. Society will consist of individuals no longer grouped into families." (1844) In 1881, some twenty-seven percent of the female population of the United Kingdom already worked outside the home, compared with thirty-two percent today. But Dame Margery and her generation did fight for the right of women to be admitted to the professions: the law, the civil service, and the diplomatic service.

It was a world of *legal* change, well illustrated by the Married Women's Property Act of 1882, which effected a major advance in women's rights. Women were now allowed to retain and own property independently of their husbands. This reasonable measure, which stopped the married woman from being a mere chattel of her husband, caused much distress in its passage through Parliament. One Member felt that its enactment should be delayed until 1885 "in order to give men who were contemplating matrimony time to change their minds when they found the law altered." Another feared that "no man would marry a woman with property, knowing that she could set him at defiance. The Bill was against Scripture." He had obviously never reflected on the words of the marriage service when, as the man said: "With all my worldly goods I thee endow." Until then it had really been the other way round.

Change is an essential characteristic of the human condition. But history is shaped by the way in which men and women *respond* to that change. They may resist it absolutely, so that all its opportunities are wasted, like the religious sect who will not use buttons [Mennonites] because they regard them as a product of decadent modern civilisation! Or they may accept it so wholeheartedly that novelty becomes a virtue in itself, and all these lessons of history and experience are dismissed. This attitude has caused much political upheaval, as whole regimes and civilisations have sometimes been swept away in the name of change which is assumed to be beneficent just because it is change.

There is another response which welcomes and uses change, but refuses to be ruled by it, testing each new development against the eternal verities. I believe that this last was the attitude of Dame Margery in her great contributions to the century of change through which she lived, in her services to women and to society in Britain and throughout the world. She was co-founder of the Townswomen's Guilds, of the Commonwealth Countries' League, and the National Women Citizens Association. She was president of the International Women's Suffrage Alliance from 1923-46 and an office-bearer in it for seventy years. She gave her first presidential speech at the Sorbonne in 1926 and presided at Berlin in 1929, Istanbul in 1935, Copenhagen in 1939, and Interlaken in 1946.

Her first concern was that women should have the same *political* rights as men. With that end in view, she became secretary of the National Union of Women's Suffrage Societies in 1907, working tirelessly until full adult female suffrage was achieved in 1928. The task was not made easier by the fact that the leader of her chosen party, Mr. Asquith, was resolutely opposed to votes for women. He followed the tradition of Mr. Gladstone, who in 1884 and then prime minister, had spoken against women's suffrage. He "feared [that] voting would trespass upon their delicacy, their purity, their refinement, the elevation of their whole nature." Dame Margery is proof that it did none of those things.

I am very conscious of the fact that it is due to the efforts of Margery Corbett Ashby and others like her that women today are able to play such a major part in political life. All women received the vote in 1928, and 1929 saw the appointment of the first woman cabinet minister, Margaret Bondfield. But this was not enough for Dame Margery. In her speech of that year to the British Commonwealth League, she deplored the fact that women did not have the right to sit in the House of Lords. Almost thirty years later, in 1958, the Life Peerages Act gave women that right. This was extended in 1963 when the same government admitted hereditary peeresses to the House of Lords. Last year we achieved another "first" when I asked Baroness Young, who has done so much for public life, to become the first woman leader of the Upper House. I think that Dame Margery would have approved.

In the House of Commons, more than half a century after all women got the vote, there are only twenty-one women Members of Parliament out of a House of Commons total of 635 Members. This would have been a great disappointment to the early suffragettes, whose main fight was for the rights of women to full participation in politics, local government, and the community. They did that partly because it is just and equitable that women should have such rights, but also because they wanted public life to be shaped and influenced by the special talents and experiences of women. To quote Dame Margery again, in her 1926 presidential address to the Congress of the International Alliance at Paris: "No woman is so busy in her home or profession that she can't by a better adjustment of her time, spare some energy to work for her neighbours, her town and her country. [We] seek to deepen a woman's sense of responsibility and to widen her sphere of activity from the home to the city, from the city to the nation."

What are these special talents and experiences which women have to bring to public life? Are they any different in kind from those of men? Yes, because women bear the children and create and run the home. It is noticeable that many suffragettes were very womanly. Like Dame Margery, they had the inestimable privilege of being wives and mothers, and they pursued their public work against the background of full and happy domestic lives. They neglected no detail of those lives, so that they were *warm* as well as immensely capable women. And it was these enriched lives, with their breadth of experience, that they devoted to public service. The many practical skills and management qualities needed to make a home give women an ability to deal with a variety of problems and to do so quickly. It is that versatility and decisiveness which is so valuable in public life.

After the victory for women's suffrage had been won here, Dame Margery went on to work for it in other countries, through the International Alliance. Their 1935 congress was held in Turkey where, despite promises and statements of relevant legislative intent in 1930, 1931, and 1934, Turkish women had still not received the vote. On her arrival in Istanbul, Dame Margery told the mayor that it was a pity "that the women will come from all over the world to Turkey and find Turkish women without the vote." This remark found its way to the president of Turkey, Kemal Ataturk, and very soon Turkish women had been granted the vote on the same terms as men, and seventeen women Members of Parliament were elected. What quiet power she had.

It was also after 1928 that she turned to the second great strand of her work, the Townswomen's Guilds, born in 1929 out of the earlier suffrage societies. The significant achievements of the Townswomen's Guilds in the last half-century owe much to her example and vigour. It is useful to remind ourselves of the objectives which guide your work: "To advance the education of women, irrespective of race, creed, or party, so as to enable them to make the best contribution towards the common good. To educate women in the principles of good citizenship and to provide facilities for women to improve their own social conditions and those of their fellows."

Margery Corbett Ashby worked hard for *legislative* change. She and others knew that only legislation could give women the vote and certain fundamental rights. But she knew too that legislation is not enough. As she said, when I was privileged to share a platform with her in Westminster Hall in 1978 at the celebration of fifty years of women's suffrage: "It's comparatively easy to change the law. What is difficult is to change the attitudes of the community." She set out to change those attitudes through the Townswomen's Guilds. Her work in them illustrated the belief that legislation can provide only a foundation for action. To give a person a vote is a remarkable achievement. But to help people to understand how democracy works and its dependence on the exercise of personal responsibilities is much harder. And is that not part of the role of the Townswomen's Guilds?

The benefits which law is intended to promote can only be achieved by the effort of *individuals*. A government may provide incentives for industrial development. But it is the brains and hands of men and women which must translate those into action, into industrial wealth and success. A government may provide a framework of social services, a safety net through which none may fall. But the many deeds of mercy, the myriad acts of human kindness which give life its dignity and meaning, these are the work of individuals. The loving care which should generate and inform such activities is a feature of the human spirit. It cannot be manufactured or decreed by politicians. "What's the government going to do about it?" is a common phrase. But surely the better approach was that expressed by President Kennedy in his Inaugural Address: "Ask not what your country can do for you. Ask what you can do for your country." Recently [in the Falklands] we have seen that philosophy abundantly fulfilled by our people when called upon to defend freedom and justice many thousands of miles away.

The achievements for which we honour Dame Margery today, although great in themselves, have been a comparatively small part of the enormous changes which have transformed our lives over the years—changes in transport, communications, automation, fuel and energy, science and medicine, in the environment and the life of our cities, above all in *prosperity* so that the luxuries of the few have become the necessities of the many. It is not therefore possible to isolate the effect of the changing status of women on our society. Nevertheless, if we are to shape our future, we must take a dispassionate look at what has happened to the structure of society across the century.

Throughout history great emphasis has been laid upon the importance of the *family*. But in family matters today there are some very disquieting features. For example, in 1882 there were 43,000 illegitimate births in England and Wales. Some eighty years later, in 1960, there were approximately the same number. In 1980 the numbers had risen to 77,000. Worse still, the number of girls who conceived children under the age of sixteen has risen from 6,600 in 1970 to 8,100 in 1979. Further, the number of juvenile offenders has doubled in less than twenty years, rising from 100,000 in 1965 to nearly 200,000 in 1979. Moreover, today one in ten marriages is expected to break down after five years, and one in three after thirty years.

It is, of course, difficult to make valid comparisons with a century ago. But the figures do tell us what has happened in the last twenty years, and we cannot fail to be worried by them. Indeed, I wonder whether the family has been sufficiently highly regarded in recent years. Much emphasis has been placed on individual rights, less on our duties to each other. Children have been encouraged to grow up faster and to see themselves as independent of parents. Parents have been told by self-appointed experts that their duties to each other and to their children should be balanced by more emphasis on self-fulfillment. In other words, we have seen the birth of the permissive society. Has that benefitted women? Far from it.

Women know that society is founded on dignity, reticence, and discipline. We know instinctively that the disintegration of society begins with the death of idealism and convention. We know that for our society as a whole, and especially for the children, much depends on the family unity remaining secure and respected. It is significant that so many women who have reached the top have families of their own, like Dame Margery, and as I can personally testify, they are our greatest joy and strength.

It is, of course, true that women of our generation are often still comparatively young by the time our children are grown up, and therefore we have an opportunity further to develop our own talents, an opportunity which in Dame Margery's day was rarely available. For many that experience can enhance their lives and enlarge their interests.

But I remain totally convinced that when children are young, however busy we may be with the practical duties inside or outside the home, the most important thing of all is to devote enough time and care to their needs and problems. There are some things for which only a parent will do. I will never forget the comment of a headmaster of a school I visited when Secretary of State for Education. He said that as many problem children came from rich as from poor homes. Some were from homes where the children have everything they wish for except perhaps enough of their parents' attention. Material goods can never be a substitute for loving care. Too much money can create problems as well as solve them.

The battle for women's rights has been largely won. The days when they were demanded and discussed in strident tones should be gone forever. We must now see them in perspective and turn our attention to how we use *human* rights to build the kind of world we wish our children to inherit. It is no use looking through rose-tinted spectacles or pretending that human imperfections and evil will disappear if we get the economy or the environment right. They won't. They are as old as humanity itself, and we have to fight them constantly, fight them by making and enforcing laws to protect the weak, by upholding conventions and customs which serve the larger and limit the selfish purpose.

In international affairs the only protection for civilised values against the tyrant is a sure defence. Dame Margery's generation learned that so vividly and at so great a price. It is a tragedy that since the last world war there have been over one hundred and forty conflicts in various parts of the world, and they continue even as we meet here today. The danger for democracy is that

FIGURE 19.1 U.S. Transportation Secretary Elizabeth Dole with Thatcher at 10 Downing Street. (*Source:* British Information Services, New York.)

too many people will say, "what can one person do among fifty-five million?" Dame Margery never took that view.... Burke put it so well so long ago: "All that is necessary for evil to triumph is for good men to do nothing." But our generation has reason to be thankful that those noble and brave acts which brought fame and renown to Britain's name are matched by deeds of courage and valour in our time.

It is a rare honour to be Prime Minister of the United Kingdom. It is a supreme privilege to occupy that high office when great human causes have to be defended. It is an inspiration to witness the young generation of today setting the most glorious standards for the young of tomorrow. I am very aware of how much I owe to Dame Margery. I honour and thank her for her sense of purpose, for her selfless service, and for that tireless spirit which sustained her until her works were well and truly accomplished—to stand on the ancient ways to see which is the right and good way and in that to walk.

FIGURE 20.1 Winston S. Churchill with Franklin D. Roosevelt. (*Source:* George C. Marshall Library.)

20

Address to a Joint Session of the U.S. Congress

February 20, 1985

My thoughts turn to three earlier occasions when a British prime minister—Winston Churchill—has been honoured by a call to address both houses. Among his many remarkable gifts, Winston held a special advantage here. Through his American mother he had ties of blood with you. Alas for me, these are not matters we can readily arrange for ourselves. Those three occasions deserve to be recalled because they serve as lamps along a dark road which our people trod together, and they remind us what an extraordinary period of history the world has passed through between that time and ours. And they tell us what later generations in both our countries sometimes find hard to grasp—why past associations bind us so closely. Winston Churchill's version of a union of mind and purpose between the English speaking peoples was to form the mainspring of the West.

No one of my generation can forget that America has been the principal architect of a peace in Europe which has lasted forty years. Given this shield of the United States, we have been granted the opportunities to build a concept of Europe beyond the dreams of our fathers: a Europe which seemed unattainable amid the mud and slaughter of the First World War and the suffering and sacrifice of the Second. When, in the Spring of 1945, the guns fell silent, General Eisenhower called our soldiers to a service of Thanksgiving. In the order of service was the famous prayer of Sir Francis Drake: "O Lord God, when thou givest to thy servants to endeavour in great matter, grant us to know that it is not the beginning but the continuing of the same, until it be thoroughly finished, which yieldeth the true glory." On this day, close to the fortieth anniversary of that service, and of peace in Europe, one of the longest periods without war in all our history, I should like to recall those words and acknowledge how faithfully America has fulfilled them. For our deliverance from what might have befallen us, I would not have us leave our gratitude to the tributes of history. The debt the free peoples of Europe owe to this nation generous with its bounty, willing to share its strength, seeking to protect the weak, is incalculable. We thank and salute you.

Of course, in the years which separate us from the time when Winston Churchill last spoke to Congress, there have been disappointments as well as hopes fulfilled, the continued troubles in the Middle East, famine and oppression in Africa, genocide in South East Asia, the brutal occupation of Afghanistan, the undiminished agony of tortured Poland, and above all, the continued and continuing division of the European continent.

A New Europe

From these shores it may seem to some of you that by comparison with the risks and sacrifices which America has borne through four decades, and the courage with which you have shouldered unwanted burdens, Europe has not fully matched your expectations. Bear with me if I dwell for a moment on the Europe to which we now belong. It is not the Europe of Ancient Rome, of Charlemagne, of Bismarck. We who are alive today have passed through perhaps the greatest transformation of human affairs on the continent of Europe since the fall of Rome. In but a short chapter of its long story, Europe lost the position which it had occupied for two thousand years: and it is your history as much as ours. For five centuries that small continent had extended its authority over islands and continents the world over. For the first forty years of this century, there were seven great powers—the United States, Great Britain, Germany, France, Russia, Japan, and Italy. Of those seven, two now tower over the rest—the United States and the Soviet Union.

To that swift and historic change, Europe—a Europe of many different histories, many different nations—has had to find a response. It has not been an easy passage to blend this conflux of nationalism, patriotism, and sovereignty into a European community. Yet I think that our children and grand-children may see this period, these birth pangs of a new Europe, more clearly than we do now. They will see it as a visionary chapter in the creation of a Europe able to share the load alongside you. Do not doubt the firmness of our resolve in our march towards this goal. But don't underestimate what we already do.

Today, out of the forces of the alliance in Europe, ninety-five percent of the divisions, eighty-five percent of the tanks, eighty percent of the combat aircraft, and seventy percent of the fighting ships are provided, manned, and paid for by the European allies. Europe has more than three million men under arms and more still in reserve. We have to. We are right in the front line. The frontier of freedom cuts across our continent. Members of Congress, the defence of that frontier is as vital to you as it is to us.

The Superpowers and Deterrence

It is fashionable for some commentators to speak of the two super powers, the United States and the Soviet Union, as though they were somehow of equal worth and equal significance. That is a travesty of the truth. The Soviet Union has never concealed its true aim. In the words of Mr. Brezhnev: "The total triumph of socialism all over the world is inevitable, for this triumph . . . we shall struggle with no lack of effort." Indeed, there has been no lack of effort.

Contrast this with the record of the West. We do not aim at domination, at hegemony in any part of the world. Even against those who oppose and would destroy our ideas, we plot no aggression. Of course, we are ready to fight the battle of ideas with all the vigour at our command. But we do not try to impose our system on others. We do not believe that force should be the final arbiter in human affairs. We threaten no one. The alliance has been a solemn assurance to the world: "None of our weapons will be used except in response to attack."

In talking to the Soviet Union, we find great difficulty in getting this message across. They judge us by their ambitions. They cannot conceive of a powerful nation not using its power for expansion or subversion. And yet they should remember that when, after the last war, the United States had a monopoly of nuclear weapons, she never once exploited her superiority. No country ever used such great power more responsibly or with such restraint. I wonder what would have befallen us in Western Europe and Great Britain if that monopoly had been in Soviet hands.

Wars are not caused by the build-up of weapons. They are caused when an aggressor believes he can achieve his objectives at an acceptable price. The war of 1939 was not caused by an arms race. It sprang from a tyrant's belief that other countries lacked the means and the will to resist him. Remember Bismarck's phrase: "Do I want war? Of course not, I want victory." Our task is to see that potential aggressors from whatever quarter understand plainly that the capacity and the resolve of the West would deny them victory in war and that the price they would pay would be intolerable.

That is the basis of deterrence. It is the same whatever the nature of the weapons. Let us never forget the horrors of conventional wars and the hideous sacrifice of those who have suffered in them. Our task is not only to prevent nuclear war, but conventional war as well. No one understood the importance of deterrence more clearly than Winston Churchill when, in his last speech to you, he said: "Be careful above all things not to let go of the atomic weapons until you are sure, and more than sure, that other means of preserving peace are in your hands." Thirty-three years on, those weapons are still keeping the peace.

But since then technology has moved on, and if we are to maintain deterrence, as we must, it is essential that our research and capacity do not fall behind the work being done by the Soviet Union. That is why I firmly support President Reagan's decision to pursue research into defence against ballistic nuclear missiles—the Strategic Defense Initiative. Indeed, I hope that our own scientists will share in this research. The United States and the Soviet Union are both signatories to the 1972 Anti-ballistic Missile Treaty, a treaty without any terminal date. Nothing in that treaty precludes research, but should that research on either side lead to the possible deployment of new defence systems, that would be a matter for negotiation under the treaty.

But despite our differences with the Soviet Union, we have to talk with them, for we have one overriding interest in common: that never again should there be a conflict between our peoples. We hope too that we can achieve security with far fewer weapons than we have today and at lower cost. Thanks to the skillful diplomacy of Secretary Shultz, negotiations of arms control open in Geneva on 12 March. They will be of immense importance to millions. They will be intricate, complex, and demanding. We should not expect too much too soon. We must recognize that we shall face a Soviet political offensive designed to sow differences among us, calculated to create infirmity of purpose, to impair resolve—and even to arouse fear in the hearts of our people.

Hope is such a precious commodity in the world today that some are tempted to buy it at too high a price. We shall have to resist the muddled arguments of those who have been induced to believe that Russia's intentions are benign and that ours are suspect, or who would have us simply give up our defences in the hope that where we lead, others would follow. As we learned cruelly in the 1930s, from good intentions can come tragic results. Let us be under no illusions: it is our strength, not their goodwill, that has brought the Soviet Union to the negotiating table in Geneva. We know that our alliance, if it holds firm, cannot be defeated. But it could be outflanked. It is among the unfree and the underfed that subversion takes root. As Ethiopia demonstrated, those people get precious little help from the Soviet Union and its allies. The weapons which they pour in bring neither help nor hope to the hungry. It is the West which heard their cries. It is the West which responded massively to the heartrending starvation in Africa. It is the West which has made a unique contribution to the uplifting of hundreds of millions of people from poverty, illiteracy, and disease.

The Third World

The problems of the Third World are not only those of famine. They face also a mounting burden of debt, falling prices for primary products, protectionism by the industrialised countries. Some of the remedies are in the hands of the developing countries themselves. They can open their markets to productive investment. They can pursue responsible policies of economic adjustment—we should respect the courage and resolve with which so many of them have tackled their special problems. But we also have a duty to help.

How can we help? First, and most important, by keeping our markets open to them. Protectionism is a danger to all our trading partnerships. For so many countries trade is even more important than aid. So we in Britain support President Reagan's call for a new GATT round. The current strength of the dollar, which is causing so much difficulty for some of your industries, creates obvious pressures for "special cases," for new trade barriers to a free market. I am certain that your administration is right to resist such pressures. To give in to them would betray the millions in the developing world, to say nothing of the strains on your other trading partners. The developing countries need our markets, as we need theirs. We cannot preach economic adjustment to them, and refuse to practise it at home.

Economic Recovery in the United States and Britain

Second, the way in which we in the developed countries manage our economies determines whether the world's financial framework is stable, the level of interest rates, the amount of capital available for sound investment the world over, and whether or not the poor countries can service their past loans, let alone compete for new ones. Those are the reasons why we support so strongly your efforts to reduce the budget deficit. No other country in the world can be immune from its effects—such is the influence of the American economy on us all. We in Europe have watched with admiration the burgeoning of this mighty American economy. There is a new mood in the United States. A visitor feels it at once. The resurgence of your self-confidence and your national pride is almost tangible. Now the sun is rising in the West.

For many years our vitality in Britain was blunted by excess reliance on the state. Our industries were nationalised, controlled, and subsidised in a way that yours never were. We're having to recover the spirit of enterprise which you never lost. Many of the policies you are following are the policies we are following: You have brought inflation down. So have we. You have declared war on regulations and controls, so have we. Our civil service is now smaller than at any time since the war. Controls on pay, prices, dividends, foreign exchange—all are gone. You have encouraged small business, so often the source of tomorrow's jobs. And so have we.

Above all, we are carrying out the largest programme of denationalisation in our history. Just a few years ago in Britain, privatisation was thought to be a pipe dream. Now it is a reality, and a popular one. Our latest success was the sale of British Telecommunications. It was the largest share issue ever to be brought to the market—on either side of the Atlantic. Some two million people bought shares. That is what capitalism is: a system which brings wealth to the many and not just to the few.

The UK economy is in its fourth year of recovery. It is lower than yours, but it is positive recovery. We have not yet shared your success in bringing down unemployment, although we are creating many new jobs. But output, investment, and standard of living are all at record levels, and profits are well up. And the pound—it is too low. But whatever the proper international level of sterling, it is a marvellous time for Americans not only to visit Britain, but to invest with us. And many are. America is by far the largest direct investor in Britain. I am delighted to say that Britain is the largest direct investor in the United States.

Foreign Policy

The British economy has an underlying strength. And, like you, we use our strength and resolve to carry out our duties to our allies and to the wider world. We were the first country to station cruise missiles on our territory. Britain led the rest. In proportion to our population, we station the same number of troops as you in Germany. In Central America we keep troops stationed in Belize at the government's request. That is our contribution to sustaining democracy in a part of the world so vital to the United States. We have troops in Cyprus and in the South Atlantic and a small force in the Sinai at your request. British servicemen are now on secondment to some thirty foreign countries. We were alongside you in Beirut. We work with you in the Atlantic and in the Indian Oceans. Our navy is on duty across the world. Britain meets her responsibility for the defence of freedom throughout the world. She will go on doing so.

Closer to home, here is a threat to freedom both savage and insidious. Both our countries have suffered at the hands of terrorists. We have lost some of our best young lives. And I have lost some close and dear friends. Free, strong, democratic societies will not be driven by gunmen to abandon freedom or democracy. The problems of the Middle East will not be solved by the cold-blooded murder of American servicemen in Lebanon, nor by the murder of American civilians on a hijacked aircraft. Nor will the problems of Northern Ireland be solved by the assassin's gun or bomb.

Garret Fitzgerald and I and our respective governments are united in condemning terrorism. We recognize the differing traditions and identities of the two parts of the community in Northern Ireland, the Nationalist and the Unionist. We seek a political way forward acceptable to them both, which respects them both. So long as a majority of people of Northern Ireland wish to remain part of the United Kingdom, their wishes will be respected. If ever there were to be a majority in favour of change, then I believe that our Parliament would respond accordingly, for that is the principle of consent, enshrined in your constitution and an essential part of ours.

There is no disagreement on this principle between the United Kingdom government and the government of the Republic of Ireland. Indeed, the four constitutional nationalist parties of Ireland, North and South, who came together to issue the New Ireland Forum Report, made clear that any new arrangements could only come about by consent. I welcome, too, their outright condemnation and total rejection of terrorism and all its works. Be under no illusions about the provisional IRA. They terrorise their own communities. They are the enemies of democracy, and of freedom, too. Do not just take my word for it: ask the government of the Irish Republic— where it is an offence even to belong to that organisation, as, indeed, it also is in Northern Ireland.

I recognize and appreciate the efforts which have been made by administration and Congress alike to bring home this message to American citizens who may be misled into making contributions to seemingly innocuous groups. The fact is that money is used to buy the deaths of Irishmen, North and South of the border—and seventy percent of those killed by the IRA are Irishmen—and that buys even the killing and wounding of American citizens visiting our country. Garret Fitzgerald—I salute him for the very brave thing he did yesterday in passing a special law to see that money did not get to the IRA—Garret Fitzgerald and I will continue to consult together in the quest for stability and peace in Northern Ireland. We hope we will have your continued support for our joint efforts to find a way forward.

Anglo-American Partnership

Our two countries have a common heritage as well as a common language. It is no mere figure of speech to say that many of your most enduring traditions—representative government, habeas corpus, trial by jury, a system of constitutional checks and balances—stem from our own small islands. But they are as much your lawful inheritance as ours. You did not borrow these traditions. You took them with you, because they were already your own, no less than ours. Human progress is not automatic. Civilisation has its ebbs and flows. If we look at the history of the last five hundred years, whether in the fields of art, science, technology, religious tolerance or in the practise of politics, the conscious inspiration of it all has been the belief and practise of freedom under law, freedom disciplined by morality, under the law perceived to be just.

I cannot conclude this address without recalling words made immortal by your great President Abraham Lincoln in his second inaugural address, when he looked beyond an age when men fought and strove, towards a more peaceful future. "With malice toward none, with charity for all: with firmness in the right as God gives us to see the right, let us strive on to finish the work that we are in... to do all which may achieve and cherish a just and lasting peace, among ourselves and with all nations." May our two kindred nations go forward together, sharing Lincoln's view, firm of purpose, clear of vision, and warm of heart, as we approach the third millennium of the Christian era.

21

Justice

*Address to the American Bar Association Meeting
in London, July 15, 1985*

Perhaps you will make a pilgrimage of professional piety to St. Ives in Cornwall, named after the patron saint of advocates. He was renowned for espousing the causes of the poor and the oppressed. In his native Brittany his anniversary is celebrated by a High Mass, at which it is customary to sing this eulogy: "*Advocatus quo non latro res miranda populo.*" A popular translation runs as follows: "An advocate but not a thief, a thing well nigh beyond belief." No profession is more sadly misunderstood by the public than that of the advocate—unless it be that of the politician. We lead not so much with the chin as with the mouth: *Violenti non fit injuria* would be a complete defence to any complaint that any of us might make. But the theme of your meeting—justice for a generation—is a fit subject for lawyers and for politicians. We both have a special responsibility to see that our generation gets justice.

What do we understand by justice? For justice to prevail, the most basic requirement is the rule of law. It was your Felix Frankfurter who said: "Limited as law is, it is all that we have standing between us and the tyranny of mere will and the cruelty of unbridled feeling." How those words ring out today across a world that is wracked by terrorism, hijacking, mob violence, and intimidation. How thin is the crust of order over the fires of human appetite and the lust for naked power.

The rule of law has only prevailed for comparatively short periods of history. It exists today in only a small part of the world, of which your country and mine are the centre. We share the Magna Carta. We share the

Bill of Rights. We share Habeas Corpus. We share the Common Law. You have enshrined all that we hold dear in that most splendid statement of liberty, the Declaration of Independence. But the rule of law itself does not guarantee justice. As Edmund Burke, a most ardent advocate for your cause, put it: "It is not what a lawyer tells me I may do: but what humanity, reason and justice tell me I ought to do." That is why the law needs to be fashioned and administered with an awareness of the contemporary concerns of the world outside the court. The law cannot stand separate from the society of which it is part.

Law and Politics. This indeed is the frontier on which the politician and the lawyer meet and mingle. The desire for justice imposes very firm requirements on the politician. First, a recognition that he can never be above the law. Second, his unstinting support for the courts which administer the law and for the police who enforce it. And third, in constructing legislation, his duty to give an honest account of what is practicable and not merely a rhetorical account of what is desirable.

Justice also requires those in public life to repudiate a number of fashionable heresies. The first heresy is that if only a determined minority gather together in large enough numbers to bully or to intimidate others, the law either will not, or cannot be enforced against them. The inference is not only that there is safety in numbers but that this brings with it some kind of collective immunity from legal process. It does not. And it must not. No matter whether those numbers are mobilised by football hooligans, political agitators, or industrial pickets: crime is no less crime just because it is committed *en masse.*

A second fashionable heresy is that if you feel sufficiently strongly about some particular issue, be it nuclear weapons, racial discrimination, or animal liberation, you are entitled to claim superiority to the law and are therefore absolved. This is arrogant nonsense and deserves to be treated as such.

It brings me to a third heresy, namely that the law can be obeyed selectively. Those groups who would pick and choose among our laws, obeying some and breaking others, imperil liberty itself. The law must stand as a whole and be obeyed as a whole. "Liberty is the right to do anything which the law permits" wrote Montesquieu in 1745, "and if a citizen were able to do what the law forbids, he would no longer have liberty, since all other citizens would have the same ability."

Justice and Democracy. I passionately believe that there is a further prerequisite for justice, and that is democracy. Order we need, but not arbitrary order. This year Britain and the United States celebrate together the fortieth anniversary of the defeat of the Third Reich. It called itself the New Order: order there certainly was, a despotic order with no system of justice independent of the ruling party. In our own day we can gaze across

FIGURE 21.1 Thatcher meets in London with a group of U.S. senators, escorted by Ambassador Charles H. Price, under a portrait of Winston S. Churchill. They are (left to right): David Boren (Okla.), Sam Nunn (Ga.), Clairborne Pell (R.I.), Mrs. Thatcher, Amb. Price, John Warner (Va.), and Robert Byrd (W.Va.). (*Source:* British Information Services, New York.)

the brutal Berlin Wall in the direction of those vast land masses where there is order but no liberty, where there are people's courts but no justice for people. You cannot have justice unless you have the right to challenge the government in the courts. Nor can you have it without the right to change a government and the laws by constitutional means if the majority so desire.

But there is more to democracy than one man, one vote. What good is it to vote unless you are offered a real choice? A choice of views as well as a choice of candidate? After all, Soviet communism gives everyone the vote. There is no tyranny on earth today which does not make some ritual bow in the direction of universal suffrage. The foundation of these two great principles, democracy and the rule of law, is not only the rule of the majority; it is a recognition and acceptance that everyone has a basic right to freedom and to justice, a right which is God-given not state-given, a right so fundamental that no mere government is entitled to take it away.

Protection Against Crime. If we are to obtain the justice for our generation which is the theme of your meeting, we must find more effective ways of protecting our citizens from crime. This is not just a matter of giving the police more men and equipment, important as that is. The police cannot do the job on their own. They deserve—and need—our active support. Those who refuse to speak up for them when their support is needed are little better than the carping critics whose voice is so often heard today. Every one of us has to accept our responsibility as a citizen. No one can opt out.

The ease with which we sometimes say "Better ninety-nine guilty men go free than one innocent man be convicted" may make us forget how essential it is to the preservation of ordered and civilised society that the guilty should be convicted and adequately punished. Our systems are rightly weighted in favour of the accused. But this should not blind us to the fact that the acquittal of a guilty person constitutes a miscarriage of justice just as much as the conviction of the innocent. It also exposes law-abiding citizens and the police to more danger—and as always, it is the weak who suffer most.

The feeling is also growing in our country—and elsewhere—that some of the *sentences* which have been passed have not measured up to the enormity of the crimes. This government therefore recently brought before Parliament a bill including a clause which would have enabled the court of appeal to review the appropriateness of a sentence passed in the lower court. Decisions would not affect the sentence in the case in question. But it would give a guide to the kind of sentence which might be expected in similar cases in the future.

22

American Bombing of Libya

Speech to the House of Commons, April 15, 1986

The House is aware that last night the United States forces made attacks on specific targets in Libya. The government have evidence showing beyond dispute that the Libyan government has been and is directly involved in promoting terrorist attacks against the United States and other Western countries, and that it had made plans for a wide range of further terrorist attacks. The United Kingdom has itself suffered from Libyan terrorism. The house will recall the murder of woman Police Constable Fletcher in St. James' Square. There is no doubt, moreover, of the Libyan government's direct and continuing support for the Provisional IRA, in the form of money and weapons.

Two years ago we took certain measures against Libya, including the closure of the Libyan People's Bureau in London, restrictions on the entry of Libyans into the United Kingdom, and a ban on new contracts for the export to Libya of defence equipment. Yesterday the foreign ministers of the European Community reaffirmed their grave concern at Libyan-inspired terrorism, and agreed on new restrictions against Libya.

Since we broke off diplomatic relations with Libya, we have had no choice but consistently to advise British nationals living and working there that they are doing so on their own responsibility. Our interests there have been looked after by the Italian government. Our representative in the British Interests Section of the Italian Embassy will continue to advise the British community as best he can.

The United States has tried by peaceful means to deter Colonel Qadhafi and his regime from their promotion of terrorism, but to no effect. President

Reagan informed me last week that the United States intended to take military action to deter further Libyan terrorism. He sought British support for this action. He also sought agreement, in accordance with our long-standing arrangements, to the use in the operation of some United States aircraft based in this country. This approach led to a series of exchanges including a visit by Ambassador Walters on Saturday 12 April.

Article 51 of the United Nations Charter specifically recognizes the inherent right to self-defence. In view of Libya's promotion of terrorism, the failure of peaceful means to deter it, and the evidence that further attacks were threatened, I replied to the President that we would support action directed against specific Libyan targets demonstrably involved in the conduct and support of terrorist activities. Further, that if the President concluded that it was necessary, we would agree to the deployment of United States aircraft from bases in the United Kingdom for that purpose. I reserved the position of the United Kingdom on any question of further action which might be more general or less clearly directed against terrorism.

The President assured me that the operation would be limited to clearly defined targets related to terrorism, and that the rest of collateral damage would be minimised. He made it clear that the use of F-111 aircraft from bases in the United Kingdom was essential, because by virtue of their special characteristics they would provide the safest means of achieving particular objectives with the lowest possible risk both of civilian casualties in Libya and of casualties among United States service personnel.

Mr. Speaker, terrorism is a scourge of the modern age. Libya has been behind much of it and was planning more. The United Kingdom itself has suffered from Libya's actions, so have many of our friends, including several in the Arab world. The United States, after trying other means, has now sought by limited military action to induce the Libyan regime to desist from terrorism. That is in the British interest. It is why the government supports the United States' action.

23

Interview on Soviet Television

March 31, 1987

INTERVIEWER: Your negotiations with Mikhail Gorbachev are now over....what are your conclusions and your assessment of the result of those negotiations and discussions?

Nuclear Weapons, Deterrence, and Arms Control

PRIME MINISTER: First, I am immensely grateful to Mr. Gorbachev for having given so much time. We had talks lasting seven hours and then at dinner another two hours. I do not think there has ever been such a thorough discussion between two leaders, and when he came to London, we learned to discuss very openly and frankly. That is good. You know, sometimes when you are talking to leaders, you get rather stilted or formal discussion—we do not, and they are all therefore done in a very friendly atmosphere.

I think I have a much better idea now of his hopes and this tremendous challenge for the Soviet people under your restructuring and the new open society. We wish you well in this great endeavour, and we hope it will be very successful. We also talked about all the regional problems because, really, foreign affairs, you know, affect us at home now—they are not something that happens out there in the world—and is something that makes a difference to our lives in the home.

Of course, we spent a long time on arms control. We both want, above all, peace, because that matters more than anything else, but we want peace with the right to live our own way of life within secure borders. So it is not just a question of saying: "no nuclear weapons—no weapons at all." We know that would not ensure peace. You have to be prepared to defend your own country, because then you are far less likely to be attacked. So we have had very good conversations, indeed—we also talked about trade, cultural relations—and I hope they will lead to more frequent contacts, because we do not see enough of people from the Soviet Union, and the greater the understanding, the better it will be for all of us, and the more open the society, the greater the trust and confidence we shall develop in one another.

INTERVIEWER: Can we speak of concrete results of your meetings with Mr. Gorbachev?

PRIME MINISTER: First, we have signed some agreements—an important one on what is called the "hot line," so that if we need to get in touch with one another, we can do it quickly and with great efficiency—more on cultural exchanges where perhaps there will be more school children coming to London from the Soviet Union and the other way round, too—quite a number on trade, which is very, very important, indeed.

Those are the detailed ones, but I think perhaps the most important talks were on arms control, where we more or less agreed on the approach to intermediate nuclear weapons. We would rather there had never been any, but there were—they were stationed here and then we replied with Cruise and Pershing. We would rather now that we had all of them taken down, not only in Europe but the world over. That would be much better. But in the meantime, we accept the zero-zero Europe with one hundred for the Soviet Union to the East of her country and one hundred to the United States. We would like there not to be those, but that is the proposal at the moment. There are some missiles very similar in range which we shall have to have follow-on negotiations about, and we recognize that.

Also, we had special talks on chemical weapons. We in Great Britain abolished our chemical weapons—we destroyed them—towards the end of the 1950s, so we have not got any. The United States did not modernise hers, but the Soviet Union not only has them but has modernised them and has a large stockpile. You can imagine this gives us cause for great concern, so we are very pleased that Mr. Gorbachev has accepted our proposals for inspection, to try to ensure that these weapons are destroyed—and we know they are destroyed—because, you know, after the First World War in Europe when they were used, they were so terrible that they were never used in the Second, and we hope therefore they will all be destroyed.

INTERVIEWER: What specifically is Great Britain planning to improve the international situation, to strengthen universal security?

PRIME MINISTER: We believe—I think as you believe—that every nation has the right to defend its own security, and defence is your only means of knowing that you are secure within your own boundaries. You have the

Warsaw Pact Organisation, we have NATO. We do talk across that. We have proposals for reducing the number of nuclear weapons. We ourselves believe in a nuclear deterrent. I will tell you why. Conventional weapons have not stopped two world wars in Europe this century, no matter how many there were, and when we had a conventional war, the race was on for who got the atomic weapon first. Had Hitler got it first, we should not be sitting here now talking as we are—it would have been devastating.

I think there has never been such a powerful deterrent as the nuclear weapon. Anyone who started a war knowing that that existed would know he could never reach victory, and we believe that one of the reasons we have had peace in Europe for forty years—and peace matters to us very much, with freedom and justice—is the existence of that nuclear deterrent. Although one has dreamed that one day there might be a world without nuclear weapons, you cannot disinvent the knowledge, the information, the fact that there have been. So we will believe in some nuclear deterrent, but we are trying to get down the numbers of nuclear weapons and chemical weapons, and trying to get some balance in conventional weapons. And never think that conventional war is some cosy alternative. It would be terrible. We know that.

INTERVIEWER: You just said that nuclear weapons preserved peace for forty years, but many times we were at the verge of nuclear war during those forty years. Many times we were saved only by accident, by chance. In the beginning, they threatened cities. Now they threaten the whole of humanity. How can one speak of nuclear weapons as a guarantor of peace?

PRIME MINISTER: Are you not making my point? If you say that many times we were at the verge of war and we did not go to war, do you not think that one of the reasons we did not go to war was the total horror of nuclear weapons? After all, I think conventional weapons are awful. It did not stop a war, a terrible war, in which the Soviet Union suffered enormously. You cannot just act as if there had never been nuclear weapons. If conventional war started again, the race would be on as to got the nuclear weapon first. That person would win. It would be far better if any tyrant or fascist country knew that if they started a war, there would be no prospect of victory, because the other side has nuclear weapons. It has kept the peace. Some people want to get rid of nuclear weapons. One would like to. There is something much more important. It is to keep the peace—and it has kept it—we have had peace for forty years.

INTERVIEWER: Yes, but one can follow the way of eliminating nuclear weapons, follow the way of reducing conventional armaments. This exactly has been proposed by us. This is the essence of the proposals put forward in Budapest by the Warsaw Treaty nations, so why should we...

PRIME MINISTER: Can I just answer this one first? Look, Europe this century has been disfigured by two world wars. The Soviet Union suffered millions of losses in the Second World War. The Soviet Union had a lot of conventional weapons. That did not stop Hitler attacking her. Conventional weapons have never been enough to stop wars. Since we have had the nuclear weapon, it is so horrific that no one dares risk going to war. Let me put to you this question: Would you rather have the absence of war because of the existence of some nuclear weapons, or would you rather have no nuclear weapons but the risk of another conventional war? I have not the slightest shadow of doubt what my answer would be. I value peace, with freedom and justice, above everything else, and because at the moment I believe that the nuclear deterrent stops anyone from starting a major war, I believe in keeping it.

There is another reason for smaller countries like us: the nuclear deterrent is the only thing which enables smaller countries actually to stand up to a bigger country. You could never do it on conventional weapons alone—you could not afford them—but a smaller country standing alone could stand up to a bigger one with the nuclear weapon. You ask why I raise it. Historically, Britain had to stand alone. But Europe was occupied by Hitler. We were alone. America had not yet come into the war. Hitler had not yet attacked the Soviet Union. So it is within our experience that we might be alone.

INTERVIEWER: The thing is that there is a possibility of an accidental outbreak of a nuclear conflict. Time passes, nuclear weapons are improved and more and more sophisticated. There is a great possibility of an accident—not political that politicians will decide, but computers. The flight time of a Pershing 2 to the Soviet Union would be only eight minutes. Who will be deciding? Who will be in charge?

PRIME MINISTER: There are more nuclear weapons in the Soviet Union than any other country in the world. You have more intercontinental ballistic missiles and warheads than the West. You started intermediate weapons—we did not have any. You have more short range ones than we have. You have more than anyone else and you say there is a risk of a nuclear accident. I believe that you and we know how dangerous these weapons are, and for forty years we have had a fail-safe mechanism which has in fact worked. You have worked it, whether it be on ground, in the air, or in submarines. These are so dangerous. Yes, we are careful with them.

Conventional weapons, conventional missiles, are also extremely dangerous. These explosives can go off and have a terrible time. Chemical weapons are terribly dangerous. All weapons of war are dangerous. Would it not be marvelous if we did not have to have them, but we can only get to that stage when we have more trust and confidence in one another. That means much more open societies. And let me put this to you: since the First World War, which finished in 1918, there has been no case where one democracy has attacked another. That is why we believe in democracy.

So you want to get rid of the weapons of war. It would be marvelous if we could, but we have to get more trust and confidence. In the meantime, may I assure you that the Soviet Union has been very careful with the massive amount of nuclear weapons that she has, she has been very careful with them—as has the West. We know how to be and rightly we are.

INTERVIEWER: Is not this doctrine of nuclear deterrence based on a policy of threat? If we from time to time will not substantiate the reality of this threat, the threat will become inefficient. So do you not think that the nuclear deterrence doctrine invites the party which sees a threat to actually eventually make use of its nuclear forces in order to substantiate the threat?

PRIME MINISTER: Is not a policy of conventional weapons, with the terrible bombs raining down, with the missiles, with the aircraft, with the submarines, the torpedoes, with the tanks, with chemical weapons—is that not based on the possibility of threat? And were you not only threatened but invaded? Are not all weapons of war based on the possibility of threat and is not your response to anyone, "Look, if you attack us, you will have such a terrible time that you cannot win." Is that not the best defence to anyone who threatens you? Does not the bully go for the weak person, not for the strong?

If you take this view, I wonder why you have so many nuclear weapons. Look. You are based, you tell me—and Mr. Gorbachev tells me—the Warsaw Pact is based on defence—not on attack, on defence. In the NATO alliance, we issued a statement at the beginning of 1980: We threaten no one, and what we said is: "None of our weapons will be used except in response to an attack from someone else." We are talking about defending ourselves from a threat we know not whence it might come, and we are saying to anyone who dares to attack us: "Do not do it. You could not win. The results would be devastating." I think you are saying the same.

INTERVIEWER: I think that your parallel with conventional weapons cannot be substantiated, because when we speak of nuclear weapons, we speak practically of a nuclear suicide even of that side that would try to make use of its nuclear forces. When we discuss nuclear weapons in Europe, the Soviet government does not touch nuclear forces of Britain, but in Reykjavik, as you know, there were agreements on disarmament. They could have become practical treaties. The process is underway, but on which stage does Britain envisage to get involved in that process?

PRIME MINISTER: You said: "Yes, nuclear weapons would be suicidal." That is why they are the most powerful deterrent we have ever known. That is why you have got them to a greater extent than anyone else—because they are such a powerful deterrent that no one would ever dare to attack you. In other words, they defend your peace. Where I think that we could profitably go ahead is that you do not need anything like the number you have got at the moment to act as a deterrent and we really want to get them down in numbers.

On the Intercontinental Ballistic Missiles—and I agree—we should have at least a fifty percent reduction. I said to Mr. Gorbachev, "That will be my objective." Intermediate ones which you stationed first—we had to respond to—you put the SS20s up first. We begged you to take them out and you did not, so we stationed ours and now we agreed that they should both go. And then there are the shorter range ones. We have got far too many. Let us go step by step and try to get them down. It will be better for the world— you do not need it for nuclear deterrence, and it will release resources which people can use in another and better way. Yes, I would like fifty percent down in the next five years of the large ones, the intercontinental. We have only four submarines with them on. That is our minimum nuclear deterrent, that is only 2.5 percent of the numbers you have got, very small, and we have to have our own deterrent. So yes, get the big ones down, get the medium ones out, yes, get chemical abandoned and then look at conventional, because you have far more conventional weapons than we have, far more tanks, far more aircraft. Get those down to balance, and then we will be making really practical progress. People will be immensely pleased, and in the meantime let us do everything we can to have a more open society. You see, all of our defence estimates are published every year. Everyone knows what we have got. We have an open society—let us have a much more open society, much more trade. Then we might be able to make further advances.

INTERVIEWER: I am returning to your words of the necessity to reduce strategic arms. First of all, I am not in total accord with you when you say the Soviet Union has more nuclear weapons than any other country in the world. It is well known that there is a military parity between us and the United States. In some fields we are ahead, in some fields they are ahead.

PRIME MINISTER: Launches of warheads, since every launcher and weapon had six, seven, or eight warheads put on, we count in warheads and really, we can get a lot of them down. Get fifty percent down and we will all be much better pleased.

Strategic Defence Initiative

INTERVIEWER: Well, I agree, but as Reykjavik has shown, on the way to such a radical reduction there is the so-called Strategic Defence Initiative, which destabilizes the situation in the world. How can we renounce one type of weapon only for the sake of creating another?

PRIME MINISTER: First, a Strategic Defence Initiative is only in a research stage. Every new weapon has brought forth a new defence from the time when spears brought forward defence of shields, aircraft brought forward anti-aircraft guns, and then the aircraft learnt to throw off the missiles. The nuclear weapon, as you have just said, is the worst one in the world, and it would seem very strange if you did not try to get a defence against it. Now that is only the research stage. The United States is not the only country doing research on that. The Soviet Union has a very good anti-ballistic missile defence system around Moscow. It has recently updated it. It has had twenty years' experience of the theory of tackling incoming missiles with missiles fired from the ground—more experience than anyone else.

In 1977, a number of us started to be very concerned by the extent to which the Soviet Union was going ahead on laser development and electronic pulse beams. You were way ahead of us, and you may still be, as far as I know. But you also are doing quite a lot of work on anti-ballistic missile defence. You have the only Anti-satellite System in the world. You are tackling it in a different way from the United States, but I do not understand you when in one and the same breath you say to me "the nuclear weapon is the worst in the world"—which I agree—"and yet you must not try to get a defence to that weapon." Do you not think it would be better if you did have a defence to that weapon? Some might fail, like aircraft which still get through the defences. But I happen to think that even if a few—there is the possibility of a few getting through—the threat would be so terrible that no one would embark upon war. Nuclear weapons are a deterrent—they are not for use. They have been the most successful deterrent against world war we have ever known, and they have kept this half of the century free from the world wars which disfigured us for the first half of the century. That really is worthwhile. It is peace which I am after. I do not understand why you concentrate only on abolition of nuclear weapons. It is peace I am after.

INTERVIEWER: You have called [SDI] a defensive research program. But if this is a research program, why then, already now, the American administration stand to the so-called broad interpretation of the ABM Treaty—that very treaty which, as you know, allows that system around Moscow mentioned by you. But that treaty prohibits testing and, of course, deploying such a system in space. And now with the so-called broad interpretation of the ABM Treaty, we are speaking of deploying in space in the mid-90s the first stages of SDI. The old treaty will be torpedoed.

PRIME MINISTER: You are getting very technical. All right, I will follow you, because you are asking me a technical question, so I will give you the technical answer. When I first went to see President Reagan at Camp David in 1984, when the strategic defence research started, there was no such thing as a narrow or broad interpretation. That whole language has come in since 1985. There was a question of what you did with new defences based on new physical principles. Those are not dealt with in the main part of the treaty, as you know; they are dealt with on a separate part called Agreed Statement D, New Physical Principles. You have to deal with them separately, because it did not exist at the time. So what you call the broad interpretation of the Treaty boils down to whether you should not only be able to do research, but whether you should be able to test your research before you start to negotiate on deployment. I can only give you an answer, not based on legal technicalities which you are raising on the interpretation of the Treaty. I can only give you an answer based on common sense. How can you start negotiating on deployment before you know whether or not a thing works? So, of course, you have to do the research. Of course, you have to test. Only then do you know whether you have anything which it is possible to work.

INTERVIEWER: In other words, you are for a broad interpretation of the ABM Treaty?

PRIME MINISTER: I am for the common sense interpretation. How can you start to negotiate on deployment before you know whether what you have got will work or not? If it will not work, you do not start to negotiate. If it does work, you have to negotiate. What I have tried to say is extend that treaty, because the terms of notice are too short. Everyone must have some kind of security in times stretching into the future, but you are the signatories, you can interpret it. I am for common sense. I cannot see how I could negotiate on deployment unless I knew the thing would work. To know the thing would work, you have to test it. Good heavens, you know yours works. The Galosh system around Moscow, we know that you have updated it. We do not know whether your anti-satellite system works. We would have reason to believe it does, but we did not stop you testing it. We know that you are working on lasers very heavily, we know that you are expert at working on lasers, and we are not complaining.

INTERVIEWER: Such a broad interpretation of the ABM Treaty, the deployment in space of components of SDI, means deploying weapons in space. This is a relatively new stage in the arms race. Can you be for such a development?

PRIME MINISTER: But if you have an anti-satellite missile, and you are the only people in the world that has it, and the satellites are in space, are you suggesting that that anti-satellite missile does not go into space, or are you suggesting that an intercontinental ballistic missile which goes right up into space and does not go down, does not go through space? It does. I am suggesting that it is reasonable to develop a defence to the most powerful weapon the world has ever known. You already have one under the ABM Treaty which is a ground defence. I believe some of yours are nuclear weapons against nuclear weapons. The SDI is not a nuclear defence against a nuclear weapon—it is a non-nuclear defence. So it would be reasonable to say that a non-nuclear defence against a nuclear weapon is better than a nuclear defence against a nuclear weapon, which is what you have got. . . .

Perestroika in the Soviet Union

INTERVIEWER: What do you think of the process we call restructuring?

PRIME MINISTER: You are having a much more open society; you can discuss things much more openly than you ever have done before. This is part of our very belief, that this goes to the depth of our fundamental freedoms: freedom of speech, freedom of worship, freedom from fear, and freedom from want. A much more open society means that you discuss all of the things in the same way as we do. We have to lay out far more details of what you have been talking about. You can find the facts about the warheads and so on, but on restructuring, you really have two ways in which you can work. You either have a completely centralised control system in which you are told what to produce, how much it will cost, how much you are paid, and that does not really work to best advantage, as you have discovered, because it does not pay people if they do better. Or, you go to what is called an incentive society when the harder your work, the more reward you get.

One has to recognize, you know, that people work not only for their country, but they work to better their families. They work for a higher standard of living. So if they see the point of working harder, they will. And, you know, no matter what the theory, and there are lots of political theories—I wish there were fewer—there is no person alive and no computer which can plan a country as large as the Soviet Union, take into account all its various different conditions and all its various republics, all the various ambitions and need, the wants, the requirements of the people. You have got to disperse your responsibility to the people who are much nearer to the life in those republics, towns, and rural areas. You have got to give them responsibility, and for that they must have incentives. That is what I understand you are doing. What you do internally is wholly up to you, obviously not for us to interfere, but we are interested.

Thatcher's Daily Routine

INTERVIEWER: People say that you are able, a workaholic, a work-monger. I read somewhere that you sleep for no more than five hours. Often you do not have any time for lunch, you only drink a cup of coffee and a tablet of Vitamin C. Is that true? What is your daily time schedule? How difficult is it to be Prime Minister and to be wise and a mother of two children?

PRIME MINISTER: I have worked hard all my life. I was brought up in a family that worked hard. We had to work hard. The only way we could get on was working hard, and frankly, it is much more interesting than anything else. Work is interesting—I enjoy it. I have trained all my life, first as a chemist and then as a lawyer, and I have had to work at both. Then I was interested in politics. Yes, I can get on with about five hours sleep a night for quite a long time. Eventually, you do want a longer rest. But I can do it, and sometimes I have to do, because do not forget, our political system is a very tough one. I have my own constituency which I represent in Parliament. I have to attend Parliament as a Member of Parliament. I also have to attend Parliament as Prime Minister. Twice every week I am answering questions before Parliament. I do not know what those questions will be—they will be right across the whole sphere of government. I have to work very hard each day when I get those questions to make certain I know the answers, because they would trip me up if I did not. When I get back from this visit, I will have to make a statement to Parliament—fifteen minutes or so—and then I will be cross-examined on it—questioned, before the whole of Parliament, before the public, on radio, for an hour. They will want to know what I saw. And then we have Cabinet meetings over which I preside, and we have cabinet committees. I preside over the Defence Committee, and I preside over the Economic Committee.

And then we go out and about a bit. I will do at least one tour round the country, possibly every month, certainly, and possibly more frequently than that. And then I will go to address meetings of businessmen, I will go to visit hospitals, I will go to visit schools to see how things are going, because if you are in politics, you have got to get out and about. All this means some days I will have ten engagements. I had ten engagements day after day, and then I began to complain a bit, because it was a little bit much, so we are down to about eight engagements a day now. That is quite a lot. You have to work hard. It is the most fascinating work I have ever done. Then there is the overseas aspect. How do you cope?

No, I do not have very much breakfast, you are quite right, a cup of black coffee and two Vitamin C, and I have a very, very light lunch. If I am answering questions, just some clear soup and fruit. If you have got to have all your concentration on answering questions, you do not want too much in your tummy. You know, you want all the blood to go there and not to digesting your meal. We live "over the shop," as it were. We have a flat over Number 10 Downing Street which is the office of the Prime Minister. At the end of the day, all the papers which all other ministers—they put a paper up for decision or to come before a committee—have been prepared for me all day. My most marvelous staff go home, having been working all day. I have been working all day, and then I start about ten o'clock at night to work on my papers. I think it is the most fascinating thing I have ever done. I have been doing it for eight years. Experience is cumulative, and I do not wish to do anything else.

Links Between Britain and the Soviet Union

Life in Britain, you know, the standard of living is high. It is higher than it has ever been. We are working very hard. In our housing we have perhaps a different system from you: sixty-four families out of every hundred own their own home. It is my ambition to get that up to seventy-five families out of every hundred. We have an excellent health service, very, very good indeed, and we are building more and more hospitals. The education service is variable. In some places it is extremely good and in some places not so good. Unfortunately, we do have unemployment, and I do not run away from it. When you get technological change, you are almost bound to get some unemployment. It is now falling. But let me make this clear: the people who are unemployed live like other people in houses. They are rented. Their rent is paid for them because they have not the income to pay, and every week they get a weekly benefit, a considerable weekly benefit. It is more if they have children. The weekly benefit for some of them will be as much as some of the wages which some people get in industry, and they will get that weekly sum for as long as they are unemployed. After six months when they have been unemployed, we will take each one of them in, and if they have been unemployed, we will try to get them a job or will try to get them fresh training or we will put them on what is called a community programme. So we are tackling our problems and we are hoping that we shall gradually get unemployment down so that those people, too, may have the higher standard of living which our other people enjoy. The arts flourish, the science is excellent as, indeed, yours is, so we have a richness to life as well as the working life. . . .

We want peace, I want peace. You know that each country has to be prepared to defend itself to keep peace, and we recognize the equal rights of all nations to do that. We want to be able to do it at far less weapons than we have now. We also want to know one another better. We want to know more about you. We want you to travel more frequently to us, because we think it is more and more and more important to build up trust, friendship, and confidence between the people of the Soviet Union and the people of Western Europe, in particular, the United Kingdom. I have loved my visit here. I have very much enjoyed the warm welcome you have given me. I will not forget it. . . . I am very grateful.

FIGURE 24.1 Winston S. Churchill with his daughter, Mary, greeted by U.S. Ambassador John G. Winant the day after V-E Day, 1945. (*Source:* George C. Marshall Library.)

24

Britain and Europe

Speech Delivered at the Opening Ceremony
of the 39th Academic Year of the College of Europe,
Bruges, September 20, 1988

You have invited me to speak on the subject of Britain and Europe. Perhaps I should congratulate you on your courage. If you believe some of the things said and written about my views in Europe, it must seem rather like inviting Genghis Khan to speak on the virtues of peaceful co-existence! I want to start by disposing of some myths about my country, Britain, and its relationship with Europe. And to do that I must say something about the identify of Europe itself.

Europe is not the creation of the Treaty of Rome. Nor is the European idea the property of any group or institution. We British are as much heirs to the legacy of European culture as any other nation. Our links to the rest of Europe, the continent of Europe, have been *the* dominant factor in our history. For three hundred years we were part of the Roman Empire, and our maps still trace the straight lines of the roads the Romans built. Our ancestors—Celts, Saxons, and Danes—came from the continent. Our nation was—in that favourite Community word—"restructured" under Norman and Angevin rule in the eleventh and twelfth centuries.

This year we celebrate the three hundredth anniversary of the Glorious Revolution in which the British crown passed to Prince William of Holland and Queen Mary. Visit the great Churches and Cathedrals of Britain, read our literature, and listen to our language: all bear witness to the cultural riches which we have drawn from Europe— and Europeans from us. We in Britain are rightly proud of the way in which, since Magna Carta in 1215, we have pioneered and developed representative institutions to stand as bastions of freedom. And proud, too, of the way in which for centuries Britain was a home for people from the rest of Europe who sought sanctuary from tyranny.

But we know that without the European legacy of political ideas, we could not have achieved as much as we did. From classical and medieval thought we have borrowed that concept of the rule of law which marks out a civilised society from barbarism. And on that concept of Christendom—for long synonymous with Europe—with its recognition of the unique and spiritual nature of the individual, we still base belief in personal liberty and other human rights. Too often the history of Europe is described as a series of interminable wars and quarrels. Yet from our perspective today, surely what strikes us most is our common experience. For instance, the story of how Europeans explored and colonised and—yes, without apology—civilised much of the world is an extraordinary tale of talent and valour.

We British have in a special way contributed to Europe, for over the centuries we have fought and died for her freedom, fought to prevent Europe from falling under the dominance of a single power. Only miles from here lie the bodies of [thousands of] British soldiers who died in the First World War. Had it not been for the willingness to fight and die, Europe *would* have been united long before now—but not in liberty and not in justice. It was British help to resistance movements throughout the last war that kept alive the flame of liberty in so many countries until the day of liberation came. Tomorrow, King Baudouin will attend a service in Brussels to commemorate the many brave Belgians who gave their lives in service with the Royal Air Force. It was from our island fortress that the liberation of Europe itself was mounted. And still today, we station 70,000 British servicemen on the mainland of Europe. All these things alone are proof of our commitment to Europe's future.

The European Community is one manifestation of that European identity. But it is not the only one. We must never forget that East of the Iron Curtain peoples who once enjoyed a full share of European culture, freedom, and identity have been cut off from their roots. We shall always look on Warsaw, Prague, and Budapest as great European cities. Nor should we forget that European values have helped to make the United States of America into the dynamic defender of freedom which she has become.

This is no arid chronicle of obscure historical facts. It is the record of nearly two thousand years of British involvement in Europe and contribution to Europe, a contribution which is today as strong as ever. Yes, we have looked also to wider horizons—and so have others—and thank goodness, we did, because Europe would never have prospered and never will prosper as a narrow-minded, inward-looking club. The European Community belongs to *all* its members and must reflect the traditions and aspirations of *all* of them in full measure. And let me be quite clear. Britain does not dream of an alternative to the European Community, and some cosy, isolated existence on its fringes. Our destiny is in Europe, as part of the Community. That is not to say that it lies *only* in Europe, nor does that of France or Spain or indeed any other members.

The Community is not an end in itself. It is not an institutional device to be constantly modified according to the dictates of some abstract theory. Nor must it be ossified by endless regulation. It is the practical means by which Europe can ensure its future prosperity and security of its people in a world in which there are many other powerful nations and groups. We Europeans cannot afford to waste our energies on internal disputes or arcane institutional debates. They are no substitute for effective action. Europe has to be ready both to contribute in full measure to its own *security* and to *compete*—compete in a world in which success goes to the countries which encourage individual initiative and enterprise, rather than to those which attempt to diminish them. I want this evening to set out some guiding principles for the future which I believe will ensure that Europe *does* succeed, not just in economic and defence terms but in the quality of life and the influence of its people.

Guiding Principles for the Future

My first guideline is this: willing and active cooperation between independent sovereign states is the best way to build a successful European Community. To try to suppress nationhood and concentrate power at the centre of a European conglomerate would be highly damaging and would jeopardise the objectives we seek to achieve. Europe will be stronger precisely because it has France as France, Spain as Spain, Britain as Britain, each with its own customs, traditions, and identity. It would be folly to try to fit them into some sort of identikit European personality.

Some of the founding fathers of the Community thought that the United States of America might be its model. But the whole history of America is quite different from Europe. People went there to get away from the intolerance and constraints of life in Europe. They sought liberty and opportunity; and their strong sense of purpose has, over two centuries, helped create a new unity and pride in being American—just as our pride lies in being British or Belgian or Dutch or German.

I am the first to say that on many great issues the countries of Europe should try to speak with a single voice. I want to see them work more closely on the things we can do better together than alone. Europe is stronger when we do so, whether it be in trade, defence, or in our relations with the rest of the world. But working more closely together does *not* require power to be centralised in Brussels or decisions to be taken by an appointed bureaucracy.

Indeed, it is ironic that just when those countries such as the Soviet Union, which have tried to run everything from the centre, are learning that success depends on dispersing power and decisions *away* from the centre, some in the Community seem to want to move in the opposite direction. We have not successfully rolled back the frontiers of the state in Britain, only to see them reimposed at a European level, with a European super-state exercising a new dominance from Brussels. Certainly, we want to see Europe more united and with a greater sense of common purpose. But it must be in a way which preserves the different traditions, Parliamentary powers and sense of national pride in one's own country, for these have been the source of Europe's vitality through the centuries.

My second guiding principle is this: Community politics must tackle present problems in a practical way, however difficult that may be. If we cannot reform those Community policies which are patently wrong or ineffective and which are rightly causing public disquiet, then we shall not get the public's support for the Community's future development. That is why the achievements of the European Council in Brussels last February are so important. It wasn't right that half the total Community Budget was being spent on storing and disposing of surplus food. Now those stocks are being sharply reduced. It was absolutely right to decide that agriculture's share of the budget should be cut in order to free resources for policies such as helping the less well off regions and training for jobs. It was right, too, to introduce tighter budgetary discipline to enforce these decisions and to bring total EC spending under better control.

Those who complained that the Community was spending so much time on financial detail missed the point. You cannot build on unsound foundations; and it was the fundamental reforms agreed last winter which paved the way for the remarkable progress which we have since made on the Single Market. But we cannot rest on what we have achieved so far. For example, the task of reforming the Common Agricultural Policy is far from complete. Certainly, Europe needs a stable and efficient farming industry. But the CAP has become unwieldy, inefficient, and grossly expensive. And production of unwanted surpluses safeguards neither the income nor the future of farmers themselves.

We must continue to pursue policies which relate supply more closely to market requirements, and which will reduce overproduction and limit costs. Of course, we must protect the villages and rural areas which are such an important part of our national life—but not by the instrument of agricultural prices. Tackling these problems requires political courage. The community will only damage itself in the eyes of its own people and the outside world, if that courage is lacking.

My third guiding principle is the need for Community policies which encourage enterprise if Europe is to flourish and create the jobs of the future. The basic framework is there: the Treaty of Rome itself was intended as a Charter for Economic Liberty. But that is not how it has always been read, still less applied. The lesson of the economic history of Europe in the '70s and '80s is that central planning and detailed control *don't* work, and that personal endeavour and initiative *do*; that a state-controlled economy is a recipe for low growth; and that free enterprise within a framework of law brings better results.

The aim of a Europe open for enterprise is the moving force behind the creation of the Single European Market by 1992. By getting rid of barriers, by making it possible for companies to operate on a Europe-wide scale, we can best compete with the United States, Japan, and the other new economic powers emerging in Asia and elsewhere. It means action to *free* markets, to *widen* choice and to produce greater economic convergence through *reduced* government intervention. Our aim should *not* be more and more detailed regulation from the centre: it should be to deregulate, to remove the constraints on trade, and to open up.

Britain has been in the *lead* in opening its *markets to others*. The City of London has long welcomed financial institutions from all over the world, which is why it is the biggest and most successful financial centre in Europe. We have opened our market for telecommunications equipment, introduced competition into the market for services and even into the network itself—steps which others in Europe are only now beginning to face. In air transport, we have taken the lead in liberalisation and seen the benefits in cheaper fares and wider choice. Our coastal shipping trade is open to the merchant navies of Europe. I wish I could say the same on many other Community members.

Consider *monetary matters*. The key issue is not whether there should be a European Central Bank. The immediate and practical requirements are: to implement the Community's commitment to free movement of capital—we have it; to abolish throughout the Community the exchange controls—we abolished them in Britain in 1979 so that people can invest wherever they wish; to establish a genuinely free market in financial services, in banking, insurance, investment; and to make greater use of the ECU. Britain is this autumn issuing ECU-denominated Treasury bills, and hopes to see other Community governments increasingly do the same. These are the *real* requirements, because they are what Community business and industry need, if they are to compete effectively in the wider world. And they are what the European consumer wants, for they will widen his choice and lower his costs.

It is to such basic practical steps that the Community's attention should be devoted. When those have been achieved, and sustained over a period of time, we shall be in a better position to judge the next moves. It is the same with the *frontiers* between our countries. Of course, we must make it easier for goods to pass through frontiers. Of course, we must make it easier for our people to travel throughout the Community. But it is a matter of plain common sense that we cannot totally abolish frontier controls if we are also to protect our citizens and stop the movement of drugs, of terrorists, of illegal immigrants. That was underlined graphically only three weeks ago, when one brave German customs officer, doing his duty on the frontier between Holland and Germany, struck a major blow against the terrorists of the IRA.

And before I leave the subject of the Single Market, may I say that we emphatically do not need new regulations which raise the cost of *employment* and make Europe's labour market less flexible and less competitive with overseas suppliers. If we are to have a European Company Statute, it should contain the minimum regulations. And certainly, we in Britain would fight attempts to introduce corporatism at the European level—although what people wish to do in their own countries is a matter for them.

My fourth guiding principle is that Europe should not be protectionist. The expansion of the world economy requires us to continue the process of removing barriers to trade, and to do so in the multilateral negotiations in the GATT. It would be a betrayal if, while breaking down constraints on trade to create the Single Market, the Community were to erect greater external protection. We must ensure that our approach to world trade is consistent with the liberalisation we preach at home. We have a responsibility to give a lead here, a responsibility which is particularly directed towards the less developed countries. They need not only aid, but more than anything, they need improved trade opportunities if they are to gain the dignity of growing economic independence and strength.

European Defence

My last guiding principle concerns the most fundamental issue, the European countries' role in defence. Europe must continue to maintain a sure *defence* through NATO. There can be no question of relaxing our efforts, even if it means taking difficult decisions and meeting heavy costs. We are thankful for the peace that NATO has maintained over forty years. The fact is things *are* going our way; the democratic model of a free enterprise society *has* proved itself superior; freedom *is* on the offensive, a peaceful offensive, the world over for the first time in my life-time.

We must strive to maintain the U.S. commitment to Europe's defence. That means recognizing the burden on their resources of the world role they undertake and their point that their Allies should play a full part in the defence of freedom, particularly as Europe grows wealthier. Increasingly, they will look to Europe to play a part in out-of-area defence, as we have recently done in the Gulf. NATO and the WEU have long recognized where the problems with Europe's defences lie and have pointed out the solutions. The time has come when we must give substance to our declarations about a strong defence effort and better value for money.

It's not an institutional problem. It's not a problem of drafting. It's much more simple and more profound: it is a question of political will and political courage, of convincing people in all our countries that we cannot rely forever on others for our defence, but that each member of the Alliance must shoulder a fair share of the burden. We must keep public support for nuclear deterrence, remembering that obsolete weapons do not deter, hence the need for modernisation. We must meet the requirements for effective conventional defence in Europe against Soviet forces which are constantly being modernised. We should develop the WEU, not as a alternative to NATO, but as a means of strengthening Europe's contribution to the common defence of the West.

Above all, at a time of change and uncertainty in the Soviet Union and Eastern Europe, we must preserve Europe's unity and resolve so that whatever may happen, our defence is sure. At the same time, we must negotiate on arms control and keep the door wide open to co-operation on all the other issues covered by the Helsinki Accords. But our way of life, our vision, and all that we hope to achieve is secured not by the rightness of our cause, but by the strength of our defence. On this, we must never falter or fail.

Conclusion

I believe it is not enough just to talk in general terms about a European vision or ideal. If you believe in it, you must chart the way ahead. That's what I have tried to do this evening. This approach does not require new documents—they are all there: the North Atlantic Treaty, the Revised Brussels Treaty, and the Treaty of Rome, texts written by far-sighted men, a remarkable Belgian—Paul Henri Spaak—among them. What we need now is to take decisions on the next steps forward rather than let ourselves be distracted by Utopian goals. However far we may all want to go, the truth is that you can only get there one step at a time. Let us concentrate on making

FIGURE 24.2 Thatcher addressing delegates from 124 countries during the opening session of the Saving the Ozone Layer Conference in London, March 1989. (*Source:* British Information Services, New York.)

sure that we get those steps right. Let Europe be a family of nations, understanding each other better, appreciating each other more, doing more together, but relishing our national identity no less than our common European endeavour. Let us have a Europe which plays its full part in the wider world, which looks outward, not inward, and which preserves that Atlantic Community—that Europe on both sides of the Atlantic—which is our greatest inheritance and our greatest strength.

25

Shaping a New Global Community

Delivered to the Aspen Institute in Colorado,
August 5, 1990

Britain's destiny lies in Europe as a full member of the Community. We shall not be standing on the side-lines or, as you would say, watching from the bleachers. On the contrary, we shall bring to it our own distinctive point of view—practical and down-to-earth. We fight hard for what we believe in, namely: a Europe based on willing cooperation between independent sovereign states; a Europe which is an expression of economic freedom, without which political freedom could not long endure; a Europe which rejects central control and its associated bureaucracy; a Europe which does not resort to protectionism but remains open to the outside world; and—of supreme importance for Britain—a Europe which always seeks the closest possible partnership with the United States.

You have chosen for this conference the theme "Shaping a New Global Community." That theme reflects the boldness, energy, and vision of this remarkable country which has led the free world for over four decades. The willingness to think ahead on a world scale, when many countries are self-absorbed, preoccupied, even obsessed with their regional problems, is very refreshing and very necessary. The president gave you his vision of the way ahead in a marvelous speech on Thursday. Anyone who had doubts—and I certainly had none—about America's willingness to continue to give leadership to the world will realize how wrong they were. I am an undiluted admirer of American values and the American dream, and I believe they will continue to inspire not just the people of the United States, but millions upon millions across the face of the globe.

FIGURE 25.1 Harry S. Truman and Winston S. Churchill meeting at the Potsdam Conference, 1945. (*Source:* George C. Marshall Library.)

Your theme is also very timely, because it has been given to us, in the last decade of this century, to fashion a new global community. For today we are coming to realise that an epoch in history is over, an epoch which began in 1946, when an American president and a former British prime minister shared a platform here in the United States at Fulton, Missouri. They saw with foreboding what Winston Churchill famously called an Iron Curtain coming down across Europe, and they forged the great Western Alliance which bound us together through a common sense of danger to the lives of free peoples.

For more than forty years that Iron Curtain remained in place. Few of us expected to see it lifted in our life-time. Yet, with great suddenness, the impossible has happened. Communism is broken, utterly broken, and Soviet citizens are talking democracy. The mayors of Moscow and Leningrad discuss Milton Friedman—I have heard them. And anyone who talks to Mr. Gorbachev and other Soviet leaders recognizes a complete change in the nature of their aspirations. We do not see this new Soviet Union as an enemy, but as a country groping its way towards freedom. We no longer have to view the world through a prism of East-West relations. The Cold War is over.

As the Iron Curtain goes up, a new drama unfolds before us, and one in which we are both the authors and the players. Our freedom of action is enlarged and our horizons broadened. The unity and strength which we in the West have found from joining together in defence can now be turned to serve more positive and ambitious purposes.

Essentials for Democracy

The first and most exalted of these is to create a world in which true democracy and the rule of law are extended far and wide. In its heyday, Communism believed that it would inevitably dominate the world, subsuming all national feeling and everything which gives life its infinite variety, replacing it with what was alleged to be a scientific system of conformity and uniformity. The very inhumanity and arrogance of the proposition makes one wonder how anyone could ever have believed in it, for Communism is so plainly contrary to the human spirit.

Not that there is anything inevitable about the spread of democracy. If anything, the difficulties of sustaining it are greatly underestimated. The heady sense of freedom which comes from throwing off totalitarian rule is short-lived. Building a true democracy is a lengthy and painstaking task. It is easy enough to transfer the institutions of democracy from one country to another, as Britain did to much of Africa in the 1960s. But it soon becomes apparent that it is no guarantee that democracy as we know it will be realized. The one-party state in which there is no possibility of choosing an alternative government is hardly what we mean by democracy.

The essentials for democracy [are]: first, a sense of personal responsibility. People need to realize that they are not just pawns on a chessboard, to be moved around at the whim of politicians. They can influence their destiny by their own efforts. Second, democracy means limitation of the powers of government and giving people the greatest possible freedom. In the end the strength of a society depends not on the big battalions, but on the foot-soldiers, on the willingness of ordinary men and women who do not seek fame or glory or high office, to play an active part in their community, not as conscripts but as volunteers.

Third, democracy and freedom are about more than the ballot and universal suffrage. At the beginning of this tumultuous century, Britain rightly believed herself a free country. Yet, we went into the First World War with only a thirty percent franchise. A strong rule of law is the essential underpinning of democracy. The steady growth of the common law over centuries, the process by which statute law is passed by an elected parliament or congress, the independence of the judiciary, these are as much the pillars of democracy as its parliamentary institutions.

The fourth essential is an economy based on market principles and a right to private property. Wealth is not created by regulation and instruction, but by ordinary enterprising people. It is hard for those who have only experienced life in totalitarian societies to think in these terms because it is outside anything they have ever known. That is why one sometimes wonders whether some of the countries trying to introduce economic reform have yet understood what a market economy is really about.

So the challenge of spreading democracy and the rule of law is an awesome one. But we must not be pessimistic. One can point to countries—for example, Spain, Portugal, Chile, Nicaragua—where the transition from authoritarian rule to democracy has succeeded. And to those who suggest that some countries are perhaps too large for democracy, there is the remarkable example of India with its 700 million people, where democracy is well established.

Our Plan of Campaign

It will take the united efforts of the West to shape a new global community based on democracy, the rule of law, and market principles. We need a plan of campaign and I suggest that these should be its main elements. At the East-West summit of thirty-five nations to be held in the autumn, I propose that we should agree on a European Magna Carta to entrench for every European citizen, including those of the Soviet Union, the basic rights which we in the West take for granted. We must enshrine certain freedoms for every individual, such as freedom of speech, of worship, of access to the law, and of the market place; freedom to participate in genuinely democratic elections, to own property, and to maintain nationhood; and last, freedom from fear of the over-mighty state.

Next, we must bring the new democracies of Eastern Europe into closer association with the institutions of Western Europe. And I propose that the Community should declare unequivocally that it is ready to accept all the countries of Eastern Europe as members if they want to join, provided that democracy has taken root and that their economies are capable of sustaining membership. We cannot say in one breath that they are part of Europe and in the next our European Community club is so exclusive that we will not admit them. Of course, it will be some time before they are ready for membership, so we are offering them intermediate steps such as Association Agreements. But the option of eventual membership should be clearly, openly, and generously on the table. The European Community has reconciled antagonisms within Western Europe; it should now help to overcome divisions between East and West in Europe.

This does not mean that the further development of the existing Community has to be put on ice. Far from it. The completion of the Single Market by 1992 will be an enormous change, one of the biggest since the Community began in 1957. It should herald a fair and open Europe, and one which should be immensely attractive to the newly free peoples of Eastern Europe. The same is true of closer cooperation in foreign policy. But if, instead, we set off down the path of giving more and more powers to highly centralised institutions, which are not democratically accountable, then we should be making it harder for the Eastern Europeans to join.

They have not thrown off central command and control in their own countries only to find them reincarnated in the European Community. With their new freedom, their feelings of patriotism and national identity flooding out again, their newly restored parliaments are full of vitality. We must find a structure for the Community which accommodates their diversity and preserves their traditions, their institutions, and their nationhood. We need to do this without introducing the concept of first and second-class membership of the Community, which would be divisive and defeat much of the purpose of bringing their countries into Europe.

Still the messages we are getting indicate that the Soviet Union and Eastern Europe desperately want to share the policies of economic freedom, but they just do not know how to acquire them. Many of us are providing practical assistance through know-how, funds, and joint ventures. But such is the scale of the problem that we shall need to devise new and more imaginative ways to help. For example, we might identify a whole sector of the Soviet economy such as transport and distribution or food processing or oil exploration or the banking system, and offer to help run it on market principles to demonstrate what can be achieved. After all, the Soviet Union has natural wealth in abundance. It is not resources it lacks, but the ability to turn them to advantage. One day the Soviet Union will be a highly prosperous country—and so will China—and it is not too soon to be thinking how to bring them into the world economy.

But the most difficult step is for governments which have been accustomed to running a regimented economy to think in a different way. If we can begin to associate them with the international institutions which have done so much to help ensure our own prosperity, in particular the GATT and the IMF, that could make it easier for them. We might also bring the Soviet Union gradually into closer association with the economic summit. Britain will be hosting next year's economic summit in London, and if my colleagues agree, I would not be averse to taking the first step along the road on that occasion. So there are three points in our plan of campaign: a European Magna Carta; closer association of East and West in Europe; and eventually bring the Soviet Union into the Economic Summit and the Western economy.

A Secure Defence

There is a further crucial point. None of this could be contemplated unless we in the West had been resolute to maintain a secure defence. The fact that our peoples were willing to bear the burdens, sustain the expense, and brave the dangers of defence for over forty years, is a proof of how much they value liberty and justice. We failed to do this after the First World War. Instead, armies were disbanded, weapons were laid aside, and American forces went home. The result was once again World War—war in Europe and war in the Pacific—and a whole generation paid a terrible price. After the Second World War, we were wiser. We threatened no one, but we kept up our defences. We halted the great expansion of Communism. Today, nations and peoples are free, who would otherwise be in bondage were it not for our perseverance and, above all, that of the United States.

But now, in the moment of success, it is wise to be cautious. History has seen too many false springs. The Soviet Union, as the president said, remains a formidable military power. Even the Russian Republic—on its own—would be the largest country in the world, stretching from the Baltic to the Pacific across eleven time zones. Moreover, with the spread of ballistic missiles and chemical weapons, it is all too likely that we shall face ugly situations in other parts of the world, as we are seeing now. We shall continue to need NATO. And that means we shall continue to need American forces in Europe—in your own interests as well as in ours.

Do you remember some of the lines from T.S. Eliot's "Chorus on the Rock"? He said this:

> It is hard for those who live near a police station to believe in the triumph of violence
> Do you think that the faith has conquered the world
> and that lions no longer need keepers?
> Do you need to be told that whatever has been, can still be?

What a pity more poets were not also politicians. That is marvelous language and its meaning so wonderfully clear.

Need for International Cooperation

As we look to the future, there are other issues which call for a much higher level of international cooperation, more intensive than anything we have achieved so far: the spread of drugs, terrorism and intimidation, a decaying environment. No country is immune from them. Our ability to come together to stop or limit damage to the world's environment will be the greatest test of how far we can act as a world community. Science is still feeling its way and some uncertainties remain. But we know that very high population growth is putting an enormous pressure on the Earth's resources. Primitive methods of agriculture are extending deserts and destroying tropical forests, and as they disappear, nature's capacity to correct its own imbalance is seriously affected.

We know, too, that our industries and way of life have done severe damage to the ozone layer. And we know that within the lifetime of our grandchildren, the surface temperature of the Earth will be higher than at any time for 150,000 years; the rate of change of temperature will be higher than in the first 10,000 years; and the sea level will rise six times faster than has been seen in the last century. The costs of doing nothing, of a policy of wait and see, would be much higher than those of taking preventive action now to stop the damage getting worse. And the damage will be counted not only in dollars, but in human misery as well. Spending on the environment is like spending on defence: if you do not do it in time, it may be too late. Most of us have been brought up to give praise and thanks for the miracle of creation. But we cannot give thanks with our words if our deeds undermine the beauty of the world to which we are born.

The same lessons apply to the evil of drugs. We must use every means to warn young people of the blandishments which will be used to entice them into drug addiction. We must ram home that to succumb would utterly ruin their lives and devastate their families. The contemptible and callous men who prey upon the young for their own material gain must be hunted ruthlessly until they are brought to justice. This problem is not limited to a handful of countries. There are now forty million addicts world wide, and the number continues to rise. We have to grapple with every aspect of the problem: cutting the demand, the production, the money-laundering, and the international networks. Hard as we have tried, we are still far from success. And there is only one way to attack the problem wherever it occurs, and that is by bringing together all the resources and knowledge of every country to slay this dragon.

That goes for terrorism and intimidation, too. The terrorists fight with weapons of war. We respond with the rule of law. The dice are loaded against the law-abiding and the innocent.Terrorism will only be beaten when all civilised governments resolve that they will never harbour or give safe haven to terrorists. Anything less than a proven total dedication to hunting down the terrorists within should make those countries the outcasts of the world. Let it be plain—we shall never surrender to terrorism.

Intensified economic international cooperation is needed just as much on more familiar problems. A world which formed itself into inward-looking blocs of nations would be taking a sad step backwards. Yet, I see a real danger of that: a European bloc based on the European Community's proposed economic and monetary union; a Western-hemisphere bloc based on a United States-Canada-Latin American free trade area; and then a Pacific bloc with Japan and some of the East and North East Asia countries. Such an arrangement would encourage protectionism and stifle trade at the very time we need to be driving forward to a positive outcome for the Uruguay Round of world trade negotiations. That means we shall all need to make concessions, particularly on agriculture, where we are all far from perfect. To slide back into protectionism would be damaging for every one of us, and none more than the developing countries who, as well as aid, need trade. Of course, they need help, particularly the poorest, and they all seek investment. But there is going to be unprecedented demand for the world's savings over the next decade.

When you look at the problems of developing countries, you frequently find it is the politics which have led the economics astray. These problems do not always stem from lack of resources or natural wealth or some other similar handicap. Quite often they are the result of bad government, corruption, and the breakdown of law and order, or cynical promises which could never be kept. And that is not a view which I have invented, in case you thought it sounded like me. It comes from an excellent report by the World Bank. The problems will not be solved by abstractions such as a new international economic order, nor by the verbose vocabulary of the North-South dialogue. The developing countries need sustained help. But they also need democracy, good government, and sensible economic policies which attract foreign investment. That investment will go to the countries which offer the best prospect of stability, which welcome enterprise, and give a fair rate of return, with the right to repatriate a reasonable proportion of the profits. Investment will not come into a country unless it can also get out.

Rediscovering the United Nations

All these problems underline the need for an effective global institution where we can agree on certain basic standards, resolve disputes, and keep the peace. We thought we had created that at San Francisco in 1946, when we founded the United Nations. Sadly, it has not quite worked out that way. Iraq's invasion of Kuwait defies every principle for which the United Nations stands. If we let it succeed, no small country can ever feel safe again. The law of the jungle would take over from the rule of law. The United Nations must assert its authority and apply a total economic embargo unless Iraq withdraws without delay. The United States and Europe both support this. But to be fully effective, it will need the collective support of all the United Nations' members. They must stand up and be counted, because a vital principle is a stake: an aggressor must never be allowed to get his way.

As East-West confrontation diminishes, as problems which have long dominated the United Nations' agenda, such as apartheid in South Africa, are being resolved, we have an opportunity to rediscover the determination that attended the founding of the United Nations. And the best time is now, with our present very able and widely respected Secretary-General. It was never realistic to think of the United Nations as a world government. But we can make it a place where truth is told and objective standards prevail. The five Permanent Members of the Security Council have acquired authority in recent times by working together—not enough, but a basis on which to build. Some would say all this is a triumph of hope over experience. But let us not be hypnotized by the past, otherwise, we shall always shrug our shoulders and walk away. Shakespeare reminded us:

> Our doubts are traitors
> And make us lose the good we oft might win,
> By fearing to attempt.

If we are to do better than our best, Europe and the United States must continue to make common cause, attracting others as we do, but remaining faithful to the principles which have brought us so far. Winston Churchill expressed so well the positive approach we shall need. In his description of the journey of life, he said this:

> Let us be contented with what has happened to us and thankful for all we have been spared,
> Let us treasure our joys but not bewail our sorrows.
> The glory of light cannot exist without its shadows.
> Life is a whole, and good and ill must be accepted together.

We must work together for more joy and less sorrow, to ensure more light and less shadow. If we achieve that, we shall have done well.

FIGURE 26.1 The House of Commons. In the center is the Speaker's Chair and seating for the Clerk of the House and assistants. (*Source:* British Information Services, New York.)

26

House of Commons No-Confidence Debate

November 22, 1990

PRIME MINISTER THATCHER: I remind this House that under socialism, this country had come to such a pass that one of our most able and distinguished ambassadors felt compelled to write in a famous dispatch, a copy of which found its way into *The Economist,* the following words. He said: "We talk of ourselves without shame as being one of the less prosperous countries of Europe. The prognosis for the foreseeable future," he said in 1979, was "discouraging."

Conservative government has changed all that. Once again, Britain stands tall in the councils of Europe and of the world, and our policies have brought unparalleled prosperity to our citizens at home. Mr. Speaker, over the last decade. we have given power back to the people on an unprecedented scale. We have given back control to people over their own lives and over their livelihood, over the decisions that matter most to them and their families. We've done it by curbing the monopoly power of trade unions to control, even victimize, the individual worker. Labour would return to conflict, confrontation, and government by the consent of the TUC. We have done it by enabling families to own their homes, not least through the sale of one and a quarter million council houses. Labour opposed our new rents to mortgage initiative that will spread the benefits of ownership wider still.

And we have done it by giving people choice in public services. Which school is right for their children, which training course is best for the school-leaver, which doctor they choose to look after their health, and which hospital they want for their treatment. Labour are against spreading these freedoms and choice to all our people. They are against us giving power back to the people by privatising nationalised industries. Eleven million people now own shares, and seven and a half million have registered an interest in buying electricity shares. Labour want to renationalise electricity and water and British telecoms, they want to take power back to the state, back into their own grasp, and that is a fitful and debilitating grasp.

MEMBER: When the right honourable lady says that she's giving power back to the people, those people—over two million of them—are unemployed. Has she given power back to them? And 10.9 percent inflation—is that power back to us? Is the hundred billion of North Sea oil frittered away, that no other nations have, giving power back to the people? Will she kindly explain these particular points and let us know where pushing large numbers of people into cardboard boxes and taking power away from them is somehow giving power back to them.

PRIME MINISTER THATCHER: Two million more jobs since 1979 is a great deal more opportunity for people. Yes, 10.9 percent inflation is much higher than it should be; it's a lot less then the 26.9 that there was under Labour. Yes, we have benefitted from North Sea oil, and this government has seen to it that there are great investments abroad that will give us an income in this country long after North Sea oil has ceased. And therefore, we have provided colossal investment for future generations. Honourable gentlemen opposite ran up debts which we have repaid. We are providing investment for the future. We do not believe in living at the expense of the future.

MEMBER: If things are quite so good as the prime minister is outlining today, why aren't all her colleagues behind her, happy to have her continue in the job of defending that record?

PRIME MINISTER THATCHER: Mr. Speaker, these are the reasons why we shall win a fourth general election. We have been down in the polls before when we've taken difficult decisions. The essence of a good government is that it is prepared to take difficult decisions to get the long-term prosperity. That is what we have accrued, and that is why we shall win, handsomely, when a general election comes.

Now, I was talking about the Labour Party wanting to renationalise privatised industry. Four of the industries we have privatised are now in the top ten British businesses, and at the very bottom of the list of one thousand British businesses lie four nationalised industries. Labour's industries consume the wealth others create and give nothing back. Mr. Speaker, it is because individuals and families now have more power and more choice, that they have more opportunities to succeed; more jobs, two million more than in 1979; better rewards for hard work; income tax down from thirty-three pence on the pound to twenty-five on the pound, and no—[MEM-

BERS: Hear, hear!]—and no surcharge on savings income either. Living standards up by a third; more new businesses, 400,000 new businesses since 1979, over seven hundred every week; and a better future for our children.

Thanks to their hard work, success, and enterprise, our people are better off than ever before. [MEMBERS: Hear, hear!] Indeed, the average pensioner—just listen, just listen. You might hear something which you didn't know—listen. [Laughter] The average pensioner now has twice as much to hand on to his children as eleven years ago. [Cheers] They are thinking about the future. This massive rise in our living standards reflects the extraordinary transformation of the private sector. I give way to the honourable gentleman.

MEMBER: There is no doubt that the prime minister has in many ways achieved substantial success. [MEMBERS: Hear, hear!] There is one statistic that I understand is not, however, challenged. And that is that over her eleven years, the gap between the richest ten percent and the poorest ten percent in this country has widened substantially. How can she say, at the end of her chapter in British politics, that she can justify that many people in a constituency such as mine feel relatively much poorer, much less well-housed, and much less well-provided than it was in 1979. Surely, she accepts that is not a record that she or any prime minister can be proud of.

PRIME MINISTER THATCHER: Mr. Speaker, all levels of income are better off than they were in 1979. But what the honourable member is saying is that he will rather the poor be poorer, provided the rich were less rich. That's why you will never create the wealth for better social justice that we have. And what a policy. Yes, he would rather have the poor poorer, provided the rich were less rich. That is the Liberal policy. Yes, it came out. He didn't [mean] it to, but it did. Now, it is an extraordinary transformation of the private sector which has created the wealth for better social services, for better pensions to enable pensioners to have twice as much as they did ten years ago to leave to their children. No longer the sick man of Europe, our output and investment grew faster over the '80s than any of our major competitors. If you'll be a little bit patient, then we'd get on a little bit further. No longer a doubtful prospect when American and Japanese companies invest in Europe, we are their first choice. But—there's no longer an overmanned, inefficient, backward manufacturing sector, but modern dynamic industries.

The right honourable gentleman referred to the level of inflation. Yes, in 1987 and 1988, the economy did expand too fast. There was too much borrowing, and inflation rose. And that's why we had to take the tough, unpopular measures to bring the growth of money supply within target. Inflation has now peaked and will soon be coming down. Inevitably, the economy has slowed, but we firmly expect growth to resume next year, for the fundamentals are right. Our industry is now enterprising. It has been modernised and restructured. In sector after sector, it is our companies which lead the world in pharmaceuticals, in telecommunications, and in aerospace. Our companies have the freedom and talent to succeed and the will to compete. I give way to the honourable gentleman.

MEMBER: I'm extremely grateful. The prime minister is aware that I detest every single one of her domestic policies and I've never hid that. It's always our greater pleasure to tackle a political heavyweight opponent than a lightweight leader of the opposition—[General commotion. SPEAKER: Order!]—who is afraid to explain why, after a lifetime of campaigning to get rid of nuclear weapons, is going to plant three Tridents in my country. But can I take the prime minister back—[MEMBERS: No! No! General uproar]—to the question of the poor getting poorer? Doesn't she realize, even at this point, which is five minutes after midnight for her, because there was a transfer of resources from the poor to the wealthy, that's why the poll tax was unacceptable, and it's because of the poll tax she has fallen?

PRIME MINISTER THATCHER: And I think that the honourable gentleman knows that I have the same contempt for his socialist policies as the people of East Europe who have experienced it have. [Uproar among members.] I think I must have hit the right nail on the head when I pointed out that the logic of those policies are they'd rather have the poor poorer. Once they start to talk about the gap, they'd rather the gap were that! [Laughter and commotion] Down here, that, not that or that. So long as the gap is smaller, so long as—[Commotion. SPEAKER: Order!]—the gap is smaller, they'd rather have the poor poorer. You do not create wealth and opportunity that way, you do not create a property-owning democracy that way.

Can I get back to the industry—to an industrial policy from which Scotland has benefitted so much, but which it could never have benefitted under the government he used to support and under a political policy he espouses now. [MEMBERS: Hear, hear, hear!] Yes, our companies have the freedom and talent to succeed and the will to compete. And compete we must. Our competitors won't be taking a break. There must be no hankering after soft options and no going back to the disastrous economic policies of Labour governments. No amount of distance lends enchantment to the lean years of Labour which gave us the lowest growth rate in Europe, the highest strike record, and, for the average family, virtually no increase in take-home pay. Labour's policies are a vote of no-confidence in the ability of British people to manage their own affairs. We have that confidence—confidence in freedom and confidence in enterprise—and that is what divides Conservatives from Socialists.

Mr. Speaker, our stewardship of the public finances has been better than that of any government for nearly fifty years. It's enabled us to repay debt and cut taxes, and the resulting success of the private sector has generated the wealth and revenues which pay for better social services—to double the amount being spent to help the disabled, to give extra help to war widows, and vastly to increase spending on the National Health Service: over one million more patients being treated each year, another 8,000 more doctors and 53,000 more nurses to treat them. That is the record of eleven and a half years of Conservative government and Conservative principles. Mr. Speaker, all these are grounds for congratulation, not censure, least of all from the right honourable gentleman who had no alternative policies. [SPEAKER: Order!] I will give way to the right honourable gentleman, and then I'd like to move on and say something about Europe, because what the right honourable gentleman said was, to say the least of it, opaque. [Laughter]

MEMBER: The prime minister mentioned disabled people, and she is, as always, anxious to be honest with the house. But would she care to give a wider perspective about what has happened to disabled people under her government? Would she care to confirm the official figures that, in the first ten years of her reign, average male earnings in real value lowered by twenty percent, whereas the benefits of disabled people over that period, in real terms, rose one percent? How well did disabled people do under that? [Cheers]

PRIME MINISTER THATCHER: Mr. Speaker, the right honourable gentleman is very selective indeed—[Cheers]—in what he chooses. He knows full well that, in the last eleven years, we have spent twice as much on he disabled, over and above inflation—not twice as much in cash terms, but twice as much in what the benefits will buy, in particular in mobility, and, of course, a motorability scheme. This has been quite outstanding, and has been brought about because we have been able, under our policies, to create the wealth which created the resources to do that, among other things. [MEMBERS: Hear, hear!]

Now, Mr. Speaker, over the last eleven years, this government has had a clear and unwavering vision of the future of Europe and of Britain's role in it. It's a vision which stems from our own deep-seated attachment to parliamentary democracy and this government's commitment to economic liberty, to enterprise, to competition, and to a free market economy. No government in Europe has fought more resolutely against subsidies, state aid to industry, and protectionism, against unnecessary regulation and bureaucracy, against increasing unaccountable central power at the expense of national parliaments. No government has fought more against that in Europe than this one. We've fought attempts to put new burdens and constraints upon industry, such as a social charter, which would take away jobs, in particular, part-time jobs.

For us, part of the purpose of the Community is to demolish trade barriers and to eliminate unfit subsidies so that we can all benefit from a great expansion of trade both within Europe and with the outside world. The fact is that Britain has done more to shape the Community over the past eleven years than any other member state. It is Britain which is leading the reform of the common agricultural policy, getting surpluses down, putting a ceiling on agricultural spending. We have been the driving force towards a single market, which when it is completed will be the most significant advance in the Community since the Treaty of Rome itself. And we've done more than any other government to resist protectionism, to keep Europe's market open to trade with the rest of the world, and to make a success of the GATT negotiations.

Mr. Speaker, we have worked for our vision of a Europe which is free and open to the rest of the world, and above all to the countries of Eastern Europe as they emerge from the shadows of socialism. It wouldn't help them for Europe to become a tight-knit little club, tied up in regulation and restrictions. They deserve a Europe where there's room for their rediscovered repression. And with all this, Mr. Speaker, we have never hesitated to stand up for Britain's interest. The people of Britain want a fair deal in Europe, particularly over our budget contribution. We have got back nearly ten billion pounds, which would otherwise have been paid over to the European community under the arrangements negotiated by the party opposition when they were in power.

Indeed, what sort of vision do they have, Mr. Speaker? None, according to the right honourable gentleman. They want a Europe with subsidies, a Europe with socialist restrictions, a Europe of protectionism. They want it because that's how they would like to run—or is it to "ruin"—this country. Every time we've stood up and fought for Britain and British interests, the front bench opposite have carped and criticized and moaned, and on the central issues of Europe's future they will not tell us where they stand. Do they want a single currency? The right honourable gentleman doesn't even know what it means. Only the—[Uproar and cheers among members. SPEAKER: Order!] Absolute nonsense. It was appalling. So he says it's a hypothetical question. It's not going to be a hypothetical question. Someone has to go there and argue knowing what it means. [MEMBERS: Hear! Hear! SPEAKER: Order!]

PRIME MINISTER THATCHER: Are they prepared to defend the rights of the United Kingdom Parliament? No, for all that the right honourable gentleman said. For them it's all compromise—sweep it under the carpet, leave it for another day, it might sort out and sort itself, in the hope that the people of Britain will not notice—[SPEAKER: Order!]—what's happening to them, and how the powers would be gradually slipping away.

This government will continue to take a positive and constructive approach to the future of Europe. We welcome economic and monetary cooperation. Indeed, no other member state has gone further than Britain in tabling proposals for the next stage, including the hard ECU. But our proposals would work with the market, and give people and governments real choice. [MEMBERS: Hear! Hear!] We want the community to move forward as twelve. And from my talks in Paris with other European leaders over these past few days, I'm convinced that that is their aim, too. Europe is strongest when it grows through willing cooperation and practical measures, not compulsion or bureaucratic dreams. I give way to the honourable gentleman.

MEMBER: I'm most grateful to the prime minister. Would she tell us whether she intends to continue her own personal fight against a single currency and an independent central bank when she leaves office?

MEMBER: No, she's going to be the governor! [Laughter]

PRIME MINISTER THATCHER: Under the present structure—[MEMBERS: Hear, hear! SPEAKER: Order!] What a good idea! [Laughter] I hadn't thought of it. But if I were, there would be no European central bank accountable to no one, least of all to national parliaments. It was the point of that kind of European central banking—no democracy, taking powers away from every single parliament, and being able to have a single currency and a monetary policy and an interest rate which takes all political power away from us. As my right honourable friend said in his first speech after the proposal of a single currency, a single currency is about the politics of Europe, it is about a federal Europe by the back door. [Commotion] So I'll consider the honourable gentleman's proposal.

Now, where were we? I'm enjoying this. I'm enjoying this. [Laughter and more commotion]—now Mr. Speaker, I was asked—[MEMBER: You can wipe the floor with it!] I was talking about—[Drowned out by extended uproarious commotion]—Yes, we know. [SPEAKER: All order! Order!] Now, Mr. Speaker, we were on Europe and what is—and the socialist ideal of Europe. Not for us the corporatism, socialism, and central control; we leave those to the benches opposite. Ours is a larger vision of the Community whose member states cooperate with one another more and more closely to the benefit of all. Are we then to be censured for standing up for a free and open Britain—[Commotion]—in a free and open Europe? No, Mr. Speaker, our policies—are—[SPEAKER: Order!]—in tune with the deepest instincts of the British people. and we shall win the censure motion. So we shall not be censured for what is thoroughly right. [MEMBERS: Hear! Hear!]

Mr. Speaker, under our leadership, Britain has been just as influential in shaping the wider Europe and the relations between East and West. Ten years ago, the Eastern part of Europe lay under totalitarian rule, its people knowing neither rights nor liberties. Today, we have a Europe in which democracy, the rule of law, and basic human rights are spreading ever more widely, where the threat to our security from the overwhelming conventional forces of the Warsaw Pact has been removed, where the Berlin Wall has been torn down and the Cold War is at an end. These immense changes didn't come about by chance; they have been achieved by strength and resolution in defence—[MEMBERS: Hear! Hear!]—and by a refusal ever to be intimidated. No one in Eastern Europe believed that their countries would be free had it not been for those Western governments who are prepared to defend liberty, who kept alive their hopes that one day Eastern Europe, too, would enjoy freedom.

But it was no thanks to the party opposite nor to their campaign for nuclear disarmament, of which the right honourable gentleman—[MEMBERS: Hear, hear!]—is still a member. It is this government which kept the nuclear weapons which insured that we would never be blackmailed or threatened. When Brezhnev deployed the SS-20s, Britain deployed the cruise missiles and was the first to do so. And all these things were done in the teeth of the opposition of honourable gentlemen opposite and their ladies. [MEMBER: Honourable right gentlemen! Laughter and commotion. SPEAKER: Order!] The SS-20s could never have been negotiated away without the bargaining strength which cruise and Pershing gave to the West. Should we be censured for our strength or the party opposite for their weakness? I have no doubt that the people of this country will willingly entrust Britain's security and future to a Conservative government which defends them rather than to socialists who put expediency before principles. [MEMBERS: Hear, hear, hear!] And it is principle which is at stake—[Commotion].

MEMBER: Could I offer to my right honourable friend one measurement of the immense international respect and affection that she enjoys as a result of her policies of peace through strength? A public opinion poll published in West Coast America last month—[Interrupted by House Members]—gave these figures—[Continued interruption from the House Members].

SPEAKER: Order! Order! It takes a lot of time. But I think the honourable gentleman is seeking to participate in the debate. Will you ask a question, please?

MEMBER: These figures: Gorbachev 74 percent, Bush 75 percent, and Thatcher 94 percent.

PRIME MINISTER THATCHER: Thank you very much—and I am sure they were quite right, too. Now, may I say a word or two about the Gulf because it—[SPEAKER: Order! Order!] May I say a word or two about the situation in the Gulf? It is the thing which will dominate politics until the matter is resolved. But it's principle which is at stake there, Mr. Speaker, principle and the rule of international law. In my discussions with other heads of government at the CSCE summit in Paris, I found unanimous and impressive determination that Iraq's aggression must not succeed; the resolutions of the United Nations must be implemented in full. That is the peaceful option, Mr. Speaker, and it is there to be taken if Saddam Hussein so chooses. But there is also a very widespread recognition among my colleagues in Paris that the time is fast approaching when the world community will have to take more decisive action to uphold international law and compel Saddam Hussein to leave Kuwait. No one can doubt the dangers which lie ahead. Saddam Hussein has many times shown his contempt for human life, not least for the lives of his own people. He has large armed forces; they are equipped with peculiarly evil weapons, both chemical and biological.

Twice in my time—[Interruptions from the floor] No, Mr. Speaker. No, Mr. Speaker, not now. [SPEAKER: Order!] Twice in my time as prime minister we've had to send our forces across the world to defend a small country against ruthless aggression. First, our own people in the Falklands, and now to the borders of Kuwait. To those who have never had to take such decisions, may I say to them that they are taken with a heavy heart and the knowledge of the manifold dangers, but with tremendous pride in the professionalism and courage of our armed forces.

There's something else that one feels as well, Mr. Speaker, that is a sense of this country's destiny, the centuries of history and experience which ensure that when principles have to be defended, when good has to be upheld, when evil has to be overcome, then Britain will take up arms. It is because we on this side have never flinched from difficult decisions that this House and this country can have confidence in this government today.

FIGURE 27.1 Cadet at the Virginia Military Institute salutes Lady Thatcher. On her right are Major General and Mrs. John W. Knapp; on her left are Mr. and Mrs. Belton Kleberg Johnson. (*Source:* Thomas Bradshaw, Lexington, Virginia.)

27

Politicians and Soldiers

Speech Delivered to the Corps of Cadets,
Virginia Military Institute, Lexington, Virginia, January 24, 1992

Being at a military institution, I wish to describe my experience of having to work both with political decisions against a background of the need for military decisions and ensuring that they both work together. The military serves the purposes of politics, and your country and mine serve the purposes of liberty and justice. Many is the time in my period of office when they were challenged. And always it had seemed to me that the Thatcher law of politics was very true, namely that the unexpected happens. So may I tell you how the unexpected happened in the military and political sphere, how we tackled it, what we did about it, and also then go on to tell you about the great changes that have come about between East and West and in the Soviet Union, how I see them, and the other still very troubled area of the world, which is the Middle East.

Soviet Invasion of Afghanistan

I had not long been in power as prime minister when I received a telephone call from the president of the United States over the Christmas of 1979 to say that the Soviet Union had invaded Afghanistan. It came as a big surprise. What were we to do about it? We were very, very far away. There was no question of being able to argue against it or send forces there, but we could clearly be very, very condemnatory of it. We could clearly take certain action, have certain sanctions. We needed to do it because it came shortly in the aftermath of the U.S. and the Soviet Union having negotiated in good faith the SALT I agreement. That particular action of the Soviets going into Afghanistan did not lead to a military reply although it did lead to helping and training those inside who were prepared to resist aggression.

One of the great joys of these circumstances is that there are always brave men and women who are prepared to risk their lives to defend their country, and we were all very active in trying to help them do that. We were also very active in the political sphere in totally condemning it, in getting the support of unaligned states, as well as those aligned as we are in defence of freedom totally to reject it. Some of us were able to prevail upon those who would otherwise have gone to the Moscow Olympics to say this is far from being a free country, it has just invaded someone else, please do not go. Shortly after that telephone call, we held in London those people who are normally not at their desks over Christmas, and I'm proud to report that London was prepared. We had a meeting very quickly of all the nations to decide what we should do. That was my first experience in office of the unexpected happening on the overseas front.

Iran-Iraq War

I did not have to wait very long for the next thing to happen on the overseas front. I got a telephone call, also on a Sunday, to say that Iraq had invaded Iran in 1980. Again unexpected, it was shortly after the Ayatollah Khomeini had gone back. He had in fact invoked a reign of terror in Iran with terrible executions, and Iraq went into Iran. I remember it very well because immediately one could see the strategic significance of it. This was the oil seaway. Down that seaway we have to get our essential supplies of oil for the rest of the world, and if we hadn't, then we were very, very much constrained in what we could do. Our whole tactic of that time was in fact to try politically to contain this great warlike action between the two nations, to contain it to that end of the Gulf. We were successful for many years, but towards the end it flared up long before the other thing in the Middle East happened.

The interesting thing looking back was that immediately we in Britain and some other nations moved some of our great naval forces to stand outside the Gulf in case there should be any need for them to escort ships of commerce up the Gulf and out. And so from that day in 1980, we moved three of our destroyers through the Gulf to make certain anyone in difficulty who needed the protection of the Royal Navy should have it as they went about their daily commerce. That was the second unexpected thing. I remember contacting some of my fellow heads of government and some other advisers and saying, "How long do you think this will last?" The advice I received varied from about five days to five years. It lasted in fact eight years and turned toward the end extremely nasty as it expanded throughout the Gulf. Our Royal Patrol Boats in fact were attacked in the Gulf. There was a very great deal of anxiety and a very great deal of action, some of it very tragic, throughout the Gulf in those days.

Falklands War

Those were the first two experiences. I didn't have to wait very long for the next. The next one was when people came in to see me urgently in 1982 on a Wednesday evening, late at night, in the House of Commons where we were still debating—we're always talking in the House of Commons, often in front of television these days—to say that the Argentine fleet had sailed. We didn't know whether it was on another lot of exercises, or whether this time it was going to be different, and they were going to land on the Falklands. By Friday we knew they had landed on and invaded the Falklands. On the Wednesday, I had to turn round and see with my advisers, military and political, precisely what we should do if they did land, because one thing I was certain: if they landed and took those islands, which were the Queen's islands—every single person on them was British and had been British for a hundred and fifty years—if they took those islands they couldn't keep them, we would have to recover them. They were eight thousand miles away. When one landed on them, they would have three weeks advance notice that a task force was on its way.

To me it was fascinating as I got our advisers, both political and defence, together. The thing I learned then was to be very thankful we were members of NATO. Not that NATO would help us under those circumstances—we were absolutely alone—but the fact that we were members of NATO meant that all our ships, all our air force, all our soldiers, every one of them, had to be on forty-eight hours' notice, fully equipped, to move to whatever was their NATO station. So as my military advisers came in, they said one after the other: within forty-eight hours we can move so many ships, we can send a task force of aircraft carriers, destroyers, support and supply ships, we can have the full army on board, as many as they can take, we can have the Harriers ready to go, and so on. That was the consequence, the benefit, the advantage, of being part of a NATO military alliance which had been formed to defend the freedom of the West against communism. How important the drill, the discipline, the regular planning, the regular procedures are, in military ways, and how important they are to politics! Because of that we were able to move very quickly, and a task force went down to the Falklands.

I was very interested again as I looked in the history to see that the walls of Number 10, Downing Street, the home of prime ministers, had seen it all before. In 1770, when the colonies were still the colonies of the British Empire, a task force had gone down to the Falklands to turf off the Spanish who had landed on our islands. The difference was, in those days, the Spanish left before we got there. Not in my day, as you know. We had in fact to fight to get the invader off.

I learned a very great deal of the work and relationship between the politicians and the military. You will have read it all in military history; at any rate, if you haven't, do. It is fascinating, because the fact is if you ever commit your armed forces in defence of your cause, they should never be wanting for a political decision as to what their objectives were. And they should never be wanting a political decision to get the supplies where they needed them at the time they needed them at the time to take action. I was very lucky. A former prime minister came in to see me and said: "Now let me give you a little bit of advice. . . ." Believe you me, always take the advice of those who have had experience. It was Harold Macmillan. He came in and said, "I'm the senior Conservative prime minister living. I want to give you this advice. Set up an emergency committee day by day. Only have a few people on it, not more than five, but for heaven's sake, don't include the Treasury." This advice I followed meticulously. It was sound advice. When the objective is to recover the liberty of people, that is your first objective, and it matters rather more than anything else. So you're not going to be constrained, nor will you put your forces in the field and constrain them by limiting the amount which you spend. And so day by day that emergency committee met, every single day, sometimes twice a day. It was my pride that never, never, never were the people in the field wanting their political objective, their rules of engagement, and never, never, never were they wanting the equipment, never, never never were they short of the men they needed.

We started by sending a small task force, something like four or five thousand men. In the end we sent a hundred ships, twenty-five thousand when you include all the support services, and I marvel at its success. We had no air cover from land. All our air cover had to be from aircraft carriers, and it was carried out. And although I was not told by any advisers, I thought we must get our commanders together, our chiefs of staff with our politicians, and every Sunday we did that. Now that was absolutely right, and every civilian here would know and understand what I meant when I said if we were ever committing our armed forces in defence of our country or its interests, we put our whole weight, our whole might, our whole economy behind then. We did, and it was successful.

We started by sending a small task force, something like four or five thousand men. In the end we sent a hundred ships, twenty-five thousand when you include all the support services, and I marvel at their success. We had no air cover from land. All our air cover had to be from aircraft carriers, and it was carried out. And although I was not told by any advisers, I thought we must get our commanders together, our chiefs of staff with our politicians, and every Sunday we did that. Now that was absolutely right, and every civilian here would know and understand what I meant when I said if we were ever committing our armed forces in defence of our country or its interests, we put our whole weight, our whole might, our whole economy behind then. We did, and it was successful.

Bombing of Libya

The next unexpected thing that happened is one of the most interesting and one of the most difficult decisions that I have ever had to take. It was when I got a telephone call in the mid-1980s from President Reagan that Libya had engaged in state terrorism for a very long time. It was continuing to do so. It was taking the view that it was free to do so, that no one dare challenge it. He was thinking of having a raid on Libya and would need to use the bases in Britain from which to conduct that raid. I was always very careful that whatever we did should never be contrary to international law, but should uphold it. And so we looked at that very carefully and came to this conclusion: If we were ever to leave the sanction of force to those countries which have no scruples, no moral scruples about its use, they would continue to use force, they would continue to use terrorism, and we would leave our people in jeopardy. For that reason we thought it was legitimate, a legitimate act of self defence of the innocent, provided the target was a military one. For that reason I said "Yes, you can use the British bases on which to conduct that raid."

I had a very difficult debate in Parliament afterwards, but they accepted the validity of the argument. The forces went from the air fields in Britain. What is the good of having air fields in another country if you can't use them when you need to? So long as the cause was just and valid, we granted that, and I have to report that we were the only European country that did. Those bombers were in fact not able to go right across the Continent of Europe from Britain, across land. They had to go all the way around the sea outside with an enormous long journey, refueling before they did their bombing run.

Iraqi Invasion of Kuwait

The next one came in August 1990. As chance would have it, I had been invited to give a major lecture to close a conference in Aspen, and the president had been asked to open it. The president accepted, and I had already accepted to close it, but as he was opening I felt I simply must go to Aspen for the opening as well as for the rest of the occasion. So I got to Aspen late one evening, very late, and at 1:00 A.M. when I had just in fact retired for the night, a telephone call came. Saddam Hussein had gone into Kuwait.

Fortunately, the president and I were meeting later that morning and decided that the invasion simply could not stand. If ever you appease a tyrant, the tyranny will go on, and you must stop it in its tracks. Later, after he had the United Nations resolution and Saddam Hussein had not obeyed them, I went to Washington on the Monday. That day we sent the forces which once again were always standing in readiness—we the Tornadoes, the Buccaneers, and the Maritime aircraft, and the United States its big aircraft to get to the northern part of Saudi Arabia to see that that invasion in the initial stages went no further. It was justified on two grounds. One, they had wrongfully invaded someone else's territory, and that couldn't stand. Second, if they went any further, they could very quickly have gone down the rest of the oil states and have got something like sixty percent of the world's oil reserves and therefore have held the rest of the world to ransom. Gradually we sent more and more forces. It was a very bold, a very brave decision, and carried out magnificently.

Lessons of Military Crises

I have to draw two conclusions from this. First, at no stage in that eleven- to twelve-year period could we have defended liberty when the unexpected happened unless we had taken the right decisions on defence. For example, we could not have gone to the Gulf with the latest equipment, with the equipment in the volume in which it went, with the equipment with the very latest aircraft, the very latest Stealth aircraft, the very latest missiles, the very latest anti-missile missiles, unless ten years, nine years, eight years before, the government in power, especially Reagan here and myself in Britain, had taken the decision to spend enough on defence, to keep up the strength of our armed forces and to give them the very best equipment which a free nation with excellent research and technological capability could field.

That was the first lesson, and it has lessons for us now. The unexpected won't stop happening. Tyrants won't stop being born, and the very, very best defence of freedom is assurance that the tyrants will not succeed. The assurance that liberty will triumph is to retain your defence in peak condition. If a politician needs to be able to take a decision quickly, you need to know that the armed forces are trained, equipment is there, and you have got the latest technology, better than anyone else could produce. Let us not shrink from that lesson, and let us learn it in case we should put the freedom of future generations in jeopardy. You don't know where the threat will come from. No one was discussing Saddam Hussein the June before he moved in August, but it came, and we were ready.

The second conclusion is that both the military and the politicians must each understand one another's problems and make provision to work together as we did during the whole of the Falklands campaign. I might say there is a third one, and I should in fact introduce it and parade it before you today. The moment the armed forces of a free country are committed in the cause of that country, the support of the entire civilian population is fantastic, it is remarkable, it is inspiring. Let me give you an example. Down in the Falklands, we had to send bombers from the Ascension Islands. In fact, in order to get to the Falklands they had to refuel twice on the way there, and they had to refuel twice on the way back. It was a great operation. We hadn't done refueling exercises before; it wasn't normally done in the Air Force. It is now, since then. So over Scotland they practised for three weeks We had to get the equipment made, every person in a factory. They didn't give a damn the hours they worked. They were doing something for our armed forces. All the equipment was made; it was their pleasure and pride to get it ready over the three weeks. We needed one of our ships in the Mediterranean to be converted into a Red Cross ship for taking the injured. It was all done in Gibraltar in ten days, and down it went. The kind of cooperation you get from a free people under those circumstances is remarkable. They understand what is at stake, and they rally totally together.

Of course, this brings me to another point. We are a country born in liberty, founded upon justice, with a spirit of enterprise, believing in the sanctity of human rights and the sanctity of the individual. This country was created by those people, by pioneers who believed in liberty, who believed in hard work, who believed in responsibility, who came to build a nation they knew to be a great example to the rest of the world. And so it has proved. They had faith that their work would bear fruit, and it has. But we've had during this century to fight two or three great battles against tyranny. The first was World War I against Germany and the Austro-Hungarian Empire, victoriously. It couldn't have been won without America, which gives security to the whole world. We in Europe couldn't have done it without America.

Second, fascism and nazism of a terrible kind rose in Germany, and also an ambitious tyranny arose in Japan, and the tyranny and the cruelty there also was terrible. We had to beat those tyrannies by the expenditure of a great many lives, a great deal of sacrifice, a great deal of resources, a great deal of money. And we did because if there's tyranny in the world, then our very freedom itself is threatened, the more so as science brings missiles able to go further and payloads ever yet more terrible. We beat those tyrannies off by having to go to war.

Communism and the Soviet Union

The third one was different, and it is about that one and the future which I particularly wish to speak. In addition to those two tyrannies, we had a new one come in 1917 in the Soviet Union as Lenin seized power by a coup from Kerenski, who had previously toppled the czars and who had started the first steps of Russia towards democracy. He had an election, and the Kerensky forces won it by something like nineteen million votes. The Soviets only got eleven million, so the Soviets had a coup. That was the first coup, and along came communism, a creed which had no respect for human freedom, no respect for human spirit, a creed which said the government could plan everything. It had a plan of production, would dispossess everyone of their property and did, and if they resisted, as peasant farmers did, they were shot. It is one of the greatest purges ever of innocent people. They dispossessed everyone of his job, so everyone had to get his job from communism. It was a total tyranny invented by Karl Marx in the free atmosphere of the British Library. Had he experienced it, he could never have written that book.

Communism held sway by force, by the KGB. It was a terrible tyranny. It had the idea that it would spread all over the world, that everyone would conform, that everything would be planned, that eventually the state would wither away, that nationalism would be suppressed. In the Second World War, Hitler attacked Russia, and for a time we had to work together to defeat Hitler. We had hoped that after that war both Russia and we would disarm. She didn't. She had her objectives then of world domination, and she went on increasing her military might, and she went on with her subversion. The purpose of that military might and subversion was to insure that other countries became communist either by threat or internal subversion, that communists would seize power as they had in the Soviet Union.

Opposing this creed was America, Britain, a newly free Europe. But for a time our whole doctrine was not in any way, certainly not, to attack militarily. We were a defensive alliance, and our doctrine was the containment of communism. Now, eventually we noticed, when President Reagan and I came to power—not really noticed, we knew!—that our expenditure on defence had weakened, and expenditure on defence, particularly on new nuclear weapons, in the Soviet Union had increased. We were therefore in danger. We said immediately that within a limited budget, we will put more priority on defence, both President Reagan and I, so that we could say to the Soviet Union: "You will never win militarily. Never. We will always match you, and we will probably be technologically ahead of you." Then President Reagan took the crucial decision to go ahead with SDI, and a marvelous decision it was! Wonderful! It got the whole technology ahead of anything they could do.

So when they had their SS-20s, we deployed cruise and Pershing, and we took the whole technology ahead. This was for the purpose of saying to them: "We will not tolerate the extension of your terrible, wicked creed, we will stop it, you will not get it by military might, so you may as well drop it." We also then said, one to another: "We're going to take the battle of ideas into the enemy territory." We'd never really fought the battle of ideas; we'd never really taught the great benefits of liberty. We knew that the Russian people had no freedom; it wasn't permitted. They had no freedom of worship; it wasn't permitted. No travel. They couldn't, in fact, read news-papers; they couldn't read what other people's views were. They were totally, totally controlled by the state. So we started, and more information gradually got into the Soviet Union. Eventually they couldn't jam it all as we spoke on Radio Liberty, on the BBC. And there grew up a number of dissidents in the Soviet Union, marvelous brave people, such as Sakharov, a brilliant physicist, and Solzhenitsyn. You know their bravery, you know the famous Nobel Prize–winning speech of Solzhenitsyn. What can we do? We can make certain that we will not cooperate with the lie that the Soviet government produces. One word of truth can outweigh the greatest tyranny. We decided that whenever we came up against the Soviet politicians, we would say to them: "What are you doing about human rights?" It's not enough to sign a treaty about it. There are no rights in the Soviet Union. Gradually we overcame with greater military strength, and we started to fight the battle of ideas.

Mikhail Gorbachev

It wasn't only President Reagan and myself. There was a third player in the game, one called Mr. Gorbachev. I decided after the 1983 elections, which I won, that we would look for a future leader in the Soviet Union, because there must be another generation that might have different ideas. If we could only get them over to see our way of life, we might give them different ideas and see what poverty—poverty of spirit and poverty of existence—the Soviet Union's creed had led to. Fortunately, the Foreign Office went talent-spotting, and they were very good. They came back and said: There's one person called Mikhail Gorbachev whom we think you should see. They were absolutely right. I got him over to London, and as always happens, when they come to the Western world for the first time, they see things they never knew existed—freedom of discussion, freedom of information, freedom of speech everywhere, freedom of association, things debated freely in our House of Commons, in our Congress, and they see shops with goods galore. And they say to you: But there are goods in the shops even at the end of the day. We say, Yes. They just cannot understand the plenty.

The moment he came I knew that we had found someone very, very different. I'd had a good deal of experience dealing with Soviet politicians. They have a standard line. It's very wooden, very rigid. Whatever question you ask, you get the standard answer. It may have nothing whatever to do with the question you asked, but nevertheless that's their answer. Not a bit with Mr. Gorbachev! Straight away he would admit the defects, admit the faults of the Soviet system. It was from him I first learned that thirty percent of the harvest in the Soviet Union never gets to market. It's not properly harvested; it's not properly stored there, and the equipment is not properly transported. It's not properly distributed, and a lot of it goes on the black market. They were admitting that in this glorious centrally planned economy everything went wrong.

As you know, he became leader of the Soviet Union, and gradually he started to make very different speeches. Gone was the rigid total control. He started to say that the people in charge must exercise initiative, they must exercise responsibility. You will understand that people work better if they have some control, some stake, some control over their own lives, some sort of stake in their own future, if they accept some responsibility. He gave them that, and never underestimate what he gave the world: He restored freedom of speech, he restored freedom of association, he restored freedom of worship, he restored the right to vote to the local councils and to the state councils and to the Supreme Soviet. He brought the television cameras in so everyone could see what their elected representatives were saying. It was the most remarkable change.

That was not all. He in fact took steps which led Poland once again to be free and leave the Warsaw Pact—Poland, where the church had played such a large part in keeping up the spirit. I remember going to Poland and visiting the Gdansk shipyard when Lech Walesa was still there, giving hope and help to those people and addressing a meeting of fifty thousand, and seeing and going back to Jaruzelski and saying: "This is a movement which no one, but no one, can ignore. They will have their way." And Poland became free. Hungary became free, Czechoslovakia. You'll remember that previously, when Hungary tried to be free in 1956, the tanks rolled in. Previously in Czechoslovakia, in the Prague Spring of 1968, the tanks rolled in. Not this time. They became free. He also withdrew support from the revolutionary forces in Nicaragua, reduced support for revolutionary forces in Angola, reduced support for the revolutionary forces of many countries in Africa.

So the whole ambition of communism the world over had fallen, and he was trying to change it even in the Soviet Union. The world owes that man a very great deal. It was leadership of a very high order. Of course, it provoked a reaction from the eighteen million bureaucrats who didn't want to lose their privileges and their jobs. Leadership looking into the future, acting as a searchlight into the future, always evokes a great deal of opposition and a great deal of enmity. If a politician who endures what he or she thinks is right, hasn't made a few enemies, then he really hasn't been bold enough in what he thinks he should do. You never worry in politics about making enemies if what you're doing is right. It was quite remarkable.

Post-Communist Eastern Europe

You will want to know what the future holds there, because you will say that it is now breaking up. Please do not worry that the Soviet Union is breaking up. After all, the British Empire at one time was, after 1776, the British Empire. That would have been handled better had I been there at the time. [Hearty laughter] The British Empire which came out of World War II, with five independent dominions—the United Kingdom, Canada, Australia, New Zealand, South Africa—brought to full independence another forty-five nations which belonged to the British Empire, ranging from India of seven hundred million, to Pakistan, to Bangladesh, to Nigeria, to Kenya, to Uganda, to Zambia, to Zimbabwe, to the Bahamas, to the East Caribbean, to the South Pacific islands, and so on and so forth. So there are now fifty votes in the United Nations of independent countries once the British Empire, now the British Commonwealth.

So you don't worry if an empire breaks up. The Habsburg Empire broke up, it was defeated; the Ottoman Empire broke up, it was defeated. The Spanish Empire broke up, the Portuguese broke up, the French broke up, the Belgian broke up. Yugoslavia, put together artificially, is now breaking up because it had no natural sense of identity. Nations put together artificially or held by force will break up. The empire of the twentieth century was the artificial communist empire. It is not surprising that it, too, will result in its component nations of fifteen separate nations. Do not be afraid of it. What we have to do is bring each one through to democracy, to freedom, with a full market economy, with private property—because where there are no private property rights, you will get no human rights—with limited government, with people acting under a framework law and letting enterprise have its full play.

If countries were rich according to the natural resources they possess, Russia should be the richest nation in the world—oil, gas, gold, silver, diamonds, platinum, all the minerals you need for an advanced economy, timber, good soil. She had all the natural resources, but she didn't have a political system which allowed the enterprise of her people to flower. She held them down. Now we have to get the political system of freedom under a rule of law, with private property, with enterprise. They know what they want; they don't know how to do it.

Worse still, the communist system has crumbled through inefficiency, and some of them haven't enough to eat in the main cities. They are reaching out, crying out for liberty. It didn't cost us a penny to beat them, to beat communism, to release the people into freedom, no sacrifices, no third world war, no sacrifice of life. It crumbled without that. No sacrifices of equipment; it crumbled without that. We got it all intact. Wouldn't it be right for those who love liberty to give them a much greater helping hand when we have surpluses of food in the United States and in Europe? We need to get them through the winter so that they have time to bring their agriculture up and gather their crops, and so that we have time to help them to change their law, to help them to help themselves. They are a very proud people. You have to be very careful how you help people, but that surely should be done on a larger scale than we've thought so far. It's not only part of our creed, our belief, our generosity, our sense of duty to fellow human beings. It is in our interest to do so.

It's my pride that I, for twelve years, represented the staunchest ally the United States has ever known. We have been partners in defending liberty. We have the same heritage. We have the same rule of law, the same democratic instincts, the same sense of liberty, that individuals have certain rights which are so fundamental that no government can take them away. It has been our duty to try to spread this all over the world. The English language is soaked in values, the values for which we stand, the values which you teach and uphold here. So, nourished in truth, brought up in freedom, we have, if we are true to those values, a better chance than ever before of having a century, the twenty-first century, better than ever we have known in this one, when we have, after all, succeeded in defeating the evil creeds that have stood in the way of liberty for all.

Questions from Cadets

CADET: In looking back through your career as prime minister, and seeing the unpopularity greeting some of your views and actions, how could you know the British people would support you by reelecting you for such a long time?

MRS. THATCHER: Well, I think the answer is that you don't know. You don't know. I faced each election not knowing what the result would be. What I did know was that we were setting Britain on a course which was right for liberty and justice, right for the talent, character, and ability of her people. As always, when you have an economy which has kind of been the sick man of Europe and which has sunk into defeatism, you have to do some pretty drastic things. Now, it's like getting an ill person better. You have to do some pretty drastic things, and you feel awful when you take the medicines and when you have the requisite operations. So long as you know you are doing the right thing, of course, you'll be unpopular when they hurt. But I believe firmly that as I had a good majority, and I had four years before I had to come up to an election, that the British people would respect honesty. They would respect doing the right thing. They would object to it while it was being done, but they would admit it was right when it succeeded.

CADET: Having been the leader of a great nation for a little over a decade, what words of advice, wisdom, or experience would you give to us as future leaders of our country?

MRS. THATCHER: You must first go right back to fundamental principles and decide what it is you believe, and reaffirm the enormous principles which are enshrined in your constitution. The constitution of the United States is the greatest expression of liberty in the English language, and was fashioned by very great men. Starting from there, you must fashion the right policies. And, believe you me, if you're in politics, the first thing you must do is learn to say No to every demand for taxpayers' money for every cause whether good or bad. You must learn to say No to the infinite number of people who ask you to put on extra controls on this or that because they don't like it. You must keep free enterprise, you must keep freedom of speech. So long as you have a framework of laws in which people can operate, and you have orthodox, sound finance, you can rely on people to use their talents to go ahead. I just say this in my own defence. We did it in my last four years in office. We had a budget surplus in each year. We were able to redeem debt, and we took off control after control. We took away organisation after organisation from state control and put them into private control, and we got capital ownership spread evermore widely throughout the community. I can recommend that recipe to your question.

CADET: Considering the dramatic developments that have occurred in Eastern Europe and the former Soviet Union, and the subsequent application of these nations, especially Russia, for admission into NATO, what do you see as the future purpose of NATO, and what role do you see the nuclear arm of the United Kingdom playing in NATO's future?

MRS. THATCHER: I think certainly the countries of Eastern Europe and the new ones in the Soviet Union might want some form of association with NATO. I don't think it could be full membership. First, we have to deal with the great nuclear weapon problem in the old Soviet Union. We can do that very much more easily if they are in association, and therefore, we can regularly monitor and watch precisely what needs to be done. There are twenty-seven thousand warheads at present in the Soviet Union. Thirteen thousand of them are strategic warheads on the big intercontinental ballistic missiles. They are in four states—Russia, Kazakhstan, Byelorussia, and the Ukraine—and those states have given undertakings that the four of them will keep control. The other fourteen thousand are tactical nuclear weapons. They are on a hundred sites scattered over the Soviet Union, and the danger is always that someone will manage to sell one of those or smuggle one of those to some of these states, terrorist states, who would only be too delighted to get hold of them and their three thousand nuclear scientists. This is really a great job to make certain that we don't get proliferation of those nuclear weapons. It is, I might say, another reason why you must continue to go ahead with SDI and the brilliant pebbles concept to stop them if anyone got hold of one. So, yes, we must keep closely in touch.

The role of NATO must always be to be prepared to tackle any tyrant, anywhere, whatever happens. Nearly ten years ago, I was already making speeches saying that NATO must act out of area. The NATO area of action has a line drawn across the North Atlantic; that might be all right for an alliance, but tyrants don't respect that line. NATO should be, in fact, able to act out of area; at the moment it is not NATO that acts out of area, but individual nations that act out of area. Note that on the Gulf, it wasn't the United Nations that took action; it passed the resolutions. It was individual sovereign states that fulfilled them. But the variedness and the preparedness you get is by being members of NATO, and it's very, very good discipline, it's very good preparation, and, as I started off by telling you, the unexpected does happen. The price of freedom is eternal vigilance; it is the oldest saying, it is the truest; we must respect it and be prepared for what happens, and NATO's the best organisation.

CADET: How would you evaluate the threat the Irish Republican Army poses today, and what do you believe is the best way to solve the problems in Northern Ireland?

MRS. THATCHER: The Irish Republican Army is not an army at all. It's a bunch of terrorists and thugs and murderers. Northern Ireland—the six northern counties, the Ulster counties—said they weren't going with the new Republic of Ireland. The Ulster counties weren't going with terror. They refused to. They fought a civil war about it. They weren't going to have it. Eventually in 1921, there was a settlement, and the border line was drawn in Number 10 Downing Street—not very well, but those were the borders. So you've got the six counties still being Northern Ireland, and they were determined to stay with the United Kingdom. We said so long as they wished to stay with the United Kingdom, they will have the right of self-determination to stay with the United Kingdom.

Everyone in Northern Ireland, whether of the Unionist persuasion, or whether he prefers to be Republican, everyone has the same vote. They send seventeen members to the Westminster Parliament every election. Some of them are Unionist, some are Republican, we had one who was neither, and we have another type of Unionist. They all have the ballot box. They also have the ballot box for their local authorities. From time to time we have a border poll to say, "Do you still wish to stay with the United Kingdom?" They vote overwhelmingly to do so, and continue to do so, and that pledge remains to them. It is the pledge of self-determination. There are some people who do not like the result of the ballot box, and they try to bomb and maim and frighten people out of it.

Now, I don't know what the answer is. I tried to have an Anglo-Irish agreement between the United Kingdom, which, of course, included Northern Ireland and the Republic of Ireland, so that we could consult together on new items of policy. The Nationalist community, Republican community, in Northern Ireland might perhaps have more confidence and, on that basis, agree with the Republic of Ireland that Northern Ireland should stay with the United Kingdom as long as that were the wish of her people. I thought we'd got it fair and evenhanded for both sides. The Unionists didn't like it, but it took us about three years to get back the confidence of the Unionists that it wasn't against their interest. In the meantime, I'm afraid that terrorism has been stepped up recently, and the Unionist terrorists have responded to it.

Now, I don't see a solution, but there are some things in politics which, for a time, are like that. One day it will be solved because circumstances will change. We had hoped that all the families would get together and say: "We must, in fact, give the children a better future." They haven't. The Pope has been marvelous, totally and utterly condemning violence. The president of the United States and your members of Congress have totally and utterly condemned it. Never give a penny to NORAID. It will find its way into terrorism, into bombs which bomb people, maim them, and bomb and hurt and harm innocent people. So we will have to go on, because in the meantime, there is one thing every government must make certain of: that terrorism never wins over the ballot box. The ballot box will prevail in Northern Ireland. We will see that it does. That is why the army is there, not as in charge, but as the aid to the civil power in Northern Ireland. It's a difficult role, but the ballot box must and will prevail. Otherwise, it would be a message to terrorists the world over that they could get their way by maiming and taking the lives of innocent people. That is Northern Ireland.

CADET: When you became prime minister in 1979, what gave you the strength, desire, and motivations to set a new course for Britain and cure its economic disease?

MRS. THATCHER: Because what had happened to Britain in the postwar period was flatly contrary to everything in the British character. The British character had been adventurous, independent. It had been the forerunner of democracy and have the oldest parliament. For nine hundred years alone among the European nations we had not been occupied. We developed a taste for running our own affairs. We'd had governments which slowly and slowly encroached upon the liberties of the people toward more money and taxation. The top rate of tax on earnings when I came into power was 83 percent, the top rate of tax on savings was 98 percent. There were controls after controls after controls: controls on prices, controls on incomes, controls on exchange, on foreign exchange, controls on where you could develop your factory even though you got planning permission elsewhere, control after control. The trade unions had so many powers that they practically ran the country and could bring any company to ruin. All of this was wrong.

Somehow the people of Britain had accepted decline. It wasn't in their character, it wasn't in their nature. I knew that if I could do the right things, all of the old things, the old spirit of adventure, the old spirit of enterprise, the old spirit of doing good things would come out once again because we're a people who did things voluntarily. That is why, having faith in that character, having faith in everything which people like Winston Churchill stood for, having faith in what I myself had seen at the end of the war and during times of difficulty, that if we could get our policies right, we could encourage the right things to come out and push down the bad things, and once again, we should be an influence in the world. It was right; it was believing in the things, the values which you believe in; it was believing that there are certain fundamental values which transcend the passage of time. It is believing that the task of government should be limited. Government shouldn't take as many powers as it can get, but it should take as few powers as it needs to run the nation well and to let the people have maximum powers themselves. And it should always have a good rule of law. That is really what motivated me. And I think we defeated defeatism and became once again a power for liberty and a power prepared to defend liberty and uphold international law. It was a good decision. The electorate chose well in 1979.

Selected Bibliography

General

Airst, Paul. *After Thatcher*. Glasgow: Collins, 1989.

Beaton, Alistair, and Andy Hamilton. *The Thatcher Papers. An Expose of the Secret Face of the Conservative Government*. London: New English Library, 1980.

Cockerell, M. *Live from Number 10*. London, 1988.

Cole, John. *The Thatcher Years*. London: BBC, 1987.

Filo della Torre, Paolo. *Viva Britannia: Mrs. Thatcher's Britain*. London: Sidgwick and Jackson, 1985.

Flamini, Roland. *Ten Years at Number 10: Images of a Decade in Office*. London: Aurum, 1989.

Harriman, Ed. *Thatcher: A Graphic Guide*. Illus. by John Freeman. London: Camden, 1986.

Ingham, Bernard. *Kill the Messenger*. London: Harper Collins, 1991.

Ingrams, Richard, and John Wells. *Bottoms Up!* Illus. by George Adamson. London: Private Eye, 1984.

_____. *Down the Hatch!* Illus. by Brian Bagnall. London: Private Eye, 1985.

Little, Graham. *Strong Leadership: Thatcher, Reagan, and an Eminent Person*. Oxford: Oxford University Press, 1988.

Manwaring, Tony, and Nick Sigler, eds. *Breaking the Nation. A Guide to Thatcher's Britain*. London: Pluto Press and New Socialist, 1985.

McFadyean, Melanie, and Margaret Renn. *Thatcher's Reign: A Bad Case of the Blues*. London: Chatto and Windus, 1984.

Mullin, Mark H. "United Kingdom" and "Ireland." In Wayne C. Thompson, *Western Europe*. Harpers Ferry, W.Va.: Stryker-Post, annually updated.

Riddell, Peter. *The Thatcher Government*. Updated ed. Oxford: Oxford University Press, 1985.

_____. *The Thatcher Decade: How Britain Has Changed During the 1980s*. Cambridge, Mass.: Basil Blackwell, 1989.

_____. *The Thatcher Era And Its Legacy*. Cambridge, Mass.: Basil Blackwell, 1991.

Skidelsky, Robert, ed. *Thatcherism*. Cambridge, Mass.: Basil Blackwell, 1988.

Smith, Geoffrey. *Reagan and Thatcher*. New York: W. W. Norton, 1991.

Warner, M. *Monuments and Maidens*. London, 1985.

Wilson, Edgar. *A Very British Miracle: The Failure of Thatcherism*. London: Pluto, 1991.

Biographies, Autobiographies, Memoirs

Abse, Leo. *Margaret, Daughter of Beatrice; A Politician's Psycho-Biography of Margaret Thatcher*. London: Jonathan Cape, 1989.

Arnold, Bruce. *Margaret Thatcher. A Study in Power*. London: Hamish Hamilton, 1984

Callaghan, James. *Time and Chance*. Glasgow: Collins, 1987.

Campbell, John. *Edward Heath*. London: Jonathan Cape, 1993.

Castle, Barbara. *The Castle Diaries, 1974–76*. London, 1980.

Faber, Doris. *Margaret Thatcher: Britain's "Iron Lady"*. New York: Viking Kestrel, 1985.

Gardiner, G. *Margaret Thatcher: From Childhood to Leadership*. London: William Kimber, 1975.

Garfinkel, Bernard. *Margaret Thatcher*. Introduced by Arthur M. Schlesinger, Jr. New York: Chelsea House, 1985.

Geelhoed, E. Bruce. *Margaret Thatcher: In Victory and Downfall*. New York: Praeger, 1992.

Foster, Leila Merrell. *Margaret Thatcher; First Woman Prime Minister of Great Britain*. Chicago: Children's Press, 1990.

Harris, Kenneth. *Thatcher*. London: Weidenfeld and Nicolson, 1988.

Harris, Robert. *Good and Faithful Servant*. London: Faber and Faber, 1990.

Healey, Denis. *The Time of My Life*. Harmondsworth: Penguin, 1989.

Hole, Dorothy. *Margaret Thatcher, Britain's Prime Minister*. Hillsdale, N.J.: Enslow, 1990.

Hughes, Libby. *Madam Prime Minister: A Biography of Margaret Thatcher*. Minneapolis: Dillon, 1989.

Hurd, Douglas. *An End to Promises*. Glasgow: Collins, 1977.

Jenkins, Roy. *A Life At the Centre*. London: Pan, 1992.

Junor, Penny. *Margaret Thatcher: Wife. Mother. Politician*. London: Sidgwick and Jackson, 1983.

Lawson, Nigel. *The View From No. 11: Memoirs of a Tory Radical*. London: Bantam, 1992.

Levin, Angela. *Margaret Thatcher*. Illus. by Peter Wingham. London: Hamish Hamilton, 1981.

Lewis, Russell. *Margaret Thatcher: A Personal and Political Biography*. London: Routledge and Kegan Paul, 1975.

Linklater, Magnus, and David Leigh. *Not Without Honour*. London: Sphere, 1986.

Maitland, Lady Olga. *Margaret Thatcher: The First Ten Years*. London: Sidgwick and Jackson, 1989.

Mayer, Allan J. *Madam Prime Minister: Margaret Thatcher and Her Rise to Power*. New York: Newsweek Books, 1979.

Mikdadi, Faysal. *Margaret Thatcher: A Bibliography*. Westport, Conn.: Greenwood, 1993.

Millar, Ronald. *A View from the Wings*. London: Weidenfeld and Nicolson, n.d.

Minogue, Kenneth, and Michael Biddiss. *Thatcherism: Personality and Politics*. London: Macmillan, 1987.

Money, Ernle. *Margaret Thatcher: First Lady of the House*. London: Leslie Frewin, 1975.

Moskin, Marietta. *Margaret Thatcher of Great Britain*. Englewood Cliffs, N.J.: Julian Messner, 1990.

Murray, Patricia. *Margaret Thatcher*. London: W. H. Allen, 1980.

Ogden, Chris. *Maggie: An Intimate Portrait of a Woman in Power*. New York: Simon and Schuster, 1990.

Prior, Jim. *A Balance of Power*. London: Hamish Hamilton, 1986.

Pym, Francis. *The Politics of Consent*. London: Hamish Hamilton, 1984.

Raban, Jonathan. *God, Man and Mrs. Thatcher*. London: Chatto and Windus, 1989.

Ridley, Nicholas. *My Style of Government: The Thatcher Years*. London: Hutchinson, 1991.

Russell, Lewis. *Margaret Thatcher: A Personal and Political Biography*. London: Routledge and Kegan Paul, 1975.

Thatcher, Margaret. *In Defence of Freedom: Speeches on Britain's Relations with the World, 1976-1986*. Introduced by Ronald Butt. London: Aurum, 1986.

_____. *The Revival of Britain: Speeches on Home and European Affairs, 1975-1988*. Compiled by Alistair B. Cooke. London: Aurum, 1989.

_____. *The Downing Street Years*. London and New York: Harper Collins, 1993. A second volume on her life before 1979 is forthcoming.

Thomson, Andrew. *Margaret Thatcher: The Woman Within*. London: W. H. Allen, 1989.

Walker, Peter. *Trust the People*. Glasgow: Collins, 1987.

Wapshott, Nicholas, and George Brock. *Thatcher*. London: Macdonald, 1983.

Webster, Wendy. *Not A Man to Match Her*. London: Women's Press, 1990.

Young, Hugo. *The Iron Lady: A Biography of Margaret Thatcher*. New York: Farrar Strauss Giroux, 1989. This was first published in the U.K. under the title, *One of Us*. London: Macmillan, 1989.

Young, Hugo, and Anne Sloman. *The Thatcher Phenomenon*. London: BBC, 1986.

Domestic Politics and Policies

Adonis, Andrew, and Tim Hames, eds. *Conservative Revolution? The Thatcher-Reagan Decade in Perspective*. Manchester: Manchester University Press, 1993.

Bruce-Gardyne, Jock. *Mrs. Thatcher's First Administration*. London: Macmillan, 1984.

Butcher, Hugh, et al. *Local Government and Thatcherism*. London: Routledge and Kegan Paul, 1990.

Budge, Ian, and David McKay, eds. *The Developing British Political System: The 1990s*. 3d ed. New York: Longman, 1993.

Bulpitt, Jim. *Territory and Power in the United Kingdom*. Manchester: Manchester University Press, 1983.

Cooper, Barry, Allan Kornberg, and William Mishler, eds. *The Resurgence of Conservatism in Anglo-American Democracies*. Durham, N.C.: Duke University Press, 1988.

Cosgrave, Patrick. *The First Term*. London: Bodley Head, 1985.

Derbyshire, J. Denis, and Ian Derbyshire. *Politics in Britain: From Callaghan to Thatcher*. Edinburgh: Chambers, 1990.

Donoughue, Bernard. *Prime Minister*. London: Jonathan Cape, 1987

Drucker, Henry, et al., eds. *Developments in British Politics*. Rev. ed. New York: St. Martin's Press, 1988.

Dunleavy, Patrick, and Christopher T. Husbands. *British Democracy at the Crossroads*. London: George Allen & Unwin, 1985.

Dunleavy, Patrick, et al., eds. *Developments in British Politics 4*. Manchester: Manchester University Press, 1993.

Dutton, David. *British Politics Since 1945: The Rise and Fall of Consensus*. Cambridge, Mass.: Basil Blackwell, 1991.

Foley, Michael. *The Rise of the British Presidency*. Manchester: Manchester University Press, 1993.

Hall, Stuart, and Martin Jacques, eds. *The Politics of Thatcherism*. London: Lawrence and Wishart, 1983.

Hall, Stuart. *The Hard Road to Renewal: Thatcherism and the Crisis of the Left*. London: Verso, 1988.

Hass, Richard, and Oliver Knox, eds. *Policies of Thatcherism: Thoughts from a London Thinktank*. Lanham, Md.: University Press of America, 1991.

Hennessy, Peter. *Cabinet*. Oxford: Basil Blackwell, 1986.

Hennessy, Peter, and Anthony Seldon, eds. *Ruling Performance: British Governments from Attlee to Thatcher*. Oxford: Basil Blackwell, 1987.

Holmes, Martin. *The First Thatcher Government, 1979-1983: Contemporary Conservatism and Economic Change*. Boulder, Colo.: Westview, 1985.

Holmes, Martin. *Thatcherism: Scope and Limits, 1983-87*. New York: St. Martin's, 1989.

James, Simon. *British Cabinet Government*. New York: Routledge, 1992.

Jenkins, Peter. *Mrs. Thatcher's Revolution: The Ending of the Socialist Era*. Cambridge, Mass.: Harvard University Press, 1987.

Kavanaugh, Dennis A. *Margaret Thatcher: A Study in Prime Ministerial Style*. Studies in Public Policy No. 151. Glasgow: Centre for the Study of Public Policy, 1986.

_____. *Thatcherism and British Politics: The End of Consensus?*. Oxford: Oxford University Press, 1987.

_____. *British Politics*. Oxford: Oxford University Press, 1990.

Kavanaugh, Dennis A., and Anthony Seldon, eds. *The Thatcher Effect*. Oxford: Oxford University Press, 1989.

King, Anthony, ed. *The British Prime Minister*. Rev. ed. Durham, N.C.: Duke University Press, 1985.

Letwin, Shirley Robin. *The Anatomy of Thatcherism*. London: Fontana, 1992.

Marsh, David, and R. A. W. Rhodes. *Implementing Thatcherite Policies: Audit of an Era*. Buckingham: Open University Press, 1992.

Middlemas, Keith. *Power, Competition and the State*. 3 vols. London: Macmillan, 1986-91.

Moon, Jeremy. *Innovative Leadership in Democracy: Policy Change under Thatcher*. Brookfield, Vt.: Dartmouth Publishing Co., 1993.

Norton, Philip. *The British Polity*. 3d ed. New York: Longman, 1994.

Rasmussen, Jorgen S. *The British Political Process: Concentrated Power Versus Accountability*. Belmont, Calif.: Wadsworth, 1993.

Savage, S. P., and L. Robins, eds. *Public Policy Under Thatcher*. London: Macmillan, 1990.

Stephenson, Hugh. *Mrs. Thatcher's First Year*. London: J. Norman, 1980.

Party Politics and Elections

Anderson, Bruce. *John Major: The Making of the Prime Minister*. London: Fourth Estate, 1991.

Atkinson, M. *Our Masters' Voices*. London, 1984.

Blake, Robert. *The Conservative Party from Peel to Thatcher*. London: Methuen, 1985.

Butler, David. *Governing Without a Majority*. London, 1983.

Butler, David, and Dennis Kavanagh. *The British General Election of 1979*. London: Macmillan, 1979.

_____. *The British General Election of 1983*. London: Macmillan, 1983.

_____. *The British General Election of 1987*. London: Macmillan, 1988.

Cosgrave, Patrick. *Margaret Thatcher: A Tory and Her Party*. London: Hutchinson, 1978.

Gamble, Andrew. *The Conservative Nation*. London, 1974.

Garner, Robert, and Richard Kelly. *British Political Parties Today*. Manchester: Manchester University Press, 1993.

Garrison, Terry. *Mrs. Thatcher's Casebook: Non-Partisan Studies in Conservative Policy in the Eighties*. Kings Ripton, Cambs.: Elm, 1987.

Gilmour, Ian. *Inside Right: A Study of Conservatism*. London: Quartet, 1977.

_____. *Britain Can Work*. Oxford, 1983.

Heald, Gordon, and Robert Wybrow. *Gallup Survey of Britain*. London: Croom Helm, 1986.

King, Anthony, et al. *Britain at the Polls, 1992*. Chatham, N.J.: Chatham House, 1992.

MacGregor, Ian. *The Enemies Within*. Glasgow: Collins, 1986.

Norton, Philip, and A. Aughey. *Conservatives and Conservatism*. London: Temple Smith, 1981.

Ross, John. *Thatcher and Friends: The Anatomy of the Tory Party*. London: Pluto, 1983.

Shepherd, Robert. *The Power Brokers: The Tory Party and its Leaders*. London: Hutchinson, 1991.

Srlvik, Bo, and Ivor Crewe. *Decade of Dealignment: The Conservative Victory of 1979 and Electoral Trends in the 1970s*. Cambridge: Cambridge University Press, 1983.

Thatcher, Carol. *Diary of an Election: With Margaret Thatcher on the Campaign Trail*. London: Sidgwick and Jackson, 1983.

Tyler, Rodney. *Campaign! The Selling of the Prime Minister*. London: Grafton, 1987.

Watkins, Alan. *A Conservative Coup: The Fall of Margaret Thatcher*. London: Duckworth, 1991.

Worcester, Robert M., and Martin Harrop, eds. *Political Communications: The General Election Campaign of 1979.* London: Allen & Unwin, 1982.
Worcester, Robert M. *British Public Opinion: A Guide to the History and Techniques of Public Opinion Polling.* Oxford: Basil Blackwell, 1991.

Foreign and Defense Policy

Byrd, Peter. *British Foreign Policy Under Thatcher.* New York: St. Martins, 1988.
Byrd, Peter. *The Politics of Defence Under Thatcher.* Hemel Hempstead: P. Allen, 1991.
Bartlett, C. J. *The Special Relationship: A Political History of Anglo-American Relations Since 1945.* New York: Longman, 1992.
Croft, Stuart, ed. *British Security Policy: The Thatcher Years and the End of the Cold War.* New York: Unwin Hyman Academic, 1992.
Cronin, James E. *The Politics of State Expansion: War, State, and Society.* New York: Routledge, 1991.
Dalyell, Tom. *Thatcher's Torpedo.* London: C. Woolf, 1983.
――――――. *Thatcher: Patterns of Deceit.* London: C. Woolf, 1986.
――――――. *Misrule: How Mrs. Thatcher Has Misled Parliament from the Sinking of the Belgrano to the Wright Affair.* London: Hamish Hamilton, 1987.
Gavshon, A., and D. Rice. *The Sinking of the Belgrano.* London, 1984.
Freedman, Lawrence. *Britain and the Falklands War.* Cambridge, Mass.: Basil Blackwell, 1988.
Freedman, Lawrence, and Virginia Gamba-Stonehouse. *Signals of War: The Falklands Conflict of 1982.* London: Faber & Faber, 1990.
Gaffikin, Frank, and Mike Morrissey. *Northern Ireland: The Thatcher Years.* Atlantic Highlands, N.J.: Humanities Press, 1990.
Haig, Alexander. *Caveat: Realism, Reagan and Foreign Policy.* London: Weidenfeld and Nicolson, 1984.
Hastings, Max, and Simon Jenkins. *The Battle for the Falklands.* London: Michael Joseph, 1983.
Henderson, Nicholas. *Channels and Tunnels.* London: Weidenfeld and Nicolson, 1987.
Middlebrook, Martin. *Task Force: The Falklands War 1982.* Harmondsworth: Penguin, 1987.
Nicoll, Sir William, and Trevor C. Salmon. *Understanding the New European Community.* Old Tappan, N.J.: Prentice Hall, 1993.
Salmon, Trevor C. *Unneutral Ireland.* Oxford: Oxford University Press, 1989.
Smith, Michael, and Steve Smith and Brian White. *British Foreign Policy: Tradition, Changes and Transformation.* London: Unwin Hyman, 1988.
Tugendhat, C. *Making Sense of Europe.* London, 1986.
Verrier, A. *The Road to Zimbabwe.* London, 1986.
Ward, Alan, ed. *Northern Ireland: Living with the Crisis.* New York: Praeger, 1987.
White, Brian. *Britain, Detente and Changing East-West Relations.* New York: Routledge, 1992.

Economy

Aaronovitch, Sam. *The Road From Thatcherism: The Alternative Economic Strategy.* London: Lawrence and Wishart, 1981.

Adeney, Martin, and John Lloyd. *The Miners' Strike, 1984-5.* London: Routledge and Kegan Paul, 1986.

Alt, James E. *Cabinet Studies.* London: Macmillan, 1975.

_____. *The Politics of Economic Decline.* Cambridge: Cambridge University Press, 1978.

_____. *Perspectives on Positive Political Economy.* Cambridge: Cambridge University Press, 1991.

Beenstock, Michael, et al. *Could Do Better: Contrasting Assessments of the Economic Progress and Prospects of the Thatcher Government at Mid-Term.* London: Institute of Economic Affairs, 1982.

Brittan, Samuel. *How to End the 'Monetarist' Controversy.* London: Institute of Economic Affairs, 1981.

_____. *A Restatement of Economic Liberalism.* London, 1988.

Butler, Nick, ed. *The Economic Consequences of Mrs. Thatcher: Speeches in the House of Lords.* London: Duckworth, 1983. Also published in London by the Fabian Society, 1983.

Coates, P., and J. Hillard, eds. *The Economic Decline of Modern Britain: The Debate Between Left and Right.* Brighton: Harvester, 1986.

Cronin, James E. *Industrial Conflict in Modern Britain.* London: Croom Helm, 1979.

_____. *Labor and Society in Britain, 1918-1979.* New York: Schocken, 1983.

Gamble, Andrew. *A Britain in Decline.* London: Macmillan, 1981.

_____. *The Free Economy and the Strong State. The Politics of Thatcherism.* Durham, N.C.: Duke University Press, 1988.

Hall, Peter. *Governing the Economy: The Politics of State Intervention in Britain and France.* Oxford: Oxford University Press, 1986.

Hanson, Charles G. *Taming the Trade Unions: A Guide to the Thatcher Government's Employment Reforms, 1980-1990.* London: Macmillan, 1991.

Hardy, Peter. *A Right Approach to Economics? Margaret Thatcher's United Kingdom.* London: Hodder & Stoughton, 1991.

Holmes, Martin. *Political Pressure and Economic Policy: British Government 1970-4.* London: Butterworth, 1982.

_____. *The Labour Government, 1974-9: Political Aims and Economic Reality.* London: Macmillan, 1985.

Johnson, Christopher. *The Economy Under Mrs. Thatcher, 1979-1990.* Harmondsworth: Penguin, 1991.

_____. *The Grand Experiment: Mrs. Thatcher's Economy and How it Spread.* Boulder, Colo.: Westview, 1993.

Keegan, William. *Mrs. Thatcher's Economic Experiment.* Harmondsworth: Penguin, 1984.

Krieger, Joel. *Reagan, Thatcher, and the Politics of Decline.* Oxford: Oxford University Press, 1986.

Letwin, O. *Privatising the World.* London, 1988.

MacInnes, John. *Thatcherism At Work: Industrial Relations and Economic Change.* Milton Keynes: Open University Press, 1987.

Minford, Patrick. *The Supply Side Revolution in Britain.* Aldershot, Hants: E. Elgar, 1991.

Norpoth, Helmut. *Confidence Regained: Economics, Mrs. Thatcher, and the British Voter.* Ann Arbor: University of Michigan Press, 1992.

Overbeek, Henk. *Global Capitalism and National Decline: The Thatcher Decade in Perspective.* London: Unwin Hyman, 1990.

Rentoul, J. *The Rich Get Richer.* London, 1987.

Tomlinson, Jim. *Hayek and the Market.* London: Pluto, 1990.

Walters, Alan. *Britain's Economic Renaissance: Margaret Thatcher's Reforms, 1979-1984.* Oxford: Oxford University Press, 1986.

Wilsher, Peter. *Strike: Thatcher, Scargill, and the Miners.* London: Hodder and Stoughton, 1985.

Social Policy and Civil Rights

Bagwell, Philip. *End Of The Line? The Fate of Public Transport Under Thatcher.* London: Verso, 1984.

Boyle, A. *The Climate of Treason.* London, 1979.

Brown, Gordon. *Where There Is Greed: Margaret Thatcher and the Betrayal of Britain's Future.* Edinburgh: Mainstream, 1989.

Bull, David, and Paul Wilding, eds. *Thatcherism and the Poor.* London: Child Poverty Action Group, 1983.

Burton, John. *What Became of the Thatcher Revolution: Lessons for Australia.* Perth: Australian Institute for Public Policy, 1986.

Campbell, B. *The Iron Ladies.* London, 1987.

Cashmore, E. Ellis. *United Kingdom? Class, Race, and Gender Since the War.* London: Unwin Hyman, 1989.

Deakin, N. *The Politics of the Welfare State.* London, 1987.

Edgell, Stephen, and Vic Duke. *A Measure of Thatcherism: A Sociology of Britain in the 1980s.* New York: Routledge, 1991.

Ewing, K. D., and C. A. Gearty. *Freedom Under Thatcher: Civil Liberties in Modern Britain.* Oxford: Oxford University Press, 1990.

Foot, Michael. *Another Heart And Other Pulses: The Alternative to the Thatcher Society.* Glasgow: Collins, 1984.

Loney, Martin. *The New Right and the Welfare State.* London: Pluto, 1986.

MacKinnon, Kenneth. *The Politics of Popular Representation: Reagan, Thatcher, AIDS, and the Movies.* Rutherford, N.J.: Fairleigh Dickinson University Presses, 1992.

Pierson, Paul. *Dismantling the Welfare State?* Cambridge: Cambridge University Press, 1994.

Thomas, Harvey, with Judith Gunn. *In The Face of Fear.* Basingstoke, Hants.: Marshalls, 1985.

Waine, Barbara. *The Rhetoric of Independence: The Ideology and Practice of Social Policy in Britain.* Oxford: Berg, 1991.

Williamson, Bill. *The Temper of the Times: British Society Since World War II.* Cambridge, Mass.: Basil Blackwell, 1990.

Index